WORKING WITH ANGLO-SAXON MANUSCRIPTS

'Every medieval manuscript is unique. Though a text or drawing may be copied from an earlier version, no manuscript is identical to its source. An edited, printed version, despite its convenience for the scholar, cannot render the fundamentally dynamic nature of medieval textuality. Even a facsimile edition, however technically accomplished, is at best only a collection of photographs, which flatten and drain the vitality from a manuscript. The immediacy of personal contact with the artefact brings a thrill which cannot be over-emphasised.'

from Chapter 1

Working with Anglo-Saxon Manuscripts is an authoritative, clearly written demystification of manuscript study by a group of scholars at the forefront of their fields. It brings together the full range of activity involved in the making of Anglo-Saxon manuscripts: the writing and compilation of a book, the textual content, and the decorative material.

Editor: Gale R. Owen-Crocker is Professor of Anglo-Saxon Culture at the University of Manchester and Director of the AHRC-funded Project 'The Lexis of Cloth and Clothing in Britain c. 700–1450'. She was co-founder and is co-editor (with Robin Netherton) of the journal *Medieval Clothing and Textiles*. Her books include *The Four Funerals in Beowulf: and the structure of the poem* (2000), *Dress in Anglo-Saxon England* (2004), *King Harold II and the Bayeux Tapestry* (2005), for which she was editor, and *Medieval Textiles of the British Isles c. 450–1100: An annotated bibliography* (2007), co-written with Elizabeth Coatsworth.

EXETER MEDIEVAL TEXTS AND STUDIES

Series Editors: Vincent Gillespie and Richard Dance

Founded by M. J. Swanton
and later co-edited by Marion Glasscoe

Working with Anglo-Saxon Manuscripts

edited by Gale R. Owen-Crocker

with contributions by:
Maria Cesario, Timothy Graham, Catherine E. Karkov
Stuart D. Lee, Daniel Paul O'Donnell, Alexander R. Rumble
Donald Scragg, Elaine Treharne, Gernot R. Wieland

UNIVERSITY
of
EXETER
PRESS

Cover image: Perseus from Cicero's *Aratea*:
detail from London, British Library, MS Cotton Tiberius B. v, fol. 34r.

First published in 2009 by
University of Exeter Press
Reed Hall, Streatham Drive
Exeter EX4 4QR
UK

www.exeterpress.co.uk

© Gale R. Owen-Crocker and the individual contributors 2009

The right of Gale R. Owen-Crocker
and the individual contributors
to be identified as authors of this
work has been asserted by them in accordance with
the Copyright, Designs and Patents Acts 1988.

British Library Cataloguing in Publication Data
A catalogue record for this book is available
from the British Library.

Paperback ISBN 978 0 85989 841 6
Hardback ISBN 978 0 85989 840 9

Typeset in 11/13.5 Minion Pro
by Carnegie Book Production, Lancaster

Printed in Great Britain
by JF Print Ltd, Sparkford

Contents

List of illustrations   vii

Acknowledgements   xv

Introduction   1
   Gale R. Owen-Crocker

1   Handling Anglo-Saxon manuscripts   7
   Gale R. Owen-Crocker and Maria Cesario

2   The construction and writing of Anglo-Saxon manuscripts   29
   Alexander R. Rumble

3   Manuscript sources of Old English prose   61
   Donald Scragg

4   Manuscript sources of Old English poetry   89
   Elaine Treharne

5   A survey of Latin manuscripts   113
   Gernot R. Wieland

6   Glosses and notes in Anglo-Saxon manuscripts   159
   Timothy Graham

7	Manuscript art *Catherine E. Karkov*	205
8	From manuscript to computer *Stuart D. Lee and Daniel Paul O'Donnell*	253

Further reading	285
Glossary	289
Index of manuscripts	296
General index	302
List of contributors	319

Illustrations

1.1 Paris, Bibliothèque Nationale, MS fonds latin 8824 (The *Paris Psalter*), fols 1v–2r. Psalms 2–3   6

1.2 London, British Library, MS Cotton Vespasian D. xiv, fol. 75v. Opening of a prognistics text   12

1.3 London, British Library, MS Harley 603 (The *Harley Psalter*), fol. 66v. Psalm 127 (128): 1–3   13

1.4 London, British Library, MS Cotton Claudius B. iv (The *Old English Hexateuch*), fol. 57v. Genesis 39:4   14

1.5 Offset of a Latin text of Arator's *Historia apostolica* formerly used as pastedowns on the wooden book covers and visible as a mirror image in the remaining glue. Oxford, Bodleian Library, MS e Mus 66, front cover   17

1.6 Würzburg, Cathedral Library MS M.p.th.q. 2, fol. 1r. Ownership note   21

1.7 Munich, Bavarian State Library MS Clm 6433 fol. 12v. Anglo-Saxon minuscule and Insular decoration by an Anglo-Saxon scribe working in Freiburg   22

1.8 Hereford, Cathedral Library, MS O.VI.11 fol. 48v. An eleventh-century miscellany, held open by a 'book snake'   26

2.1 Oxford, Bodleian Library, MS Hatton 48, fols 24v–25r. Opening of *Regula Benedicti*. Latin: Insular Uncial, late seventh/early eighth century, with rubrics and red initials   38

2.2 Durham, Cathedral Library MS A.II.16, fol. 91r (Gospel of Luke). Latin: Insular Half-Uncial, eighth century; from Northumbria   39

2.3 Cambridge, University Library MS Kk.5.16 (The *Moore Bede* version of Bede's *Historia Ecclesiastica*), fol. 89v. Latin: Phase II

	Insular minuscule, early eighth-century; from Northumbria (?Wearmouth-Jarrow)	40
2.4	Facsimile by Alexander R. Rumble of letter-forms, ligatures and abbreviations in the Moore MS of Bede, *Historia Ecclesiastica*	40
2.5	London, British Library, MS Royal 2 A. xx, fol. 17r (The *Royal Prayerbook*). Latin: early ninth-century Insular Set minuscule; from Southumbria	41
2.6	Cambridge, Corpus Christi College MS 144, fol. 31r (Glossary). Latin: early ninth-century Insular Hybrid minuscule; from southern England	41
2.7	Cambridge, Corpus Christi College MS 173, Part I (Anglo-Saxon annals MS A, The *Parker Chronicle* 824–36), fol. 12r. Old English: early tenth-century Anglo-Saxon minuscule which retains some features of the Pointed variety; from Winchester	42
2.8	Cambridge, Corpus Christi College MS 12 (Gregory, *Cura pastoralis*), fol. 4r. Table of contents; Old English: late tenth-century Anglo-Saxon Square minuscule, perhaps written at Worcester. Interlinear glosses by the 'Tremulous Hand'	43
2.9	Paris, Bibliothèque Nationale, MS lat 987 (The *Ramsey Benedictional*), fol. 7r. Latin: English Caroline minuscule (Style I) with rubrics, etc. in Uncials and lines 9–10 in Square Capitals; produced in the later tenth century at the Old Minster, Winchester	45
2.10	Oxford, Bodleian Library, MS Auct. F.4.32 (*Dunstan's 'classbook'*), fol. 47r. Latin verse (Ovid, *Ars amatoria*, book i): mid-tenth-century Caroline minuscule (with some Insular features) by a scribe associated with Dunstan, abbot of Glastonbury (later archbishop of Canterbury)	46
2.11	Hanover, Kestner-Museum, Hs. W.M. XXIa 36 (the *Eadwig Gospels*), fol. 183v. Latin: written in the earlier eleventh century in English Caroline minuscule (Style IV) and Rustic Capitals by the Christ Church, Canterbury, scribe Eadwig Basan followed (lines 9–12) by his colophon to the volume. A slightly later German scribe added the bottom seven lines	46
2.12	London, British Library, MS Cotton Tiberius B. i (The *Anglo-Saxon Chronicle* MS C), fol. 141r. Old English prose and verse annals written at Abingdon: early eleventh-century Anglo-Saxon Round minuscule. Underlining and marginal note (*Kyngston*) by Robert Talbot (d. 1558)	47

List of illustrations ix

2.13 London, British Library, MS Additional 37517 (The *Bosworth Psalter*), fol. 81r. Latin: late tenth-century Anglo-Saxon Square minuscule, with continuous Old English gloss added slightly later; produced at Canterbury — 48

2.14 Cambridge, Corpus Christi College MS 57 (*Regula S. Benedicti*), fol. 120v. Latin: tenth/eleventh-century Anglo-Saxon Square minuscule. From line 11 on this page a later hand has changed the letter *a* to a Caroline form. Produced at Abingdon or Canterbury — 49

2.15 Manchester, John Rylands Library, Rylands Latin MS 155, fol. 4r. Part of the Tribal and Burghal Hidages, early thirteenth-century; Old English in Gothic Textura script — 50

3.1 London, British Library, MS Royal 7 C. xii, fol. 64r — 62

3.2 Oxford, Bodleian Library, MS Bodley 340, fol. 1r — 68

3.3 Oxford, Bodleian Library, MS Bodley 342, fol. 1r — 69

3.4 Cambridge, Corpus Christi College MS 140, fol. 1v. Gospel Book with legal items added — 72

3.5 Cambridge, Corpus Christi College MS 41, p. 300. Homilies in margin of Bede — 73

3.6 Cambridge, Corpus Christi College MS 41, p. 272. With addition of charm — 73

3.7 Cambridge, Corpus Christi College MS 173, Part I fol. 29v. The *Parker Chronicle* for 993 with marginal additions (actually 991) — 74

3.8 London, British Library, MS Cotton Tiberius A. iii (*Regularis Concordia*), fol. 3r — 79

4.1 Exeter, Cathedral, Dean and Chapter Library MS 3501 (The *Exeter Book*), fol. 8r — 94

4.2 Cambridge, Corpus Christi College MS 173, Part I (The *Parker Chronicle*), fol. 28v — 96

4.3 Vercelli, Biblioteca capitolare CXVII (The *Vercelli Book*), fol. 104v — 103

4.4 London, British Library, MS Cotton Vitellius A. xv (The *Beowulf Manuscript*), fol. 132r — 105

4.5 London, British Library, MS Cotton Vitellius A. xv (The *Beowulf Manuscript*), fol. 175v — 105

4.6 Cambridge, Corpus Christi College MS 201, p. 166 — 109

4.7 Cambridge, Corpus Christi College MS 201, p. 167 — 109

5.1	London, British Library, MS Cotton Vitellius E. xviii (Psalter), fol. 18r. Mid-eleventh-century	129
5.2	London, Lambeth Palace Library MS 149 (Bede's *In Apocalypsin*), fol. 10r. Third quarter of the tenth century	133
5.3	Durham, Cathedral Library MS A.IV.19 (The *Durham Ritual* or *Durham Collectar*), fol. 27v. Ninth-/tenth-century	136
5.4	London, British Library, MS Additional 37517 (Calendar), fol. 2r. Tenth-/eleventh-century	137
5.5	Oxford, Corpus Christi College MS 197 (The *Benedictine Rule*), fol. 28v. From the last quarter of the tenth century	139
5.6	Cambridge, Corpus Christi College MS 23 (Prudentius, *Psychomachia*), fol. 7r. From the end of the tenth century	147
5.7	London, British Library, MS Cotton Tiberius B. v, fol. 34r. A mid-eleventh-century manuscript. Perseus from Cicero's *Aratea*.	153
6.1	London, British Library, MS Cotton Vespasian A. i (The *Vespasian Psalter*), fol. 55v. With the opening of Psalm 56; with interlinear gloss	161
6.2	Cambridge, University Library MS Ff.1.23, fol. 5r. With the opening of Psalm 1; with Old English gloss	162
6.3	London, British Library, MS Cotton Nero D. iv (The *Lindisfarne Gospels*), fol. 255r. With text from John 19 glossed by Aldred	164
6.4	Brussels, Bibliothèque Royale MS 1650 (Aldhelm, prose *De virginitate*), fol. 25r. Glossed in stages	168
6.5	Cambridge, Corpus Christi College MS 352 (Boethius, *De institutione arithmetica*), fol. 4v. With marginal *scholia* linked to the text by pairs of matching *signes-de-renvoi*	171
6.6	Cambridge, Corpus Christi College MS 214 (Boethius, *Consolation of Philosophy*), fol. 107r. With paving letters	172
6.7	London, British Library, MS Cotton Vitellius A. xix (Bede, *Life of St Cuthbert*), fol. 32r. With syntactical glossing	173
6.8	Cambridge, Corpus Christi College MS 23 (Prudentius, *Psychomachia*), fol. 8v. With gloss entered on the page before the frame	175
6.9	Cambridge, Corpus Christi College MS 173, Part II (Sedulius, *Paschale carmen*), fol. 61v. With glosses in a different hands	176

6.10	Cambridge, Corpus Christi College MS 57, fol. 58v. With drypoint gloss visible under cold fibre-optic light	177
6.11	Cambridge, Corpus Christi College MS 183, fol. 70r. With the opening of a set of *glossae collectae*	179
6.12	Cambridge, Corpus Christi College MS 144 (The *Corpus Glossary*), fol. 13v. With *bu*, *by*, and *ca* sections	180
6.13	Cambridge, Corpus Christi College MS 12, fol. 3r. With a portion of King Alfred's *Pastoral Care Preface* glossed by the 'Tremulous Hand' of Worcester	184
6.14	Cambridge, Corpus Christi College MS 383, fol. 57r. Showing Robert Talbot's annotations to the opening of the treaty between Alfred and Guthrum	188
6.15	Exeter, Cathedral, Dean and Chapter Library MS 3501 (The *Exeter Book*), fol. 9r. With Laurence Nowell's interlinear gloss to a portion of *Christ I*	189
6.16	London, British Library, MS Cotton Tiberius B. iv (The *Anglo-Saxon Chronicle* MS D), fol. 20r. With annotations by John Joscelyn	193
6.17	Oxford, Bodleian Library, MS Laud Misc. 636 (The *Anglo-Saxon Chronicle* MS E), fol. 34v. With annotations by William L'Isle	196
6.18	Oxford, Bodleian Library, MS Laud Misc. 509, fol. 24r. The lower margin carries a passage transcribed (with alterations) by William L'Isle from another manuscript	198
6.19	Cambridge, Corpus Christi College MS 162 (Homiliary), p. 531. With underlinings and marginalia attributable to William L'Isle	199
6.20	Cambridge, Corpus Christi College MS 191 (*Rule for Canons* by Chrodegang of Metz, in Latin and Old English), p. 95. With interlinear transcription of the faded chapter title by Abraham Wheelock	201
6.21	Cambridge, University Library MS Kk.3.18 (Old English Bede), fol. 41r. With marginal annotations by Abraham Wheelock	203
7.1	London, British Library, MS Cotton Nero D. iv (The *Lindisfarne Gospels*), fol. 29r (*Chi-Rho* page)	207
7.2	Stockholm, Royal Library MS A.135 (*Codex Aureus*), fol. 150v (John)	208
7.3	Stockholm, Royal Library MS A.135 (*Codex Aureus*), fol. 16r (purple page with crosses)	209

7.4	Stockholm, Royal Library MS A.135 (*Codex Aureus*), fol. 11r (*Chi-Rho* page)	210
7.5	Cambridge, University Library MS Ll.1.10 (The *Book of Cerne*), fol. 31v (John)	212
7.6	Cambridge, University Library MS Ll.1.10 (The *Book of Cerne*), fol. 32r (John *incipit*)	212
7.7	Cambridge, University Library MS Ll.10 (The *Book of Cerne*), fol. 56r (prayer)	213
7.8	London, British Library, MS Cotton Vespasian A. i (The *Vespasian Psalter*), fol. 53r (initial of David with lamb)	215
7.9	Cambridge, Corpus Christi College MS 422 (The *Red Book of Darley*), p. 52 (Preface to Mass)	217
7.10	Rheims, Bibliothèque Municipale MS 9 (Gospels), fol. 23r (Matthew)	218
7.11	London, British Library, MS Cotton Nero D. iv (The *Lindisfarne Gospels*), fol. 25v (Matthew portrait)	219
7.12	London, British Library, MS Cotton Nero D. iv (The *Lindisfarne Gospels*), fol. 27r (Matthew *incipit*)	219
7.13	Hanover, Kestner Museum, Hs. W.M. XXIa 36 (The *Eadwig Gospels*), fol. 9v (Canon Table)	220
7.14	Hanover, Kestner Museum, Hs. W.M. XXIa 36 (The *Eadwig Gospels*), fol. 10r (Canon Table)	220
7.15	Hanover, Kestner Museum, Hs. W.M. XXIa 36 (The *Eadwig Gospels*), fol. 17v (Matthew)	221
7.16	Hanover, Kestner Museum, Hs. W.M. XXIa 36 (The *Eadwig Gospels*), fol. 65v (Mark)	221
7.17	Hanover, Kestner Museum, Hs. W.M. XXIa 36 (The *Eadwig Gospels*), fol. 96v (Luke)	222
7.18	Hanover, Kestner Museum, Hs. W.M. XXIa 36 (The *Eadwig Gospels*), fol. 147v (John)	222
7.19	London, British Library, MS Additional 49598 (The *Benedictional of Æthelwold*), fol. 97v (St Swithun)	225
7.20	London, British Library, MS Additional 495958 (The *Benedictional of Æthelwold*), fol. 118v (Dedication of a church)	226
7.21	London, British Library, MS Additional 49598 (The *Benedictional of Æthelwold*), fol. 102v (Dormition of the Virgin)	228

7.22	London, British Library, MS Cotton Titus D. xxvii (*Ælfwine's Prayerbook*), fol. 65v (Crucifixion)	230
7.23	London, British Library, MS Cotton Galba A. xviii (The *Galba Psalter*), fol. 21r (Christ enthroned)	232
7.24	London, British Library, MS Cotton Tiberius C. vi (The *Tiberius Psalter*), fol. 6v (*Vita* and *Mors*)	234
7.25	London, British Library, MS Cotton Tiberius C. vi (The *Tiberius Psalter*), fol. 14r (Harrowing of Hell)	234
7.26	London, British Library, MS Stowe 944 (The New Minster *Liber Vitae*), fol. 6r (Ælfgifu/Emma and Cnut)	236
7.27	London, British Library, MS Cotton Vespasian A. viii (The *New Minster Charter*), fol. 2v (Edgar)	238
7.28	London, British Library, MS Cotton Julius A. vi (Calendar), fol. 4v (April)	239
7.29	London, British Library, MS Cotton Julius A. vi (Calendar), fol. 5v (June)	240
7.30	London, British Library, MS Cotton Vitellius A. xv (The *Beowulf Manuscript*), fol. 103v, detail (Donestre)	243
7.31	London, British Library, MS Cotton Tiberius B. v, fol. 82r (Blemmyae)	244
7.32	London, British Library, MS Cotton Claudius B. iv (The *Old English Hexateuch*), fol. 26r (Abraham)	245
7.33	Oxford, Bodleian Library, MS Junius 11 (The *Junius Manuscript*), p. 16 (fall of angels)	247
7.34	Oxford, Bodleian Library, MS Junius 11 (The *Junius Manuscript*), p. 47 (birth of Abel)	248
7.35	New York, Pierpont Morgan Library MS 709 (*Judith Gospels*), fol. 1v (Crucifixion)	250
8.1	Non-contact digitization; the book or manuscript is held in an angled cradle	256
8.2	Non-contact digitization; overhead scanning of an object laid flat	257
8.3	Ultra violet image overlaid on the original image of damaged manuscript London, British Library, MS Cotton Otho A. vi	262
8.4	Browsable web page from the Bodleian Library's digitization project	264

8.5	The folder structure of the *Electronic Beowulf*	265
8.6	'Page-turning' in the Bodleian Library's digitization project	266
8.7	'Turning the Pages' system developed by the British Library: the *Lindisfarne Gospels* (London, British Library, MS Cotton Nero D. iv)	266
8.8	Page containing diplomatic and semi-normalised texts of *Cædmon's Hymn*	268
8.9	Link in digitized edition of *Cædmon's Hymn*	269
8.10	Images derived from the opening 'h' of *Beowulf*	270
8.11	The Bodleian Library's digitization project, MS Junius 11, top and bottom of image	271
8.12	Table-based web page layout	274
8.13	Order of reading of table-based web page by automatic indexer or aural screen browser	275
8.14	Different apparatus views, digital edition of *Cædmon's Hymn*	283

Acknowledgements

The publication of this book has been assisted by grants from The British Academy Neil Ker Memorial Fund, The Scouloudi Foundation in association with the Institute of Historical Research and the University of Manchester School of Arts, Histories and Cultures Research Support Fund.

Illustrations appear by permission of:
  Bayerische Staatsbibliothek, Munich: 1.7
  Bernard Muir: 4.1, 6.15, 7.33–7.34
  La Bibliothèque municipale, Rheims: 7.10
  La Bibliothèque nationale de France, Paris: 1.1, 2.9
  La Bibliothèque Royale, Brussels: 6.4
  The Bodleian Library, Oxford: 1.5, 2.1, 2.8, 3.2–3.3, 6.17–6.18, 7.33–7.34, 8.4, 8.6, 8.11
  The British Library, London: 1.2–1.4, 2.5, 2.12–2.13, 3.1, 3.8, 4.4–4.5, 5.1, 5.4, 5.7, 6.1, 6.3, 6.7, 6.16, 7.1, 7.8, 7.11–7.12, 7.19–7.32, 8.7
  The Cathedral Library, Durham: 2.2, 5.3
  The Dean and Chapter of Hereford Cathedral: 1.8
  The eBeowulf Project and the British Library Board: 8.5
  The eBoethius Project and the British Library Board: 8.3
  Kestner Museum, Hanover: 2.11, 7.13–7.18
  Kungl. Biblioteket (National Library of Sweden), Stockholm: 7.2–7.4
  Lambeth Palace Library, London: 5.2
  The Master and Fellows of Corpus Christi College, Cambridge: 2.6–2.8 2.14, 3.4–3.7, 4.2, 4.6–4.7, 5.6, 6.5–6.6, 6.8–6.14, 6.19–6.21, 7.9
  The Morgan Library, New York: 7.35
  The President and Fellows of Corpus Christi College, Oxford: 5.5

The University Librarian and Director, The John Rylands University Library, The University of Manchester: 2.15

Universität Würzburg: 1.6

University Library, Cambridge: 2.3, 6.2, 7.5–7.7

The editor would like to thank the authors and also to acknowledge the many colleagues who have helped this project in individual ways, especially Patricia Buckingham, Alun Ford, Anne Klinck, Bernard Muir, Hans Sauer, Susan Thompson, and Chris Tuckley.

Introduction

Gale R. Owen-Crocker

The young doctoral student had crossed the Atlantic to examine the sixth-century, Gothic manuscripts. The philology classes, the months of correspondence with the Italian library, the carefully composed reference from his supervisor, had all led up to this moment. He watched in awe as a procession of ecclesiastical librarians approached carrying great boxes containing delicate manuscript sheets layered with tissue paper. The curator slowly removed a single leaf from its container and held it up by the top corners. The vellum shivered, and dissolved into dust.[1]

This true and tragic tale from the 1960s illustrates why access to medieval manuscripts is restricted. Today, parchment or vellum from the Anglo-Saxon period is normally kept in climate-controlled conditions (usually 80° Celsius) with limited light. Anyone handling manuscripts is normally required to wear white cotton gloves, to read the manuscript only at a designated table and to use prescribed equipment; to hold a codex open, for instance, or to prevent a single leaf from curling and tearing.

Now that photographic facsimiles, microfilms, microfiche and digitized copies are readily available, readers are naturally encouraged to make use of these rather than to handle the manuscript itself – one *bona fide* scholar reports making an international journey only to have a protective monk hand him a facsimile edition which was available in his home university library. However, the availability of good copies has itself increased awareness of, and enthusiasm for, manuscript study. Many a teacher raised on edited texts in printed editions is now showing students the script, the punctuation and

---

[1] I am grateful to Anne Klinck for forwarding this story. Its victim prefers to remain anonymous. The doomed manuscript had apparently been treated with nut gall in the nineteenth century to make the letters clearer, and this had eaten into the thin vellum.

the textual cruces of those texts in digitized close-up. A lively interest in material culture and social history means that palaeography and codicology are no longer inaccessible subjects to most, but are instead desirable tools for appreciating the book as artefact. We live in a time when imaginative leaps are encouraged: for example the knowledge that the production of the *Codex Amiatinus* and two similar manuscripts at Jarrow/Monkwearmouth in the seventh century required 1,545 calf-skins[2] raises questions about monastic cattle breeding programmes and gives a new dimension to the responsibilities of the cowman Cædmon at another major Northumbrian monastery.[3]

About this book

Every piece of research is different and scholars' requirements of their manuscript sources are correspondingly varied. Some will focus on a single text, others will need to collate versions of the same text in different manuscripts, sometimes in different libraries, each with their own rules and conventions. While one scholar may wish to examine every image in numerous illuminated manuscripts in pursuit of some detail of costume or architecture, another may focus on the minutiae of letter forms in order to identify different scribes. A majority may wish to work on the main body of text on a page but others may be interested chiefly in marginal or interlinear glosses, or in decorated initials.

This practical guide, written by leading scholars in Anglo-Saxon studies, is aimed principally at advanced undergraduates, graduate students and their teachers; young scholars and overseas scholars (particularly non-Europeans who may be unfamiliar with manuscripts); scholars particularly wishing to read text, both Old English and Latin, in manuscript form for themselves, having relied on printed editions hitherto; and established scholars searching for material slightly outside their own area. It seeks to prepare readers so that they maximise their opportunities, since visiting libraries may involve expensive travel and accommodation, and since time, prescribed by pre-arranged bookings and other commitments, may be limited. It brings together the full range of scholarly activity involved in the making of Anglo-Saxon manuscripts: the writing and compilation of a book, the textual content, and the decorative material.

---

[2] R.L.S. Bruce-Mitford, *The Art of the Codex Amiatinus*, Jarrow Lecture, 1967, p. 2 (reprinted from *The Journal of the Archaeological Association*, 3rd series, 32, 1969).

[3] Cædmon was to become the first documented Old English poet. Bede, *Historia Ecclesiastica*, IV, xxiv; Bertrand Colgrave and R.A.B. Mynors, ed., *Bede's Ecclesiastical History of the English People*, Oxford, Clarendon, 1969, pp. 414–19.

The book also caters for researchers who are unable to travel to libraries or who in fact do not need to do so, giving information on electronic editions, and on websites which will give access to digitized manuscripts. As such it should be of use to undergraduates, theatrical and film designers, graphic artists, independent researchers, reconstructors and re-enactors.

The Anglo-Saxon focus

Working with Anglo-Saxon Manuscripts has a deliberately tight focus on the manuscripts produced and owned in Anglo-Saxon England, rather than attempting to cover the manuscripts of the medieval period in general or the output of western Europe. This allows a thorough treatment of the material under consideration and brings to the fore many of the lesser-known resources of this period.

All information coming in or out of Anglo-Saxon England had to be transmitted by human means – either in the memory of travellers or in manuscripts carried in their baggage. Every person making such a journey – whether merchant, missionary, student, teacher, envoy or other – risked his or her life in making the voyage, whether they used the short English Channel crossing or travelled the rougher waters of the North or Irish Seas. To reach their destination they had to walk or ride on horseback, enduring wind, rain and the dangers of theft. It is remarkable that books reached Anglo-Saxon England at all, and we should not be surprised that imports and exports are in the minority among extant Anglo-Saxon manuscripts – though some of those survivors are of enormous importance and scholarly interest. Yet despite England's geographical isolation, her manuscript culture was inspired by imported scholars and books. English book learning was initially a Christian innovation grafted onto a pre-established Germanic civilization, and Anglo-Saxon scholarship continued to evolve in response to influences from outside, as the following chapters will demonstrate. The rapidity of its development was remarkable. Its variety and sophistication are celebrated here.

Literacy was an esoteric skill in the Anglo-Saxon period, largely confined to men and women who had been educated by the Christian Church, many of whom continued to dedicate their lives to it; and even though the Anglo-Saxon population included enormous numbers of professed monks, nuns and priests, and in the later part of the period non-monastic canons, there must have been many, many more lay persons who never handled a book or even saw one, except distantly in church.

Manuscripts, then, were for the educated minority in Anglo-Saxon England. However, the breadth of the education enjoyed by that élite was remarkable, and these privileged few regularly crossed what today would be seen as academic boundaries. Not only were many scholars bilingual in English and Latin, they were capable of writing different scripts to convey the discrete languages. They did not simply read their books and learn passages by heart (though memorisation was undoubtedly part of their learning method); they carried out research, using libraries; they made notes; they glossed and developed existing texts. Coloured inks and decoration were not simply ornament but devices to help readers navigate the text. Illuminations did not simply reinforce narrative, they might reflect doctrinal complexities and so confirm and manifest scholarship.

In our own era education has become divided into 'subject areas' such as art history, English language, English literature and Latin, to the extent that many highly educated people are ignorant of areas outside their own specialisation and unaware of relevant interdisciplinary material in and around the period and region they are studying. Recent scholarly approaches to the medieval period, however, are emphasising the multilingualism, cross-culturalism and integration of disciplines which was taken for granted in the Middle Ages. This requires greater versatility on the part of students than heretofore. It is in order to facilitate cross-fertilisation, and to encourage researchers to explore across modern subject divisions, that this book presents an interdisciplinary approach to Anglo-Saxon manuscript study.

The arrangement of the book

The book begins with a chapter on the practicalities of viewing and using the manuscript, jointly authored to give a balance of perspective, by myself and Maria Cesario. Since it is essential for those new to manuscript study to have a working knowledge of the terminology used to describe the physical characteristics of the codex and the attributes of a script, Alexander R. Rumble sets out these principles in Chapter 2.

Separate chapters by Donald Scragg and Elaine Treharne respectively discuss Old English prose and poetry, expanding beyond the 'canon' of works commonly taught in universities to show the full range of material surviving. Following on from discussion of the better known Old English material, Gernot Wieland enumerates and explains the Latin texts which survive in amazing quantity in Anglo-Saxon manuscripts, revealing the extensive learning that was available in the English classroom and monastic library, material which is only appreciated by a handful of scholars working in the Anglo-Saxon field today.

The development of a manuscript did not necessarily end with the completion of the work of the original scribe and artist. Texts or groups of texts seem to have been carried around in unbound booklets, enabling them to be read by travellers and copied with relative ease, but the possibility always existed of binding booklets together, and compiling a codex with material of different origins. Many of the manuscripts which survive today are thought to be copies of earlier material, so although an extant manuscript may be written entirely in the same hand (such as the famous poetic codex known as the *Exeter Book*), the material it contains may have originated from different times and places. Additional texts were sometimes copied into spare space in the margins of existing texts. Sometimes these were relevant to the main text, such as the Old English metrical versions of *Cædmon's Hymn* copied into manuscripts of Bede's *Historia Ecclesiastica*, in which a Latin, prose paraphrase of the *Hymn* is given; sometimes the additions were disparate, such as the homily and Latin charm added to a manuscript containing the Old English version of Bede's work, illustrated at Figs 3.5–3.6. Readers of a manuscript, from Anglo-Saxon to early modern, added their own definitions and comments between the lines and in the margins and even rearranged the order of the leaves. Several chapters in this book refer to this additional material and a chapter by Timothy Graham is devoted to glosses and annotations.

The decoration, illumination and illustration of manuscripts is considered by Catherine Karkov in a discussion which contextualises art in relation to the Anglo-Saxon world and especially to Anglo-Saxon book-learning, showing that the symbolism and sequence of pictures in a manuscript can be just as intellectually probing as written text.

Anglo-Saxonists were quick to see the potential of digitization. The combination of the fragility of manuscript material and the number of scholars working at long distances from the libraries where manuscripts are located means that digitized material has rapidly become a part of mainstream research in the discipline. It is likely that every young scholar working on the Anglo-Saxon period will use digitized material: anything from a single illumination or passage of text from a manuscript supplied by the library which owns it, to a sophisticated digitized edition. A dedicated chapter co-authored by Stuart Lee and Daniel Paul O'Donnell, 'From Manuscript to Computer' explains what can, and has, been achieved by digitizing manuscripts, highlighting some outstanding recent projects and discussing the responsibilities inherent in following this path.

The text of the book is followed by a short list of further reading (pp. 285–8) and a glossary of terms (pp. 289–95). There is an index of the manuscripts mentioned in the book arranged by country (pp. 296–301) and a general index (pp. 302–18).

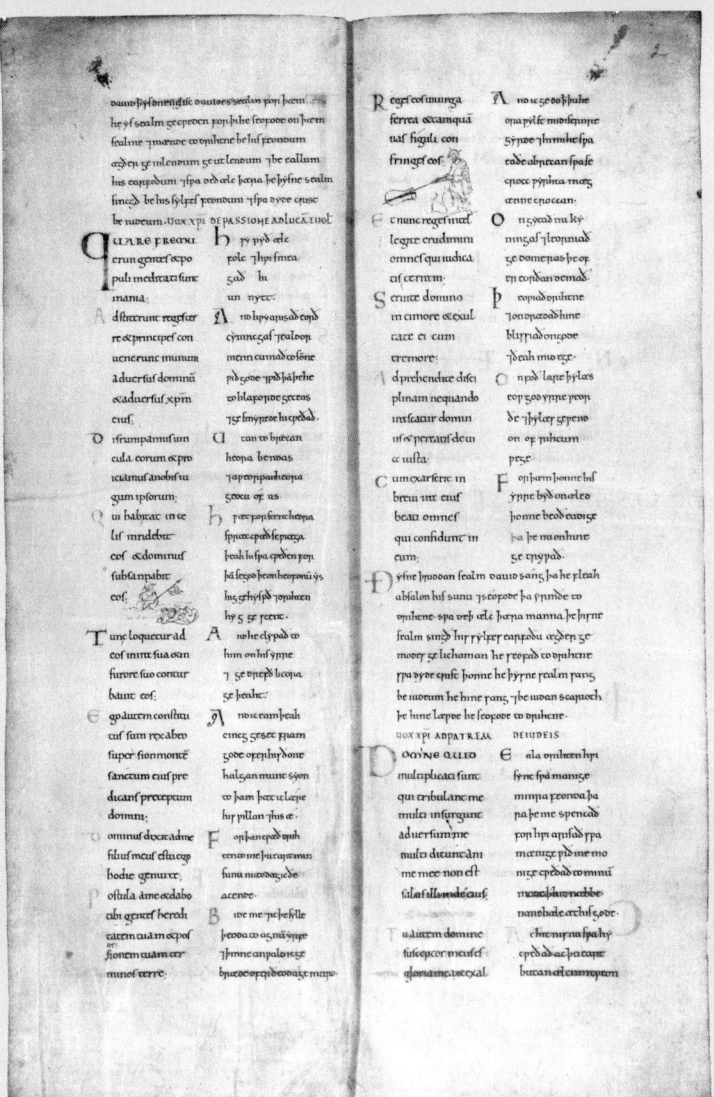

1.1 The *Paris Psalter*, Paris, Bibliothèque Nationale, MS fonds latin 8824, fols 1v–2r. Psalms 2–3.

The tall, narrow pages (526 × 186 mm) have been ruled horizontally and vertically with a hard point and the text keeps neatly to its boundaries. The bilingual text is set out in two columns with coloured marginal initials. This is the only surviving continuous translation of the psalms into Old English, all the other Old English texts being interlinear glosses. Psalms 1–50 are translated into prose (shown here). The dialect of the prose is West Saxon and the text may have been produced by King Alfred's ninth-century translation programme. Psalms 51–150 are rendered metrically (not shown). The mid-eleventh-century manuscript may derive from St Augustine's Canterbury. It was all written in the same hand, probably by the Wulfwine who is named in a colophon on fol. 186r., and exhibits facility with a variety of scripts. The Latin, in the left hand column, is in Anglo-Caroline minuscule; the Old English texts are written in an English vernacular minuscule which has the effect of matching the Latin text but which includes the traditional Anglo-Saxon letters æ ð þ and ƿ and some letter forms derived from Insular minuscule script. Each psalm is preceded by an *argumentum* in rather rhetorical English prose (paraphrased from a Latin source), contextualising King David's composition of the psalm, and explaining its use for others who sing it; and a heading in Latin, written in rustic capitals.

The first line of the Latin texts is in Uncial letters. Different punctuation conventions are used for the two languages, the Latin punctuated with the *punctus elevatus*, the Old English with pointing. The Latin text is from the Roman psalter. The Old English is a translation of a different text, also Roman but with some readings from St Jerome's Gallican version. The English text is longer than the Latin, but the scribe maintains parallelism by using smaller script for the English and leaving gaps at the end of Latin verses. Up to fol. 6r, some gaps are filled with tiny coloured ink drawings in typical St Augustine's style. Mostly derived from the Carolingian *Utrecht Psalter* (Utrecht, Universiteitsbibliotheek 32, Script. Eccl. 484), they depict part of the psalter text literally. Here, illustrating Psalm 2.4, a bearded God, with a cruciform nimbus and holding a banner with a decorated with a cross mounted on a lance, appears from the clouds above a pit filled with men; and Psalm 2.9, again bearded and with a cruciform nimbus, he breaks a pottery vessel with an iron rod. There is a gloss near the bottom of fol. 1v and an erasure near the bottom of fol. 2r.

1

Handling Anglo-Saxon manuscripts

Gale R. Owen-Crocker and Maria Cesario

The importance of seeing the manuscript

Every medieval manuscript is unique. Though a text or drawing may be copied from an earlier version, no manuscript is identical to its source. An edited, printed version, despite its convenience for the scholar, cannot render the fundamentally dynamic nature of medieval textuality. Even a facsimile edition, however technically accomplished, is at best only a collection of photographs, which flatten and drain the vitality from a manuscript.

The immediacy of personal contact with the artefact brings a thrill which cannot be over-emphasised. New dimensions are brought to the experience of research by the impact of a first-hand appreciation of the proportions of a manuscript, which mathematical measurements can only approximate – of the texture and thickness of the vellum; of the freshness of script and illustrations; and of the recognition of a deliberate and meaningful layout. In addition, for the imaginative, there is the *frisson* that comes from knowing that one is following the hands of all those who have worked with the manuscript before, most, but not all of them, anonymous. They include the scribe(s) and Anglo-Saxon owners; later medieval scholars who have read, glossed, added to or erased text, learning, borrowing and teaching from it; early modern collectors like Archbishop Matthew Parker; and recent giants in the field of scholarship such as J.R.R. Tolkien.

However, such emotive, but essentially selfish, reasons are not sufficient to disturb a fragile manuscript and the student should not rush into the experience prematurely; s/he may find that access is limited, and having used up the permitted allowance of visits, or available travel money, in pursuit of the 'thrill-factor' there is no possibility of revisiting the manuscript to scrutinize the scratched gloss or erasure which has become crucial at a more sophisticated stage of research.

Where there is no facsimile of any kind available, it is of course desirable to see the manuscript, especially if you are aware that an editor is uncertain of a reading, that editors disagree, or report an impenetrable stain; in such cases you need to see for yourself, perhaps with modern lighting. Even if no such ambiguities have been documented, it is wise to see a manuscript personally before you commit yourself in print. Something that is obvious on a first-hand examination may take you by surprise and cause you to change your mind about some aspect of your work.

For the researcher who has been working from printed material that isolates image or text, one language or another, and records additions such as glosses and emendations in footnotes, certain features may not have been properly considered. These include the size and shape of the book, the *mise-en-page* and the context surrounding the material on which the research is focussed. The visual impact of the original is demonstrated to some extent by the photograph of the *Paris Psalter*, Fig. 1.1. This manuscript is unusual among Anglo-Saxon works for its size and shape, though such tall, narrow books are sometimes clutched by figures in Anglo-Saxon illuminations (such as the Virgin in London, British Library, MS Stowe 944, Fig. 7.26). The layout of the *Paris Psalter* was clearly intended to draw attention to its bilingualism. The Old English *argumenta* and the Latin rubrics, written across both columns, visibly apply to both versions and so do the lively little drawings. The scribe has set out the text neatly and clearly, with verse divisions clearly marked. This is a rather grand book, scholarly, yet accessible to a person who preferred to read in English rather than Latin. Its very appearance has information to give us.[1]

It is often possible to purchase a copy of a manuscript from the library where it is kept, in the form of microfilm, electronic copy or individual plates, but, unless you have specified your requirements precisely, you are subject to the selection chosen by the library, and they may have omitted something: royal charters, for example, are usually endorsed in English. The endorsement, which was originally written on the outside of the folded document, may be on the verso of a leaf and may be ignored when a copy of the charter is made.[2]

---

[1] Bertram Colgrave, ed., *The Paris Psalter: MS Bibliothèque Nationale fonds latin 8824*, Early English Manuscripts in Facsimile 8, Copenhagen, Rosenkilde & Bagger, 1956; T.H. Ohlgren, ed., *Anglo-Saxon Textual Illustration: photographs of sixteen manuscripts with descriptions and index*, Kalamazoo, MI, Medieval Institute Publications, 1992, Item 4, pp. 3–4, 50–2, 298–302; Richard Emms, 'The scribe of the Paris Psalter', *Anglo-Saxon England*, 28, 1999, pp. 179–83.

[2] Susan D. Thompson, *Anglo-Saxon Royal Diplomas: a Palaeography*, Woodbridge, Boydell and Brewer, 2006, pp. 50–4. I am grateful to Dr Thompson for bringing the matter of endorsements to my attention.

Scratched glosses, made with a stylus, are not visible on a microfilm. It is not possible from a facsimile to determine the quality of the membrane, and certainly not to distinguish between parchment (sheepskin) and vellum (calfskin) – though the latter is not always possible with the original manuscript either. Details such as quiring, stubs left by leaves that have been removed, page size, pricking and the dimensions of the writing grid, and changes of ink colour which may sometimes indicate a change of scribe or glossator, can only be established by examining the original manuscript.

As a trusting young researcher, the editor of the present book arrived at the British Library (at considerable expense) to be told that the manuscript she had ordered, and on which she was writing her first article, was unknown. Fortunately, informed guesswork soon produced the precious single leaf: knowing that many Anglo-Saxon manuscripts are in the Cotton collection she tried substituting 'Cotton' for 'Harley'. The famous editor of the printed text on which she had been relying had mis-identified the manuscript collection of this item as Harley. Experience shows that such errors are surprisingly frequent, even in classic editions on which generations of scholars have relied, though mistakes with numbers are more common than erroneous collection names. Mistakes left uncorrected in published works result in false manuscript numbers and wrong folios. Library cataloguing systems may change and much time can be wasted by searching for an outdated shelfmark listed in an old edition. In all such cases, errors can be perpetuated by scholars copying from one another. The researcher should not take it for granted that a published author has worked with the original text; the number of identical errors in different books demonstrates that this is not so. Advance checking and cross-checking by the researcher prevents panic and wasted time. Published reference works by Ker, Gneuss and Lapidge are available in University libraries[3] and many library catalogues can be checked on line in advance of a visit, though even here errors may be found. The researcher should not only confirm the library and shelfmark of the text required, but also the folio numbers. In checking the contents of a manuscript Thorndike and Kibre's *Catalogue of Incipits* may prove useful.[4] Information

---

[3] A manuscript can be checked in N.R. Ker, *Catalogue of Manuscripts Containing Anglo-Saxon*, Oxford, Clarendon (1957), 1990; Helmut Gneuss, *Handlist of Anglo-Saxon Manuscripts: a hand-list of manuscripts and manuscript fragments written or owned in England up to 1100*, Arizona Center for Medieval and Renaissance Studies, Tempe Arizona, 2001, and 'Addenda and corrigenda to the *Handlist of Anglo-Saxon manuscripts*', *Anglo-Saxon England*, 32, 2003, pp. 293–305; Michael Lapidge, *The Anglo-Saxon Library*, Oxford, Oxford University Press, 2007.

[4] Lynn Thorndike and Pearl Kibre, ed., *A Catalogue of Incipits of Medieval Scientific Writings in Latin*, Cambridge MA, Medieval Academy of America, 1937, revised and enlarged edition, 1963.

on drawings and illuminations in specific manuscripts can be checked in the series A Survey of Manuscripts Illuminated in the British Isles [5] and Ohlgren's *Iconographic Catalogue* may prove valuable in listing images according to subject matter and cross-referencing them to manuscripts.[6]

Colour

It pays to keep in mind that Anglo-Saxon manuscripts are not black and white and thus many photographs are misleading in this respect. Firstly, the tone is quite different. The famous *Beowulf* manuscript, for example, pages of which are reproduced in black and white in many editions, is in fact written in ink which is now brown, on brown vellum. Secondly, there are distinctions visible to the naked eye that may be lost in a photograph. Inks used by the same hand writing text at different times, or inks used by different hands, correcting, inserting and glossing, may be dissimilar. For example, in Oxford, Bodleian Library, MS Digby 86, there are additions in a different ink to the text on wind and Christmas Day prognostications, but possibly by the same hand. Annotations include the writing of the days of the week on the right-hand side of the folio, which ensured that a reader could find the day in question easily, and attest the care taken by the scribe in his revisions and the importance given to a prognostics text, a genre which has been largely overlooked by modern scholars until recently. The difference in ink is not visible in a black and white copy. A forthcoming doctoral thesis on the *Exeter Book*, which relies on first-hand examination of the manuscript, is able to suggest distinctions between punctuation which may be the work of the original scribe, and pointing which is probably later; details that are not always visible even in the recent digitized facsimile.[7]

Colour facsimiles of entire manuscripts are still relatively uncommon.

---

[5] J.J.G. Alexander, *Insular Manuscripts, 6th to the 9th century*, Insular Manuscripts of the British Isles, 1, London, Harvey Miller, 1978 and Elżbieta Temple, *Anglo-Saxon Manuscripts, 900–1066*, A Survey of Manuscripts Illuminated in the British Isles, 2, London, Harvey Miller, 1976. For Corpus Christi College, Cambridge see Mildred Budny, *Insular, Anglo-Saxon and Early Anglo-Norman Art at Corpus Christi College, Cambridge: an illustrated catalogue*, Kalamazoo MI, Medieval Institute Press, 1997.

[6] Thomas H. Ohlgren, *Insular and Anglo-Saxon Illuminated Manuscripts: an iconographic catalogue c. A.D. 625–1100*, New York and London, Garland, 1986.

[7] Abdullah Alger, 'The Verbal and Visual Rhetoric of Old English Poetry: an analysis of the punctuation and formulaic patterns in the *Exeter Book* (Exeter, Cathedral Library, MS 3501)', unpublished Ph.D. thesis, The University of Manchester, forthcoming 2009. The *Exeter Book*, Exeter, Cathedral, Dean and Chapter Library MS 3501, is digitized as Bernard J. Muir, ed., *The Exeter DVD: The Exeter Anthology of Old English Poetry*, Exeter, University of Exeter Press, 2006.

Printed facsimile books are usually partially or entirely in black and white, and digitized images on the web can be selective. While recent and forthcoming full colour digital editions such as Bernard Muir's *MS Junius 11*[8] are likely to satisfy most of the needs of researchers, in at least the immediate future, the expense of producing them means that the manuscripts selected for this process are likely to be the most famous items in a library's collection.

The absence of colour in a facsimile limits reader perception. Consider again Fig. 1.1. In the case of this black and white photograph, as in the facsimile edition of the *Paris Psalter*, the colour in text and drawings is effectively lost, though differences of tone are apparent if you look for them. It is significant that the introduction to the facsimile edition, which was published in 1956, makes no reference to colour in the lettering or the drawings, preferring to concentrate on full page illuminations once present, but now missing from the book. Greater access to colour photography in our own time may mean that today's scholars are more sensitive to the subtle messages of coloured text and will seek them out. Contemporary readers would have instantly understood information about the structure of a text from coloured rubrication and initials, messages that are lost in a black and white reproduction. As Elaine Treharne says of Cambridge, Corpus Christi College MS 201 'it seems that the later scribe ... copying *Lord's Prayer II* at p. 167, understood that coloured initial capitals and spacing introduced new sections of text within the layout of this manuscript' (p. 111). Effective use of colour is demonstrated by the beginning of a prognostics text in London, British Library, MS Cotton Vespasian D. xiv, fol. 75v (Fig. 1.2). The opening initial is red with green inside, a combination preparing the reader for a decorative programme of initials alternately coloured red and green, which are mostly set within the text line, not in the margin, yet which mark out sections of text clearly by virtue of being coloured. This is a fairly esoteric text in a manuscript which was probably not intended for display, yet it is set out carefully in a way that guides the reader. The colouring, and the distribution of red and green, would have acted as a mnemonic tool to help the process of memorizing which was an essential feature of education and scholarship.[9]

Black and white photographs of coloured line drawings are also misleading because they direct the modern viewer into false assumptions, not only that the drawings are monochrome but also that each figure, tree or building is the product of a single creative act. As Richard Gameson perceptively

---

[8] Bernard J. Muir, *MS Junius 11: the origins of English poetry, a masterpiece of Anglo-Saxon art; Bodleian Library Digital Texts 1*, software by Nick Kennedy, distributed for the Bodleian Library, University of Oxford, 2004.

[9] Mary J. Carruthers, *The Book of Memory: a study of memory in medieval culture*, Cambridge, Cambridge University Press, 1990, p. 9.

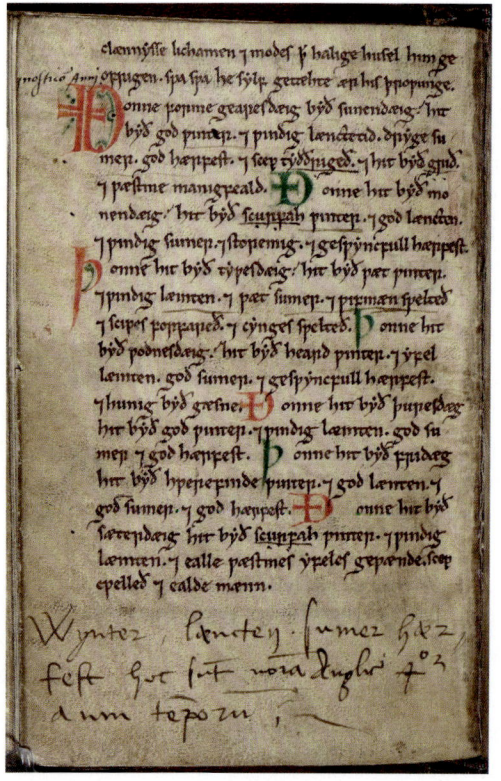

The opening of one of only two prognostics texts in the manuscript's extensive collection of catechetical, educative and homiletic material, including 53 pieces in Old English. This text concerns the day of the week on which the kalends of January falls. Coloured initials in alternating colours appear at the beginning of the prophecy for each day of the week, which would have helped the reader identify the day of the week immediately. Prognostics were part of a monk's training, and this text is set out carefully, just as are the religious texts among which it appears. The prophesy for the first day of the week reads:

Ðonne forme geares dæig byð sunendæig. hit/
byð god winter. 7 windig lænctetid. dryge su/
mer. god hærfest. 7 scep tyððrigeð. 7 hit byð grið./
7 wæstme manigfeald.

'Then [if] the first day of the year is on a Sunday, there will be a good winter, and a windy spring, and a good autumn [harvest], and sheep will be good and there will be abundant peace and wealth'.

The manuscript belongs to the first half of the twelfth century. It may have originated at Christ Church, Canterbury, or Rochester.

1.2 London, British Library, MS Cotton Vespasian D. xiv, fol.75v.

notes, with regard to the copying of the Carolingian *Utrecht Psalter* (Utrecht Universiteitsbibliotheek MS 32/484) by Anglo-Saxon artists in a range of coloured inks (in the manuscript now known as the *Harley Psalter*, London, British Library, MS Harley 603): 'The use of coloured lines also required the Anglo-Saxon artists to approach their task in a different way from their ninth-century predecessors. Instead of working through the composition, drawing one illustration after another, they had to proceed piecemeal, drawing one small part of a figure or building in one colour and consequently returning to draw the next part of the figure when they had changed to a different colour ink'.[10] Since such 'piecemeal' composition requires the division of bodies, costumes, architecture and plants into their component parts, an appreciation of the way colour is used involves an adjustment in our appreciation of the drawing, from something which, though copied, involving an element of spontaneity, to something more mechanical (Fig. 1.3).

---

[10] Richard Gameson, *The Role of Art in the Late Anglo-Saxon Church*, Oxford, Clarendon Press, 1995, p. 13. It should be noted, however, that the *Utrecht Psalter* itself is not monochrome. The drawings are executed in light and dark brown.

1.3 London, British Library, MS Harley 603 (*Harley Psalter*), fol. 66v, Psalm 127 (128): 1–3. The manuscript is a copy of Utrecht, Universiteitsbibliotheek 32, Script. Eccl. 484 (*Utrecht Psalter*).

The use of colour in Anglo-Saxon textual illustrations is not realistic. The artist had a restricted range of colours with which to convey differences of texture and tone, and the viewer responds accordingly. The tree in the bottom right of Fig. 1.3, for example, is not seen as the absurdity of a red trunk and branches with blue-black twigs and leaves, but an entity in which leaves are clearly distinguished from trunk and the branches from twigs. In 'reading' the images of the colourful Old English illuminated *Hexateuch* (London, British Library, MS Cotton Claudius B. iv) we do not see men with blue hair and buildings of blue, green, red and brown, but men with brunette hair and buildings with distinctive architectural features (Fig. 1.4).

Colour in more formal illuminations, however, may have specific significance. The yellow of the large cross which Queen Ælfgifu and King Cnut present to the New Minster at Winchester suggests that the cross

1.4 London, British Library, MS Cotton Claudius B. iv, fol. 57v, The *Old English Hexateuch*. Joseph as a servant in the household of Potiphar. Genesis 39:4.

was gold; the cross and the coloured names of the benefactors stand out against the pen-and-ink drawing of the donor portrait in the New Minster *Liber Vitae* (MS Stowe 944, fol. 6r; Fig. 7.26). The purple cloak of King Athelstan in Cambridge, Corpus Christi College MS 183 fol. 1v suggests royal magnificence, even though the king bows respectfully before the figure of St Cuthbert. Purple-stained leaves were used for the most magnificent Antique and Carolingian books, and the technique was copied in some of the most prestigious Anglo-Saxon books: Fig. 7.3 shows a purple page with inlaid crosses in the eighth-century *Codex Aureus* (Stockholm, Royal Library MS A. 135, fol. 16r). The significance of the purple background to the tenth-century donor portrait in the *New Minster Charter* (London, British Library, MS Cotton Vespasian A. viii, fol. 2v; Fig. 7.27) is pointed out by Catherine Karkov in this volume (p. 237). Yet even the best-quality, published, colour reproductions may convey no more than pinkish patches.[11]

---

[11] See Stuart D. Lee and Daniel Paul O'Donnell, 'From manuscript to computer', p. 259 in this volume for the difference in colour quality between JPEG and TIFF images.

> Table 1: What to take with you
>
> Depending on what the researcher wishes to study, some of the following will be necessary:
>
> - Pencils. It is not normally permitted to use a pen near manuscripts. Propelling ('non-stop') pencils avoid the awkwardness of sharpening.
> - Notebook. This should be big enough to write on one side of the page only (which will be clearer to read) and to allow for sketches.
> - The printed text – or the text on a laptop.
> - A hand-size Latin dictionary.
> - A dictionary of Latin abbreviations.*
> - A hand-size Old English dictionary. A University library will no doubt have dictionaries, but obtaining them takes time and they are not always shelved in the same place as the manuscripts.
> - A hand-held magnifying glass. (The Librarian may have one to lend. If not, they are difficult to find in Britain; try a fancy gift shop.)
> - A tape measure.
> - Laptop.
> - An international plug converter if a laptop is to be plugged in (can be bought at international airport of departure).
> - Mirror to read offsets (may be best bought locally to avoid broken glass in transit).
> - Some useful work to do while waiting for archive material to arrive.
>
> * Adriano Capelli, *Lexicon abbreviarum. Dizionario di abbreviature latine ed italiane*, 6th edition, Milan, Ulrico Hoepli, 2001.

Holes and other damage

Moððe word fræt, 'A moth ate words', exclaims an Anglo-Saxon riddler, expressing astonishment that *se wyrm forswealg wera gied sumes*, 'the worm should swallow the song of a man'.[12] 'Bookworms', actually caterpillars or insect larvae which feed on parchment, glue and the moulds in books, have sometimes damaged surviving manuscripts. More common are natural holes in the animal skin of which the pages are made; scribes were used to these and worked round them: they do not interfere with the continuity of a text. Later tears may be much more damaging. Some holes are visible in photographic reproductions; others are not. One Anglo-Saxon scholar reports being unable to make any sense of the text at one point in a manuscript, which he was reading in microfilm reproduction. On examining the manuscript first hand,

---

[12] Riddle 47, lines 1, 3; George Philip Krapp and Elliott Van Kirk Dobbie, ed., *The Exeter Book*, The Anglo-Saxon Poetic Records 3, New York, Columbia University Press, 1936, p. 205. The Old English riddle is related to Latin Riddle 16 of Symphosius, *Tinea*.

however, he discovered that there was a hole in the parchment and the text from the next folio was showing through.

Examination of post-scribal damage may be instructive to codicologists. First-hand examination of a wormhole has proved so on at least one occasion: the drawing of the Crucifixion that is now the frontispiece to one volume of an eleventh-century Old English homiliary, Cambridge, Corpus Christi College MS 421, p. 1, has been shown to have originally belonged in the companion volume (CCCC MS 419), and to have been reversed, so that it is now on the recto of the folio, facing the reader as the book is opened, rather than on the verso, facing text.[13] Cambridge, Corpus Christi College MS 391, page 713 has a hole which continues through the remaining leaves of the manuscript, getting steadily larger towards the end of the book. Examination suggests that the damage was caused by a stud on the back board: the parchment around the edges of the hole has been discoloured by rust. However, the folio preceding page 713 has no hole or stain of any sort, suggesting either that there is more than one leaf missing, or that the final quire was once bound in a different order. There is confirmation of the disruption in traces of ink, particularly higher up on the page, which do not match the text or any shine-through; they probably derive from a facing page that is now missing.[14]

Many Anglo-Saxon manuscripts have been despoiled, 'improved' or damagingly repaired by their owners. Not all such alterations are obvious, but close examination may sometimes indicate the nature of the interference: stitch holes may indicate where a leaf has previously been bound; missing text or decoration may show that a manuscript has been trimmed; strips of paper or parchment, stuck down to reinforce damaged edges, may cover some original material. Partial reconstruction is sometimes possible. If a leaf has left offsets on a remaining folio, a weak mirror image of the original gives some evidence (for example the remains of a frame to a now-missing illuminated page dividing the psalter from the canticles, visible on fol. 176r of the *Paris Psalter*); special lighting may reveal text underneath a pasted repair strip, a stain, or other damage. There is nothing new about such discoveries: a previously illegible word at a climactic part of *Beowulf* was read from an ultra violet photograph in 1938.[15] Technology

---

[13] First noted by Neil Ker and described in detail in Timothy Graham, 'Changing the context of medieval manuscript art: the case of Matthew Parker' in *Medieval Art: recent perspectives. A memorial tribute to C.R. Dodwell*, ed. Gale R. Owen-Crocker and Timothy Graham, Manchester, Manchester University Press, 1998, pp. 183–205, at pp. 194–5.

[14] These might have been erased glosses, but this appears unlikely, since the parchment is usually quite smooth.

[15] John C. Pope, *The Rhythm of Beowulf: an interpretation of the normal and hypermetric verse-forms in Old English poetry*, New Haven and London, Yale University

1.5 Oxford, Bodleian Library, MS e Mus 66 (inside front cover board).

Sheets containing sections from Arator's *Historia apostolica* were used as pastedowns on the insides of the front and back wooden book covers, probably some time in the late twelfth century. At some later date, these pastedowns were removed, but not without leaving an imprint of the writing in the glue where they can be read with the aid of a mirror. The scribe has been identified as coming from either Northern Italy or France, and as having written in the late sixth or early seventh century. It is especially interesting that the text is written as though it were prose, and not, as is customary, one dactylic hexameter per line. (Extended caption provided by Gernot R. Wieland)

does advance, however, and there is always the possibility that a patch of runny ink created by an earlier attempt to improve a text with chemicals may yield its secrets to more modern, non-intrusive techniques. Manuscript contexts which have been taken for granted for well over a century may be questioned by modern palaeographers. Kevin Kiernan's arguments for the rearrangement of the *Beowulf* manuscript both before and after its damage in the Ashburnham House fire of 1731 are perhaps the best-known challenges to preconceptions,[16] but many Anglo-Saxon manuscripts have been re-ordered and added to in both medieval and early modern times,

---

Press, pp. 232–3. The reading itself is anticlimactic in literary-critical terms: it reveals that the woman mourner at Beowulf's funeral is *geatisc* ('Geatish'), hardly surprising since Beowulf was king of the Geats.

[16] Kevin Kiernan, *Beowulf and the Beowulf Manuscript*, New Brunswick, NJ, Rutgers University Press, 1981; see Elaine Treharne, 'Manuscript sources of Old English poetry' in this volume, pp. 104–6.

and there is scope for the recognition of such changes as students work on less famous manuscripts.

Numerous medieval manuscripts were dismembered when they were no longer useful or readable. Although it is generally assumed that many Anglo-Saxon manuscripts were wilfully destroyed at the Reformation, pre-modern habits of recycling did mean that old parchment was routinely re-used in the repair of books and the making of new books. Old folios were cut up to repair damaged leaves, to line spines, to act as endpapers or to be used as pastedowns on the insides of book covers. Text recovered from an offset in the glue left from such a pastedown is illustrated in Fig. 1.5: fragments of folios containing Arator's *Historia apostolica* had been glued onto the wooden book covers of Oxford, Bodleian Library, MS e Mus 66. Although the folios were later removed, traces of writing remained in the glue, which, with the help of a mirror, could be deciphered. Reading a medieval manuscript, then, may not involve working with a codex, a single leaf or even a fragment. It might mean detective work with the ghost that was once a text or an illumination.

When to make your visit

Preparation is essential. Although every researcher's requirements are different, it is important for every scholar to familiarise him/herself as fully as possible with the material before approaching the manuscript. It is sensible to have acquaintance with the relevant script or scripts. This point stands even if the researcher's primary aim is art rather than text. While combing through manuscripts the student may find some useful additional material; it is frustrating if it cannot be contextualised because one cannot read the associated text.

If the research concerns a text that has been edited, the student should get to know the text well, identifying any areas of ambiguity or difficulty. Subsequently s/he may wish to compare this edited version with the manuscript to see if the editor has transcribed it faithfully or, as sometimes happens, has misrepresented some parts of it. An editor may transcribe what s/he expects to see rather than what is really there such as writing *bið* ('is') when the manuscript has *bid*. Adding macrons to indicate (supposed) vowel length may impose an editor's interpretation of words. Some editions omit to note mixed scripts, standard conventions for abbreviations, contractions, capitalization, punctuation, additions, deletions, marginalia or spelling variations. The repetition of a reading in more than one edition need not mean this is an accurate transcription of the manuscript, since, as already noted, an editor may copy a predecessor's work. Punctuation is not consistent in either Latin or Old English manuscripts of the Anglo-Saxon period, but an individual scribe may have consistent habits which an editor may obscure by replacing original punctuation with modern. Modern punctuation itself may be controversial, since the placing of a pause may affect the interpretation of the text.

If no edited text exists, it may be possible to order a copy of the manuscript for personal research, in the form of microfilm, prints, or digitized photographs which can be received by email. The speed with which requests are carried out can vary tremendously. Some libraries are extremely efficient; others are notoriously slow and can take several months to supply material, which may be too long for a short-term project. It is wise to check

---

Table 2: What not to do

- Do not eat or drink in the vicinity of a manuscript. Normally there will be notices strictly forbidding this. If a well-intentioned but misguided member of the administrative staff should bring you a cup of coffee do not to drink it near the archival material.
- Smoking is forbidden in most public buildings today, but the smell of cigarettes can linger on the hands, so any reader taking a 'smoke break' should wash their hands before returning to the manuscript.
- Do not rest anything on the manuscript (such as a stand-alone magnifier).
- Do not attempt to trace any letter or image.
- Do not turn down pages.
- Do not 'bookmark' the manuscript with scraps of your own paper or anything else; if you need to cross-reference ask the duty librarian to supply markers made of harmless materials.
- Never take an unauthorized sample of parchment, ink or paint.
- Do not place a codex face-down: this may break the binding and damage the text or image on the page.
- Do not attempt to take photographs without permission. Manuscripts are normally kept under controlled lighting and flash photography may cause damage. Archival material is copyright; to take an unauthorised copy is to break the law. Applications for reproduction should be made to the Library's Office of Reproduction and Rights.
- Do not pull out a mobile phone (cellphone). Library staff may think unauthorised photographs are being taken. Phones should be switched off or set to 'silent' in libraries, and only used outside the reading rooms.
- Do not indicate that an item is 'finished with' and have it returned to store only to countermand this. Librarians will usually be able to keep an item available if a reader is likely to want to consult it again.
- Do not leave archival material unattended on a desk unless the librarian says it is acceptable to do so.
- Do not leave your library card and identification inside the library: you may not be able to get back in without them
- Do not remove any library property from the library.

the timetable for supply before committing to a piece of work dependent on the reproduction. Even when such research materials are supplied, as outlined above, it is desirable to check your finds against the manuscript in case more exists than has been transmitted, or there are further details not visible in the reproduction.

Study of a text in isolation may obscure the importance of context. The conscientious researcher will wish to know if the text being studied has habitual 'companions'. One of the authors of this chapter (Maria Cesario) found hitherto unstudied texts of prognostics by analysing the manuscript contexts of known texts and identifying common patterns. Having established the occurrence of the *Kalendae ianuariae* (first of January) text in manuscripts also containing *computus* texts, she decided to examine other *computus* manuscripts for more texts of this prognostication and was rewarded with finding them. The contents of a manuscript can generally be identified from published research tools and library catalogues.

If the research interest is palaeographical or codicological it is obviously essential to examine the manuscript, though unless the scholar is part of a major, funded research project and has full permission and co-operation from the library, access is likely to be restricted; for example modern bindings cannot be removed. It is important for the researcher to come to the manuscript with a full check-list of what s/he is looking for; experience and a responsible, professional approach are desirable. In preparation for such work, many University Masters Programmes offer palaeography modules and there are online courses and teaching software, such as the University of Melbourne's Evellum software which includes a DVD about the practicalities of making manuscripts and the Ductus Project intended to teach Latin palaeography, as well as digitized editions. Some major libraries offer short palaeography courses on site, and these can offer invaluable preliminary experience of working with medieval manuscripts under the guidance of experienced scholars.

Accumulating information from images is another skill, which may require researching many manuscripts. Though Ohlgren's *Iconographic catalogue* offers a useful starting point, it has few reproductions and those included are not of good quality. The volumes by Temple and Alexander in the Survey of Manuscripts Illuminated in the British Isles series are invaluable in terms of identifying the images in specific manuscripts, and contain a useful range of reproductions, but there is no attempt at comprehensive illustration. From these works, however, the researcher should be able to establish whether there is a facsimile edition or an individual reproduction in a published work. Not all images have been photographed, and some artwork, especially decorated initials, may have been paid little attention. In such cases a researcher should request a copy, and if the library offers a print, s/he may wish to invest in the

This manuscript has the right to be called an Anglo-Saxon manuscript since it contains an ownership note in Old English testifying that it belonged to an English abbess: *Cuthsuuithae boec thaera abbatissan*, 'A book of Cuthswitha, of the abbess'. The owner is presumed to be the Cuthswitha who was abbess of Inkberrow, in the diocese of Worcester, from 693 to 709. The manuscript itself, however, was old and foreign when it came into the abbess's possession, and, after only a short time in England, has spent the rest of its life on the Continent. A Latin manuscript of St Jerome's *In Ecclesiasten*, it was written in Italy in the fifth century. It was almost certainly taken to Würzburg by the eighth-century English mission to Germany. The English tradition was strong in Würzburg: the bishopric was founded by the Anglo-Saxon missionary St Boniface in 742, and the first bishop, Burkhard (742–753) was also English.

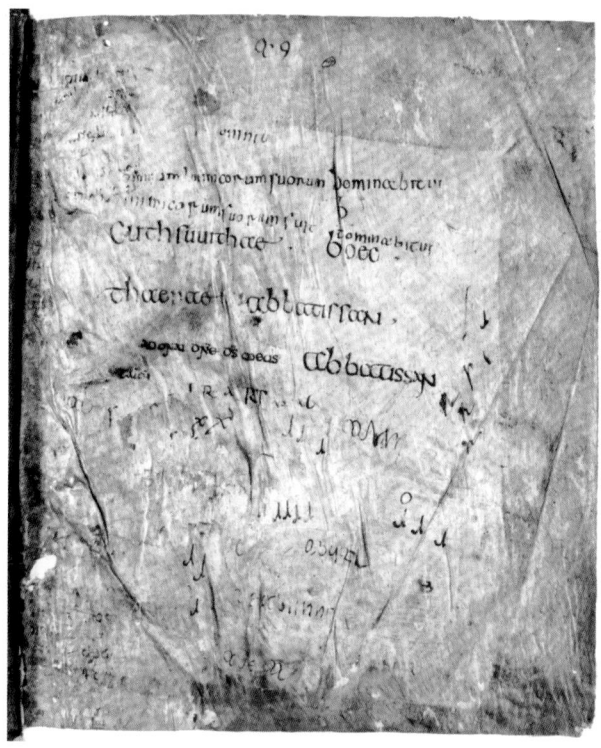

1.6 Würzburg, Cathedral Library MS M.p.th.q. 2, fol. 1r.

extra expense of a colour reproduction. Digital scans, which are increasingly the standard format, generally come in colour.

Not all manuscripts are accessible to scholars. The eighth-century *St Petersburg Gospels* (St Petersburg, National Library of Russia, MS Lat. F.v.I. 8), displayed under glass but disbound, was revealed briefly to members of the International Society of Anglo-Saxonists in the course of a symposium following the conference in Helsinki in 2001. A few of the images were already well known, but the exhibition of familiar Insular details in an unfamiliar and magnificent context proved a delight. A digital facsimile version is in preparation, but the manuscript is not normally available for study.[17]

It may be that the researcher genuinely does NOT need to see the manuscript. If a text is well known, has been edited several times, and

---

[17] See the catalogue of the parallel exhibitions held in Helsinki and St Petersburg on this occasion: Matti Kilpiö and Leena Kahlas-Tarkka, ed., *Ex Insula Lux: manuscripts and hagiographical material connected with medieval England*, Helsinki, Helsinki University Library, The National Library of Finland, 2001, pp. 87–8, 118, Plates 11–12, 27.

1.7 Munich, Bavarian State Library MS Clm 6433, fol. 12v.

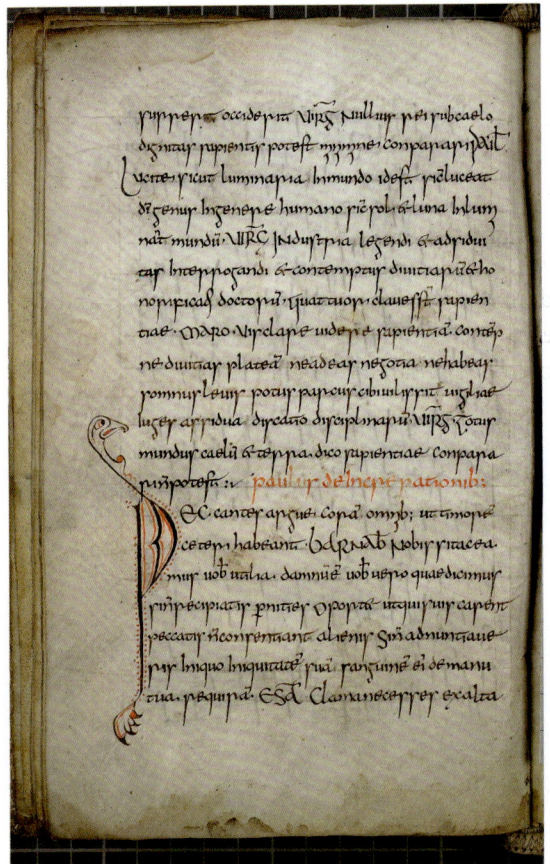

A theological miscellany or *Florilegium*, the eighth-century manuscript was written and decorated by the scribe of several Freiburg manuscripts, who calls himself *Perigrinus*. He was probably a Northumbrian. The script is Anglo-Saxon minuscule and features the diminuendo in script size from the large initial letter, which is typical of Insular work. The initial has characteristic Insular zoomorphic terminals and red dotting.

detailed editorial notes and versions can be compared, it may be more responsible not to disturb the manuscript for the sake of its preservation, especially if photographs have been studied. However, this should be a rational judgement, not an opt-out! The well-known Old English poetic texts from the four major codices have been repeatedly edited, exist in hard-copy facsimiles and all have either been digitized or are in the process of being digitally published. Access to these manuscripts is now severely restricted.

Planning a journey

Establish the location of the manuscript using the reference works already mentioned. As a glance at the index of manuscripts at the end of this book (pp. 296–301) will show, the British Library in London, the Bodleian Library in Oxford and the Cambridge libraries of Corpus Christi College, Trinity College and Cambridge University have outstandingly extensive collections of Anglo-Saxon manuscripts, but others are to be found in Cathedral,

University and National libraries of the United Kingdom and still more are abroad. Comparative work, such as examining the output of a particular scribe, different versions of a homily or independent illustrations of the same basic text, will very often require the examination of manuscripts from more than one library, so the scholar should take into account travelling time and the need for inductions into different libraries (see below, pp. 25–7) when planning a research trip.

Although it is entirely possible that a scholar's interest may focus on material written/illuminated in England between the conversion and the Norman Conquest, the researcher studying Anglo-Saxon culture and scholarship, for example, should be prepared to widen his/her net to include works which do not fit into a straightforward pattern of English production and ownership. Some manuscripts spent time in England before being taken to the Continent. A famous example is the *Vercelli Book* (Vercelli, Biblioteca capitolare CXVII) which contains some of the best-known Old English poems as well as a substantial collection of Old English homiletic prose.[18] A less-known case is the fifth-century Italian manuscript illustrated in Fig. 1.6 (Würzburg Cathedral Library MS M.p.th.q. 2, fol. 1r.), which bears an ownership note demonstrating that it belonged to a seventh-century Anglo-Saxon abbess, before being taken to Würzburg during the eighth-century missions to Frisia and Old Saxony.

Likewise, a researcher might include manuscripts produced by English-trained scribes/artist working on the Continent, such as the Freising scribe who names himself as *Perigrinus* ('foreigner'; Fig. 1.7).

Sometimes manuscripts produced abroad were deliberately imported into England.[19] An illuminated Carolingian psalter, probably produced in Rheims in the ninth century, was taken to England in about AD 1000, where its impressionistic line-drawings were hugely influential. It returned to the Continent in the seventeenth century and is now known as the *Utrecht Psalter*; but for a significant period of its existence it was in Anglo-Saxon ownership.

Manuscripts containing Old English may have been written as late as the twelfth century and so historically belong to the Norman period rather than the Anglo-Saxon, but they may be relevant to a research project on Anglo-Saxon material.

---

[18] See Donald Scragg, 'Manuscript sources of Old English prose', pp. 61–87 in this volume; and Elaine Treharne, 'Manuscript sources of Old English poetry', pp. 89–111 in this volume.

[19] See Gernot Wieland, 'A survey of Latin manuscripts', pp. 113–57 in this volume.

Arranging access to the manuscript

Study the library's web pages to establish its policies on handling manuscripts, how many manuscripts can be studied simultaneously (generally not more than three) and the opening days and hours. Most libraries are open from 9.00 a.m. to 5.00 p.m. Monday to Friday – opening hours in municipal libraries may seem relatively short for those accustomed to University Library access. Hours are reduced at weekend and some libraries are closed on Sundays. Visiting on weekdays is recommended, preferably in the morning. Access to some libraries, such as the Wren and the Parker in Cambridge, is restricted by the number of seats. Competition can be particularly strong during traditional University research periods, such as summer vacation.

Requests for access should include precise details of which manuscript or manuscripts are required. If an item is in a special exhibition it is not likely to be available for study during the duration of the exhibition and advance enquiry can save a wasted journey. Likewise, if a manuscript is in a display case on long-term exhibition the curator or librarian may be unwilling to disturb it and negotiations may be necessary. However, individual libraries may go to an extraordinary amount of trouble to help researchers.

Write well in advance for permission to work with a manuscript. It is usually possible to correspond by email: there are links on web pages and major libraries on the Continent have English-language links. If writing personally to a small, continental library consider the courtesy of writing in their language, which may produce a more rapid reply than a letter in English would do. A reference is normally required. For a graduate student this should normally come from the research supervisor/advisor, and should explain the research, give reasons for visiting the library and assert the reliability of the student. Graduate level is normally expected. If for any reason a potential reader does not have a 'first degree', or is working outside normal academic circles, the reference should make it clear that the research is at graduate level. If the visit does not involve study at this level, other supporting information should be supplied.

If there is need for special lighting (ultra violet or fibre optic lights or a video spectral comparator for palimpsests) this should be discussed in advance. The library may be able to provide it or the researcher may have to bring it, if permitted. If the researcher wishes to use a laptop, permission should be granted and facilities established in advance. Absence of a wireless connection, or even of conveniently placed electric sockets, is to be expected in older buildings.

If the researcher wishes to photograph the manuscript, the library's policy should be established in advance. Permission is quite likely to be refused, though the librarian may be willing to have the manuscript photographed professionally at your expense. This is likely to take place at a later date; do not expect to take photographs home with you.

Finally, it is wise to confirm precise details of date, time and requirements close to the time of the visit. Libraries have been known to deny all knowledge of a foreign visit and to refuse access to a traveller who has made an expensive journey. On the scholar's arrival librarians may offer a microfilm rather than the expected manuscript, claiming that authorisation to view the original will take too long; so allow plenty of time. Missing keys, or staff with the authority to grant access being absent for the day may not seem like good reasons to block your work, but these things do happen and having a public argument about it will probably not forward your case. Be firm but patient.

Beware closure for national and local holidays. Do not assume that the library will be open: ask the question specifically. A foreign library may take it for granted that everybody knows the date of a local festival! Much as the visiting student might enjoy participating in the town celebrations, the diversion can be frustrating if unexpected.

What to expect from the library

The whole procedure may take a considerable amount of time, especially on the first visit. The researcher may have corresponded with manuscript curators and their staff, but the 'Manuscripts Department' may be a separate entity within a library, the entry criteria of which also have to be met. It may be necessary to produce identification (such as the library card from the home university) and a copy of the letter of recommendation, even if this item has been sent in advance. The student should be prepared to queue to be photographed for a library card and even to swear an oath not to inflict damage on library property. The researcher may be treated with caution, which might be interpreted as rudeness, but is merely unwillingness to release fragile material to an unauthorised person. Getting back into the library after a break will probably mean producing identification, or a barcoded card on each occasion.

There may be a long wait for the archive material, despite ordering in advance. Library staff will advise on the delivery time. Orders placed after 4.00 p.m. will not normally be processed until the following day. Manuscripts are not simply kept on shelves like modern library books. They are maintained in controlled temperature and humidity, and in fire-proof environments. There are national and international standards of practice in manuscript storage and conservation. It may take a good deal of time and effort to bring a manuscript from its place of storage to a reading room some distance away, which explains the need to alert the library well in advance.

1.8 Working with a 'book snake' to hold open a manuscript. The manuscript is Hereford Cathedral Library O.VI.II, fol. 48v.

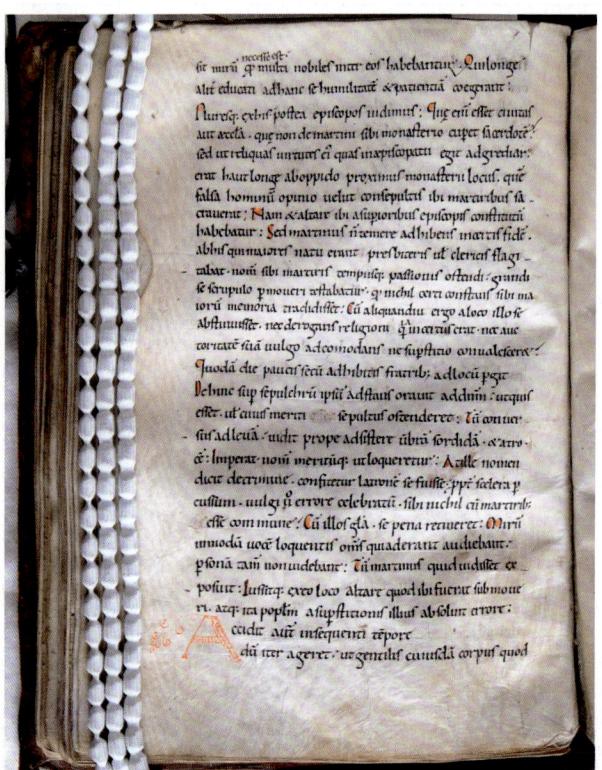

While examining the archive material, the reader may be required to wear washable cotton gloves to protect the manuscript material from dust, dirt and sweat; they may also protect the researcher. Many manuscripts are kept in purpose-made boxes which fit them exactly, providing support and protection. The manuscript may be delivered to the reader's table in its box and should be removed carefully. If an inexperienced reader is left to do this alone and the book is heavy or awkward s/he should not hesitate to ask library staff for help. It is likely that the manuscript will not simply be placed on the table. It may be supported on a wooden reading stand, a cradle made of synthetic foam or by a book support bag: a kind of cushion made of felt and filled with polystyrene granules. Foam supports of various kinds may be inserted under the book and a spine-support strip may be necessary. Once a codex is opened on its support, the pages may start to close, especially if the binding is tight. To prevent this happening the reader may be provided with a 'snake' which looks deceptively like a string of beads, but in fact consists of a series of small, non-toxic lead weights covered in leather or cotton (Fig. 1.8).[20] The 'snake' is intended to lie on the pages, not in the central gutter. Conservation weights are also available. Made of smooth wood, leather or cotton, they can be wedged against the manuscript to stop it moving. A single leaf may start to curl and be in danger of tearing. Some kind of archival weight should prevent this.

The furniture provided by the library as appropriate for reading their manuscripts may prove to be uncomfortable. One professor speaks of a table so high that she had to stand for two full days. The top of a large book on a sloping reading stand may prove difficult for the myopic. Generally

---

[20] See *Recommendations for the storage and exhibition of archival documents* BS 5454: 2000, London, BSI, 2000. I am grateful to Alun Ford for information about the British Standards document and for answering my questions; and to Chris Tuckley for the image.

speaking, one puts up with some discomfort if it is in the best interests of the archival material. However, if it is impossible to work, the researcher should not be afraid to ask for help, and will usually meet with kindness and sensitivity. Manuscript rooms are generally more intimate than reading rooms for printed books, and librarians may offer personal attention and interest. However, the student should never take advantage of this. Members of the library staff are not academic supervisors, nor are they there to do the students' research for them.

Table 3: Reproducing manuscript material

Images are copyright and should not be reproduced without permission. Most libraries will allow a graduate student to reproduce, without charge, images of manuscripts in a thesis or dissertation which is not to be published, though there may be a limit to the number of images permitted.*

If an author wishes to illustrate a book or article with photographs it is essential to discuss the matter in advance with the editor or publisher. Book publishers may budget for a certain number of illustrations but additional ones will have to be paid for, either personally by the author or by means of a grant, which should be applied for well in advance of need. Reproduction of colour is particularly expensive; it requires high quality paper, and is unusual in journals.

To reproduce an image in a printed text, the author should expect to pay both for the photograph and for publication rights. Costs vary tremendously from library to library and also depending on the quality of the image required, its size (full, half or quarter page) and whether it is to be in colour or black and white. The author should establish in advance from the editor/publisher what quality of reproduction is needed and is usually required to give full details of the publication to a library before permission is granted: author/editor, title, publisher, date of publication, print run, hardback and paperback editions, price, nature of publication, single country/single language/world rights. There are different charge rates for book jackets and film/television publications. Some libraries will not give permission to reproduce any image from a secondary source, so it is necessary to purchase their own photograph. All fees for photographs have to be paid in advance, though the reproduction rights, in some cases, only have to be paid on publication. Some libraries require an exact form of words to accompany each image used. Do not attempt to edit permission statements to make them uniform, however unwieldy they appear; there may be penalties if the correct form of words is not used. It is common for a library to request a copy of the published work either in addition to, or in lieu of, a rights fee. However, many libraries generously reduce or waive reproduction fees for academic publications with limited circulation.

* The Bodleian Library, Oxford, for example, would waive the reproduction fee for up to ten images of its copyright material; but above this number there is a nominal charge of £5 per image plus VAT if appropriate. Information from Patricia Buckingham, Principal Library Assistant, Western Manuscripts Photographic Research, Bodleian Library, 18 December 2007.

Introduction to Chapter 2

The analytical techniques of codicology and palaeography are often overlooked by students studying text in a modern printed edition. Yet it is the pioneering research of deciphering the manuscript that has made possible the transcription of texts into modern lettering and led to the resultant boom in editions, commentaries and the whole 'industry' of textual criticism. New technical developments, particularly in lighting and digitization, mean that this once-neglected area is now expanding rapidly and there is room for new research both on well-known texts and on manuscripts which have received little attention before. The recent Manchester-based Project 'An Inventory of Script and Spellings in eleventh-century English' and the work of the University of Lethbridge-based 'Digital Medievalist' group testify to the lively growth of this type of study.

The following chapter explains the details which should be examined by codicologists and palaeographers, and gives a great deal of practical guidance to those new both to reading the findings of experts and to making their own observations. It includes explanations of the processes by which quires of leaves came to be assembled and available to be bound into codices; details of how to describe them and why deviation from the norm may be significant; examples of the conventional 'shorthand' used to express the dating of material; and an account of styles of script and the abbreviations commonly used in both Latin and Old English writing.

While modern mass-production of printed material may seem very distant from an era where every process was carried out by hand, it is fascinating to find that many conventions used in Anglo-Saxon times continued for centuries of printed-book production and in most cases are still used today – lists of contents, running headings, enlarged initials at chapter openings, carefully observed margins, the use of different scripts within a single manuscript. Anglo-Saxon manuscripts seem less remote when one recognises that they are the direct ancestors of the books we handle daily in our own lives.

2

The construction and writing of Anglo-Saxon manuscripts

Alexander R. Rumble

Being able to transcribe or check a text in an original manuscript gives real meaning to 'primary' source study. If it happens to be the only surviving manuscript of that text, then this is the closest one can physically get both to the text's creator and to its first known copyist. Such a manuscript contrasts wholly to printed editions which replace all original physical features with a modern homogenized regularity of appearance affording little difference between a tenth- and a twenty-first-century text. However, only by understanding the processes that occurred in the making of the physical artefact represented by the manuscript, and by learning what each of its individual features signify, can the modern user take full advantage of the huge privilege of gaining access to it.

The present chapter aims to provide some guidance to modern users of Anglo-Saxon manuscripts, particularly those using them for the first time. It concerns two closely interrelated disciplines: 'codicology', the examination of the physical characteristics of the manuscript book or *codex*; and 'palaeography', the classification and description of former styles of handwriting. The focus is on manuscripts preserved as books, but much of what follows is also relevant to fragments and to documents written on single-sheets of parchment.

It is desirable for new researchers to be as proficient as possible in the reading of Anglo-Saxon and later scripts before seeing the manuscripts themselves. Librarians and curators cannot be expected to read the text for their 'customers' but will usually give advice in cases where a manuscript is damaged, if only by the provision of aids such as cold fibre-optic lights or magnifying glasses.

The increased availability of facsimiles of manuscripts has provided the student with the essential tools needed for practice in transcription and description. Photographs (or digital images) of specific pages of manuscripts for private study may usually be ordered from the libraries where they are now preserved, unless the physical state of the manuscript does not allow this. Many of the most important surviving contemporary manuscripts from the Anglo-Saxon period have in fact already been published in facsimile or microfiche and should be available in major libraries around the world. The researcher may thus consult and study the volumes of the two serial publications Early English Manuscripts in Facsimile (Copenhagen, 1951–2002) and Anglo-Saxon Manuscripts in Microfiche Facsimile (Tempe, Arizona, 1994–, in progress). CD-ROMs of some manuscripts can also be purchased and there are a growing number of digital images on the world wide web.

The other essential preparation for work on a particular manuscript or collection is to read closely the extant catalogues, not only Ker's *Catalogue* and Gneuss's *Handbook*, but also the catalogue of the specific library concerned. The latter are increasingly available online in searchable electronic form. Notes should be made from them not only in relation to the content of a manuscript but also regarding its physical make-up and the current view as to the number and date of its scribes.

A note on dates and dating conventions

Anglo-Saxon manuscripts can only very rarely be dated to an exact year of production. Palaeographical dating usually represents the opinion of an expert as to roughly which quarter of a century the manuscript belongs, based on the style of script and sometimes also of the decoration. The palaeographical date assigned to the manuscript and its contents is given in a standard formula where 's.' stands for 'from the ... th century' (Latin *saeculo*) and a roman numeral with an added modifier indicates a sub-division of a particular century. An example of the sequence of possible dates within the tenth century, set out in the conventionally accepted way, is given in Table 1. (Note that, according to this convention, 900 × 920 etc means a date between 900 and 920, as opposed to 900–20 which means continuously in these years.)

Table 1 Palaeographical dating: examples of dates in the tenth century.

s.ix/x	= *c.*900
s.x in.	= 900 × 920 [in. = Latin *ineunte* 'at the beginning of ...']
s.x^1	= 920 × 940
s.x med.	= 940 × 960 [med. = Latin *mediante* 'in the middle of ...']
s.x^2	= 960 × 980
s.x ex.	= 980 × 1000 [ex. = Latin *exeunte* 'at the end of ...']
s.x/xi	= *c.*1000

Binding(s) and associated features

The first thing that confronts the reader in a library on being handed the manuscript requested is usually a bound volume. This often contains extra leaves between the covers and the textblock (the leaves containing the text). It is very important to spend time on examining these outer features of the manuscript before going on to read the text. Some careful note-taking at the start about these features will not only give a preliminary idea of the context in which the main text survived and was used but will also later save time in finding one's way around the *codex*.

Binding(s)

The purpose of the covers and associated material was to protect the textblock from physical damage. The binding structure may be Anglo-Saxon (rarely), medieval, or modern; those of any date may give clues about the origin or provenance of the manuscript not contained in the text itself. The materials, motifs and methods used in the binding should be observed and noted, for example wooden boards covered with decorated or stamped leather and/or metal and jewels or ivories; or, alternatively, covers made of stiff parchment or pasteboard. Variation in the number and arrangement of the leather bands to which individual quires were sewn and to which the boards were attached can be used to give an approximate date to a particular binding. In general, the later the binding the more bands will be present. Some medieval books have the title (and sometimes the press-mark) of the volume on a parchment slip pasted to the outside of the binding. A previous owner's coat of arms, badge or initials sometimes appears on the cover, although further work may be needed to identify the full name, biography and significance of the person concerned.

'... only by understanding the processes that occurred in the making of the physical artefact represented by the manuscript, and by learning what each of its individual features signify, can the modern user take full advantage of the huge privilege of gaining access to it.'

Pastedowns

A piece of parchment or paper was usually stuck on the inside of each of the two boards of the binding in order to hide the grooves into which the ends of the leather bands were channelled. Such pastedowns were sometimes made from fragments of books which had been dismembered, identification and study of which may provide clues as to the provenance of the *codex*.

Flyleaves

Extra leaves were normally placed between the pastedowns and the first and last pages of text in order to act as a protective buffer between the textblock and the cover. The parchment or paper used for such flyleaves may be blank or it may be pages from dismembered manuscripts; even if originally blank, they were often written upon by later owners or users and may give pointers as to the provenance of the *codex*.

Binding fragments

Throughout the medieval period it was common practice to take apart books that were no longer of interest or of which the script or language was regarded as archaic and difficult to read. The parchment of individual leaves was then re-used as pastedowns, or flyleaves or, often cut into strips, as stiffening material within new bindings. Because of their small size the identification of the text contained in such manuscript fragments sometimes proves difficult. As their provenance and/or origin are even more difficult to ascertain, it is all the more important to make a careful record of their discernible external features as this may lead to the discovery of other fragments from the same manuscript elsewhere.

Marks of previous ownership

Both institutional librarians and individual owners often added inscriptions to books identifying them as part of a particular collection, occasionally including a curse against potential thieves. The signatures of owners, or donors, of manuscripts may also be found, usually on a flyleaf or a pastedown, but also sometimes in the margin of the text itself. Similarly, coats of arms and personal or family badges also appear. Further study based on these marks can provide evidence for provenance.

Library press-marks were sometimes added to a flyleaf or a pastedown, and may correspond to references in a surviving library catalogue. Some libraries use a distinctive stamp to safeguard their property rights, often in former times adding it rather obtrusively to the leaves containing the text or illustrations, a practice now generally discontinued. Details about the acquisition of the volume by a particular owner are also occasionally to be found written somewhere within it and may include the date of purchase, the price paid, and the source of acquisition.

Table of contents or index

From time to time internal finding aids were added to manuscript books in the form of a table of contents or an index. Such tables of contents consist of lists of texts in the order of their occurrence in the volume, usually referring each item to the number of the folio or page on which it begins. Occasionally, however, tables of contents are to be found as an original part of a text (Fig. 2.8), giving easy access to a complex entity divided into books and/or chapters. Thus, in Cambridge, Corpus Christi College MS 173, Part I, fols 33r–35r, the preliminary table of contents to this early tenth-century copy of the *Alfred-Ine Law-code* gives a quick overview of the whole text, listing topics of legislation in chapter order, for example *xix Be preosta gefeohte* ('concerning fighting by priests'). Care should be taken, however, in using such finding aids, as sometimes the table does not correspond exactly with what follows in the main text. Such lack of correspondence may be a clue to a revision of the text during copying.

A medieval index usually only gave a rough alphabetical order of names or subjects, with folio or page or section references added. Careful analysis of both tables of contents and indexes may give the researcher information about an earlier ordering of the contents of a volume or evidence for the loss of items from it.

The construction of the textblock

Leaves

Anglo-Saxon texts surviving in contemporary manuscripts and in most medieval copies were written on treated animal skins, the generic term for which is 'parchment'. The better type (vellum) was made from calf skin, the less fine from that of sheep or goats. The method of preparation of the skin included its cleaning in a solution of lime, the removal of the animal's hair or wool by shaving, smoothing the skin with a knife or plane, whitening it with chalk, and cutting it to the required size. Despite the skill of the parchment-maker, there usually remains a noticeable difference between the hair and the flesh sides of a parchment leaf, the hair side being darker in colour and often less smooth. There is also a difference, in the early Anglo-Saxon period of literacy, between the parchment produced in the British Isles and that produced on the Continent, the former being darker in colour, thicker and more suede-like than the latter.

Anglo-Saxon texts surviving in early modern copies will usually be found written on hand-made paper rather than parchment and such paper often has distinctive watermarks from which it may be possible to date and locate the place of its manufacture.

With both parchment and paper, the following details should be recorded: the nature, texture, and colour of the material; the outside dimensions of the leaves, measuring height × width in millimetres; and the presence of holes, tears or repairs (and whether these were made before or after the writing of the text).

Preliminary page-design: pricking and ruling

Before any writing was added to a page its layout was planned and marked out by means of ruled lines guided by patterns of prickings made in the margins with a sharp point. Sometimes a pricker in the form of a spiked wheel may have been used in order to get an even distribution of pricks. The use of a template, a piece of wood or leather with holes at the required intervals, is also possible. A few vertical lines, often in pairs, were ruled in order to mark the sides of the space intended for writing. Many more lines were ruled horizontally as a guide to help the scribe to keep each line of text even across the page. In Insular manuscripts up to the tenth century, it was the practice that the whole quire (usually of four *bifolia*) was pricked together as a folded booklet, and therefore the manuscripts exhibit pricks in both margins of each page, not just in the outer one. Two or more *bifolia* were then ruled together to create the writing grid using the prickings. Before the mid-twelfth century it was normal to use a hard point, of metal or bone, to make the ruling; later, lead (plummet) was used. There was a short transitional period in the mid- to late twelfth century when both hard point and lead were used together. By the late medieval period, ruling in ink is also found, but often merely as a frame for an internally unruled space for writing. The presence in a manuscript of one of these methods of ruling rather than another may thus be used as a general indication of the period of production.

'The full analysis of the varied physical details to be found in any surviving Anglo-Saxon manuscript may to some appear arcane and overly time-consuming. It is well worth the effort, however, as it can provide unique evidence that adds greatly to our knowledge of the written culture of the period.'

The maximum size of the space taken up by the text on each page should be measured and recorded, giving height × width in millimetres. The shape of the written space in Anglo-Saxon manuscripts for most purposes is usually a rectangle of which the height is greater than its width. It will normally be found that the maximum height of the written space approximates to the width of the actual leaf. Where the text is arranged in more than one column, these columns should also be measured individually. Although double columns are unusual in vernacular manuscripts of the Anglo-Saxon period, they are more common in Latin and bilingual texts (Fig. 1.1). In glossaries and some psalters triple columns also occur. Where a Latin work has a parallel commentary this may be in a column, or columns, of different width from that of the principal text. The use of a single wide column of long lines was usual for vernacular texts. It should be noted that poetic lines were not used in the manuscripts of Old English verse (Figs 4.2–4.7), despite their appearance in printed editions, though they were used in some Latin verse composed or copied in the period (Fig. 2.10).

A variable allowance of blank parchment within the written space was often left by the scribe for the later insertion of coloured initials, rubrics, line drawings, music, or interlinear glosses. Full-page illustrations or miniatures, however, were sometimes added on half-sheets inserted within or at the beginning of quires; such decorative works need not therefore always be strictly contemporary with the associated text.

Foliation(s) or pagination(s)

Individual leaves within a *codex* are identified for reference by a sequence either of folio or of page numbers. Foliation, the name given to the former of these methods, is the standard one used in manuscripts. In this, each leaf is numbered once, with the addition of v for 'verso' to refer to the back of the leaf, and sometimes of r for 'recto' to refer to the front. Pagination, in contrast, numbers each side of the leaf separately, as in modern printed books. Such numbers are found added to the leaves in ink or pencil; earlier medieval ones (though rare) will be in roman numerals, later ones in arabic numerals. Some foliations or paginations can be related to the construction of a table of contents or index. A series of different foliations or paginations within a *codex* may be an indication of its having been constructed from a number of pre-existing smaller volumes. Variations between medieval and (sometimes more than one) modern numerations should be carefully noted, as individual early modern and modern editors may differ from each other as to which they quote in their printed versions of texts.

Collation

The internal construction of individual quires (groups of leaves, usually consisting of sheets of parchment or paper folded into pairs of conjoint folios or *bifolia*, but often with associated half-sheets) should be recorded. The normal number of pairs used per quire in the Anglo-Saxon and medieval period was four, but five, six, or more, occur. Quires of five pairs, giving ten folios, seem to have been common in early Insular manuscripts. The conventional abbreviated formulas used in the recording of the collation of a manuscript volume assume an ideal quire of several paired folios to which modifications may be made by the addition or omission of half-sheets. Examples of notation and explanations are given in Table 2.

In Anglo-Saxon manuscripts up to the beginning of the eleventh century the leaves were normally arranged within each quire so that all the hair sides faced outwards, thus giving a hair-flesh arrangement (HFHF) to all the openings (two facing pages) within a quire, except for that in the middle, but giving a hair-hair one where quires met. Later on, the internal arrangement was changed so that hair faced hair and flesh faced flesh (HFFH), as was usual on the Continent, resulting in a greater consistency of appearance across openings.

Table 2
Conventional abbreviated formulas used in recording the collation of a manuscript volume.

4^8	The fourth quire (containing eight leaves) is made up of four conjoint pairs.
5^8 3 and 6 are half-sheets	The fifth quire (containing eight leaves) consists of three conjoint pairs, with the third and sixth leaves being half-sheets.
9^6 + 1 leaf after 3	The ninth quire (containing seven leaves) consists of three conjoint pairs, with a half-sheet used by the original scribe after the third leaf.
10^6 + 1 leaf inserted after 3	The tenth quire (containing seven leaves) is similar to the preceding, but the half-sheet has been added at a date later than that of the original make-up.
11^{10} wants 4	The eleventh quire (containing nine leaves) contains a gap in the text which shows that the fourth leaf is now missing.
12^{10} wants 10, probably blank	Similar to preceding quire, but the loss of a leaf is suggested by the fact that the scribe finished writing his text at the ninth leaf.
14 nine	The fourteenth quire consists of nine leaves but its make-up is uncertain.

Quire-numbers or quire-signatures

It was the practice to add a sequence of numbers or letters at the foot of the last folio verso (but occasionally the first folio recto) of each quire in order to guide the binder of the volume in getting the quires, and thus the text, in the correct order (Figs 2.1, 2.3, 4.3).

The later addition or insertion of quires into a volume, or the re-ordering of quires, can sometimes be detected from the lack of, or disorder in, such numbers or letters. In Cambridge, Corpus Christi College MS 41 (Old English Bede, *Historia ecclesiastica*; s.xi[1]) two different sequences of contemporary quire-signatures occur and can be related to the work of two separate copyists; one sequence appears on the last verso of quires 1–13 (with surviving letters F, G, I–M) and the other in quires 14–31 (with letters A–R).

Unfortunately, however, such quire-numbers or signatures are often now missing, having been lost when the leaves were trimmed to a consistent size as the last part of the binding process.

Catchwords

A few words from the text were sometimes written at the foot of the final folio in a quire, being an anticipation of those to come on the first line of the following quire. These were intended, in addition to (or instead of) the use of quire-signatures or numbers, to help preserve the correct sequence of quires before or during binding. Other catchwords were also occasionally used within quires, in order to maintain the correct sequence of individual folios prior to binding, preceding the addition of a foliation or a pagination to the whole *codex*. In most cases, however, they too are now missing having been written on that part of the leaf trimmed by the binder.

Booklets

Careful study of the external features of a *codex* may sometimes lead to the conclusion that within what is now treated as a single volume there exists more than one unit of production. In these cases we may be dealing with a collection of structurally (and textually) independent booklets, each with its own physical history, origin and previous provenance, which should be examined and described as separate entities. Where the main text in such booklets ends before one or more blank leaves, it is common that other quite unrelated texts have been added to these, diversifying the contents of the *codex*. Thus, in Cambridge, Corpus Christi College MS 173, Part I, after the end of the booklet (fols 1–32r) containing the 'A' version of the *Anglo-Saxon Chronicle*, a later set of Latin annals relating to the archiepiscopate of Lanfranc was added, while after the booklet (fols 33–52) containing the *Alfred-Ine Law-code*, sets of papal, episcopal and regnal lists were added.

The writing of the text(s)

Writing materials: inks and pens

The text was normally written in an acidic ink intended to burn into the surface of the page just enough to give it permanence, but not enough to burn right through and cause irreparable damage. Recipes consisted of various mixtures of oak galls, iron sulphate, gum, and water, wine or vinegar. Other types of ink which included ingredients such as carbon and thorn branches were also used.

The ink was added to the surface of the page by means of a quill pen, usually made from the tail feather of a goose, its thicker end cut to shape and re-sharpened as necessary during the course of the writing. Marked changes within a text, both in the colour of ink used and in the width of the nib, should be noted as they may be clues which help in distinguishing between the work of different scribes. Black ink is taken to be characteristic of the early Insular period.

Scripts in Anglo-Saxon England

It should be kept in mind that palaeographical dating is subjective and can only be expressed in sub-divisions of a century rather than in specific years. Particular scripts remained in use for several generations and individual scribes probably in the main tended to keep fairly closely throughout their career to the styles in which they were first trained, although from time to time some may have been forced to change due to their patron's wish to employ a different style. The broad succession of scripts used in Anglo-Saxon England is, however, quite firmly established through the evidence of dated manuscripts and original documents, as are some local styles. Familiarity with the main characteristics of each of the scripts used in Anglo-Saxon England is thus needed. The various categories of script used (both for the text and for headings, glosses, rubrics or initials) should be referred to by their respective standard names.

Writing in England before the Benedictine Reform

Although the earliest Anglo-Saxons would have been familiar with runes used for inscriptions on stone or metal, and some would have been aware of the existence of other forms of writing from seeing Roman remains or from contact with various Romanised peoples, it was only with their conversion to Christianity from the end of the sixth century that they (that is, their priests and administrators) became literate in the Latin alphabet. Christian missionaries, coming from Ireland to the north and west of England and from Rome to the east and south, brought both a new religion and an emphasis on the importance and use of the written word. Although most of these

2.1 Oxford, Bodleian Library, MS Hatton 48, fols 24v–25r (*Regula S. Benedicti*). Latin prose monastic rule written in late seventh-/early eighth-century Insular Uncial, with rubrics, red initials and quire-number (*III*); from Southern England or Mercia.

The Vulgate Latin text written in eighth-century Insular Half-Uncial, with versal letters highlighted with red dots; from Northumbria.

writings were in Latin and related to the Church, certain texts such as the Anglo-Saxon laws were written down in the vernacular from the earliest days of the Conversion, requiring an early adaptation of certain letters in the Latin alphabet to suit Old English sound-values. Thus we find the creation of the Anglo-Saxon letters ash (æ, Æ) and eth (ð, Ð), adapted from the Latin diphthong *ae* and the letter *d*, respectively. A little later, two runic letters thorn (þ, Þ) and wynn (ƿ, Ƿ) were also appropriated, although in the case of thorn rather unnecessarily, as it stood for an identical sound to that of eth.

Latin texts in seventh- and eighth-century England were usually copied in local versions of the formal book-scripts used in late Roman ecclesiastical manuscripts. The earliest Anglo-Saxon bibles and gospel books were written in majuscule or semi-majuscule scripts (Uncials or Half-Uncials). In general, the Half-Uncials were normally used in books produced in churches associated with the Irish mission, while Uncials are found in those with closer links to Rome. Uncials are rounded majuscules, with characteristic shapes for *A*, *D*, *E*, *G* and *M* (Fig. 2.1). Half-Uncials often look more like minuscules, with ascenders and descenders on certain letters, but have a particular form of *a* (like an overlapping double-*c*) and the peculiarity of retaining majuscule forms for *N*, *R*, *S* as the norm, though sometimes alternating with the respective minuscule shapes (Fig. 2.2). Monumental Square Capitals, often infilled with interlace or colour and with zoomorphic terminals, were used for headings in some of these early manuscripts (Figs 7.6, 7.12).

2.2 Durham, Cathedral Library MS A.II.16, fol. 91r (Gospel of Luke).

RIGHT

2.3 Cambridge, University Library MS Kk.5.16, fol. 89v (The Moore MS of Bede, *Historia Ecclesiastica*).

Latin prose history written in Phase II Insular Cursive minuscule, early eighth-century, showing the quire number (*uiiii*); from Northumbria (?Wearmouth-Jarrow).

BELOW

2.4 Facsimile by Alexander R. Rumble of letter-forms, ligatures and abbreviations in the Moore MS of Bede, *Historia Ecclesiastica* (see Fig. 2.3).

From the eighth century onwards, books were more usually written in minuscule scripts, that is, those which have a number of letters containing ascenders and descenders. The earliest varieties are described as forms of 'Insular minuscule', signifying a generic style of script produced in the British Isles but not being specific to any one of its constituent regions. In its Phase I, before c.700, the minuscule script was cursive and had many ligatures (links between adjacent letters). In Phase II, from c.700 to the mid-ninth century, several grades of the script were used in a hierarchy of increasing formality: Cursive, Set and Hybrid (Figs 2.3–2.6). A further term 'Current' is reserved for script written with speed and lack of care. Hybrid minuscule may sometimes be difficult to distinguish from Half-Uncial,

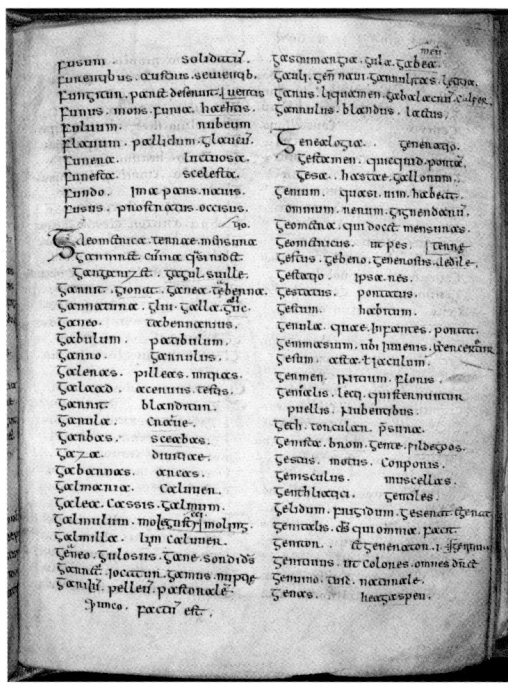

LEFT

2.5 London, British Library, MS Royal 2 A. xx, fol. 17r (The *Royal Prayerbook*).

Latin prayers written in early ninth-century Insular Set minuscule, with zoomorphic *IN* at start of text; from Southumbria.

RIGHT

2.6 Cambridge, Corpus Christi College MS 144, fol. 31r (Glossary).

Two columns of Latin words (beginning *Fu-*, *Ga-*, *Ge-*) with their Old English equivalents, written in early ninth-century Insular Hybrid minuscule; from southern England.

particularly as it too used the double-*c* form of *a*, but was formed using a slanting rather than an upright pen.

Although the occurrence of Old English text or words in a manuscript with Insular features (Figs 2.3–2.6) may suggest that it was produced in England, one must not forget the fact that English (and Irish) missionaries were active on the Continent from the late seventh century. The written remains of the churches founded by these missionaries contain both script and decoration with Insular characteristics (Fig. 1.7) and vernacular glosses. Other indications of Insular origin are the occurrence of particular forms of the abbreviations used in Latin for common words such as *autem*, *eius*, *est*, and *quae*, or for syllables like *con-* and *pro-*, which differed from Continental usage.

By the late ninth century it is possible to differentiate an English style of script (Anglo-Saxon Pointed minuscule (Fig. 2.7)) as separate from Irish or Welsh varieties. This script developed from Insular Cursive minuscule and

LEFT

2.7 Cambridge, Corpus Christi College MS 173, Part I, fol. 12r (Anglo-Saxon annals MS A, The *Parker Chronicle*).

Old English prose annals (the end of 824 to the start of 836), written in early tenth-century Anglo-Saxon minuscule which retains some features of the Pointed variety (e.g. 'underslung' *l* in *fronclond*, last line); from Winchester.

RIGHT

2.8 Cambridge, Corpus Christi College MS 12, fol. 4r (Gregory, *Cura pastoralis*).

Table of contents to the Old English translation of this text, written in late tenth-century Anglo-Saxon Square minuscule, perhaps at Worcester. Interlinear glosses by the thirteenth-century Worcester 'Tremulous Hand'.

læden spræce læste cuðon·⁊

I. Ðæt ðe unlæredē neðyrften undērfon lareopdom·⁊

II. Ne ꝥ ða geledan de hē æfre ellas libban sħalie on bocum leornēdon ꝥ hie sceoldon· ne undērfon ða are ðæs lareopdomes·⁊

III. Be ðǣre byrðenne ðæs reccendomes· ⁊ hu hē scyle eal ēarfoðu forsion· ⁊ hu foroht hē sceal beon for ælcre onfongnesse·⁊

IIII. Ond hu oft fio birsung ðæs fulcs ⁊ ðæs reccendomes toslit ðæt mod ðæs recceres·⁊

V. Be ðǣm ðe magon on ealdordome nytte beon on byrnum ⁊ on cræftum ⁊ ðonne for hio ða gyrpeies nerre ðæt fleod·⁊

VI. Be ðǣm ðe for eadmodnesse fleod ða byrðenne ðæs lareopdomes· ðonne hie beoð ryhtlice eadmode ðonne hie ne winnað wið ðone godcundan dom·⁊

VII. Ðæt te oft ðæs lareopdomes ðenung bið swiðe untælwirðlice gewilnad ⁊ eac swiðe untælwyrðlice mon gebeod to geniedde·⁊

had a pointed top to *a*, often included an 'underslung' form of *l* and still used a number of ligatures (particularly of high *e* with a following letter). It was replaced in many writing-centres during the tenth century by a new reformed style, Anglo-Saxon Square minuscule (Fig. 2.8), in which the module of *a*, *n*, *o*, and *u* was a square shape and which included hardly any ligatures (apart from *e* + *t* and *s* + *t*). There was also an avoidance of underslung *l*. The degree of squareness varied between writing-centres and changed over time but the employment of this script is taken to be more or less confined to the tenth century and can be used as a dating criterion, as for example in relation to the two scribes of the text of *Beowulf* in London, British Library, MS Cotton Vitellius A. xv, Part 2. The second scribe of this used a Square minuscule but the first used a later Round variety which was common in the eleventh century (Figs 4.4–4.5). As they were contemporary co-workers it is surmised that they were copying the text at the end of the tenth and the start of the eleventh centuries (s.x/xi).

Writing in England after the Benedictine Reform

Latin texts

The reform of Benedictine monasticism in England under King Edgar (959–75) led directly to the importation of Caroline minuscule, a script first created at the court of the Frankish Emperor Charlemagne *c*.800 and which had soon spread widely on the Continent, but which was not used generally in England before the later tenth century. This script offered a greater degree of legibility compared to the preceding minuscule scripts, particularly Merovingian cursive in Francia and Square Anglo-Saxon minuscule in England. This was attained through a reduced use of letter-forms with descenders (there were none on *f* or *r*, while the frequent use of high *s* reduced the number of low and long forms of that letter) and an avoidance of ligatures (apart from *c* + *t* and *s* + *t* and, at first, *r* + *t*).

Variant sub-styles of English Caroline minuscule have been associated with particular churchmen regarded as leaders of the tenth-century Benedictine Reform. The monumental Style I (Fig. 2.9) was written at monasteries associated with Bishop Æthelwold of Winchester, such as the Old and New Minsters there, and Abingdon Abbey, as well as at Worcester under Bishop Oswald. The smaller Style II (Fig. 2.10) was written at churches associated with Archbishop Dunstan, such as Glastonbury Abbey and Christ Church, Canterbury. Style III was an angular variety used at Worcester in the early eleventh century. A later, rounder category (Style IV) was developed at Christ Church, Canterbury by the monk Eadwig Basan who wrote both books and documents there *c*.1010–1030 (Fig. 2.11); this category influenced later proponents of the script in England until much later in the eleventh century.

By the mid-eleventh century, the size of letters in English Caroline minuscule was generally larger than in the contemporary Norman variety: there was also a difference in the nature of the feet added to minims; thus scribes trained in England made them horizontal, while Norman scribes formed them at an angle of 45°.

There were also sub-categories of script for different purposes, such as for glossing or for documentary texts. These were generally smaller and more informal and made use of frequent abbreviations.

OLD ENGLISH TEXTS

In the eleventh century, there is a great variety of appearance in hands in the surviving corpus of vernacular manuscripts. While nearly all the samples of writing could be termed 'Anglo-Saxon minuscule', there are many differences between them in detail (Figs 1.1, 2.12). Some scribes were influenced by their knowledge of Caroline minuscule and produced more rounded letter-forms in their vernacular script but this was by no means universal. Because of the use in Anglo-Saxon minuscule of accepted variant shapes for the same letter, the opportunity for scribal individuality was greater than in Latin manuscripts of this time. In relation to the letter *s* in vernacular manuscripts,

2.9 Paris, Bibliothèque Nationale, MS latin 987, fol. 7r (The *Ramsey Benedictional*).

Latin blessings written in English Caroline minuscule (Style I) with rubrics, versal letters and AMEN in Uncials and lines 9–10 in Square Capitals; produced in the later tenth century at the Old Minster, Winchester.

2.10 Oxford, Bodleian Library, MS Auct. F.4.32, fol. 47r (Dunstan's 'classbook').

Latin verse (Ovid, *Ars amatoria*, book i). This page was written in mid-tenth-century Caroline minuscule (with some Insular features) by a scribe associated with Dunstan, abbot of Glastonbury (later archbishop of Canterbury).

2.11 Hanover, Kestner-Museum, Hs. W.M. XXIa 36, fol. 183v (the *Eadwig Gospels*).

At the top, the end of the Vulgate Latin text of the Gospel of John, written in the earlier eleventh century in English Caroline minuscule (Style IV) and Rustic Capitals by the Christ Church, Canterbury scribe Eadwig Basan followed (lines 9–12) by his colophon to the volume. A slightly later German scribe added the bottom seven lines, the beginning of a gospel chapter list.

for example, besides the low, long and round varieties, there was also an elongated version of Caroline high *s* which reached below the baseline; in Latin manuscripts, low *s* was not used, while the high *s* would normally stand on the baseline. In relation to the letter *g* in vernacular manuscripts, the scribe could choose whether its neck should originate from the left, centre or right of the horizontal bar and whether the descender should be open or closed.

2.12 London, British Library, MS Cotton Tiberius B. i, fol. 141r (Anglo-Saxon annals MS C).

Old English prose and verse annals (including under 937 the beginning of the poem on the *Battle of Brunanburh*), written at Abingdon in early eleventh-century Anglo-Saxon Round minuscule. Underlining and marginal note (*Kyngston*) by Robert Talbot (d.1558).

2.13 London, British Library, MS Additional 37517, fol. 81r (The *Bosworth Psalter*).

Latin psalms in the Roman Version, written in late tenth-century Anglo-Saxon Square minuscule, with continuous Old English gloss added slightly later in a glossing version of Anglo-Saxon minuscule; produced at Canterbury.

2.14 Cambridge, Corpus Christi College MS 57, fol. 120v (*Regula S. Benedicti*).

Latin prose monastic rule written in a tenth/eleventh-century Anglo-Saxon Square minuscule. From line 11 on this page a later hand has changed the letter *a* to a Caroline form. Produced at Abingdon or Canterbury.

A special version of Anglo-Saxon minuscule script is found in some continuous Old English glosses and commentaries. This has ascenders and descenders of exaggerated length and a correspondingly small minim height. This occurs, for example, in the vernacular gloss to the *Bosworth Psalter* from Christ Church, Canterbury (London, British Library, MS Additional 37517; s. x/xi; Fig. 2.13), where descenders on *f, r,* low *s* and *y* are unusually long; in initial position there is also a long version of not only *s* but also *f* and *þ*.

BILINGUAL TEXTS

The use of both Caroline minuscule and Anglo-Saxon minuscule continued in England until the late eleventh century and there was a two-way influence of each on the other (Fig. 2.14), most easily studied in the manuscripts of bilingual texts. The creation of dual-language versions of certain texts

2.15 Manchester, John Rylands Library, Rylands MS Latin 155, fol. 4r.

Part of the Tribal and Burghal Hidages, Old English written in the thirteenth century in Gothic Textura script.

(such as the *Regula sancti Benedicti* and glossaries) allowed the scribes who copied them to demonstrate their skill in writing the vernacular as well as Latin. Caroline and Anglo-Saxon minuscule scripts were used for the corresponding sections of the same text, for the Latin and Old English respectively. Contrasting forms of the letters *a*, *d*, *f*, *g*, *h*, *r* and *s* were normally used. There is also an opposition on the page between the symbols for the conjunction 'and': in Old English text the tironian *nota* <7> (for *and* or *ond*) and in Latin the ampersand <&> (for *et*).

LATER COPIES

In early Middle English copies of Anglo-Saxon texts some form of Protogothic minuscule script was used with varying ranges of Anglo-Saxon letter-forms being retained. From the thirteenth to the sixteenth centuries some form of Gothic minuscule will be found: formal Textura (Fig. 2.15), cursive Anglicana or cursive Secretary. In later transcripts Italic, Round or Copperplate scripts were used. There is a marked difference in competence and accuracy between the scribes of these later copies. Just because they were chronologically closer to the original author, it does not mean they had a better understanding of the text than a properly trained modern scholar. Only close analysis can establish the potential authority of scribal work.

Other aspects relating to the main text

PUNCTUATION

Although in many cases internally consistent, the systems of punctuation used by Anglo-Saxon and medieval scribes were different from those used by modern writers, being influenced both by the requirements of liturgical performance and by formulaic structures within Latin and Old English. As usage varies from manuscript to manuscript and from scribe to scribe, it is most important to study the system in operation within each particular surviving piece of writing, in order to isolate variations of practice between both authors and copyists.

The articulation of the two columns of majuscule text in the early Insular bibles and gospel books was achieved not by the use of punctuation marks but *per cola et commata*, that is by starting each verse and each of its subordinate clauses on a new line, with insetting of any run-over words. Most later manuscripts exhibit other methods, however, their scribes making use of various symbols to indicate minor and major pauses in the text and sometimes to mark word-stress or vowel-length. Thus in London, British Library, MS Cotton Claudius B. iv (the *Old English Hexateuch*; s.xi[1]) a cup-shaped suprascript sign indicates a short vowel. It became conventional for an enlarged letter (*littera notabilior*) to be employed as the initial capital to a clause, such letters sometimes being coloured or highlighted. It was not normal practice, however, for names to be given capital initials, although in some documentary texts they were written wholly in majuscules. Word-division was often irregular and causes the modern reader particular problems in reassembling compound words containing prefixes like *ge-* and *in-* in Old English; it also affects compound words such as *quapropter* and *siquis* in Latin. The most frequent punctuation-symbol was the *punctus simplex*, a single dot, which could be used to indicate a pause of either minor or major importance, as well as to distinguish numerals (one *punctus* before the number and one after), names, or a one-letter word such as Old English *æ*, 'law', from surrounding text. The *punctus versus*, looking like a semi-colon, usually indicated a major pause, such as the end of a chapter or sub-section within a work. The *punctus elevatus*, an association between a dot and a superior rising line, often indicated the internal division of a sentence. The *punctus interrogativus*, a dot and a sideways hook-shape, was placed at the end of a phrase containing a question. Punctuation with symbols made of multiple points is regarded as a feature of Insular, particularly Irish or Irish-influenced, manuscripts. The punctuation of verse, both in Latin and Old English, differed from that of prose and sometimes related to the isolation of formulaic phrases and poetic sections rather than sentences.

ORTHOGRAPHY

Scribal preferences should be looked for in relation to a range of possible variable spellings in both Latin and Old English. In the latter, one should in particular note usage in relation to dative plural *-um /-an /-un*; the prefix *an- /on-*; the diphthongs *eo /io*; and the interchangeable letters *æ /e /ea /a*; *b /f /u /v*; *y /i /e /u*; *ð /þ /th*; and *u /uu /p /w*. Some of these features were orthographical conventions that originated in variant spoken dialects, others related to broader chronological developments in the language. In Latin texts, usage as regards both *ae /ę /e* and *s /ss* (confusion of which was an Insular feature) should be recorded. Such spelling preferences may prove significant for determining the place at which the scribe was trained, but do not necessarily indicate the place of origin of the manuscript, since the mobility of Anglo-Saxon and medieval scribes should be taken into account.

RUBRICATION AND RUNNING HEADINGS

Rubrics, as their name indicates, were usually written in red ink, but sometimes are found either in ink of another colour or in the basic ink of the text. They are short headings placed at the beginning and/or within texts, which introduce the textual unit about to begin. They are usually slightly later additions made in spaces left by the scribe of the text, so that all the writing in red or coloured ink might be done at the same time. If written by someone other than the scribe of the text, they may have differences of letter-form, spelling or wording and so amount to a sub-text of the main work. It is therefore important in a transcript to distinguish them by a note and in an edition by either footnotes or the use of a different typeface.

Running headings, often in red or coloured ink, were occasionally added to an Anglo-Saxon manuscript by a later scribe. These consist of information written in the upper margin of each page, either the title of the whole work or the title or number of the chapter within it whose text appears on that particular opening or page.

CONTEMPORARY GLOSSES OR COMMENTARIES

The text of some works, particularly biblical or scholastic ones, was sometimes explained by means of words or whole sections of commentary written either between the lines of the main text or in an adjacent margin (Figs 2.13, 6.3, 6.8). These are referred to as either 'interlinear' or 'marginal' glosses. They may be in a language different from that of the main text and can develop into a continuous translation of it and sometimes require a two-column arrangement of the page. The longer commentaries and alphabetical collections of glosses (Fig. 2.6) often became works well-known in their own right which were separately copied and were then subject to their own individual manuscript tradition.

The subsidiary glosses or commentaries were differentiated from the main text by their placing on the page, but also by their (often smaller) size and less formal category of script. Where a sufficient amount of material exists and can be seen to be written by one hand this may be datable to a different period from the hand of the main text (Fig. 2.13).

Either a commentary or marginal glosses may be referenced from the main text solely by *lemmata* but often also by the use of marks known as *signes de renvoi*. These are matching symbols paired in the main text and the subsidiary text to locate each particular comment (Fig. 6.5).

Some categories of gloss are thought to have been designed for teaching or learning more difficult Latin texts. Five types of didactic gloss have been distinguished to date, each of which has left its trace upon the manuscript page. Lexical glosses relate to the explanation of items of vocabulary (Fig. 6.11). Accentual glosses indicate the proper pronunciation of Latin, marking long or short vowels or stress. Grammatical glosses identify cases; for example, the letter *o* is sometimes used above a Latin word to show it is in the vocative case. Interrogative or 'q: glosses' represent cues for questions from a master to his students. Syntactical glosses illuminate the Latin sentence structure by means of markers in the form of suprascript letters the wrong alphabetical order of which is required to be corrected by the reader (Fig. 6.6).

ALTERATIONS OR CORRECTIONS

Wherever possible, a clear distinction should be made between alterations to their own work by the scribe of the text and any corrections done as a separate process in the production of a manuscript. Whether alteration or correction is involved, the methods used were similar: either erasure (by scratching away the ink) of the incorrect letters or words and subsequent rewriting; or deleting, underlining or subpuncting of the mistake and the writing of the correct version interlineally or adjacent. The second of these methods was the more common since erasure was liable to cause damage to the surface of the parchment and made rewriting impossible without blotting. Occasionally a serious copying error such as the repetition of a whole page of text meant that a folio had to be scrapped; this would be reflected by the collation of that particular quire.

THE IDENTIFICATION OF SCRIBES

Who wrote a particular surviving manuscript, at what exact date and in what precise location are the questions that unfortunately are those to which all too often we have no answers, even after a minute examination of the artefact concerned. Only on rare occasions did an Anglo-Saxon scribe add a colophon at the end of the text he or she had copied (Fig. 2.11), stating information such as the name of the work, its author, the name of the scribe and the date and place of inscription. Even where a colophon does exist, careful thought needs to be given as to whether it refers to the particular manuscript under examination, or has been copied wholesale with the main text from the exemplar manuscript.

Although we will never know the names of most of the scribes who produced the surviving manuscripts, we should distinguish between their work and collect any information that may help to date and locate them as closely as possible. An extremely important aspect of this is the accurate description of the hands involved. The individual characteristics of each hand should be isolated and described. These amount to slight but consistent modifications in the shape of letter-forms from a norm to be expected within the type of script used and should be described in the following order:

(i) *The treatment of ascenders*: their height in relation to that of minims; whether clubbed at the top, or curved, or notched, or looped;

(ii) *The treatment of descenders*: their depth in relation to the height of minims; whether they end in a point, or curve in one direction or the other;

(iii) *Minims*: their width (reflecting the width of the nib); whether they have feet or not, and, if so, are these horizontal or oblique?

(iv) *Individual letters*. Where any letter-forms seem to be made in a consistently idiosyncratic fashion these should be described (in alphabetical order) as succinctly as possible. The terminology used in describing letter-forms is often taken from that for parts of the human body, e.g. 'head', 'neck', 'shoulder', 'waist', 'back', 'arm', 'leg', and 'foot'; but terms like 'tail', 'cross-bar', and 'bowl' also occur. Whatever terms are chosen, it is important that they should be applied in a consistent fashion. There is no need to mention letters the appearance of which is not unusual within the context of the type of script being used. The shape given to the following letters will be found to be most often significant in distinguishing between hands: *a, d, e, g, r, s, t, y, ð, þ*. Note should also be made of the usage of particular forms of a letter where more than one was available, e.g. Caroline instead of 2-shaped *r* after *o*; low, long, high and round forms of *s* (particularly in relation to *-ss-*); and the three different forms of *y* (straight-armed, with curved arms, or *f*-shaped).

(v) *Ligatures.* Any deliberate union between neighbouring letters should be noted, e.g. that of *e* with the following letter, *c* + *t*, *s* + *t* and (less commonly) *r* + *t*.

(vi) *Abbreviations.* In order to save both space and time, Latin texts were normally heavily abbreviated by the omission of letters from within (contraction) or at the end (suspension) of words. The general consistency of Latin inflexions and the frequent repetition of certain groups of letters allowed a large body of conventional abbreviation-symbols to be developed by the early medieval period. Old English texts, being less consistent in spelling, are much less abbreviated than those in Latin. In either language, however, an individual scribe might choose to vary the number of abbreviations used in copying a whole text or part of it, particularly when space was limited.

In both languages, the most common abbreviation-mark was the overline, a short suprascript horizontal line which indicates that a word has been abbreviated near to (usually just after) the place where the mark occurs. Above a vowel at the end of a word it nearly always indicates a missing *m* in Latin, *m* or *n* in Old English.

In Latin texts many common words and some syllables had their own conventional abbreviated form which could where necessary be modified according to inflexion. Table 3 (where the letters here italicised are omitted in the manuscript and the omission marked by an overline) gives just a few examples of a much more extensive vocabulary of abbreviation in Latin manuscripts.

The most frequent abbreviations in Old English manuscripts, apart from the overline above a vowel (see above), are set out in Table 4.

Before the work of any individual scribe can be isolated from that of contemporaries working in the same milieu, the occurrence in the work of a combination of several distinctive letter-forms or palaeographical features needs to be recognized. Scribal difference is likely to be less in a well-regulated writing-centre than in one without a strict training or supervisory programme.

The longer the piece of text the clearer to us should be the preferred usages

Table 3
Examples of common Latin abbreviations.

d**eu**s nominative/vocative singular 'God', d**ei** genitive singular 'of God'

d**ic**t**us** nominative singular masculine past participle 'said'

d**om**i**nu**m accusative singular 'lord', d**om**i**n**a nominative/vocative/ablative singular 'lady'

.**e.** 'he/she/it is', e**ss**e 'to be', e**sse**t subjunctive 'he/she/it might be'

ep**iscop**i either genitive singular or nominative/vocative plural 'bishop(s)'

h**abe**re 'to have', h**abe**nt 'they have', h**a**b**uit** 'he/she/it had'

o**mn**es nominative/vocative/accusative plural adjective 'all'

p**resb**it**er** nominative/vocative singular 'priest'

q**uan**do 'when'

q**uon**ia**m** 'since, wherefore'

t**am**en 'however'

Note the following abbreviations for some very common syllables:

b: or **b;** = -b*us*, 3rd declension dative/ablative plural

q: or **q;** = -q*ue* 'and'

⁹ = -*us*

of the scribe. Similarly, the larger the number of manuscripts, or sections thereof, written by a particular scribe that have survived, the more likely should it be that a scribal overlap can be recognized if the right features are sought in them.

It should not be assumed that all copyists (or indeed authors), professional or amateur, were masculine. The members of female, as well as male, religious houses are known to have copied texts and it is possible that they composed or modified some. Neither should it be assumed that all scribes were members of the regular, as opposed to the secular clergy. Some cathedrals had non-monastic communities and these also needed books and writers; there were also priests in the royal household and in minster churches. Equally we should remember not only that such secular writers had no religious constraints on their freedom of movement or association but also that some senior monks too were allowed to travel with their abbot or bishop, while others relocated as a result of promotion. It is therefore doubtful whether attempts to localise the execution of any so called 'style' as a subdivision of a particular script in the Anglo-Saxon period can ever be precise at closer than a regional level. Such attempts are limited by the exactitude of the definition of the style concerned, but also depend on how firm a control was maintained over the production of a particular writing-centre and the degree

7 = and/ ond 'and'	**Table 4** Examples of common Old English abbreviations.
æfter 'after, following'	
for 'because'	
ge- verbal prefix	
ł = oððe 'or'	
sancte 'saint'	
þ' = þæt 'that'	
ðonne 'then'	

to which its constituent scribes moved or worked elsewhere during the course of their careers. Such considerations will always affect our ability to localise the surviving manuscripts.

Decoration

Attention should be given to the type of decoration found within a manuscript, and of its location and function relative to the text. However, as the topic of Anglo-Saxon manuscript decoration is covered extensively by Catherine Karkov in Chapter 7, reference is only made here to aspects which impinge directly on the palaeography.

Latin manuscripts from the Anglo-Saxon period exhibit decorated features in styles influenced by both Irish/Celtic and Continental/Classical models. High status biblical and religious texts in Latin tended to be the most elaborately adorned with the use of coloured inks and (sometimes) gold leaf and (very occasionally) writing in gold ink. Nevertheless, some more technical texts, such as the Old English *Herbarium* (London, British Library, MS Cotton Vitellius C. iii; s. xi in.) and the bilingual *Wonders of the East* (London, British Library, MS Cotton Tiberius B. v; s. xi[1]; Figs 7.30–7.31) were also illustrated, their artists probably copying or adapting the drawings of their exemplars. The great majority of the surviving vernacular manuscripts of the time, however, even those with a religious content, are quite plain, with only the minimum of decoration.

Styles of decoration may provide clues as to the origin and date of a manuscript. As with script, one must remember that often such attributions are governed by the current opinion of experts rather than by any incontrovertible evidence. Sometimes, in any case, illustration was added to a manuscript a considerable time after the writing of the text and in a different region or even country. More reliable evidence for the localisation of the decoration may soon be forthcoming from scientific analysis of the colours used, they being mainly produced on the spot from mineral and vegetable sources.

DECORATED INITIALS AND DIMINUENDO

Large capital letters marking the beginning of a text or of an internal textual section were often executed merely in the ink of the text, but were sometimes drawn in one or more coloured inks. In certain manuscripts the construction of the initials is very intricate, being made up of biting beasts or acrobatic humans (e.g. Oxford, Bodleian Library, MS Tanner 10, the Old English translation of Bede, *Historia ecclesiastica*; s. x[1]) or having foliate terminals. In other examples, the initials are infilled with interlace patterns or surrounded by red dots (Figs 1.7, 2.5, 7.12).

An associated palaeographical feature in both Latin and vernacular manuscripts is the 'diminuendo' in which there is a gradual reduction in size and formality of script at the beginning of a text (Figs 7.6, 7.12). In less luxurious manuscripts, after a decorated initial in coloured ink the rest of the first word (or line) may be in non-coloured majuscule letters before the second word (or line) begins the minuscule script of the remainder of the copied text (Fig. 1.7). The reader is thus first attracted to the place where the text or section begins and is then led into reading it.

LINE-DRAWINGS ILLUSTRATING THE TEXT

In general, the line-drawings in coloured inks which accompany the text in Anglo-Saxon manuscripts in either Latin or Old English are of high quality, with good attention to details of anatomy, dress and gesture. Some, such as the finely executed panels illustrating the text of Prudentius, *Psychomachia* (Cambridge, Corpus Christi College MS 23; s. x: Fig. 6.8) may have been copied, or adapted, from an earlier Continental exemplar. The small outline pictures on the first folios of the *Paris Psalter* (Paris, Bibliothèque Nationale, MS Latin 8824; s. xi med.; Fig. 1.1) were placed within the column containing the Latin version, the text of which is shorter than that in the parallel column in which the vernacular translation appears. It is possible that the scribe had not foreseen the effect of using a two column arrangement for his bilingual text, rather than alternate paragraphs, and attempted to fill in with pictures the consequent gaps on the page. Although the illustrated *Old English Hexateuch* (London, British Library, MS Cotton Claudius B. iv; s. xi[1]: Figs 1.4, 7.32) had specially reserved spaces in the writing space for the addition of the coloured drawings that illustrate the text, this is not necessarily proof that they were copied from a pre-existing exemplar.

Non-contemporary marginalia and glosses

Various words or text were frequently added to a manuscript over time by its readers, either between the lines as a discontinuous gloss or in the margin as notes (Figs 6.9–6.10, 6.13, 6.15). A series of these in the same hand can provide a clue as to the purpose or main interest of one particular past user of the manuscript. It is therefore important both to read and to try to date such notes. It is sometimes possible to identify their author if he or she had a securely distinguishable hand and wrote in other surviving manuscripts. Such notes have proven of great significance in relation to the use of Anglo-Saxon manuscripts by medieval and early modern antiquaries and scholars (Fig. 2.12).

Thus, a number of surviving manuscripts with a firm Worcester Cathedral provenance carry annotations by a thirteenth-century scribe who has posthumously become well known to modern scholars as the 'Tremulous Hand', a designation first given by the palaeographer and ghost-story writer M.R. James (Figs 2.8, 6.13). The progressively more wobbly appearance of his writing suggests that he suffered from a degenerative disease, one of the symptoms of which was a tremor. Other manuscripts have been given a Worcester Cathedral provenance because they too were annotated by him. Recognition of the considerable amount of work this medieval scholar did on Old English texts has been made possible mainly because of the individuality of his writing (see Timothy Graham's chapter in this book, pp. 182–6).

Later, the occurrence of a distinctive red crayon for underlining words in several Anglo-Saxon manuscripts, now at Corpus Christi College, Cambridge and elsewhere, has been taken as evidence of their use at the time of the Tudor Reformation by Archbishop Matthew Parker and/or his son John. The group of scholars gathered by Matthew Parker at this time (see pp. 190–4) to put together evidence for the early independence of the English Church laid the foundation for the modern study of Old English and Anglo-Saxon topics and in so doing added many annotations to the manuscripts they consulted (Fig. 6.16).

The full analysis of the varied physical details to be found in any surviving Anglo-Saxon manuscript may to some appear arcane and overly time-consuming. It is well worth the effort, however, as it can provide unique evidence that adds greatly to our knowledge of the written culture of the period and to our appreciation of the human labour which contributed to the artefact as it exists today.

Introduction to Chapter 3

Old English was first written down as a result of Christian missionary activity. Christianity is a religion of the book, and literacy – in Latin – was necessary in its priests. As a preliminary educational step, Anglo-Saxon pupils were taught to read English, using an alphabet based on Latin. Anglo-Saxon law was committed to writing at an early stage and laws and charters continued to be written in English (as well as Latin), showing that the written vernacular carried status and authority. Nevertheless, little written English material survives from before the ninth century, when King Alfred established a policy of translating Latin works which he considered classic educational books, accompanied by explanatory prefaces. The same century saw the compilation of the *Anglo-Saxon Chronicle*, which was continued by means of yearly reports ('annals'). Alfred's proposal of an educational programme also established a readership for English books since it decreed that freeborn boys should be taught to read written English.

Almost certainly, all surviving Anglo-Saxon manuscripts were created in a monastic environment, and the majority were intended for a monastic audience and survived in monasteries until their dissolution in the sixteenth century. Hence the majority of surviving Old English prose is scholarly. Anecdotes from the Old English version of Bede may appear a relatively unchallenging read, but the *Historia Ecclesiastica* was an original and intellectual work. Ælfric's *Grammar and Glossary* were schoolbooks, as was his entertaining *Colloquy* (which was in fact composed in Latin; the Old English version translated by today's University students is a gloss on the Latin text, see p. 166).

Much surviving Old English prose is homiletic, including biblical commentary and doctrine as well as narratives of saints. Lesser-known texts (such as medical lore and prognostics), compiled from multiple sources, copied and recopied, were similarly part of the stock-in-trade of the scholar.

The following chapter demonstrates that many extant Anglo-Saxon manuscripts are multi-stratified artefacts: disparate items bound together; texts surrounded by marginalia; unrelated writings added on spare areas of parchment; copies made by scribes conscientiously trying to follow their exemplar but trained in different places and with different degrees of competence and interest in their work and thus inevitably altering the text by their contribution. The corpus of Old English prose includes texts surviving in multiple copies; a few texts with identifiable named authors and different texts copied by the same scribal hand.

3

Manuscript sources of Old English prose

Donald Scragg

Today, we have a clear idea of what constitutes a book. It has a subject, usually identified by the title on the cover, and its contents are organised around some principle of construction frequently stated at the outset, or implicit in the familiar formula of a beginning, a middle and an end. The medieval reader had a very different idea of a book, and therefore coming to surviving manuscripts with modern preconceptions has its dangers. Very many surviving vernacular manuscripts resemble miscellanies or commonplace books, and rarely have any sort of title. While it is always important to look at the manuscript context of any surviving text, contiguous items may not necessarily have any connection in terms of subject, at least to our eyes. A simple example is the text known as *Apollonius of Tyre*, a Latin romance containing the story found in Shakespeare's *Pericles*, which was translated into Old English probably during the tenth century and which survives in a single copy in Cambridge, Corpus Christi College 201, towards the end of a large collection consisting entirely – but for the *Apollonius* – of homilies and laws, all written (including *Apollonius*) by the same scribe. On the other hand, some manuscripts are very carefully organised around a definable theme. Typical here are the many surviving books of homilies, some, such as London, British Library, Royal 7 C. xii (Fig. 3.1) containing Ælfric's First Series of Catholic Homilies, organised on the principle of the ecclesiastical calendar, others, such as Cambridge, Corpus Christi College 162, containing many of the same pieces but excluding all of Ælfric's items that were written for saints' days. Even when a manuscript appears to have an internal consistency, however, there can be no assurance that it was planned prior to the process of writing in the form in which it survives today. The last named manuscript, CCCC 162, written throughout by a single scribe, in general has homiletic pieces ordered to follow the chronology of the church year, but it begins with items designed for preaching on any occasion. It would appear that the manuscript as originally written did not start with the items with

3.1 London, British Library, MS Royal 7 C. xii, fol. 64r.

The note in the margin comments that the matter in the marked section is discussed more fully in another place and 'we' excise it from here. This and other notes in the same hand in this manuscript show that they could only have been written by the author, Ælfric, and that this is therefore a working copy.

which it now opens but was intended to provide a simple chronological sequence. Only subsequently was it expanded with extra quires.[1]

The same may be shown of other manuscripts. In what has become a seminal article on the compilation of manuscripts, I proved many years ago that the *Vercelli Book* (Vercelli, Biblioteca capitolare CXVII), again written

---

[1] See D.G. Scragg, 'Cambridge, Corpus Christi College 162' in Phillip Pulsiano and Elaine Treharne, ed., *Anglo-Saxon Manuscripts and their Heritage*, Aldershot, Ashgate, 1998, pp. 71–83.

throughout by a single scribe, originally began with what is now item 5 and that items 1–4 were added to the collection after item 5 had been written.[2] Proof lies in the arrangement of quires, where the final leaf of the third quire, probably blank, has been removed between what are now items 4 and 5. A similar arrangement of quires leads to the conclusion of discontinuous writing in CCCC 162, while London, BL, Harley 3271 was probably constructed in the same way. The principal item of the latter is a copy of Ælfric's Latin grammar, written in English for the benefit of novices in the numerous monasteries of the period who needed to learn to communicate in the international language of the Church. The grammar in Harley 3271 is written by two scribes in tandem (that is, they were writing different parts of the grammar at the same time) on eleven regular quires; but an extra quire (now lacking the first two leaves) was added at the beginning, presumably after the grammar had been written, on which other scribes wrote four additional items. Furthermore, still more scribes added extra material after the conclusion of the grammar itself. They first used sheets that remained blank at the end of the grammar to add another seven short items, and then attached still more quires for further items after that. In all they produced a miscellany of items which might be useful in a school context, but clearly one which the original scribes of the central text had no thought of devising.

Surviving Old English prose

We can deduce this much about the development of individual manuscripts in the Anglo-Saxon period because such an extraordinary wealth of material survives, more from the eleventh century, in fact, than from any comparable period until the fourteenth. Yet, although Old English poetry has been studied with great enthusiasm for more than two centuries, close examination of the vast bulk of the much greater quantity of prose that has survived was slow to develop in recent times. Some of the most important prose texts were not edited and thus made available to the majority of readers until relatively recently. (An example is the Vercelli homilies, the earliest surviving collection of sermons in English, which were not published in their entirety until 1981.) The largest number of manuscripts containing prose in English that survive from the period were written during the half century beginning around 990. Relatively few manuscripts and documents survive from before 990: eighteen manuscripts, many of them lists of glosses, from the eighth century to the tenth, together with a scattering of single-page Latin documents with some material in English, plus a few Latin manuscripts glossed in English between

---

[2] See D.G. Scragg, 'The compilation of the Vercelli Book', *Anglo-Saxon England*, 2, 1973, pp. 189–207.

the lines. After the Norman Conquest – and more particularly after 1100 – the number of manuscripts with English as the principal or only language gradually declined, although it appears that Old English continued to be copied regularly in some scriptoria until at least 1150; but from the hundred-year period after 990 over 275 manuscripts and documents containing English survive, written by a total of more than 500 scribes. If we add to these the many more scribes who made marginal and interlinear annotations in English during the eleventh century, it becomes clear that this is a period of widespread literacy in the vernacular. When it is considered that, with changes in script and in language, these writings would have been effectively unreadable to all but a very few after the twelfth century, it is remarkable that so many books have survived. It is indicative of the many thousands – even tens of thousands – that must have been produced in the period.

Texts in multiple copies

The survival of so many manuscripts means that large numbers of texts – the ones in greatest demand in the places where they were produced, the monasteries – have come down to us in multiple copies. The largest group of texts that has survived is school texts for novices, such as copies of Ælfric's *Grammar*, and items intended for enlarging the minds of adults, both clerical and lay, particularly texts used for preaching (sermons or homilies and saints' lives) but also confessional and penitential material, and monastic rules, liturgical books and prayers. Translations too were plainly popular, both those made in King Alfred's day, including those by the king, and many made during the following century, especially parts of the Bible (the Hexateuch, the psalms and the gospels). Other materials of importance within a monastic environment are also found in multiple copies: chronicles and genealogies, law-codes, scientific, medical and computistical works, calculations of numbers and notes on the meaning of names, and texts that may be broadly classified under the heading of folklore, even though much of this matter draws on classical sources.[3]

---

[3] There are two quick means of finding texts which survive in multiple copies: the index to N.R. Ker's *Catalogue of Manuscripts Containing Anglo-Saxon*, Oxford, Clarendon, 1957, and Angus Cameron, 'A list of Old English texts' in Roberta Frank and Angus Cameron, ed., *A Plan for the Dictionary of Old English*, Toronto, Centre for Medieval Studies, 1973, pp. 25–306.

Clerical scribes and methods of production

Given the nature of the production of manuscript materials, and of the exigencies of their survival, it is unlikely that any manuscripts that remain to us today were produced anywhere but within a monastic context. Even the many hundreds of legal documents that survive were actually written by clerics and probably preserved in monastic libraries since by and large they were intended to verify the claims of monasteries to land. Although there is ample evidence that the lay aristocracy in late Anglo-Saxon England could read, it is doubtful if many of them had time for the more laborious task of writing but would employ clerks (clerics) to write for them; so the very large number of individuals that we can identify by their script were necessarily clerics – mostly men although there are some books that have been shown to be written by (or for) women too.[4] A few of the male scribes we can identify by name. Individual authors whose work is studied today, such as the homilist Ælfric and Archbishop Wulfstan of York, both wrote in their own hand in manuscripts which survive. In Wulfstan's case, no less than eight separate manuscripts have been identified with samples of his handwriting. Other individuals, both named and unnamed, can also be shown to have been involved in writing in a range of manuscripts,[5] one called Hemming from Worcester in the 1060s producing work in both English and Latin in a long list of manuscripts. Worcester, which was a rich monastery, had a very large scriptorium, and we have knowledge of significant numbers of scribes working there, many of them overlapping in the same manuscript. Most surviving manuscripts were written by more than one scribe, and it is often

> '... although Old English poetry has been studied with great enthusiasm for more than two centuries, close examination of the vast bulk of the much greater quantity of prose that has survived was slow to develop in recent times. Some of the most important prose texts were not edited and thus made available to the majority of readers until relatively recently.'

---

[4] London, British Library, Cotton Faustina A. x contains a copy of Bishop Æthelwold's translation of the *Benedictine Rule*, in which there are many references to followers of the *Rule* couched in the feminine gender, all of which have been altered to masculine by a later scribe. Clearly a version of the *Rule* for nuns has been altered for the use of monks. Salisbury Cathedral 150, which contains a continuous Old English gloss to a Latin psalter, has been linked to the nunnery at Shaftesbury, see Celia Sisam and Kenneth Sisam, ed., *The Salisbury Psalter*, Early English Text Society original series 242, London and New York, Oxford University Press, 1959.

[5] A simple route to scribes, both named and unnamed, who worked on more than one manuscript in the eleventh century can be found in the list of scriptors and their work on the Manchester online database at http://www.arts.manchester.ac.uk/mancass/C11database/data/.

possible to determine a great deal about how the books were constructed from a careful examination of layout and spacing. For example, in the case of two scribes writing in tandem, each beginning the task of copying a long item or collection of items at a different point, the first scribe would be allocated a section which was expected to be completed at the end of a quire to ensure an appropriate link to the second section, already begun on a new quire by Scribe 2. But the chances of the first scribe copying so exactly over a long period of writing that he would complete his stint precisely at the end of a quire were so remote that either a page or part of a page would remain blank, or, alternatively, the writing would become smaller and more cramped at the end of the stint to squeeze in the appropriate portion of text. When either of these happens in a manuscript, it is probably a sign that the scribes were writing in tandem rather than one taking over from the other. An understanding of this practice may have repercussions for the study of the transmission of texts. Only if the scribes were copying an existing collection of texts in their entirety could they work in tandem in this way. In some manuscripts, on the other hand, single items were written jointly by different scribes in ways that may be hard to explain. Occasionally a scribe has intervened in the writing of just a few lines.[6] If this happened at the beginning of an item, as it does in three of the Blickling homilies (Princeton, Scheide collection 71), it may have occurred because one scribe was more senior than the other, and he was indicating to a more junior scribe which item should be copied next.[7] In this case, the distribution of hands supports the suggestion that the surviving book contains a collection of items brought together in this manuscript for the first time, rather than being a collection

---

[6] There are many surviving manuscripts in which a number of scribes intervene briefly in ways that are difficult to explain. One example is Oxford, Bodleian Library, Hatton 76, which has a copy of the translation of Pope Gregory's *Dialogues* made by Bishop Wærferth of Worcester in the late ninth century. The Hatton 76 version has been heavily modernized in the late Anglo-Saxon period, and this copy (which is incomplete but nonetheless still consists of more than fifty leaves) is largely the work of a single scribe, but two others intervened five times on three pages, in each instance for no more than a few lines.

[7] The person I have assumed here to be the more senior scribe in Blickling also intervened briefly in other items, including writing the *explicit* of two of them, perhaps to ensure that no more of that copy-text was used. He also wrote brief sections in the middle of some items, in ways that are hard to explain, and copied the whole of the last two surviving items of the manuscript. The end of the manuscript is fragmentary. See D.G. Scragg, 'The homilies of the Blickling manuscript' in Michael Lapidge and Helmut Gneuss, ed., *Learning and Literature in Anglo-Saxon England: Studies presented to Peter Clemoes on the occasion of his sixty-fifth birthday*, Cambridge, Cambridge University Press, 1985, pp. 299–316.

already in existence in the copy-text. Such seemingly unimportant details are significant for any study of textual transmission, which itself may be important in recovering the history and development of a text as well as the history of the book itself. Thus palaeography and codicology may ultimately contribute to the concerns of the literary critic.

The case of a homily in a Worcester manuscript, Oxford, Bodleian Library, Junius 121, item 33, is even more complicated, showing just how complex some palaeographic puzzles can be. There are three scribes involved in the copying of this short text, one of them being the man known to us as Hemming.[8] Hemming was clearly the senior scribe, opening the item by writing the first half-page, and closing it by writing the end; but after establishing the piece by writing just thirteen lines, he handed over to a more junior colleague (identified as such by his many copying errors, some of which he corrected afterwards above the line, and by the inferiority of his handwriting).[9] This scribe wrote two pages, only to give way to Hemming again for one more page. Then the junior wrote half a page, which Hemming completed before adding the next page. The junior added one more page before Hemming added three more pages. Then Hemming handed over to yet a third scribe who again wrote just half a page, and finally Hemming completed that page and ended the item halfway down the next. In all, these three scribes wrote only eleven pages between them, five separate stints being by Hemming. It is impossible now to recover the reasons for the frequent swapping of the task, but one may speculate from the surviving evidence that Hemming was an extremely busy scribe who had assistants from time to time, and that these assistants could not be trusted with the copying of complete items but had to be closely supervised, with the master taking over the copying when he had the opportunity to do so.[10]

Varieties of book

Manuscripts in English from the Anglo-Saxon period are of variable sizes, depending on their content and use. Even the thickness of the parchment used can vary considerably, from very fine thin material, almost transparent,

---

[8] On Hemming see N.R. Ker, 'Hemming's cartulary', reprinted in A.G. Watson, ed., *Books, Collectors and Libraries*, London, Continuum, 1985, pp. 31–59.

[9] The judgement on the quality of the hand is Neil Ker's; see his *Catalogue*, p. 417.

[10] For a fuller examination of this item, see Donald Scragg, 'A late Old English Harrowing of Hell homily from Worcester and Blickling Homily VII' in Katherine O'Brien O'Keeffe and Andy Orchard, ed., *Latin Learning and English Lore: studies in Anglo-Saxon Literature for Michael Lapidge*, 2 vols, Toronto Old English Series 14, Toronto and London, University of Toronto Press, 2005, pp. 197–211.

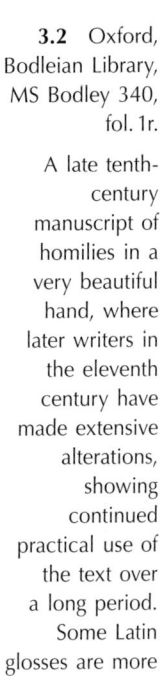

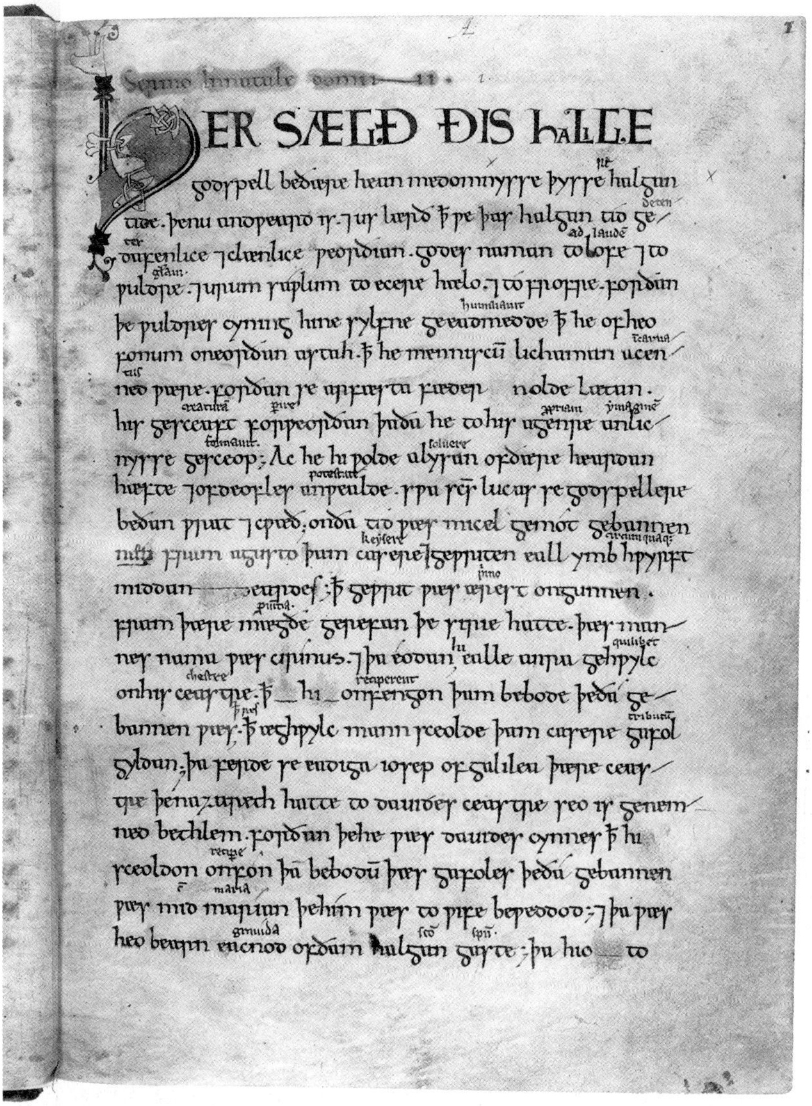

3.2 Oxford, Bodleian Library, MS Bodley 340, fol. 1r.

A late tenth-century manuscript of homilies in a very beautiful hand, where later writers in the eleventh century have made extensive alterations, showing continued practical use of the text over a long period. Some Latin glosses are more recent.

to thick heavy pages, and such variation sometimes occurs within a single manuscript. The page size (and consequently the writing) varies from large-scale, in books intended for public reading, as in the case of Oxford, Bodleian Library, Bodley 340/342, a handsome, beautifully crafted two-volume homiliary with a page size of 315 × 220 mm. (Figs 3.2–3.3),[11] to the relatively tiny pocket-books such as Oxford, Bodleian Library, Junius 85/86,

---

[11] Note that page sizes as given throughout this essay are always approximate because they may have been cut down over the centuries by binders. This is true even of binders in the twentieth century.

which again contains homilies but which was clearly intended to be carried by a preacher from place to place rather than situated permanently on a lectern or in a library because it is only 160 × 115 mm. (Bodley 340/342 was always intended to be in two volumes as we can see from the fact that the opening item of volume 2 is an introductory piece, whereas Junius 85/86 was broken up long after its copying.) Between these two extremes we find

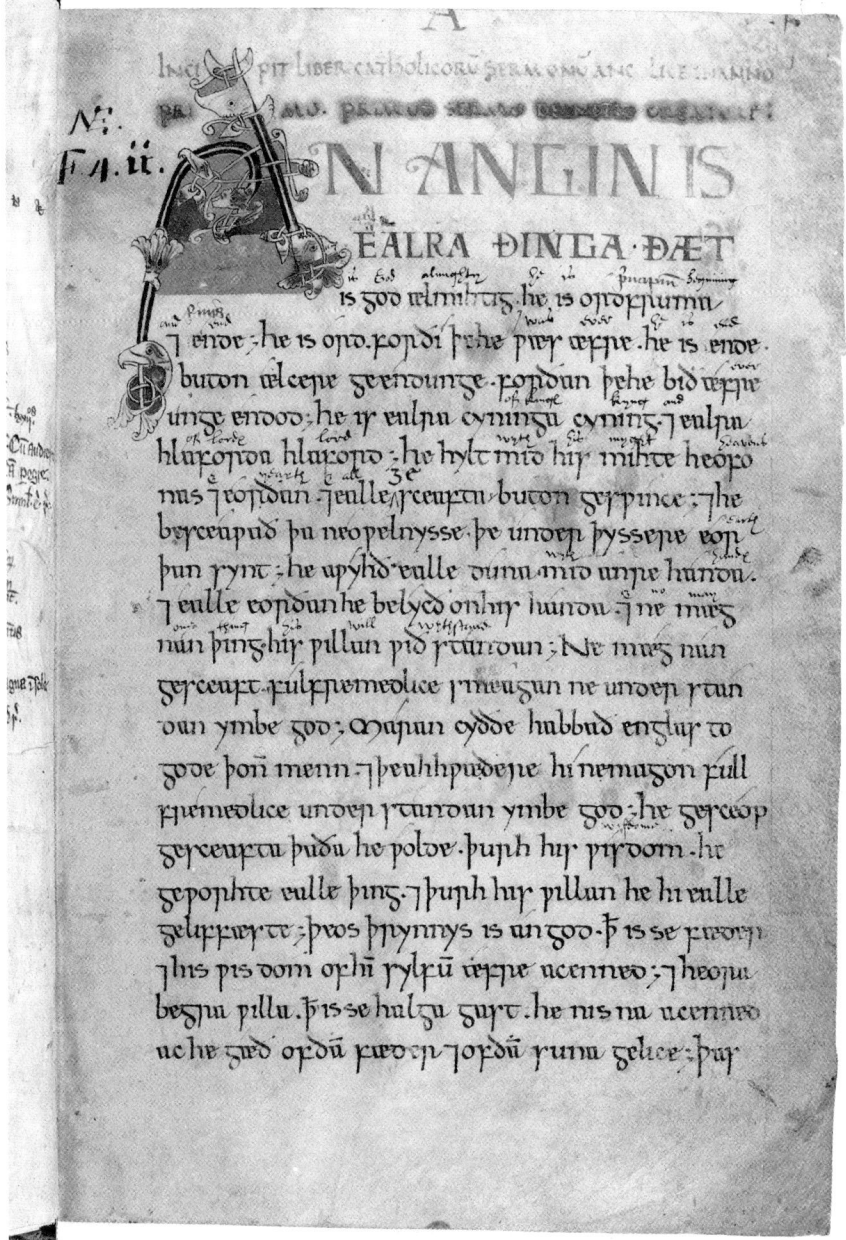

3.3 Oxford, Bodleian Library, MS Bodley 342, fol. 1r.

The opening page of the second volume of homilies, companion to Fig. 3.2. Here the care with which this large double volume (written space c.260 mm–c.150 mm) was written is apparent.

books of various shapes and sizes, intended for a variety of purposes: long, thin pocket-books such as the penitential Oxford, Bodleian Library, Laud Misc 482 (page size 202 × 91 mm.), written in a minute but beautiful script, a book which was obviously intended to travel with a confessor in his baggage, to working manuscripts such as London, British Library, Cotton Nero A. i, which is probably a commonplace book assembled for Archbishop Wulfstan (it contains some pieces by him and others known to be of interest to him). This was made at the very beginning of the eleventh century, and Wulfstan himself (who died in 1023) annotated the book, so it clearly belonged to him at an early period. The book, which contains some Latin pieces as well as many in Old English, at 165 × 105 mm. is again pocket-sized and may have been carried about by the archbishop or by one of his entourage on his behalf. Another working manuscript is Royal 7 C. xii which is an incomplete copy of Ælfric's First Series of Catholic Homilies written in his own scriptorium of Cerne Abbas, Dorset (Fig. 3.1). It is incomplete because it lacks the introductory preface, which Ælfric presumably added later, and it is a working manuscript in two respects: it has marginal comments and some alterations in Ælfric's own hand, and it has two additional slips, fragments of parchment inserted between existing leaves on which new text is written, to be included within the existing text. This book would appear to be a fair copy of homilies initially composed by Ælfric on wax tablets (which could be re-used) and then amended by the author in the light of further consideration.

Punctuation

Old English in manuscript is in general very easy to read, once the basic shapes of the letters are recognized.[12] Script has been treated by Alexander R. Rumble in Chapter 2 of this book, but it is worth making a few comments here on punctuation. In general, punctuation of the period (including capitalization and accent marks) is based on rhetoric as opposed to syntax as it is today. A phrase with two contrasting halves, for example, such as *not this but that*, is likely to have the heaviest mark of punctuation before *but*, often accompanied by the capitalization of the following word. The function of early punctuation was thus to ensure that a text was read aloud correctly, rather than that it should be understood silently as we assume. Accent marks (in the shape of an acute accent) again usually mark stress rather than the length of a vowel or the nature of its pronunciation as in modern scripts. There is evidence too that marks of punctuation were generally carried over from one copy to the next, as a single scribe might use one system of

---

[12] For an easy introduction to many variable letter forms, see the Manchester website, details of which are in note 5, above.

punctuation in one item that he copied and another in the next.[13] But it is not possible to write about punctuation in Old English prose without drawing attention to one manuscript in particular, Royal 7 C. xii, the copy of Ælfric's homilies annotated by the author. This manuscript has a regular system of punctuation throughout which so marries with the text that it must be assumed to be the author's own. One feature of it that is especially notable is that it frequently uses the *punctus interrogativus* (looking like a reversed question mark leaning at a 45° angle from the vertical) after questions, the first example of a vernacular manuscript to use this feature and almost the only one to use it for Old English.[14] It is a punctuation mark which became commonplace only much later in the medieval period and shows Ælfric's deep understanding of Latin rhetoric and his concern that his material (intended for reading to an audience) should be stressed appropriately.

Additions to manuscripts

Many surviving manuscripts were added to by later writers in a variety of ways, either by copying in extra texts, commenting or altering texts already in place, or even by fastening two books – or a series of separate (perhaps unbound) booklets – together. A gospel book might be expected by its owners to survive, and because of that it could be utilized to record pieces of information they regarded as important. Such a one is Cambridge, Corpus Christi College 140 which contains copies of the four gospels in Old English, but on blank spaces between the gospels are manumissions which the owner wanted recorded at various times during the eleventh and twelfth centuries (Fig. 3.4). Who that owner was, is made clear both by the manumissions (many issued by Abbot Ælfsige of Bath who died in 1087) and by a list of relics owned by Bath Abbey. Although we cannot be sure where the manuscript was written, there is no doubt that it was the property of Bath during the late Anglo-Saxon and early Norman periods. Other manuscripts had additional items added in the margins. Cambridge, Corpus Christi College 41 as originally written contained an eleventh-century copy of the ninth-century translation of Bede's *Historia ecclesiastica*, but it now also has a series of items added in the margins a generation after the main text was copied – charms,

---

[13] See D.G. Scragg, 'Accent marks in the Old English Vercelli Book', *Neuphilologische Mitteilungen*, 72, 1971, pp. 699–710.

[14] The principal scribe of Hatton 76 (see note 6) also uses the mark occasionally near the beginning of his task. It is possible that here it is carried over by the scribe from his exemplar since whoever revised the text in the late period must have had close knowledge of the Latin from which it was translated, and may have been influenced by Latin punctuation.

medical recipes and homilies – all in the same hand, although not the one which wrote the Bede translation (Fig. 3.5). We know that these texts were entered at different times rather than as a single copying exercise, because some time after a charm was written in the margin of page 272 (Fig. 3.6), the

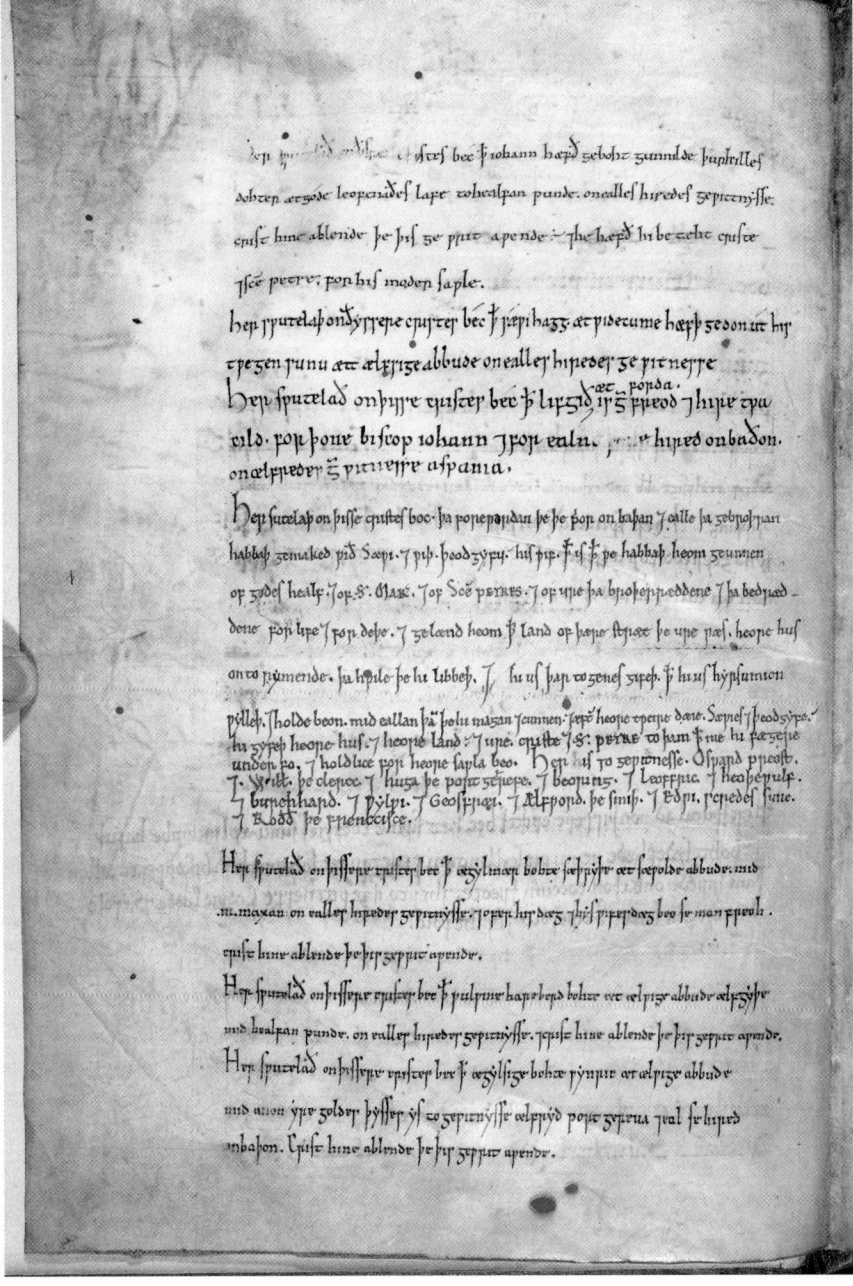

3.4 Cambridge, Corpus Christi College MS 140, fol. 1v. Gospel Book with legal items added.

The flyleaf of an early eleventh-century book containing an English version of the four gospels and belonging to Bath Abbey. The addition of a series of brief legal texts in English – which Bath clearly wanted to preserve – shows the reverence felt for the book and the certainty that anything written in it would be sure to survive. For Bibles in English to be treated in this way indicates that contemporaries felt that written English was here to stay, at a time when no other vernacular language in Europe was being recorded.

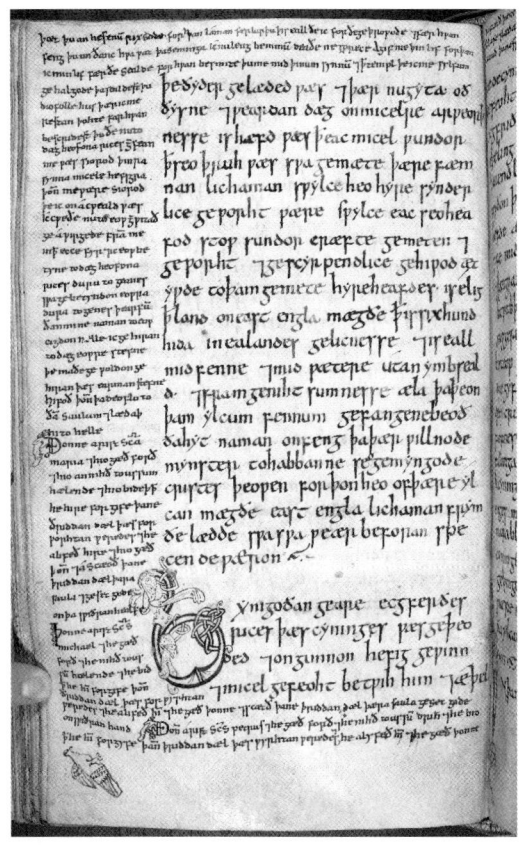

LEFT

3.5 Cambridge, Corpus Christi College MS 41, p. 300.

Parchment was such a precious commodity in the eleventh century that sometimes every inch was used. Here an additional text (a homily or sermon) – which has no relation to the main text (the English version of Bede's *Historia ecclesiastica gentis anglorum*) – has been added by someone who wished to record the homily but had no access to virgin parchment (or who felt that the item would be safer within this book).

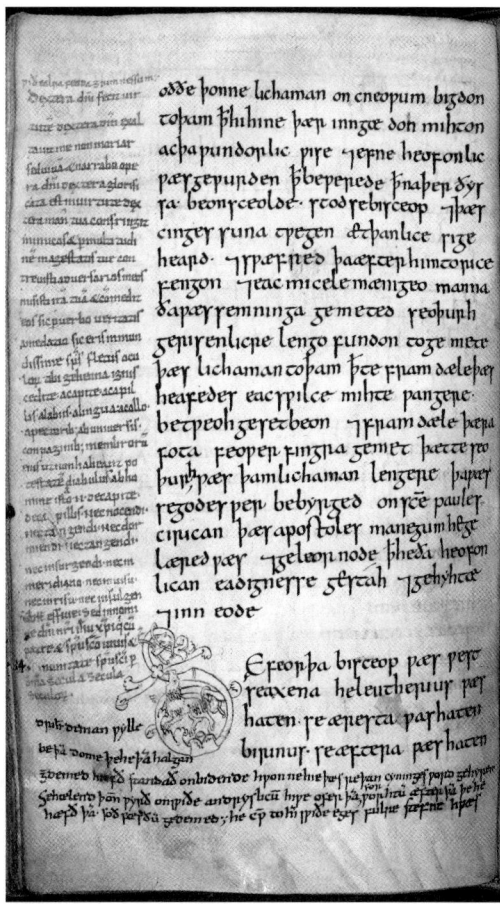

RIGHT

3.6 Cambridge, Corpus Christi College MS 41, p. 272 (additional charm).

Another page from the Bede in Fig. 3.5, added to twice. Beside the Bede text is a Latin charm, with a heading in English. At the foot of the page in a darker ink is the continuation of a homily begun earlier in the book, carried over from the previous page, and continuing onto the next one. We can see here that the charm was in position before the homily was begun, as the homily is written, in effect, round it. This gives us three layers of writing, the Bede, the charm and finally the homily. The writing cannot continue to the absolute bottom of the page because the scribe needed to be able to rest on the book in order to write.

An .dcccc.lxxxiiii Her forð ferde se welwillenda biscop Aðelwold
An .dcccc.lxxxv   ⁊ se halgung þæs æftran fylgendan biscopes Ælfheages
An .dcccc.lxxxvi se ðe oðran naman wæs geciged Godwine xiiii. kł. nou.
An .dcccc.lxxxvii ⁊ he gesæt þon biscopstol an þapa twegra apostola dæge
An .dcccc.lxxxviii Simonis ⁊ Iudæ. on Wintan ceastre.
An .dcccc.lxxxviiii An .dcccc. xc. An .dcccc. xci. An .dcccc. xcii.
An .dcccc. xciii Her on ðyssum geare com unlaf mid hys ⁊ hund nigontigon
   scypum ⁊ forhergedon þ on Ytan ⁊ forða danon to Sandwic ⁊ swa danon to Gipes-
   wic eall oferhergode ⁊ swa to Mældune ⁊ ðær heo togeanes Byrhtnoð ealdorman mid
   hys fyrde geaht ⁊ hy þon ealdorman þær ofslogon ⁊ wælstowe geweald ahtan ⁊ him ar...

(syððan grið wið   An .dcccc. xciiii Her forð ferde Sigeric arce biscop. ⁊ feng Ælfric
⁊ hine man sealde   Wiltun scire biscop to ðam arce biscop rice.
grið wið to biscop   An .dcccc. xcv
handa. Durh Siric   An .dcccc. xcvi
þare cantwara biscopes
⁊ Ælfeages Wincestres An .dcccc. xcvii
                      An .dcccc. xcviii
                      An .dcccc. xcviiii
                      M

M .i. Her on ðyssum geare wæs micel unfrið on Angelcynnes londe þurh scyphere
   ⁊ ælghwær hergedon ⁊ bærndon swa hy upp asetton on æfnesiþ þ hy
   coman to Æþelinga dene ⁊ þa com þær togeanes Hamtunscyr ⁊ hy wið
   gefuhton ⁊ þær wearð Æðelweard cynges heahgerefa ofslegen
   ⁊ Leofric æt Hwitciricean ⁊ Leofwine cynges heahgerefa ⁊ Wulfhere
   biscopes ðegn ⁊ Godwine æt Worðige Ælfsiges biscopes sunu ⁊ ealra
   manna an ⁊ hund eahtatig. ⁊ þær weard þara Denisca micle ma
   ofslegenra. healde hie wælstowe geweald ahtan.

3.7 Cambridge, Corpus Christi College MS 173, Part I, fol. 29v. *Parker Chronicle* for 993 with marginal additions (actually 991).

We can see here (in part) how the *Chronicle* came into its present form, with additional material being added as it became available. The page was written originally with one line allocated to each year, the list of years (in roman numerals) being written first down the left margin. When more information on '993' reached the scribe, he erased some annal numbers and wrote them in a line across line 6. Having written four lines of text, he still had something to add, so put it into the left margin (ending with *handa*). A later scribe added another sentence.

same scribe began to add a homily to the margin of page 254. Unfortunately, the homily proved longer than expected, and when the writer reached the beginning of the charm, he (or she) had to skip down the page to write the rest, the homily now ending on page 280. Thus the charm is now embedded within the homily. For some unknown reason, the items as a whole are added in groups at different points in the manuscript. The additional pieces have nothing in common with the Bede and must have been entered there because no other parchment was available. Every possible scrap of parchment in this instance has been used on the pages with the additional items, the texts being entered across the top margin, down the outer edge and across the bottom. The result is a manuscript with texts which are today very vulnerable, because it is impossible to turn the relevant pages without touching the writing. Other manuscripts show continued use by virtue of marginal additions which do relate to the main entries. In Cambridge, Corpus Christi College 173, which contains the earliest or A-version of the *Anglo-Saxon Chronicle*, extra material was added apparently as it became available. The most notable instance of this is the account of the battle of Maldon (commemorated elsewhere in the poem now known by that name), which has been entered partly under the year 993 (actually 991) in a space created by moving annal numbers, but was forced to spill into the outer margin because the space proved insufficient for the text (Fig. 3.7).

Many manuscripts have additional items added on blank leaves at the end of an item or in blank spaces left by the original scribe or scribes for a variety of reasons. Oxford, Bodleian Library, Hatton 114 is the second volume of a two-part collection of homilies all written by a single scribe of Worcester around 1065–1075. Soon after the completion of the homiliary, other scribes added further homilies on additional quires. That some of them are contemporary is shown by the fact that one of the scribes involved also wrote the table of contents which contains the set of homilies copied by the original scribe, and there are signs that at least one other was written by a known Worcester scribe of the same period.

Sometimes, however, items now conjoined originally belonged to different manuscripts, and it is impossible to know when they came together in their present position. This is particularly the case with manuscripts in the British Library's Cotton collection, because Sir Robert Cotton (1571–1631), the most important early modern collector of Anglo-Saxon manuscripts, had the annoying (to us) habit of dissecting manuscripts in his collection and reassembling them in ways that he found more satisfying. But that practice extended back into the medieval period itself. In some cases, it was a means of preserving manuscripts which otherwise would have been vulnerable. A case in point is Oxford, Bodleian Library, Hatton 115. Again this is a collection of homilies dating from the second half of the eleventh century and again probably from Worcester. The original scribe copied thirty-one items, but subsequently three extra layers of texts were added. In the first place, the scribe seems to have constructed two separate books, perhaps at different times, because although the book as it now stands opens with eight regular quires of eight leaves (that is, each having four double sheets folded to make a 'booklet' of eight), the ninth quire has just four single leaves. Since leaves in such a quire could easily become separated and so lost, it is impossible to suppose that the scribe actually made a quire in this way. Rather, his ninth was a regular eight-leaf quire which at some time was cut down the middle. (It is clear that there was a break in his copying at this point because there are a few blank lines at the foot of the final surviving page of this reduced quire, showing that the rest of the book was not part of the same copying exercise.) It is likely that the cut was made when the book of nine quires was added to another pre-existing book written by the same scribe, but whoever made up the new book also added an extra sheet – the first of the three additional layers in the manuscript. This single leaf, containing two short items, was written by a different but contemporary scribe. It must be assumed that the task of adding the extra leaf and the putting together of two books was all part of a single enterprise, making a book of thirty-three items. But two further additions were made subsequently. The first is a single late eleventh-century quire, added at the end, and containing a single homily, and the second a twelfth-century quire from Worcester containing non-homiletic prognostics and notes on names and numbers which the Worcester scriptorium clearly wanted to preserve. Of all of the additions, the most interesting bibliographically is the quire containing a single homily, because this is one of a series of booklets surviving from the period which allows us to see that many manuscripts were left in an unbound state (this booklet

'... from the hundred-year period after 990, over 275 manuscripts and documents containing English survive, written by a total of more than 500 scribes ... It is indicative of the many thousands – even tens of thousands – that must have been produced in the period.'

has a crease across the middle showing that it has been folded at some point and stuffed into the eleventh-century equivalent of its owner's pocket). Most of such booklets must have been lost, and only by being attached to the Hatton manuscript by a thoughtful librarian in the twelfth century has this one managed to survive.[15]

Scribal care and scribal error

Many of the manuscripts that we have today are imposing books which should realistically have been discarded after their owners found difficulty in reading them because of changes in both script and language from the thirteenth century onwards, but which have survived presumably because of their grandeur. Most of these were carefully written, with words divided along syllabic lines to ensure that the right-hand margin of the page was kept straight or justified. This is something that we, in the print age, take for granted, but with handwritten materials, it was more difficult to achieve, and it is interesting to note the trouble that some scribes took to make the page look attractive to the eye. Even quite short words with no more than five letters, and common words such as *buton* 'except, but', might be split, and short words of two or three letters might be run together. Some scribes used hyphens to indicate run on between lines but the majority did not. But because the task of accurate copying over a long period is difficult, especially in a monastic environment with all the exigencies of cold and damp that must have existed for much of the time, all manuscripts, even the most handsome ones on which considerable care has obviously been expended, have copying errors of a variety of sorts. The most common are failures on the copyists' part to keep to their place in the copy-text. Texts with repetitive or formulaic language led to the scribe's eye picking up the wrong point when looking back for the next phrase to be copied, resulting in the repeating of a word, phrase or passage (dittography) or the omission of one (homeoteleuton or eyeskip). Dittography or omission can even happen within a word, omission of a single letter or syllable usually being called haplography, as when in Modern English the word *adaptation* becomes *adaption*. Dittography and homeoteleuton occur most frequently when the same word or phrase occurs twice in a similar position in the copy-text, for example at the end of a line, and the occurrence of such errors may lead us to the possibility of linking surviving manuscripts. Given the tens of thousands of manuscripts that existed in the last decades of the Anglo-Saxon period, it is extremely unlikely that two survive of which one is a direct copy of the other, but since we

---

[15] See P.R. Robinson, 'Self-contained units in composite manuscripts of the Anglo-Saxon period', *Anglo-Saxon England*, 7, 1978, pp. 231–8.

3.8 London, British Library, MS Cotton Tiberius A. iii, fol. 3r.

The beginning of the *Regularis Concordia* which Æthelwold drew up to regularize monastic life in the 960s. This version has a running English gloss to the Latin text, and was written at Canterbury around 1050.

have considerable knowledge of a few large scriptoria (especially Canterbury, Worcester and, for a brief period, Exeter), it is just within the bounds of possibility. We can associate manuscripts by their having errors (especially copying errors) in common. Occasionally scribes repeat an error from their copy-text, and since this is more likely than two scribes making the same mistake independently, it shows that two manuscripts are in the same line of transmission, although not necessarily copied from one another but with an unknown number of copies between.

Some errors, however, may be explained by other, more specialized reasons than that of mistaking the copy-text. It is conceivable that when multiple copies of a large text were needed quickly, copying was done by dictation. When King Alfred translated Pope Gregory the Great's *Cura pastoralis* into English in the last decade of the ninth century, he noted in his preface his intention to send one copy to each of his bishops. The text is indeed long, and the number needed was probably at least twelve, and dictation has been suggested for the completion of this exercise.[16] This would explain the 'fusion' of short words in the earliest complete copy of the text to survive (Oxford, Bodleian Library, Hatton 20) whereby words ending and beginning with the same letter (e.g. *ðurh hine*) were written together with only one *h* (*ðurhine*).

Finally, as the eleventh century progressed, and more non-native speakers entered the monasteries with the growth of Norman influence following the accession of Edward the Confessor in 1042, some errors may result from texts being copied by scribes with an imperfect grasp of the language. London, British Library, Cotton Tiberius A. iii was made in the middle of the eleventh century at Christ Church, Canterbury, one of the most significant monasteries in the land, yet one of its scribes exhibits curious linguistic features such as the confusion of the native symbol *p* (*wynn*), the equivalent of modern English *w*, with similarly shaped letters like *p* and *þ* (*thorn*), the equivalent of Modern English *th* (Fig. 3.8). It is hard to see why a native speaker would make such mistakes in writing his own language.

---

[16] An assessment of the number of copies required was made by Kenneth Sisam in 'The publication of Alfred's *Pastoral Care*' in his *Studies in the History of Old English Literature*, Oxford, Clarendon Press, 1953, pp. 140–7. On copying of this text, see Dorothy M. Horgan, 'The relationship between the O.E. MSS of King Alfred's translation of Gregory's *Pastoral Care*', *Anglia*, 91, 1973, pp. 153–69.

PROHEMIUM REGULARIS CONCORDIE ANGLICAE NATIONIS

Monachoru͂ sc͂i monialiu͂q́ue oriditur :~

Gloriosus etenim eadgar xp̄i opitulante gratia anglorū
cęterarumq́ue gentium intra ambitum brittanice insule degentiū
rex egregius· ab ineunte sue puritię ętate· licet uti ipsa soleę ętatis di
uersis uteretur moribus· attamen respectu diuino attactus· abbate
quodam assiduo monente· ac regiam catholicę fidei uiam demonstran
te· cępit magnopere dn̄m timere· diligere· ac uenerari· Radiante paula
tim fidei scintilla· ne ociositatis torpore explosa delitesceret· Quibus
scorum operum meritis inferundum persecutionis ardorem accendi ua
lerit· studiose percunctari sollicitus cępit· Comperto etenim quod sacra
coenobia diuersis sui regiminis locis diruta ac pene dn̄i nr̄i ih̄u xp̄i ser
uitio destituta neglegenter tabescerent· dn̄i conpunctus gr̄a· cum
magna animi· alacritate festinando· ubicumq́ue locorum decentissime
restauraret· cięterisq́ue neglegentium clericorum spurcitias non solum
monachos· uerum sanctimoniales etiam patribus matribusq́ue constitutis
addi famulatum ubiq́ue· p̄atam sui regni amplitudinem deuotissime
constituit· bonisq́ue omnib· locupletans gratulabundus ditauit· Regali
itaq́ue functus officio uelut pastorum pastor sollicitus· antidiis p̄sidor
nibus ut i̇ianibus luporum faucibus oues quas dn̄i largiente gr̄a
studiosus collegerat / munifico eriperet contuitq́ue sue ælþryþe sc̄i
monialium mandras· ut impauidi more custodis defenderet· cautis
sime pręcepit· ut uidelicet mas· maribus feminaę feminis sine ullo
suspicionis scrupulo subuenirent· Regulari itaquę sc̄i patris benedicti

Origin, provenance and mobility

This chapter has made occasional reference to the origin or provenance of manuscripts, the difference being that the former refers to the place where a manuscript was written and the latter to the place where it was kept. On the whole, little is known about the origin of Anglo-Saxon manuscripts. The majority were written after the Benedictine Reform movement of the 960s when monastic education was closely controlled from Winchester and a uniform written language was employed nearly everywhere. Internal evidence, at least linguistic evidence, is therefore absent from the majority of texts. Even when regional forms occasionally creep in (as periodically we find vowel confusion which is associated with the Kentish 'dialect'), there is no certainty that a scribe was working where he was trained. The most reliable evidence for the origin of a manuscript comes from its script, as hands vary from region to region since professional scribes were trained to write in particular ways, although again, the mobility of scribes once trained is a factor which must be borne in mind.

We have more chance of being able to deduce the provenance of a manuscript, as has been suggested above. Manuscripts made at one centre might be moved either as soon as copied, or later, to another centre. There is no knowing for certain how soon after copying a manuscript might have been transferred to a different place, but an example of one that certainly was moved later rather than earlier is the *Vercelli Book*, now in northern Italy, because the presence of marginal annotations in the book show that it was in England long enough to be used as a copy-text (a copy from which others were made). Similarly an early copy of the first and second series of Ælfric's Catholic Homilies, Cambridge, University Library Gg. 3.28, was made somewhere in the south of England, perhaps at Ælfric's own scriptorium of Cerne Abbas, but transferred at an early period to Durham. Many manuscripts must have remained where they were written, however. Similarities of script have allowed scholars to identify a group of scribes working – or trained – at Exeter in the third quarter of the eleventh century, and the appearance of annotations in a large number of manuscripts by a scribe of the thirteenth century known as the 'Tremulous Hand' (because of the shaky appearance of the script) has suggested that they were all to be found in a single monastery, the very rich foundation at Worcester. There is evidence that many of these manuscripts were in fact written at Worcester itself. Scholars have now identified a large group of scribes working there in the 1060s. Relatively large numbers of books were made in Canterbury, although it is not always easy to be sure whether that means the monastic cathedral of Christ Church or the nearby abbey of St Augustine's, or even the scriptorium at Rochester only thirty miles away, which we know to have been the provenance of at least one surviving manuscript (Bodley 340/342) and the place of writing in the twelfth century of Cambridge, Corpus Christi College 303. But we have few manuscripts from the two monasteries at the royal seat at Winchester, none from the major monastery (and royal burial ground) at Glastonbury, and virtually no evidence of writing in London.

Ornamentation and marginalia

On the whole, surviving manuscripts containing prose are workaday copies with limited ornamentation, but there are notable exceptions, such as the lavishly illustrated Old Testament translation, London, British Library, Cotton Claudius B. iv (Figs 1.4, 7.32). There also seems to have been a tradition of illustrating the text known as the *Wonders* (or *Marvels*) *of the East* which survives in two manuscripts (Figs 7.30–7.31), in both of which it is illustrated even though the sets of pictures appear unrelated (not copied from one manuscript to another or derived by them from a common ancestor). But colour and minor decorative features are also used in a fair number of manuscripts: ornamental capitals mark the opening of new sections of a text or new texts, and red or green, occasionally blue or purple, are used for initial letters. Such capitals were undoubtedly copied from one text to another. The related manuscripts Bodley 340/342, Cambridge, Corpus Christi College 162 and CCCC 198 have the same initial drawn at the beginning of their opening item,[17] even though they are unlikely to have been copied from one another; but all three go back to a common (Canterbury) ancestor at some distance, even though there is a gap of twenty or thirty years between their copying. Occasionally we can see a copyist practising an initial on the copy-text, as at the foot of the *Vercelli Book*, fol. 112r. The margins of many manuscripts provide fascinating evidence of their use. A cock crows at the top of a page of Royal 7 C. xii and a dog runs across the foot of a page of the *Vercelli Book*. Such doodles are the work of scribes who were bored with their task of copying, but they are not the scribes of the manuscripts in question because they would be wary of spoiling their own work. Beatings were commonplace for monks who produced imperfect results. Rather they are the signs of copyists using the surviving manuscripts as copy-texts. Similar are pen-trials in margins, such as *writ ðus* 'write like this' added to Oxford, Bodleian Library, Junius 121 at the end of the eleventh century, and even, with an attempt at verse, *writ þus oððe bet, oððe þine hyde forlet* 'write like this or better, or lose your skin' added to Hatton 20 early in the

---

[17] In the case of CCCC 162, it was originally the opening item, as explained above.

twelfth century. All of these are important indications that the manuscripts in question were still in use as copy-texts at the time that the marginalia were added. There are also many instances of names written in margins – owners' perhaps – and ownership is certainly central to such notes as *of searbyrig ic eom* 'I am from Salisbury' on the flyleaf of Dublin, Trinity College 174. But marginal annotations are more frequently concerned with the content of the manuscripts. A good example of this involves the note at the end of Ælfric's sermon for Palm Sunday in his First Series of homilies which draws attention to the three 'silent days' from Maundy Thursday to Easter Saturday during which no sermon should be preached. That this was an afterthought by Ælfric is suggested by the fact that in his 'working' manuscript, Royal 7 C. xii, it is added by a different scribe on a blank line, but the comment subsequently found its way into other copies that were 'published' by Ælfric and so probably comes from the master himself. In two surviving copies, however, later scribes added *ac þis ne þynceð no us well gesæd* 'but this doesn't seem to us well said' (in Cambridge, Corpus Christi College 178, early eleventh-century, but probably annotated at Worcester in the middle of the century) and *ðis nis no well gesæd* 'this is not well said' (in Hatton 114, written at Worcester where it remained, the post-Conquest annotation being perhaps by a scribe calling himself Coleman). Clearly Ælfric's view was unfashionable at Worcester half a century after his death.[18] All of this shows readers working with Old English texts, and adapting and adjusting them to their own needs both before and after the Conquest. During the eleventh century alone hundreds of readers with pens in their hands added annotations of various sorts to earlier manuscripts, producing good evidence of their continued use. But what it also proves is the existence of the very widespread literary culture that existed in the vernacular throughout the late Anglo-Saxon period and well into the Norman era.

The roles of editors

The fact that so much English material survives from the last century of the Anglo-Saxon state makes the task of the textual critic, editing texts from manuscripts, challenging.[19] Very many prose texts survive in multiple

---

[18] It is worth noting that it was also unfashionable in Canterbury during Ælfric's lifetime since anonymous sermons for his 'silent days' were included in collections of his pieces around 1000.

[19] The bibliography of textual criticism is long, and even the shorter list of books and articles on the subject dealing specifically with Old English is growing. I recommend that the interested reader begins with the most recent and one of the best: R.M. Liuzza, 'Scribes of the mind: editing Old English in theory and practice' in

copies, and although almost all Old English prose has now been published in modern editions, many of those are unsatisfactory in a variety of ways. Nineteenth-century editions, such as Richard Morris's edition of the Blickling Homilies,[20] and Benjamin Thorpe's edition of Ælfric's Catholic Sermons,[21] were printed from a single manuscript and ignored readings in others, for their editors were concerned to make the texts available to an age that knew little about the prose tradition of the period. There were other contemporary editors who served other texts (and their readers) better, however: Henry Sweet's edition of the *Pastoral Care*[22] has two versions in parallel and variants from a third in an appendix, but still fails to exhaust all available copies of that text. Thorpe's edition of the *Anglo-Saxon Chronicle* prints six versions in parallel columns, and Arthur Napier's edition of Wulfstan[23] (which contains a much wider range of texts than those that can be safely attributed to the archbishop) has a complete set of variant readings for all of them from all of the manuscripts known to the editor when he published. In the twentieth century, the citing of variants has become the norm, but most editors of prose still print a single text, many citing only 'substantive' variants. What constitutes a substantive variant is, of course, highly subjective. It usually means those variants from manuscripts other than the base text (the one chosen as the basis for the edition) which help to establish the text or which show how it was significantly altered, deliberately or accidentally, by later writers. But the flaw in the whole procedure is the necessity of choosing one surviving manuscript version and giving it priority, so that the casual user of the edition, who is unlikely ever to work through the whole of the apparatus to re-examine the editor's chain of thought, accepts the text as authoritative. The common practice among editors is to try to establish the 'author's' text, a dangerous undertaking in

---

Hugh Magennis and Jonathan Wilcox, ed., *The Power of Words: Anglo-Saxon studies presented to Donald G. Scragg on his seventieth birthday*, Morgantown, WV, West Virginia University Press, 2006, pp. 245-77.

[20] Richard Morris, ed., *The Blickling Homilies*, Early English Text Society, original series 58, 63, 73, London, Early English Text Society, 1874-78.

[21] Benjamin Thorpe, ed., *The Homilies of the Anglo-Saxon Church: the first part, containing the Sermones Catholici or Homilies of Ælfric*, 2 vols, London, Aelfric Society, 1844-6.

[22] Henry Sweet, ed., *King Alfred's West Saxon Version of Gregory's Pastoral Care*, Early English Text Society, original series 45, 50, London, Oxford University Press, 1871.

[23] Arthur Napier, ed., *Wulfstan: Sammlung der ihm zugeschriebenen Homilien nebst Untersuchungen über ihre Echtheit*, Berlin, Weidmannsche Buchhandlung, 1883, repr. with a bibliographical supplement by Klaus Ostheeren, Dublin and Zurich, 1965.

the medieval period where anonymity is usual. On the other hand, we do have a remarkable amount of Old English prose which can be safely linked to an author, and this in itself shows the impropriety of prioritizing a single text. It is well known that Wulfstan rewrote his most famous piece, the *Sermo Lupi*, more than once, and his most recent editor, Dorothy Bethurum, acknowledges that by printing three versions independently.[24] But the case of Ælfric is more complicated. In the first place, we have more Ælfrician texts surviving than from any other single author before the fourteenth century. On the other, his work was extremely popular in the eleventh century and that popularity continued to a less extent into the twelfth. As a result, we have a huge volume of Ælfrian manuscripts of variable quality. His first series of homilies survives in many copies – a dozen or more in the case of individual homilies – and his latest editor, Peter Clemoes,[25] chose as the base text a manuscript which can undoubtedly be associated with Ælfric himself because it has annotations in his own hand.[26] But like Wulfstan, Ælfric changed his mind. Wulfstan did so because of changed political circumstances, but Ælfric was more concerned to refine his ideas and to avoid unnecessary repetition. We know that later medieval writers, and many modern ones, rewrote, so what should an editor prioritize, the earliest copy (in this case Royal 7 C. xii) which contains the closest text that we have to Ælfric's first thoughts, or the best copy, in this case probably Cambridge, University Library Gg. 3.28, which contains a full set of the homilies including the preface, or perhaps even a later manuscript which might contain Ælfric's last thoughts? The dilemma stems from the need to choose a single copy on which to base an edition of a text progressively transformed over a period of time.

There is a further problem which editors of texts surviving in multiple copies have to face and that is that modern critical approaches are as interested in what happens to a text – how it was developed by later writers and scribes for new audiences – as in its presumed author's thoughts. The only way in which this interest can be accommodated is to present the reader with several versions of the text in tandem, as Thorpe did with the *Anglo-Saxon Chronicle*.[27] In the past, manuscript copies have been associated with

---

[24] Dorothy Bethurum, ed., *The Homilies of Wulfstan*, Oxford, Clarendon Press, 1957. The three versions of the *Sermo Lupi*, her no. XX, are on pages 255–75.

[25] Peter Clemoes, ed., *Ælfric's Catholic Homilies: the first series*, Early English Text Society, supplementary series 17, Oxford, Oxford University Press, 1997.

[26] For proof that the annotations are by Ælfric, see the introduction to Norman Eliason and Peter Clemoes, ed., *Ælfric's First Series of Catholic Homilies (British Museum Royal 7 C. XII, fols 4–218)*, Early English Manuscripts in Facsimile 13, Copenhagen, Rosenkilde & Bagger, 1966, esp. pp. 19–22.

[27] See now the collaborative edition of the *Anglo-Saxon Chronicle*, initiated by

one another through the exhibition of their textual similarity by means of family trees (the so-called Lachmannian stemma, in line with the procedure developed for an edition of the Latin poet Lucretius by Karl Lachmann in the nineteenth century), but this practice is now discredited since we now know that marginal additions and alterations were copied from one Anglo-Saxon manuscript to another,[28] and that identical readings thus found their way into subsequent copies which are themselves otherwise entirely unrelated, or perhaps only distantly so. Again, the safest practice for the editor is to consider each manuscript on its merits and to print as much information from all of them as is practicably possible. In an ideal world, that would mean printing the text of each copy separately, but since this would leave the casual reader without an authoritative text to refer to, some compromise is patently inevitable. It is important, however, that an editor, who is bound by the nature of his task to make a full collation of every surviving copy of the text in order to consider the value of each, find some way of making all that hard-won material available. Just as one person's substantive variant may be of little interest to one group of readers, so minor readings may be of great interest to others. Few Old English texts survive in so many copies that it is impossible to list a complete set of variants, and this should be the lowest aim of every editor.

It might be thought from the huge output of editions of Old English prose in the last half century that the subject is all but exhausted. This is far from the case. In the first place, many early editions are out of date as noted above, or unsatisfactory for reasons that have been outlined, and occasionally even texts that have been carefully edited by major scholars may need to be updated. As I showed recently,[29] the text *De septiformi spiritu* published by Napier in his Wulfstan collection as no. VIII needs revision because a new copy has been identified (in Harley 3271) which throws doubt on some of his editorial choices. In the second place, there is a need for editions based on individual 'complete' manuscripts rather than separate texts. This is

---

David Dumville and Simon Keynes, which devotes a separate volume to each version of the text: *MS A*, ed. Janet M. Bately, Cambridge, D.S. Brewer, 1986; *MS B*, ed. Simon Taylor, Cambridge, D.S. Brewer, 1983; *MS C*, ed. Katherine O'Brien O'Keefe, Woodbridge, D.S. Brewer, 2001; *MS D*, ed. G.P. Cubbin, Cambridge, D.S. Brewer, 1996; *MS E*, ed. Susan Irvine, Cambridge, D.S. Brewer, 2004; and *MS F*, ed. Peter S. Baker, Woodbridge, D.S. Brewer, 2000.

[28] On this practice, see D.G. Scragg, *The Vercelli Homilies and Related Texts*, Early English Text Society, original series 300, Oxford, Oxford University Press, 1992, especially pp. 312–13.

[29] 'Rewriting eleventh-century English grammar and the editing of texts'; paper given at the SELIM conference at La Coruna in 2005, to be published in the conference proceedings.

particularly true where it can be shown that an individual scribe compiled a whole manuscript, with texts of his own or his master's choosing. A good example is CCCC 162 which consists of homilies that have almost all been edited already but from other manuscripts, so that no-one has presented and considered the specific selection of texts, only the minor alterations of wording by this particular scribe. Another desideratum is editions of texts which have been heavily annotated by later scribes. Very rarely do editors give appropriate coverage to the intervention of later scribes in their texts, yet, as has been suggested, this can show us much about changing fashions and attitudes to vernacular material. An edition which was structured to display how a text was modified in the century or so after its writing might tell us much about cultural and literary history. Many manuscripts have layers of interventions by later scribes sometimes scattered throughout the whole book, sometimes confined to specific texts suggesting a particular interest in individual pieces. Careful reading of Neil Ker's *Catalogue*[30] will help in the choice of such items for study, but as an example I would highlight Bodley 340/342 which has alterations by no less than eight annotators during the eleventh century, at least one of them known to be working in Rochester.

The importance of working with manuscripts

All serious students of Old English should work with manuscripts, preferably 'in the flesh', for although there are many excellent facsimiles available now, there is no substitute for examining the real thing.[31] Equally it is important that editing a text from manuscript is part of the training for all graduate students. This can be done most easily by choosing an item that survives in multiple copies, such as Catholic Homilies I.i, of which we have knowledge from thirteen manuscript copies. Peter Clemoes bases his text in his own edition on two, Royal 7 C. xii, and, where that is imperfect, CUL Gg. 3.28, but he gives substantive variants from all of the other copies.

---

[30] Comments on alterations by later hands are generally in the introductory paragraph to each manuscript.

[31] The best series of facsimiles in book form is 'Early English Manuscripts in Facsimile', published by Rosenkilde & Bagger in Copenhagen, but the Early English Text Society occasionally offers a facsimile volume such as that of CCCC 173 (Robin Flower and Hugh Smith, ed., *The Parker Chronicle and Laws*, original series 208, London, H. Milford, Oxford University Press, 1941). A very valuable relatively new series (which has the added advantage of being inexpensive) is 'Anglo-Saxon Manuscripts in Microfiche Facsimile', published under the general editorship of N. Doane by the Arizona Center for Medieval and Renaissance Studies at Tempe, Arizona, each volume of which has fiches for a series of related manuscripts with a full bibliographical introduction by distinguished scholars.

A valuable student exercise is to take a single page from another surviving copy of the text and make that the basis for an edition, citing all the other versions (including Royal and CUL) as variants. The variants may be either substantive or full, either possibility giving the student a better understanding of the way in which major modern editions of Old English texts work. The pattern of providing variants in 'decks' (in Clemoes' case, an upper deck for variants from the base manuscript and a lower deck for variants from all other copies) and of referring to manuscript copies by letter sigla (here A for Royal, K for CUL, etc) thus is learnt by the student through practice, as is an understanding of the sorts of choices that an editor has to make in selecting readings when different versions offer alternative readings that make equal sense. The exercise also produces an appreciation of the difficulty of displaying to a reader that the editor has been forced to emend a text for whatever reason (particularly when the emendation involves omitting something which is in the manuscript), and it teaches the importance (and limitations) of source study, and the value of presenting as much manuscript information as possible within a clear text, rather than one cluttered with diacritics. The total discipline thus acquired not only gives students an introduction to palaeography and to textual criticism but allows a greater appreciation of how editions that are currently in the public domain should be used, how far they can be relied upon as representing the manuscripts on which they draw, and how to make the best use of the information they offer.

The study of manuscripts is basic to the study of Old English. It provides the foundation for textual criticism, which is essentially the editing of texts, and every student of the language (and that encompasses students of literature, history and society) needs an understanding of how the editors of the texts that they constantly use arrived at the readings that are provided in their editions. Nothing is more fundamental to the study of a society than an informed understanding of the direct, immediate information about that society that has come down to us. Such information includes material objects other than books, but they can be misinterpreted, and though the evidence supplied by manuscript material is equally open to conjecture, it offers us the fullest window that we possess into the minds of the people that we study. We have no native informants from the Anglo-Saxon period, but manuscripts offer us the next best thing.

Introduction to Chapter 4

The corpus of Old English poetry is probably the best-known written material from the Anglo-Saxon period. Many of the texts, especially the heroic and elegiac poems, have long been studied for their literary qualities, their sources and their language. The whole body of poetic material is far more accessible than the body of Old English prose, since most of the surviving poetry exists in just four major manuscripts, most poems survive in only one version and the poems are readily available in modern printed editions: as individual texts, in anthologies and in *The Anglo-Saxon Poetic Records: a collective edition* edited in six volumes by G.P. Krapp and E.V.K. Dobbie (published by Columbia University Press, 1931–42). Electronic texts are also easily accessible.

However, modern printed texts of Old English poetry give a bewildering variety of versions and, as the following chapter demonstrates, are the product of both editorial convention and individual choice. This choice is manifested in terms of the physical presentation of a text and sometimes significantly reflects the editor's subjective interpretation of it in the choice of (modern) punctuation, capitalisation and even individual readings of Old English words. The very decision to print a text in poetic lines or continuous prose may be contentious since Anglo-Saxon text did not readily fall into the generic divide that contemporary literary criticism utilises. Rhythmic alliterative prose and poetic interludes in otherwise prose texts contribute to what is here described as the 'permeability' of Old English prose and poetry. The very identification of 'a poem' may be controversial given the lack of titles and inconsistent use of distinctive opening initials in Anglo-Saxon manuscripts.

This chapter demonstrates the desirability of studying the manuscript itself if you are conducting advanced research on Old English poetry. It examines those poems which exist outside the four major codices, demonstrating the advantages and disadvantages of survival in different contexts. It discusses the rare examples of texts which exist in multiple versions, highlighting the impossibility of establishing a definitive text. It concludes with detailed consideration of the four major manuscripts, focusing on issues of textual integrity in the *Exeter Book* and *Vercelli Book*, and the reasons for the scholarly debates that rage regarding the composite *Beowulf Manuscript* and *Junius Manuscript*; and of Cambridge, Corpus Christi College 201, which, with its prose and poetry content together encompassing a multiplicity of genres, demonstrates the problems and challenges involved in Old English poetic manuscript study.

4

Manuscript sources of Old English poetry

Elaine Treharne

Over thirty thousand lines of Old English poetry survive, principally from the eighth to the twelfth centuries; the majority of it is contained in four major manuscripts and the remainder is scattered throughout numerous codices and fragments, and sometimes embedded within prose texts. While the extant verse varies considerably in date, style, content, context of production and possible function, all of it shares a number of things in common. Firstly, the date of composition of the verse is often very difficult, or impossible, to determine, because much of the poetry may have existed in an earlier form before being written into the manuscript in which it now survives. Secondly, since so little is known about the composition of individual poems, very few of them can be attributed to any particular author, or place or specific setting. In addition, almost all of the poetry that survives is written out in long lines as if it were prose, often with the minimum of medieval punctuation; and almost all of it is alliterative in form, consisting of two half-lines, linked by alliteration, a form of verse ideal for oral recitation.

The manuscript and the edited text

Unlike the original manuscript text with its prose-like presentation of the poetry, modern editions arrange the text on the page in a way that visually reflects the alliterative nature of Old English poetry. Since the nineteenth century, it has been the convention to show the poem in long verse-lines with a gap in the middle called the caesura. This literal gap divides the two half-lines, linked by alliteration to form a longer, four-stress line. The following quotation of the first five lines of the famous elegiac poem known as *The Wanderer* illustrates this typographical practice:

> Oft him anhaga   are gebideð,
> Metudes miltse,   þeah þe he modcearig
> geond lagulade   longe sceolde
> hreran mid hondum   hrimcealde sæ,
> wadan wræclastas.   Wyrd bið ful aræd.
>
> (Often the solitary one experiences favour
> the mercy of the Ruler, though he, sorrowing,
> throughout the waterways must long
> stir with his hands the rime-cold sea,
> wade the paths of exile. Fate is fully resolute.)[1]

In this extract, the vowels in the first verse-line alliterate, and, as always in Old English verse, any vowel can alliterate with any other vowel (here it is *Oft*, *anhaga*, *are* that alliterate); in the second verse-line, alliteration falls on the consonant *m*; in the third *l*; the fourth *h*; and the fifth verse-line alliterates on *w*. When the poem is presented in these long lines, sundered by the caesura, it is easy to determine the alliterative structure and to recognise the impact of each verse-line.

If the same extract is examined within its manuscript context, it looks very different indeed. In the case of *The Wanderer* itself, it occurs at folios 76 verso to 78 recto of the *Exeter Book*, one of the four major manuscripts containing Old English poetry. The *Exeter Book* – Exeter, Cathedral, Dean and Chapter Library 3501 – was written by one exceptionally professional scribe in about 970, possibly in Exeter or Glastonbury (see Figs 4.1, 6.15). The passage edited above, when transcribed from the manuscript (that is, written out without any changes), looks like prose; the scribe writes across the lined grid he or she has ruled for the text, filling the central space of the manuscript page. The scribe also copies the poem in a style of script that employs numerous different letters from those we use in Modern English today. In Old English, the letters ð, þ, æ, and ƿ are, respectively, the Germanic runes eth and thorn (both realising the sound -*th*-), ash (for the sound -*a*-), and wynn (for modern -*w*-). Other letters are formed differently too: so, for example, the *g* looks like the modern number 5; the *t* has no stem protruding upwards; the *r* has the shape of a shepherd's crook, and is easily confused with the shape of *s*, because *s* is similar to a modern *r*, with a downstroke descending below the line. By using a modern typeface designed to emulate the Old English script, the same extract provided above can be made to look much more similar to its actual appearance in the *Exeter Book*:

---

[1] Edited and translated by the author.

> OFT him anhaga are gebideð metudes miltse þeah þe
> he mod ceariᵹ ᵹeond laᵹu lade longe sceolde hrepan
> mid hondum hrim cealde sæ padan wræc lastas wyrd
> bið ful aræd .

This kind of attempt at emulation is useful for illustrating a number of important aspects of working with all Old English poetic texts, besides the obvious difference in script. Principally, it is clear that the manuscript layout – in long lines – does not parallel the verse representation of modern editions; secondly, word division does not correspond with modern edited representations of Old English. One can, for example, notice the gap between *mod* and *cearig* or *lagu* and *lade* in the second line of this manuscript emulation, while these elements are compounded in modern editions to form *modcearig* ('sorrowing [in mind]') and *lagulade* ('waterways'). Thirdly, capitalisation is different in the manuscript and tends to be far less standard than modern rules about the use of capitals. So, for example, in order to display a new text, the scribe might capitalise some or all of the letters of the first few words of that text. Here, the first word *OFT* is completely capitalised by the tenth-century scribe, while modern editors only capitalise the first letter because it is the beginning of a sentence. Similarly, if editors believe *wyrd bið ful aræd* (line 5 in the modern version) is a complete sentence and not a clause, *wyrd* will be capitalised, while it remains uncapitalised in the manuscript. Such editorial intervention has significant implications for the ways in which a text is interpreted. In the excerpt above, the word *metudes* in the second line of the edited poem means 'of the ruler' or 'ruler's'. If the noun is left uncapitalised, as it appears in the first line of the poem in the *Exeter Book*, it is quite likely to mean 'fate' or 'ordaining one'; if, however, the editors choose to follow the convention of capitalising nouns referring to the Christian deity, then *Metudes* will be interpreted as meaning the Christian God, the Ruler. And because Old English conventions of capitalisation were far less standardised than Modern English conventions (not all personal or place names are consistently capitalised in Old English, for example), modern scholars cannot be sure whether *M/metudes* should or should not begin with a capital. How readers interpret this key word in the opening lines of the poem – as a Christian ruler or the more neutral 'fate' has a very serious effect on their overall understanding of *The Wanderer*.

Furthermore, Old English poetry in its manuscript context, as with all Old English writing, does not illustrate conventions of punctuation like those in use in Modern English. In the manuscript emulation above, only one mark of punctuation occurs – a point (or *punctus*) that looks similar to a full-stop.

In the corresponding edited version, there are three commas and two full-stops, and not all editions will provide the same punctuation, even for these five lines of verse. Punctuation, of course, is a major determiner of close interpretation, breaking up the flow of the language, creating pauses, marking out units of sense and meaning. As such, its occurrence in Old English editions is a matter of subjective reading by the editor, and combined with all the other editorial interventions discussed here, it demonstrates how significant the role of the modern textual editor is. A reader of Old English poetry today is usually provided with a cleaned-up or mediated version of the original text; and the greater the editor's mediation, the further the reader is moved from the manuscript context of the text.

'... editorial fixity might well shift in coming decades, with the accessibility of electronic facsimiles of the Old English manuscripts themselves, and the interpretative fluidity that could result from personal ownership of high-quality manuscript images.'

This readerly distance from the original, the sense of an editorially predetermined interpretation, is nowhere more apparent, of course, than in the provision of modern titles for Old English poems. Old English verse, almost without exception, is not given any form of title by the scribes of the various manuscripts. For some poems, this causes few interpretative difficulties. But while an epic and spectacular verse narrative outlining the life and deeds of a great hero might reasonably be given the title of its eponymous hero(ine) – as in *Beowulf*, or *Judith*, or *Andreas* – it is much less assured that *The Wanderer* actually concerns itself with one who wanders (arguably intimating directionlessness, aimlessness, physical travelling). The poem concerns an *anhaga* or 'solitary one', an *eardstapa* or 'earth-stepper', who is certainly engaged as much (if not more) upon a spiritual and psychological journey as he is an actual journey. One might equally feasibly give this poem the title 'The Exile', 'The Solitary One', or, more abstractly, 'Wisdom', or 'Remembrance', or 'Loneliness'. However, the title *The Wanderer*, like the titles of the *Exeter Book* poems *The Wife's Lament* and *The Husband's Message* (neither of which explicitly concern a 'wife' or a 'husband'), is almost certainly fixed in current scholarship for practical reasons of identification and discussion as much as anything else. However, editorial fixity – enshrined on the page of the book – might well shift in coming decades, with the accessibility of electronic facsimiles of the Old English manuscripts themselves, and the interpretative fluidity that could result from personal ownership of high-quality manuscript images where readers can access for themselves something arguably much closer to the 'original' text.

For the moment, it suffices to say that any facsimile, edition, or image clearly cannot take the scholar to the material reality of the manuscript artefact itself, and there is really no substitute for seeing the codex, even through the glass of an exhibition case. And while working with images – from black and white facsimiles to full colour digital images – or viewing the manuscript in its exhibition case may seem to replicate the original manuscript page, one cannot feel the parchment upon which the text is written, or see the gatherings into which the folios are joined as quires, or detect glosses made by dry point – scratched into the parchment by passing readers as deliberate notes on the text or simply indeterminate comments. One cannot feel the weight of the volume to assess how portable it might have been, or see erasures on folios showing where mistakes have been excised through scraping away at the surface layers of the prepared skin. In other words, without handling the manuscript, interpretation can only ever be partial.

Manuscripts in libraries

Most interested parties are able to see a number of the Old English poetic manuscripts in their cases: the British Library Exhibition has one of the four major poetry books on display year-round. This is London, British Library, Cotton Vitellius A. xv, the *Beowulf Manuscript*, or *Nowell Codex*, as it is sometimes known. It is very difficult to obtain personal access to this most famous book, but one can get a keen sense of its size, condition, and contents from a combination of viewing it *in situ* in the British Library and through Professor Kevin Kiernan's electronic version, published on CD-ROM by British Library Publications or indeed, from the Early English Text Society (original series, volume 77) facsimile, edited by Julius Zupitza in 1882 and published by Oxford University Press. In the precincts of Exeter Cathedral, too, at the Dean and Chapter Library behind the great cathedral, one can gain limited access to the small Library with its ground floor exhibition, and its upper floor reading room. If a visitor asks to see the famous *Exeter Book* of Old English poetry, the enthusiastic volunteer staff will roll back the heavy metal lid of the bomb-proof, tomb-like case to reveal a much bigger manuscript book than one might imagine from looking at any image or facsimile (such as Bernard Muir's digitized version published by University of Exeter Press as *The Exeter Anthology of Old English Poetry*), big enough indeed to be thought of as a display book or a presentation book, which is not the impression one would obtain from its imaging in any other medium. Moreover, no image can do justice to the pristine condition of the middle folios of the manuscript; it might have been written in the very recent past, so clear and undamaged do the display openings appear. Like the *Beowulf Manuscript*, however, it suffered terrible damage in the course of its history, which has significantly impacted on the legibility of some of the poetry. While the *Beowulf Manuscript*, opened at any folio, has clearly been the victim of serious (accidental) injury, burned at the edges by the fire

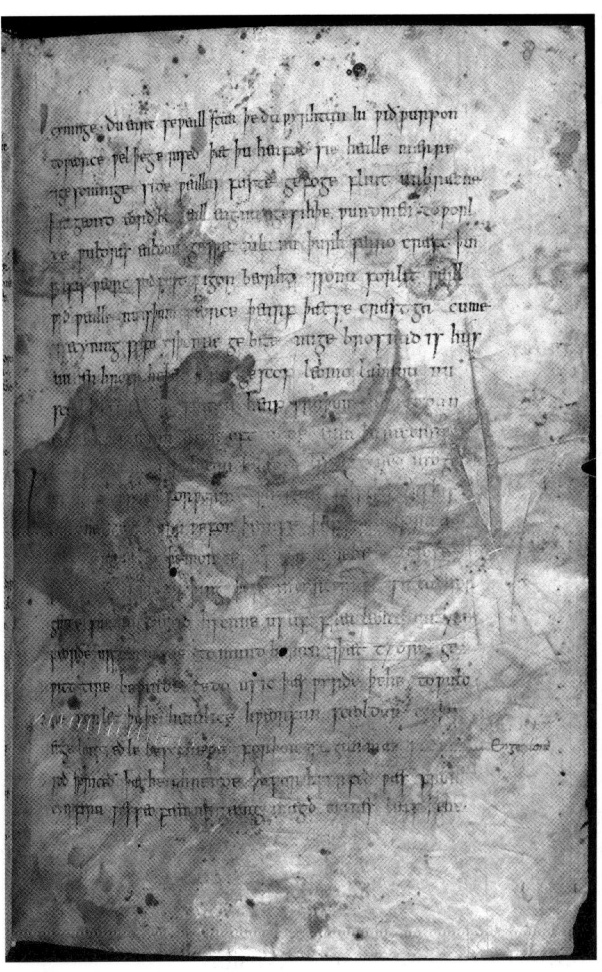

4.1 Exeter, Cathedral, Dean and Chapter Library MS 3501 (*Exeter Book*), fol. 8r.

The leaf, which shows *Advent Lyric I*, has been badly damaged by water, knife cuts and a stain from the wet base of a drinking vessel that has been carelessly placed on it.

at the Cotton Library at the rather ironically named Ashburnham House in Westminster in October 1731, the *Exeter Book* is irreparably damaged at the beginning and the end (Fig. 4.1). The manuscript, which has lost leaves before folio 8r, is damaged by water and cuts from folios 8r to 11r; and from folios 117r to 130v, there is increasing damage from a deep burn through the centre of these final leaves, until by the final folio, up to 25% of the text is lost. It is thought that the cuts at the beginning of the manuscript were caused by its use as a chopping or cutting board, and that the burn at the back was caused by even more wilful negligence: the placing of a red-hot firebrand on the book by a careless medieval monk, using the manuscript as a placemat, in an act of cultural vandalism illustrative of the easy disdain with which books and their contents were viewed, many others – many thousands of others – being lost and dismembered during centuries of disregard.

The other two major manuscripts of vernacular poems are less easy to see; in Oxford, the Bodleian Library holds the *Junius Manuscript*, or Junius 11, a wonderful illustrated manuscript containing biblical poems (Figs 7.33–7.34). In principle, this volume is accessible in the Duke Humphrey Library, though the Bodleian can be strict about who can sit and read this codex. Their display facilities are not like the British Library's either, so that for the vast majority, the closest they can get to the *Junius Manuscript* is via the electronic images on the CD edited recently by Bernard Muir, (published by the Bodleian Library, Oxford). The final major volume of poetry was taken from south-east England to Vercelli Cathedral in northern Italy in the eleventh or twelfth century, perhaps by a senior ecclesiastic on a pilgrimage to Rome, who may have left the manuscript there accidentally, or, less probably, as a gift (why would anyone leave an extensive, but unintelligible, collection of Old English homilies and religious verse in an Italian cathedral?). The cathedral library still houses the *Vercelli Book*, Vercelli, Bibliotheca capitolare CXVII (roughly the same, impressive size as the *Exeter Book*). It is currently in the process of being fully digitized by a team of scholars – a great advance, given the manuscript's difficult access.

Manuscripts and the parameters of poetry

The bulk of the surviving poetry from the Anglo-Saxon period is thus found within these four major codices. Three of them – the *Exeter Book*, the *Vercelli Book* and the *Beowulf Manuscript* – can be dated to the period c.970 to c.1010, *Beowulf* being the latest. The *Junius Manuscript*, probably datable to c.980–1030, was the last to be completed. Each of these immeasurably important manuscripts has its own interpretative difficulties, but all four of them share the physical characteristics of text outlined above: the poetry within them is written in long lines in a script employing letter forms that are no longer in use, and which evince considerable variation in spelling, punctuation, word division and capitalisation.

Moreover, in a few cases, it is not even clear where texts themselves begin and end because there are no titles or notable visual cues to show the beginnings and endings of items. In the case of the poems contained within the prose manuscripts collectively known as the *Anglo-Saxon Chronicle*, dating from the late ninth to the mid-twelfth centuries, the scribes move from copying the annals detailing events of national significance to poetic evocations of kings and battles with little more than a line break (Fig. 4.2). Within other prose texts too, as Charles D. Wright has recently shown in relation to the homilies in the *Vercelli Book*, there are occasionally instances of some texts containing highly poetic prose or perhaps, just as possibly, containing embedded poetry, disguised by the Anglo-Saxon custom of writing both verse and prose in long lines across the page. It is possible, too, as W.W. Skeat did in the nineteenth century, to lay out as verse the alliterative prose of the tenth-century homilist and hagiographer, Ælfric. It is as well to remember, then, that modern conceptions of form and genre are, at the very least, rather more fixed than they appear to have been for Old English scribes at work in the many manuscripts that survive from the period, 890–1200.

One may, indeed, look well beyond the traditional parameters of Old English verse in the case of some texts. There are, for example, an astonishing twenty-one surviving examples of the poem known to modern scholars as *Cædmon's Hymn*, dating from approximately 735 to the fifteenth century and all are edited and digitized in Daniel O'Donnell's book and CD-ROM on the poems (*Cædmon's Hymn: a multi-media study, edition and archive*, published by D.S. Brewer). The poems are embedded within, or appended to, the Latin and Old English versions of Bede's famous *Ecclesiastical History of*

AN DCCCLXVIII

B. AN DCCCLXX
AN DCCCLXX
AN DCCCLXXI
B. AN DCCCLXXII
AN DCCCLXXIII

Her Eadgar þæs Engla þeoden corðre micelre to cyninge gehalgod on ðære ealdan byrig Acemannesceastre, eac hi buend oðre worde beornas baðan nemnað. þær wæs bliþs micel on þa eadgan dæge eallum geworden þonne niða bearn nemnað 7 cigað Pentecosten. þær wæs preosta heap, micel muneca þreat, mine gefrege gleawra gaderod, 7 þa agan stenþæs tyn hund wintra geteled rimes, fra geboren wæs bremes cyninges leohta hyrdes, buton ðær to lafe þa agan þæs wintres geteles, þæs ðe gewritu secgað seofon 7 XX ig, swa neah þæs sigora frean, dusend a urnen. Ða haði gelamp, 7 Eadmundes eafora hæfde nigon 7 XX nið frea ca, hæfde wintra on worulde, þis geworden þæs, 7 þa on ðam XXX þæs ðeoden gehalgod;

AN DCCCLXXIIII
AN DCCCLXXV

Her geendode eorðan dreamas Eadgar Engla cyning, ceas him oðer leoht, wlitig 7 wynsum, 7 þis wace forlet, lif þis læne. Nemnað leoda bearn, men on moldan, þæne monað gehwær in ðisse eðeltyrf, þa þe ær wæran on rim cræfte rihte getogene, Iulius monað, þ se geonga gefor on þone eahteðan dæg Eadgar of life, beorna beahgyfa, 7 feng his bearn syððan to cynerice, cild ungeaxen, eorla ealdor, þæs wæs Eadweard nama, 7 him æþel hæleð, tyn nihtum ær, of Brytene gefor biscop se goda þurh his gecynde cræft, þam wæs Cyneweard nama;

4.2 Cambridge, Corpus Christi College MS 173, Part I (*Parker Chronicle*), fol. 28v.

The folio contains the poem *The Coronation of Edgar* (for 973) and the opening of *The Death of Edgar* (for 975) beginning at line 18. The page had been prepared for a series of one-line entries. Sixteen dates have been erased and the remaining dates altered. One line of text has been erased above *The Coronation of Edgar*.

the English Church and People (Historia Ecclesiastica), completed by the great religious and historical writer in the 730s at his monastery at Jarrow. These surviving versions of the nine-line poem, sung by the cowherd Cædmon after an angelic visitation, all differ in some way: either in terms of their dialect (Northumbrian or West Saxon); or their physical form (at the bottom margin of some of the Latin *Ecclesiastical History* manuscripts, or incorporated into the Latin or English texts, or added in the right margin within an elaborate frame, almost adjacent to the Latin rendition of the poem, as is the case in one twelfth-century manuscript); or their word-spacing; or their punctuation. Each illustrates well the complexity of working with poetic texts that survive in multiple copies: which of these, if any, might be thought of as 'THE poem'? Given the way in which multiple medieval texts of all kinds are effectively unfixed in spelling, vocabulary, structure and physical appearance, existing in subtly or dramatically different contexts and forms, modern scholars are obliged to interpret each on its own merits, cognisant of the textual variance that is so integral to medieval manuscript culture.

Unique texts and chance survivals

Not all Old English poems exist in multiple manuscripts or even survive in their original form. Much of the verse – in fact, the predominant proportion – survives in only one scribal text. This is the case, of course, with all of the poems in the *Beowulf Manuscript* and the *Junius Manuscript*. Where a poem survives uniquely, it creates particular difficulties for editors, and for interpretation more broadly. One very famous poem, *The Battle of Maldon*, survives purely by chance. Its original manuscript, London, British Library, Cotton Otho A. xii, was very badly burnt in the fire at Ashburnham House in 1731, the same fire that caused such damage to the *Beowulf Manuscript*, and to so many of Sir Robert Cotton's manuscripts, carefully collected by him in the sixteenth century, and maintained in his Library until the fire. Under Cotton's ownership, the composite volume had been assembled by combining originally separate manuscripts: the Old English poem on the battle of Maldon between the English and the Vikings; a number of Latin saints' lives; Asser's Latin life of King Alfred; and two charms in Latin and

Old English. Of the fourteen texts that formed the composite Otho A. xii only ten survived in a poor state of legibility after the fire, and *The Battle of Maldon* was completely destroyed. The poem is therefore known only from the transcript made in the early seventeenth century by John Elphinston or David Casley, and copied into pp. 7–12 of the manuscript now shelf-marked as Oxford, Bodleian Library, Rawlinson B. 203. It appears that when the text was copied, the beginning and end of the poem had already been lost. Thus, only an incomplete text survives for scholars to study the heroic deeds of the Ealdorman Byrhtnoth and his Essex *comitatus* defending Eastern England to the death against the Vikings in 991.

Numerous other poems survive by chance or in rather unexpected contexts. For example, late verse productions of the twelfth century, written in a period when some scholars would erroneously consider Old English to be all but defunct, are *The Grave*, *Durham*, and *Cnut's Song*, all surviving within the context of prose texts, and predominantly Latin ones at that. *Durham*, or *De Situ Dunhelmi*, was originally contained in at least two twelfth-century manuscripts, one of which – London, British Library, Cotton Vitellius D. xx – was badly burnt in the 1731 fire, with the loss of the poem. The poem, celebrating the city, with its English saints, scholars and kings, thus survives uniquely among historical documents relating to Durham in Cambridge, University Library Ff. 1. 27, with a provenance of Sawley, a Cistercian monastery in Yorkshire. Similarly embedded within an historical context are the five poems of the *Anglo-Saxon Chronicle*, a major source for the period up to 1154, comprised of manuscripts from different scriptoria, written at different times and for varying regional audiences (Figs 2.12, 4.2). These poems, such as *The Battle of Brunanburh*, celebrating the achievements in 924 of Athelstan, king of the English, and *The Coronation of Edgar* and *The Death of Edgar* which form the annals for 973 and 975 in four manuscripts of the *Chronicle*, are unusual in that they can be closely dated and their context of production is relatively assured: national, monastic histories, propagating the deeds and events of the English Crown and its notable subjects. Such information is usually lacking for most of the other poems that survive.

The four major manuscripts

The greater number of poems, as mentioned, is extant in the four major manuscripts and each of these offers its own challenges to the scholar, beyond the initial, and sometimes insurmountable, hurdle of access to the artefact itself.

The Exeter Book

Probably the earliest of the four manuscripts is the *Exeter Book*, which is folios 8r–130v of the current volume Exeter, Cathedral, Dean and Chapter Library 3501, the interpretation of which has been the focus of sustained research in recent years by Patrick Conner and Bernard Muir, among others. This manuscript, which may have been put together at Exeter, Crediton or another south-western monastic scriptorium in the 960s or 970s, was among the books given to Exeter Cathedral by Bishop Leofric when he donated most of his collection before his death in 1072. A donation list, datable to 1069–72, contains a reference to *mycel Englisc boc be gehwilcum þingum on leoðwisum geworht* (a 'large English book about many things written in verse'), an entry that seems to refer to the *Exeter Book*.

The *Exeter Book* is undoubtedly one of the most significant volumes to survive from Anglo-Saxon England, because it contains the largest amount of Old English religious and secular verse; in total, it contains over thirty individual poetic texts as well as more than ninety riddles. The texts, all written by one scribe, are varied in nature, complex in interpretation, and probably organised into loosely related sections reflecting concerns of their later tenth-century monastic milieu. The way in which the manuscript was put together – its codicology – is fundamental to its interpretation. It is likely that the *Exeter Book* was put together over a period of time in sections; that it was aimed at a variety of audiences in the decades at the height of the period traditionally known as the Benedictine Reform, when some English monasteries underwent changes instigated by reformers following the Benedictine Rule.

In their thorough, and differing, codicological studies of the manuscript, Conner (*Anglo-Saxon Exeter*) and Muir (*The Exeter Anthology of Old English Poetry*) argue for the classification of the poems in the volume into a number of genres, organised into three booklets. Where one might imagine that looking at a manuscript written by one scribe means that it was written linearly, in sequence from beginning to end, this is often not the case; sections of manuscripts could be copied in any order, since the basic element of the structure is the quire, then the booklet (one or more quires loosely held together, sometimes unbound, sometimes kept in wrappers), and finally the whole manuscript itself. Conner suggests, because of evidence at the crucial folios in the manuscript gatherings, that the three major booklets of the *Exeter Book* were written in the order 2, 3, 1. It seems that damage to the gatherings at the three key points in the manuscript's make-up show that the opening leaves (folios 53r, 83r, and 98r) of the respective booklets were exposed and thus unbound for a period; missing folios at these points also suggest damage from exposure; and the parchment varies in quality between the three booklets. Thematic distinctions also reinforce this theory:

demonstrating connections with Continental culture, the second booklet includes narrative and catalogue poetry, allegory, and elegy, among others (for example, *Juliana*, *The Gifts of Men*, *Maxims I*, *The Whale*, and *The Wanderer*). The third booklet reflects clerical as well as monastic interests, and represents the amalgamation of two separate collections; this third booklet contains the riddles as well as religious and elegiac material, such as *The Descent into Hell*, *Soul and Body II*, *Deor*, *Wulf and Eadwacer*, *The Wife's Lament*, *The Husband's Message*, *Resignation A* and *B*. The first booklet (containing the three *Christ* poems, and *Guthlac A* and *B*) is concerned with salvation and how to acquire it. While not all critics agree with Conner's division of the *Exeter Book* into three sections, this detailed codicological approach illustrates how scholars can provide nuance to the interpretation of medieval books, demonstrating the organisation and coherence behind a collection of texts, rather than thinking of large volumes with multiple texts as a random miscellany of disparate poetic works.

The *Exeter Book* was written in a square Anglo-Saxon minuscule by a single accomplished scribe, whose polished performance is noted for its aesthetic calligraphic appeal, its clarity and sustained regularity (evident in Fig. 4.1, despite the damage; see also Fig. 6.15). There can be little doubt that the expertise of the scribe suggests that he was very well trained, but this volume, while exceptionally executed, did not employ a large team of scribes and illustrators; the scribe was also, as all commentators agree, responsible for the capitalisation and for the decorative features of the manuscript. In addition, the evidence provided by the standard of the parchment, which Muir (*The Exeter Anthology*) remarks is inferior throughout, permits the deduction that the *Exeter Book* was not produced in a scriptorium rich in material resources. Having said that, though, there is never any sense of the script being compressed, or of a lack of space within the book's overall design. The relative lack of abbreviations also indicates that there is little pressure on the scribe to squeeze his text in. The spacing of script both laterally and vertically, the generous allowance on many occasions of blank lines between texts, and the unabbreviated nature of the text all suggest a well-resourced project, despite the seemingly poor quality of the skin itself.

Moreover, from analysing the *mise-en-page*, it becomes apparent that this is a book written with very great care and deliberate crafting of textual items' positions and relationships. The scribe usually makes the beginning of a new poem, or a new section within the poem, very clear: he uses large, slightly decorated, capitals to introduce the new item or section, and, on occasion, square capitals to begin the opening words of a new text, as is the case at the opening of *Guthlac* (fol. 33v), or the very notable opening of *The Passion of St Juliana* at fol. 65v, which is separated from the preceding text, *The Phoenix*, by a double strong punctuation mark (two sets of two dots adjacent to a seven-shaped comma), two blank lines, a large initial *H* (four lines in height), and a whole line of square capitals denoting the opening words of the poem. In some cases, however, the scribe's intentions are not as clear: the textual divide between *Riddle 60* and *The Husband's Message* at fols 122v–123r consists of a strong punctuation mark (two dots adjacent to a seven-shaped comma), and an enlarged capital *N*, opening the poem now known as *The Husband's Message* (*Nu ic onsundran* ...). It is difficult to determine the precise relationship of these texts: are they the same single text, as indeed they have been treated by some editors; or are they two completely separate poems; or is some thematic or generic relationship indicated by the relative lack of textual demarcation? In order to begin to understand the possible answers to these crucial questions, any student of the manuscript must work carefully through the facsimile or digital edition to analyse the normal patterns of textual production by this scribe.

The Vercelli Book

Directly comparable with the *Exeter Book* in some respects is the contemporary *Vercelli Book*, copied *c.*970 by one scribe, possibly at St Augustine's, Canterbury. The major difference between the *Exeter Book* and the *Vercelli Book* is that the latter contains both prose and poetry in Old English (as does the *Beowulf Manuscript*). While the function of the *Exeter Book* is difficult to determine because of the notable diversity of its contents, the *Vercelli Book* seems clearly intended to educate an audience in the fundamental tenets of Christian doctrine, an audience which might consist of a single, private reader, or a group of listeners.

The 135 folios of the *Vercelli Book* contain twenty-three prose sermons and saints' lives. These are interspersed with six poems: *Andreas* (fols 29–52), *The Fates of the Apostles* (fols 52–4), *Soul and Body I* (fols 101–3; another version of which is in the *Exeter Book*), *Homiletic Fragment I* (fol. 104), *The Dream of the Rood* (fols 104–6, which also exists in part in runic form on the earlier Ruthwell monument), and *Elene* (fols 121–33). Some of the texts are fragmentary because of the loss of manuscript pages; part of *Andreas*, for example, has been lost after folio 42; and part of *Homily IX* has also been lost through damage. As with all Old English poems, the verse is copied out as if it were prose, and not one of the poetic texts has a title in the manuscript itself; *The Dream of the Rood*, for example, might just as easily be called something else by its editors, such as *The Vision of the Rood*, or *The Vision of the Cross*.

The scribe, who copied the *Vercelli Book* in a clear and consistent square Anglo-Saxon minuscule, is thought to have been relatively mechanical in his work; that is, some scholars believe the scribe may have copied some of his source material without much thought or intervention. In most cases, it seems that he copied the dialect and the manuscript punctuation that was found in the original texts, and these aspects therefore help scholars to reconstruct the textual exemplars, because there are notable changes to spelling and punctuation within discrete sections of the manuscript. Close analysis of these features of the texts suggests that some of the homilies were copied as a set, but none of the poems offers evidence of this nature. Moreover, the texts in the *Vercelli Book* may all range widely in date for although they were copied in the later tenth century, they were not necessarily written in this period. Indeed, some of the poems, such *The Fates of the Apostles* and *Elene*, could be much earlier in date of origin. These were written by an Anglo-Saxon poet called Cynewulf who signed his name at the end of the poems using the Germanic runic alphabet, and who was also responsible for *The Passion of St Juliana* and *Christ III* in the *Exeter Book*. Although the sources of the *Vercelli Book* are varied, and scholars cannot determine any obvious chronological sequence of texts or overall thematic unity, the range of material suggests that the compiler was someone with access to a reasonable library, probably within a monastic environment. Concerns about penance and salvation are in evidence as is salvation history, particular focusing on Christ's great sacrifice and its omni-temporal significance, which is made apparent in what are, arguably, the two finest poetic pieces in the manuscript: *Elene* and *The Dream of the Rood*.

While there are discernible themes and motifs within the manuscript, there is much about this codex that remains elusive. To begin with, damage to the manuscript has made illegible parts of the text, and especially so within the facsimile and the forthcoming digitized version. A reagent, applied to try and make the manuscript more legible in the nineteenth century, has, instead, caused significant problems with legibility in reproduction, such that the opening folio of the original manuscript, for example, appears to be impossible to read. This is in addition to the damage to the texts already mentioned, occasioned by folios that are missing at intervals throughout the book (at folios 55, 85 and 103, for example). Contemporary quire signatures provided within the manuscript, assisting scholars in assessing how the manuscript was put together, also indicate significant loss. One set of signatures consists of Roman numerals in the top margins of the opening folio of a new quire (e.g, 'VI' at fol. 41r, now partially excised by the binding process) and indicates to the tenth-century binder the order in which the quires are to be bound; and a second set, comprised of letters written at the foot of the final folio of the quire, appear at the end of the majority of quires (Fig. 4.3). From the current nineteen quires, it is apparent from the sequence of signatures that quires VIII and XVI are now missing.

While at this macro-level it is clear that the volume was thoughtfully constructed with a definite order from the scribe or compiler's viewpoint,

4.3 Vercelli, Biblioteca capitolare CXVII (*Vercelli Book*), fol. 104v.

The end of the poetic *Homiletic Fragment I* (*Deceit*) and the opening of the poem *The Dream of the Rood*. There is a quire signature at the bottom of the leaf. This folio is at the end of a quire.

there are numerous puzzles within the manuscript about the sequences and discrete nature of individual texts. This scribe, rather like the *Exeter Book* scribe, is responsible for the pen-drawn initials that open the new texts, or new sections within texts and for the square capitals that form the opening words of texts or sections of texts. In the case of the lengthy poem *Andreas*, which begins on fol. 29v and ends at fol. 52v, there are numerous sections within the poem indicated by heavy punctuation at the section's end, and then enlarged pen-drawn square capitals, slightly offset into the left-hand margin, followed by slightly smaller square capital letters completing the opening word (at the top of fol. 42r 'NV'; at the penultimate line of fol. 43r, 'GE'); one or two blank lines separate the sections into discrete units, possibly designed for individual sessions of oral delivery, but certainly functioning like modern book chapters. At some section openings, though, there are very notable large initials: at fol. 49r, three quarters of the way down the page, an elaborate, zoomorphic initial *H* is designed from interlaced dragons and foliage, seeming to signify something notable, although it simply denotes another new section. Yet, at fol. 52v, after a blank line, square capitals spell out [H]WÆT, which is surely the opening of a new verse text, commonly known as *The Fates of the Apostles*, though here the elaborate *H* is missing altogether – four lines of space provided, but never used. Given the proximity of the over-elaborate *H* at fol. 49r, at what is a 'normal' section break, one might surmise that this was completed in error for the missing *H* at fol. 52v, where a new text is intended.

The opening of one of the most famous Old English poems, *The Dream of the Rood* (Fig. 4.3) illustrates this rather inconsistent process of textual demarcation and, in fact, this specific folio, fol. 104v, effectively represents the materiality of the *Vercelli Book* itself. The folio is damaged, both by damp or water damage in the outer margin and by reagent at the bottom three lines of the folio; and it has an alphabetic quire signature, 'O', at the foot of the folio, showing this to be the last folio in the quire. At the top of fol. 104v are five lines of a fragmentary poem written out, as usual, in long lines, generally punctuated by a single point, or *punctus*, indicating a minor pause. Other punctuation usually consists of a colon or point(s) and colon indicating a major pause or, as here probably, the end of a text. A heavier punctuation mark of colon+comma is followed by two blank lines, commonly used to denote the introduction of a new poem or section of text. Instead of an elaborate opening initial, however, a very plain, two-line *H* introduces the opening *Hwæt* of the poem, the *p* (*w*) being written inside the shoulder of *H*. This unremarkable initial sequence seems less visually imposing than the section breaks of *Andreas*, and invites the question of how the scribe regarded the textual integrity of *The Dream of the Rood*.

The Beowulf Manuscript

Understanding textual integrity is not the major issue in the other two poetic manuscripts: London, British Library, Cotton Vitellius A. xv (the *Beowulf Manuscript*) and Oxford, Bodleian Library, Junius 11 (the *Junius Manuscript*). The former is dated to c.1000–1010, the latter is contemporary with it, but has later additions. Both are the subjects of intense scholarly debates about their dates, their localisation, their form, function, and unity; both manuscripts are now composite volumes; both result from the work of more than one scribe; both contain illustrations (in Cotton Vitellius A. xv, the prose *Marvels of the East* is richly illustrated; Fig. 7.30); the former is badly damaged and the latter incomplete, presenting specific interpretative problems for scholars.

The *Beowulf Manuscript* is one part of the volume now shelved as Cotton Vitellius A. xv (Figs 4.4–4.5). A major surprise for students just introduced to the manuscript is that it is part of a much larger composite codex that also includes an unrelated twelfth-century manuscript usually known as the *Southwick Codex*. Within the *Beowulf Manuscript* itself, there are two poetic texts, *Beowulf* and *Judith*, which come last in the volume, despite being the primary focus of scholarly attention. Both these texts, as with all the texts in this manuscript, seem to concern themselves thematically with the battle between good and evil, or between humanity and the monstrous, and scholars have long looked for coherence between all of the texts. The principal difficulty in dealing with this manuscript is not thematic or structural, however, or even the dating or the script, but rather, the legibility of the text. Kevin Kiernan, in his *Electronic Beowulf*, deduces that there are about 2,000 letters missing from *Beowulf*, caused by the severe damage to the margins from the fire in 1731. Transcripts of the poem made in the eighteenth century preserve numerous readings now lost, and editors of the poem, of whom there have been many, rely considerably on these transcripts.

Unlike the *Exeter Book* and the *Vercelli Book*, which are both written by one scribe, there are two main scribes at work in the *Beowulf Manuscript*.

LEFT

4.4 London, British Library, MS Cotton Vitellius A. xv, fol. 132r.

The opening of *Beowulf* in the hand of the first scribe. The damage inflicted by the Ashburnham House fire is visible in the crumbled edges and faded writing; a split in the leaf from line 15 to the bottom margin has displaced letters to the right of the rift. There is an erasure at line 10 (after *hron*). Modern readers have left their marks on the page. The gloss over *egsode* (line 6) is in the hand of the sixteenth-century scholar Laurence Nowell. The blot over *of* on the same line is nineteenth-century. The folio number 129 at the right above line 2 is modern.

RIGHT

4.5 London, British Library, MS Cotton Vitellius A. xv, fol. 175v. *Beowulf*.

The first three lines on the leaf are in the first scribe's hand. The second scribe takes over at the beginning of line 4 (line 1939 in printed editions of the text). Although the first scribe shows regard for the writing of the text, completing a line before breaking off, the interruption shows no regard for content, grammar or poetry, since he stopped part way through a fitt, a sentence and a metrical unit.

The first scribe (Fig. 4.4) wrote from folios 94 (the previous folios of Vitellius A. xv contain the *Southwick Codex*) to the top three lines of folio 174v; the second wrote from line 4 of fol. 174v (Fig. 4.5) to the end of the manuscript, a sequence of stints that includes the copying of *Judith*, the fragmentary poem that is now adjacent to *Beowulf*, but does not seem to have been contiguous originally. Interestingly, despite the order in which the scribes appear, the first scribe seems to have the more contemporary hand, while the second scribe writes a square Anglo-Saxon minuscule, a type of script that was becoming somewhat outdated by the first decades of the eleventh century. These aspects of the physical context of the poems, the scribal relationships, and the precise date of the scribes' hands present some challenging questions for scholars in relation to the production of the manuscript and the date of the composition of the texts included in it. Arguably more ink has been metaphorically spilled on this manuscript – especially with regard to the date of *Beowulf* – than any other single issue in Old English literary studies, and yet, of course, one can state firmly that the only known date of the poem is the first quarter of the eleventh century, as it manifests itself in its present state in Cotton Vitellius A. xv.

Both *Beowulf* and *Judith* are written in sections that are called fitts, denoted by numbers within the poems themselves (so, akin to the introductory capitals of, say, *Andreas* in the *Vercelli Book*). These fitts may correspond to the appropriate length of text for oral readings, and thus may function in a way similar to chapters in modern books, or they may have functioned to denote some type of shift or movement. Within both poems, the fitt numbering does not function as one might expect; thus, in *Beowulf*, for example, there are forty-three fitts denoted by roman numerals within the text, but some fitts are much shorter than others; fitt VII, for example, is forty-three lines long (lines 456–99), whereas the majority tend to be more than twice that. *Judith*, which is acephalous (lacking its beginning), now opens towards the end of what seems to be section IX, causing significant debate among scholars about the amount of material that might be missing at the start of the poem. At 349 lines long, the poem that survives comprises the end of fitt IX and fitts X, XI and XII, intimating that many hundreds of lines are missing, if these numbers are meant to indicate sequential lines within one text.

The Junius Manuscript

Whereas scholars are concerned to establish the nature of the text in relation to *Judith*, and to address the relationship of *Judith* to *Beowulf* and the other works in Vitellius A. xv, with the *Junius Manuscript* the issue of unity stems less from individual texts than from the overarching structure of the current manuscript itself. The *Junius Manuscript*, written by four scribes, is unique among the four Old English poetic books because of its elaborate sequence of line-drawn illustrations accompanying the text (Figs 7.33–7.34), a sequence which was, unfortunately, never completed. Named after its donor, the seventeenth-century scholar, Francis Junius, Junius 11 is part of the major collection of medieval manuscripts in Oxford's Bodleian Library. Junius studied the four Biblical poems in the codex and published the first edition of them; the first three, given the modern titles of *Genesis*, *Exodus* and *Daniel*, are based on the Old Testament books of those names; and the fourth, written in a slightly later script and now called *Christ and Satan*, is based on three major events – the Fall of the Angels, Christ's Crucifixion to the Last Judgement, and Christ's Temptation. From studying the language and style of the poems, all four poems seem to have been composed at different times by different authors, and may have been gathered into this manuscript because they have in common the theme of Christian salvation history (a rather large and nebulous theme, it has to be said).

'... editorial intervention has significant implications for the ways in which a text is interpreted ... the greater the editor's mediation, the further the reader is moved from the manuscript context of the text.'

The structure of the manuscript and its overall unity is hinted at by the sporadic section numbers that occur through the volume up to p. 209. At the end of *Christ and Satan* is a scribal *explicit* (closing words) that reads 'Finit Liber. II. Amen', or 'Here ends the second book. Amen'. Since *Christ and Satan* seems to have been thought of by the scribe as making a second book, many scholars are of the opinion that the first three poems in the manuscript comprise an original *Liber I*, a first book, that has had its *explicit* removed because the last page or pages of the poem *Daniel* have been excised or lost through damage. This reading of the manuscript's physical make-up would therefore regard the volume as two-part, with its Old and New Testament division mirroring the structure of the Bible itself. Whether or not one views the later addition *Christ and Satan* as part of the original design or as simply an appropriate text to add on, its themes are certainly relevant to, and an extension of the themes of, the first three poems.

As is the case with most of the other manuscripts discussed, very little is known about Junius 11's immediate historical and cultural contexts. Not only do we not know how the manuscript was conceived or by whom, or when the texts were originally composed, but we are also unsure about the manuscript's date of composition and its place of production. In very important respects, the vacuum of information about the manuscript's conception and manufacture (as with all four of the poetic manuscripts, of course) means that we cannot contextualise what we do know: we do not know by whom, for whom, where, why or how the manuscript was put together. In general, scholars agree that the first three poems in the manuscript were copied by one scribe in the later tenth century, and *Christ and Satan*, written by three scribes, was added early in the eleventh century. Possible places of origin are Christ Church, Canterbury, or Winchester, capital of Anglo-Saxon England, or, less plausibly, Malmesbury in Wiltshire. These localisations are deduced from a holistic analysis of the manuscript: the similarity of the script to examples of hands from other scriptoria, the methods of manuscript production – the way the leaves are ruled, the layout of the writing, the use of capitals, punctuation, methods of corrections – are among the aspects of the page layout and scribal practice that permit comparison. These features can be relatively well detected in Muir's digital version of the manuscript, and allow for detailed examination of all aspects of the script and line-drawings. In the case of the *Junius Manuscript*, given that it is elaborately illustrated (though no drawings survive for *Christ and Satan*), and that it can therefore be considered an expensive and *deluxe* volume, it is possible that a wealthy patron paid for the volume to be put together. It was, though, as the sequence of incomplete illustrations testifies, never finished, since the scribes left gaps for illustrations, which are still large, blank spaces on the page.

Problems and challenges: a composite manuscript, Cambridge, Corpus Christi College 201

One final example will cogently demonstrate the problems and challenges inherent in working with Old English poetic manuscripts: the case of Cambridge, Corpus Christi College 201, fols 161–9 (Figs 4.6–4.7). This composite manuscript, which appears to have originated in Worcester before moving to Winchester where it was added to, was described in the sixteenth century as *Miscellanea quaedam Saxonice*, 'a miscellany of Anglo-Saxon material'. Among its current contents (constructed as it has been from the amalgamation of manuscripts), is a version of the *Regularis Concordia*, the English customary for monastic houses participating in the so-called Benedictine Reform; numerous homilies, confessional and penitential texts and law-codes; and the earliest romance in the English language, *Apollonius of Tyre*.

The intended audience of these prose texts may well have been ecclesiastical to begin with, but later, it might also have been extended to a broader range of those with the power to govern. In addition to the prose items are poetic texts written by two scribes – one early eleventh-century, who also copied the *Regularis Concordia*, and the other, mid-eleventh-century, copying pp. 1–151 and the poetry at pp. 167–9. The poems written into Corpus 201 by these two scribes are traditionally divided into five separate texts: the Old English version of Bede's *De die judicii* (pp. 161–5); *An Exhortation to Christian Living* (pp. 165–6); *A Summons to Prayer* (pp. 166–7; Figs 4.6, 4.7); the verse *Pater*

LEFT

4.6 Cambridge, Corpus Christi College MS 201 p. 166. The end of an *Exhortation to Christian Living* and beginning of *A Summons to Prayer*.

The scribe punctuates systematically indicating half-lines and uses coloured initials in a regular way.

RIGHT

4.7 Cambridge, Corpus Christi College MS 201 p. 167.

The end of *A Summons to Prayer*, and the verse *Pater Noster* added by a second scribe, who copies the careful punctuation and initialization of scribe 1.

Noster (pp. 167–9), and the *Gloria* (pp. 169–70). This manuscript then, like the *Vercelli Book* and the *Beowulf Manuscript* is mixed in form, unequivocally demonstrating the permeability of prose and poetry during this period. Moreover, the potential for the exploitation of form and function evinced in the early medieval multivalency of genre situated together – prose Romance, homily, penitential prose text, eschatological poetry, didactic and exhortatory poetry, meditation, catechesis – is much more apparent in this manuscript than one could discern from tidied-up modern editions and anthologies.

Pages 166–7 of Corpus 201 visually, and rather startlingly, demonstrate the somwwhat arbitrary nature of textual itemisation, the vagaries of poetic layout, and the aspects of medieval book production specific to Old English poetry, which are utterly erased in the long-line layout and standardisation of modern verse editions (Figs 4.6–4.7). Infinite potential for informed interpretation is dispensed with by the uniformity and fixity of the print edition. At this opening, two scribes are at work: the earlier scribe writes pp. 166 and 167 to line 9, leaving the remainder of the page blank. Anglo-Saxon scribes traditionally abhor space, and so the second scribe fills p. 167 with the verse *Pater Noster*, introduced by the large pen-drawn P. Both hands are a practised Anglo-Saxon insular minuscule, the later hand rounder than the first. Despite (or perhaps because of) the compact impression of the script, both scribes end up with a good deal of space with which to write. As the first scribe sees how much space he has, he finishes *A Summons to Prayer* on p. 167, lines 8–9, with the decoratively adorned words, *regna caelorum*, extended across the lines to ensure the poem is neatly rounded off: a true professional. Yet very little about the *mise-en-page* of the work of either scribe suggests an abundance of resource: both pages are written in a compressed and upright script, with forty-one lines to each relatively tall and narrow page, and an average of eleven words to the line. There is a notable proportion of abbreviated words, which suggests this may not have been an easy text from which to read aloud. Even so, the earlier scribe is meticulous in ensuring that lines are filled with complete words to create a neat appearance and perhaps (and rather contradictorily) for ease of reading, such that only one word on fol. 166 is hyphenated. Various devices ensure that this policy is effective; at line 4, a tilted -*s* extends 'þy læs'; at line 26, a widened final –*n* extends 'begytan' to the edge of the writing grid.

Despite not looking like poetry, there is clearly very careful pointing demarcating half-lines of verse throughout these two scribes' stints. Meticulous punctuation is rarely a feature of scribal hands in this period: while punctuation itself is common, it is often inconsistent. In the case of *The Wanderer* quoted at the beginning of this discussion, there is only one point or *punctus* in five lines of verse. At pp. 166–7 of Corpus 201, every half line is pointed, and the first scribe consistently uses the *punctus versus* (which looks like a semi-colon) to mark sections of text at lines 166/4, 7, 23, and 32. Each *punctus versus* is followed by an initial coloured in red or green, in a relatively systematic way, both instances of the large, capital *þ* on page 166 (at lines 24 and 33) being offset into the left margin, the first four lines long, the second six. The heaviest mark of punctuation, which looks like a colon followed by a hyphen, occurs at 167/9, after *cælorum*. It is precisely because this scribe is consistent in his use of punctuation that one can question the traditional textual boundaries suggested by critics: that there are two poems at pp. 165–7: *An Exhortation to Christian Living* and *A Summons to Prayer*. Modern scholars, in fact, have recently proposed that these two poems could more feasibly be thought of as one work, the apparent textual boundary at line 32 actually being the start of a new section of the first poem, which should thus extend to p. 167/9, creating a single work out of two shorter poems, the larger verse focusing entirely on penance and the means to achieve salvation. By closely analysing the *mise-en-page* and scribal habits illustrated within manuscripts, it is possible to make fresh interpretations of text, where the lack of titles and rubrics – typical in the copying of verse – creates questions about textual integrity. And it seems that the later scribe in Corpus 201, copying *Lord's Prayer II* at p. 167, understood that coloured initial capitals and spacing introduced new sections of text within the layout of this manuscript, and constructed his own verse layout to match his earlier colleague's.

Conclusion

Working with Old English poetic manuscripts thus means working with varieties of codices and fragments to determine texts themselves, and to witness and understand very different compositional and copying methods from our own. Whereas printed editions provide very standardised and mediated versions of the original texts, it is as well to return to the manuscript, through digital publications and facsimiles, to see how the actual compilers and scribes viewed the material with which they worked. The fluidity of Old English verse in its immediate physical context and the permeability of genre and form all add up to an exciting and vibrant corpus of poetry that we are still in the process of learning to read and construe as we emerge from print into new, dynamic multimedia and the possibilities that this creates for presentation, comprehension and fresh interpretation.

Introduction to Chapter 5

Being a much larger, more varied and more esoteric body of material than Old English prose or poetry, Latin texts in Anglo-Saxon manuscripts require a different approach. Using data from Helmut Gneuss's *Handlist of Anglo-Saxon Manuscripts*, this survey seeks to convey the range of texts available in Anglo-Saxon manuscripts and the uses to which the Anglo-Saxons put them. It includes manuscripts of Latin texts written in England during the Anglo-Saxon period and manuscripts written elsewhere that passed into English ownership (some of which remained, some of which were later taken abroad). Unlike written Old English, which was terminally (if not immediately) damaged as a result of the Norman Conquest, the use of Latin continued uninterrupted after 1066 and the distinction between pre- and post-Conquest manuscripts is less marked.

The chapter divides Latin manuscripts into genres. It first examines representative examples of the primary material for Christian culture: Latin biblical texts, followed by manuscripts used in the liturgy (such as sacramentaries, homiliaries and lectionaries). We then move from texts required for formal use in church to other works important to the supporting structure of monasticism, which would have been read publicly in the chapter house or refectory and might also have been studied privately by individual monks and clerics: monastic and other religious Rules and commentaries on them; and historical texts, in which ecclesiastical history featured prominently. Progressing from refectory to classroom, the chapter considers manuscripts relevant to the monastic school curriculum: those taught at the basic level, called the *trivium*, such as grammar, works by classical Latin authors, and writings of early Christian and Anglo-Latin scholars; and manuscripts pertaining to the more advanced *quadrivium*, including texts on mathematics, music, and astronomy; and finally, manuscripts containing texts on geography and medicine. The survey reveals the astonishing range of scholarly material available to the educated Anglo-Saxon by the end of the era, material almost entirely in the hands of professional ecclesiastics.

The number of manuscripts extant and the use that has been made of them – such as glossing the texts in Latin or Old English – testify to their importance. However the state of preservation of some manuscripts complicates research for the modern scholar who must be prepared to pursue fragments and to study scattered folios, palimpsests and traces of text on pastedowns of later books. For example, while complete pontificals survive in surprising numbers, anyone wishing to study all the remains of the books of the bible written or owned in Anglo-Saxon England will have to deal with numerous parts.

5

A survey of Latin manuscripts

Gernot R. Wieland

While almost all manuscripts containing Old English texts were probably written in England, manuscripts with owners in Anglo-Saxon England but containing Latin texts originate from a much wider area: present-day Austria, Belgium, France, Germany, Italy, Luxembourg and the Netherlands as well as England itself. The contents of Latin manuscripts can be diverse, often mixing prose and poetry, as well as textual genres. Though both Old English and Latin manuscripts contain a great variety of material spanning the biblical, homiletic, exegetical, hagiographic, philosophical, epic, lyric, scientific and medical, the sheer number of Latin manuscripts written or owned in Anglo-Saxon England[1] ensures that the Latin manuscripts contain more, and more sophisticated, texts than their Old English counterparts. The primary texts in the many surviving liturgical manuscripts are in Latin, since neither the Mass nor Office was celebrated in the vernacular during the Anglo-Saxon period.

Establishing a corpus of 'Anglo-Saxon Latin manuscripts' presents some problems. In particular eighth-century manuscripts in Insular script now preserved on the Continent cannot always be unambiguously attributed to scribes in England, since they might have been written by English scribes working on the Continent, or by Continental students of Anglo-Saxon missionaries. While keeping this *caveat* in mind, these manuscripts have been included in this survey when the latest expert opinion considers them

---

[1] Approximately nine hundred pre-Conquest Latin manuscripts survive; see Helmut Gneuss, *Handlist of Anglo-Saxon Manuscripts: a list of manuscripts and manuscript fragments written or owned in England up to 1100*, Medieval and Renaissance Texts and Studies, vol. 241 (Tempe, AZ: Arizona Center for Medieval and Renaissance Studies, 2001).

In this chapter the term 'Anglo-Latin' is used only for Latin texts written by Anglo-Saxons such as Æthelweard, Alcuin, Aldhelm or Bede but is not used for other Latin texts in Anglo-Saxon manuscripts. 'Old English' refers to the language spoken by the Anglo-Saxons, regardless of dialect, and 'Anglo-Saxon' refers to the West Germanic settlers in what is now England as well as their cultural products, regardless of whether these are in Old English or in Latin.

'certainly or probably English'.[2] Late eleventh-century manuscripts pose a different problem[3] and are omitted here[4] except for those that have specifically Anglo-Saxon content, such as works by Bede or lives of Anglo-Saxon saints.

'Manuscripts' discussed in the survey below are not all complete codices. Some are fragments; several are *membra disiecta*,[5] fragments of a manuscript now located in different libraries. Some are palimpsests, for example Edinburgh, National Library of Scotland, Advocates 18.7.8, which contains as the lower script on several folios Latin texts written in England during the eighth and eleventh centuries, and, as the upper script, a late eleventh-century text. Obsolete manuscripts were sometimes cut apart, and the resulting single folios used as pastedowns or flyleaves, with Anglo-Saxon folios continuing to be used as flyleaves in printed books as late as the fifteenth and sixteenth centuries. Single or several folios of an original manuscript may, of course, also survive on their own; if they have a unique layout, a unique scribe, and unique page and writing grid sizes, then we can reasonably assume that we possess remnants of an original manuscript.

Manuscripts preserved in modern libraries may actually be combinations of several medieval manuscripts, all under one modern shelf mark. Thus two or three originally different Anglo-Saxon manuscripts may be bound together, or one or two original Anglo-Saxon manuscripts may be bound with a later manuscript or one that was neither written nor owned in Anglo-Saxon

---

[2] Gneuss, *Handlist*, p. 6.

[3] I agree with Gneuss's decision to include all manuscripts written or owned in England up to 1100 since Anglo-Saxon culture did not come to a sudden end in 1066 but clearly continued for several more decades. Nonetheless, the Normans did bring with them manuscripts that reflected their interests, and, as Gneuss mentions in his Introduction, 'the *Handlist* may contain texts that were not actually known or available in Anglo-Saxon England, or at least in the period from King Alfred to Edward the Confessor and William the Conqueror' (*Handlist*, p. 7).

[4] All those manuscripts which are dated 's. xi²', 's. xi ex' or 's. xi/xii' are omitted for two reasons: if no earlier Anglo-Saxon manuscript with the same content is extant, then it would seem that the late eleventh-century manuscript constitutes part of what Gneuss calls the 'Norman library programme' (*Handlist*, p. 7). If earlier Anglo-Saxon manuscripts with the same content survive, then the late eleventh-century manuscripts do no more than to point to a continuity between Anglo-Saxon and the Norman interests. In any case, however, late eleventh-century manuscripts would have only a marginal influence, if any, on Anglo-Saxon learning.

[5] Gneuss indicates *membra disiecta* by using the preposition 'with'. Thus, for instance, Cambridge, Magdalene College, Pepys 2981 (2) (s. viii 2), a fragment of the Gospels, has a *membrum disiectum* in London, British Library, Sloane 1086, fol. 119. In the interest of brevity, I shall not list all the *membra disiecta* of a manuscript, but simply give the main manuscript as listed in Gneuss and add 'plus *membra disiecta*' or 'plus *membrum disiectum*'.

England. An example of the latter is London, British Library, Cotton Vespasian D. xv, which on folios 68–101 contains one Anglo-Saxon manuscript of the mid-tenth century, on folios 102–21 another Anglo-Saxon manuscript of about 1000, and on folios 1–67 a manuscript that was neither written nor owned in Anglo-Saxon England.[6]

Biblical manuscripts

The Bible in its various manifestations was the most important text for the monks and clergy who in Anglo-Saxon times were the almost exclusive producers and consumers of Latin books, since most lay persons would have been unable to read Latin. Only one extant Anglo-Saxon manuscript contains all the books of both Old and New Testaments: the *Codex Amiatinus*, Florence, Biblioteca Medicea Laurenziana, MS Amiatino 1 (s. vii ex or viii in).[7] The manuscript was written in either Jarrow or Monkwearmouth, and came to rest in Abbadia San Salvatore, Italy. While this is the only pandect, the Anglo-Saxons did produce Bibles in two volumes: London, BL, Royal 1 E. vii and 1 E. viii (s. x/xi) together form a complete Bible. Gneuss lists about another dozen manuscripts as 'Bible', mostly fragmentary, such as Cambridge, Gonville and Caius College 820 (h) (s. viii ex) which contains texts from the Minor Prophets, or Cambridge, Magdalene College, MS Pepys 2981 (4) (s. ix 1), with portions from Daniel. It is difficult to decide whether these fragments derive from pandects, two- or multi-volume Bibles, or just sections from the Old Testament. Durham, Cathedral Library B.IV.6, fol. 169*, which contains a text from Machabees, seems to be the oldest 'Bible' owned in Anglo-Saxon England: the fragment derives from a manuscript written in Italy some time in the sixth century. It was presumably brought to Northumbria in the mission to Anglo-Saxon England. Probably the oldest manuscript containing biblical texts actually written in Anglo-Saxon England is London, BL, Additional 37777 plus *membra disiecta*. Copied at the end of the seventh century in Monkwearmouth-Jarrow, it contains portions from Kings and Ecclesiasticus. Anglo-Saxon Bible manuscripts from between the eighth and eleventh century were all written in England. Considering the importance of the Bible to Anglo-Saxon educated society, the surviving examples – about a dozen pre-Conquest manuscripts – are surprisingly few.

The term 'Bible', however, does not exhaust all biblical texts. About another ten pre-Conquest manuscripts contain individual parts of the Old Testament,

---

[6] When I provide folio numbers for a manuscript in the survey below, I do so to indicate that only this particular portion of the manuscript is to be considered Anglo-Saxon.

[7] Abbreviations for dates of manuscripts are explained at p. 30 of this book.

such as London, BL, MS Egerton 1046 (s. viii), Oxford, Bodleian Library, Lat. bib. c.8 (P) (s. ix 1) plus *membra disiecta*, or London, BL, Cotton Vespasian D. vi, fols 2–77 (s. x med). The Egerton manuscript contains the largest number of Old Testament texts with Proverbs, Ecclesiastes, Song of Songs, Wisdom, and Ecclesiasticus (though both Proverbs and Ecclesiasticus are incomplete). The Oxford manuscript plus *membra disiecta* contains only part of Numbers and Deuteronomy, and the Cotton manuscript only the *Proverbia Salomonis*. In the latter the *Proverbia Salomonis* are paired with glosses on the *Proverbia* and with other texts, so clearly the manuscript served purposes other than simply communicating the biblical text.

Manuscripts containing only the psalms, another Old Testament text, are called 'psalters'.[8] The psalms rarely fill an entire manuscript. Mostly they accompany other texts such as canticles, collects, litanies, prayers, and responsories, as for instance in Cambridge, University Library Ff.1.23 (s. xi in or med), Cambridge, Corpus Christi College 272 (883 × 884 Rheims, in England by s. xi); or are bound together with such texts as a calendar, a litany, canticles, and prayers, as for instance in Oxford, Bodleian Library, Douce 296 (s. xi 2/4). More than thirty such manuscripts exist.[9] Only London, BL, Harley 603 (s. x/xi; Fig. 1.3) limits itself to the psalms. Other manuscripts listed in Gneuss's *Handlist* as containing only the psalms are fragmentary, and probably in their complete state the psalms would have been bound with items like prayers, litanies and calendars.

The surrounding texts imply that psalms were mostly read in the liturgical setting of the Office.[10] The utilitarian, liturgical, aspect of these codices is emphasized by heavy glossing in Old English, sometimes with continuous interlinear gloss, sometimes with glosses over a substantial number of Latin *lemmata*. Examples include Cambridge, University Library Ff.1.23 (s. xi in or med), London, BL, Cotton Tiberius C. vi (s. xi med), Cotton Vitellius E. xviii (s. xi med; Fig. 5.1), and Additional 37517 (s. x/xi), and several other manuscripts. Evidently the glossators wished to ensure that Anglo-Saxon readers, presumably clergy, would thoroughly understand the Latin texts, which had to be memorized.

See p. 129 for Fig. 5.1

---

[8] I shall here not distinguish between the Romanum, Gallicanum, and Hebraicum psalters. Except for the Hebraicum, of which only two pre-Conquest manuscripts are extant, both the Romanum and Gallicanum are represented by a substantial number of manuscripts, fifteen and eighteen respectively.

[9] On psalters, see also Helmut Gneuss, 'Liturgical books in Anglo-Saxon England and their Old English Terminology' in Michael Lapidge and Helmut Gneuss, ed., *Learning and Literature in Anglo-Saxon England: Studies presented to Peter Clemoes on the occasion of his sixty-fifth birthday*, Cambridge University Press, 1985, pp. 91–141 at 114–16.

[10] More on the Office below, pp. 134–8.

Manuscripts containing the psalms extend from the seventh or eighth centuries to the end of the Anglo-Saxon period. The earliest, such as Cambridge, University Library Ff.5.27, fol. i, as well as those of the tenth and eleventh centuries, are usually from England. Ninth-century manuscripts are imports from France/Brittany: Cambridge, Corpus Christi College 272 (883 × 884) and London, BL, Cotton Galba A. xviii (s. ix in), both in England by the beginning of the tenth century; Salisbury, Cathedral Library 180 (s. ix 1), in England by 920–40; and Utrecht, Universiteitsbibliotheek 32, Script. eccl. 484, fols 1–91 (s. ix 1), in England by the end of the tenth century. The probable dates by which at least three of these imports reached England suggest that they came in connection with the Benedictine Reform, manifesting an Anglo-Saxon attempt to restock libraries depleted by neglect and Vikings.

Manuscripts containing only the writings of the four Evangelists are listed by Gneuss as 'Gospels'. With over seventy extant examples,[11] they are much more numerous than 'Bibles' and 'Old Testament' manuscripts. Some of the best-known Anglo-Saxon manuscripts fall into this category, including the *Lindisfarne Gospels* (London, BL, Cotton Nero D. iv – s. viii in – Figs 6.3, 7.1, 7.11–7.12),[12] *Codex Aureus* (Stockholm, Kungliga Biblioteket MS A.135 – s. viii med – Figs 7.2–7.4), *Echternach Gospels* (Paris, Bibliothèque Nationale, lat. 9389 – s. vii/viii) and *St Petersburg Gospels* (St Petersburg, Public Library Codex F.v.1.8 – s. viii ex). The scribes of both early and late periods lavished care on these manuscripts. Many are illustrated or richly decorated and have survived for that reason. Since gospel books were often used in the liturgy, so-called canon tables were included at the beginning of manuscripts to indicate which text should be read on which day. Often these canon tables themselves constitute works of art (Figs 7.13–7.14). Two gospel manuscripts, the *Lindisfarne Gospels* and Oxford, Bodleian Library, Auctarium D.2.19 (s. viii/ix), are unusual in containing continuous Old English gloss, added in the second half of the tenth century, seemingly reflective of a trend at that time to make the gospels more accessible to laity.

As with Bibles, the earliest manuscripts containing the gospels were not written in England but abroad, their origins reflecting the early competing missionary influences on the Anglo-Saxons. Three manuscripts, all written in the sixth, or possibly early seventh century, were Italian: CCCC 286, which was used in England by s. vii/viii; Oxford, Bodleian Library,

---

[11] Gneuss, counting manuscripts written in the second half of the eleventh century, which are excluded in the present work, lists eighty-one.

[12] On the *Lindisfarne Gospels*, see Michelle P. Brown, *The Lindisfarne Gospels: society, spirituality, and the scribe*, Toronto, University of Toronto Press, 2003. Gneuss dates the *Lindisfarne Gospels* to 687 × 689, but Brown suggests a slightly later date, namely the second decade of the eighth century.

Auctarium D.2.14, in England at least by the end of the eighth century; and Würzburg, Universitätsbibliothek M.p.th.f.68, which was in Northumbria by the end of the seventh century, and in Würzburg by the middle of the eighth – seemingly a book used by Italian missionaries to England, and Anglo-Saxon missionaries to Germany. At least one early gospel hails from a Celtic country, namely London, BL, Add. 40618 (s. viii²), certainly in England by the tenth century but possibly earlier, and several gospel manuscripts clearly show Celtic influences though their exact origin is uncertain: Dublin, Trinity College manuscripts 57 (s. vii²) and 58 (s. viii²) could have been written in Northumbria, Iona, or Ireland; and Durham, Cathedral Library A.II.10, fols 2–5, 338 and 339 plus *membra disiecta* (s. vii med) could have been written in Northumbria or Ireland. Bede's *Ecclesiastical History* records that Oswald, the Northumbrian king, invited monks from Iona to Northumbria to convert the Anglo-Saxons.[13] Dublin, Trinity College MSS 57 and 58 show all the features of Irish manuscripts, but there is no definitive way to prove whether they were written by Irish monks on Iona or in Ireland and brought to Northumbria; or whether they were written in Northumbria by Irish monks; or possibly by Anglo-Saxon students under the guidance of these Irish monks.

The temporal distribution of the gospels manuscripts is unexpected (Table 1). Rather than a dearth of older manuscripts caused by the destruction of the Danish wars and a proliferation of tenth and eleventh manuscripts, especially gospels, reflecting the Benedictine Reform, a surprisingly low number of the seventy-six surviving gospel manuscripts were written in the tenth century, while the eighth century presents the highest count.

Table 1 Gospel book production by century.

Century	Proportion of gospel books surviving	Number of gospel books surviving (in whole or part)
Eleventh	17%	13
Tenth	14%	11
Ninth	18%	14
Eighth	38%	29
Seventh	8%	6
Sixth	4%	3

The surprising quantity of extant eighth-century gospel manuscripts confirms King Alfred's memory of *hu ða cirican geond eall Angelkynn stodon maðma & boca gefylda* ('… how the churches throughout all England stood filled with

---

[13] Bede, *Historia Ecclesiastica*, III, 3; Bertram Colgrave and R.A.B. Mynors, ed., *Bede's Ecclesiastical History of the English People*, Oxford, Clarendon Press, 1969, p. 219.

treasures and books').[14] Even though a substantial number of ninth-century manuscripts survive, only a few were written in England and most were imported to England in the tenth century, thus confirming Alfred's statement that ... *heora nan wuht ongietan ne meahton forþæmþe hie næron on hiora ægen geðeode awritene* ('... they [monks] could not understand anything of them because they were not written in their own language').[15] Alfred's estimation of the eighth century as a Golden Age in which Anglo-Saxon England abounded in scholars might also help to explain the survival of so many eighth-century gospel books, treasured because of their association with the first flowering of English Christianity.

Liturgical manuscripts

Whereas the Bible provided the foundations of the Christian faith for the Anglo-Saxons, liturgical books provided the means by which the God of the Bible would be worshipped. It is therefore not surprising to find that the Anglo-Saxons possessed a very large number of books containing liturgical texts. The line between biblical and liturgical manuscripts at times is blurred: psalms form part of the Old Testament, but were also an important part of monastic daily prayers; the gospels, though providing the entire texts written by the four Evangelists, were also used in the liturgy, as the canon tables suggest.[16]

The Mass

Sacramentaries contain texts that were read by the priest at the altar during Mass. These include the so-called *ordo missae*, the unchanging parts of the Mass; and the prayers that change every day, such as that after the *Gloria* (*oratio*), that over the bread and wine (*super oblata*, later called the *secreta*), the preface, and the final prayer (*ad complendum*, later called *postcommunio*). Sacramentaries are usually arranged according to the *circulus anni*, beginning with either Christmas or the first Sunday of Advent, and are usually subdivided into: the *Temporale* (the major feasts and seasons of

---

[14] In Alfred's preface to the translation of Gregory's *Cura Pastoralis*; Henry Sweet, ed., *King Alfred's West-Saxon Version of Gregory's Pastoral Care*, Early English Text Society, original series 45, London, Oxford University Press, 1871, p. 4.

[15] Sweet, *King Alfred's West-Saxon Version*, p. 4.

[16] 'Liturgy' will here be taken in its widest sense including the Mass as well as the monastic and clerical Offices. The texts discussed would, in the Middle Ages, be found in separate manuscripts or in substantial portions of manuscripts. Shorter texts such as individual benedictions, Offices for specific purposes and forms of excommunication will be omitted since these do not take up an entire manuscript nor a substantial portion of a manuscript.

Advent, Christmas, Lent, Easter, and Pentecost, as well as all the Sundays following them); the *Sanctorale* (special saints' days for which individual Masses had been written); and the *Commune Sanctorum*, which provides Masses for one or several martyrs, virgins, or confessors (that is, for saints for whom no individual Masses were written). This division into *Temporale*, *Sanctorale* and *Commune Sanctorum* is common to all liturgical books.

Missals are effectively sacramentaries supplemented with other texts such as the lessons of the day and the gospel readings, as well as prayers that in a high Mass are not read by the priest but by a lector; or sung by the choir.[17] The earliest extant missals in the Latin West date from the sixth century, but not until the twelfth century do missals become as common as sacramentaries. In the Anglo-Saxon period, sacramentaries are more numerous in the earlier centuries, and missals in the later.

Gneuss lists twenty-two pre-Conquest sacramentaries,[18] one of the earliest being Cambridge, Trinity Hall 24, fols 78–83, a palimpsest of which the lower text appears to be an eighth-century sacramentary. Some of the oldest Anglo-Saxon sacramentaries ended up on the Continent, presumably through the Anglo-Saxon mission. Berlin, Staatsbibliothek Preussischer Kulturbesitz Lat. fol. 877 (s. viii) plus two *membra disiecta* was at Regensburg by the end of the eighth century. Werden, the monastery to which Münster in Westfalen, Universitätsbibliothek, Fragmentensammlung IV.8 (s. viii in) traces its medieval provenance, had strong Anglo-Saxon connections, so the manuscript probably arrived there early.[19]

Most early Anglo-Saxon sacramentaries are now fragmentary, partly no doubt because they were replaced by missals and therefore discarded or re-used, and partly because Latin liturgical manuscripts, unless they had attractive art work, were not of great interest in post-Reformation England. Because most are fragmentary, it is difficult to ascertain whether they were originally bound with other texts, and what these other texts might have been. The best evidence for texts potentially surrounding a sacramentary is provided

---

[17] A 'high' Mass is one at which a choir and a lector are present; a 'low' Mass is one read only by the priest. Sacramentaries provide texts only for high Masses, and need to be supplemented by graduals and lectionaries; missals, on the other hand, provide texts for both high and low Masses, and in a high Mass the priest can simply omit the portions sung by the choir and read by the lector. Missals are more bulky, but more useful. Because of their greater usefulness, missals were produced in larger numbers over time, though the production of sacramentaries did not cease.

[18] See also Gneuss, 'Liturgical books', pp. 101–2.

[19] Other early Anglo-Saxon sacramentaries can be found in Köln, Historisches Archiv der Stadt, GB Kasten B, nos 24, 123, and 124 (s. viii med), in Paris, Bibliothèque Nationale, lat. 9488, fols 3–4 (s. viii), and in St Gallen, Stiftsbibliothek 1394, pp. 95–8 (s. viii in).

by Rouen, Bibliothèque Municipale 274 (Y.6) (1014 × 1023),[20] which contains a calendar and *computus* material. Oxford, Bodleian Library, Bodley 579, written around 900 in Saint-Vaast, Arras, originally contained a sacramentary with catchwords for mass chants,[21] a pontifical and a benedictional. After it came to England around 920, a calendar and *computus* material were added between 979 and 987, and pericope *incipits* in the middle of the eleventh century.[22] In contrast, texts found with excerpts from a sacramentary in Cambridge, Corpus Christi College 41, seem unusual: they include the Old English translation of Bede's *Ecclesiastical History*, the Old English *Martyrology*, charms, *Solomon and Saturn* and Old English medical recipes. The oddity can be partially explained by the fact that sacramentary material in this manuscript was not the original text but consists of excerpts added in the margins of a pre-existing text. The reason for adding sacramentary extracts to the Old English Bede is not immediately apparent.

Sacramentaries need to be supplemented with the texts that are sung by the choir – the introit, the gradual, the offertory, and the communion – as well as with texts read by the lector – epistles and gospels. The texts for lectors can be found in lectionaries.[23] Mass lectionaries, which contain both epistles and gospels, are more comprehensive than gospel lectionaries. Four mass lectionaries survive from the Anglo-Saxon period, all fragmentary. The oldest is Durham, Cathedral Library A.IV.19, fol. 89 (s. viii); the youngest, Cambridge, Gonville and Caius College 734/782a (s. xi¹).[24]

Six pre-Conquest gospel lectionaries survive, so we are better informed about them than about mass lectionaries. The oldest, London, BL, Cotton Claudius B. v, fol. 132v, has the distinction of coming from the court of

---

[20] This manuscript has been published by H.A. Wilson, ed. *The Missal of Robert of Jumièges*, Henry Bradshaw Society 11, London, Henry Bradshaw Society, 1896. Despite the somewhat misleading title, which refers to 'missal', Wilson fully recognizes that this manuscript is a sacramentary; see the first sentence of his introduction: 'The Sacramentary known as the Missal of Robert of Jumièges … is one of the few remaining English service books belonging to the period before the Norman Conquest' (p. xix).

[21] Because of the catchwords for the chants sung by the choir, one could make the argument that this manuscript is a precursor of a missal; a missal would, of course, have the full texts instead of just catchwords.

[22] This manuscript is edited by F.E. Warren under the title *The Leofric Missal, as Used in the Cathedral of Exeter during the Episcopate of its First Bishop, A.D. 1050–1072; together with some Account of the Red Book of Derby, the Missal of Robert of Jumièges, and a few other early Ms. Service Books of the English Church*, Oxford, Clarendon Press, 1883.

[23] On lectionaries, see also Gneuss, 'Liturgical books', pp. 105–9.

[24] The others are Oslo, Riksarkivet, Lat. fragm. 201 plus *membrum disiectum* and Oslo, Riksarkivet, Lat. fragm. 211.

Charlemagne; it was written around 800. The oldest extant gospel lectionary written in Anglo-Saxon England is London, College of Arms, Arundel 22, fols 84 and 85 (s. x 4/4). The youngest, Florence, Biblioteca Medicea Laurenziana Plut. xvii.20 (s. xi med), did not stay in England very long, arriving on the Continent during the eleventh century.

Sacramentaries also have to be supplemented by graduals to complete the texts necessary for the mass.[25] Gneuss lists six pre-Conquest graduals dating from the mid-tenth to mid-eleventh centuries.[26] The oldest is Cambridge, Pembroke College 46, fols A and B (s. x 2/4). All are fragmentary except Oxford, Bodleian Library, Bodley 775 (s. xi med), which also contains a troper.

In his edition of Bodley 775, Frere provides a Latin definition of a trope: *Tropus, in re liturgica, est versiculus quidam aut etiam plures ante inter vel post alios ecclesiasticos cantus appositi* ('A trope, in the context of the liturgy, is one or several stanzas added before, in the middle of, or after other liturgical songs.')[27] Despite its vagueness, the definition helpfully indicates that tropes are a form of song, and thus fall under the purview of the choir rather than the priest or lector. Frere also mentions that 'tropes are a later accretion [to the liturgy] and did not survive for more than a few centuries',[28] approximately the ninth to twelfth. The combination of troper and gradual in Bodley 775 is not coincidental, since the texts of both are sung by the choir. For the Mass on Christmas Day, for instance, the *Winchester Troper* provides tropes *ad Introitum*, *ad Gloriam*, *ad Offertorium*, and *ad Communionem*, and gives detailed instructions as to when they are to be inserted. Only three tropers survive from the pre-Conquest period,[29] the earliest of which is CCCC 473 (s. x/xi), and the latest Bodley 775.

Missals combine all the texts found separately in sacramentaries, graduals and lectionaries. Surviving missals are more numerous than sacramentaries (thirty, compared to twenty-two sacramentaries),[30] but none of the missals is complete. The fact that several serve as flyleaves or paste-downs in printed books (e.g. Cambridge, Pembroke College C8 and Oxford, All Souls College SR 79.g.8) suggests that some extant missals were dismantled in the

---

[25] The gradual contains the songs sung by the choir *ad gradus*, at the steps of the sanctuary.

[26] On graduals see also Gneuss, 'Liturgical books', pp. 102–4.

[27] Walter Howard Frere, ed. *The Winchester Troper from Mss. of the Xth and XIth Centuries*, Henry Bradshaw Society 8, London, Harrison and Sons, 1894, p. viii.

[28] Frere, *The Winchester Troper*, p. v.

[29] On tropers, see also Gneuss, 'Liturgical books', pp. 104–5.

[30] I exclude Oxford, Bodleian Library, Bodley 579 since I have already mentioned it above under 'sacramentaries'. Since Bodley 579 contains catchwords for the mass chants, it stands halfway between a sacramentary and a missal. On missals, see also Gneuss, 'Liturgical books', pp. 99–101.

wake of the Reformation. Dismemberment seems to have started earlier, however, since fragments of other missals appear as flyleaves or endleaves in manuscripts from the Middle English period, for example the two endleaves in Cambridge, Gonville and Caius College 466/573 (s. ix med), and the flyleaves in Cambridge, Jesus College 5 (Q.A.5) (s. xi¹). Gneuss does not always indicate the length of surviving fragments, but it seems that longer portions of the missal appear in fragments such as Worcester, Cathedral Library F.173 (s. xi med), the content of which Gneuss identifies as 'Missal (part)', or Le Havre, Bibliothèque Municipale 330, the content of which he identifies as 'Missal (incomplete)'. A considerable portion of the missal also seems to be preserved in London, Westminster Abbey Library 36, nos 17–19 (s. xi med) and its *membra disiecta*. Since all extant Anglo-Saxon missals are either fragmentary or incomplete, we have no indication with what other texts, if any, they might have been bound.

'... *monks and clergy were the almost exclusive producers and consumers of Latin books, since most lay persons would have been unable to read Latin.*'

There are no early Anglo-Saxon missals. While the earliest Anglo-Saxon sacramentaries date back to the eighth century, the first extant missal owned in Anglo-Saxon England, an import from either France or Italy (London, BL, Royal 4 A. xiv, fols 1* and 2*, s. ix²), was in England, possibly Worcester, only by the end of the ninth century, while the earliest extant missals written in England date from the second half of the tenth century. Examples are Oxford, Bodleian Library, Bodley 386, fols i and 174 (s. x ex. or x/xi), Bloomington, Indiana University, Lilly Library Poole 41 (s. x 2 or x ex), and Oslo, Riksarkivet 207, 208 and 210 plus *membra disiecta*. The youngest, such as Canterbury, Cathedral Library and Archives Add. 128/52, date from the middle of the eleventh century.

The pontifical is a type of missal for the use of bishops, containing the texts for rites only bishops (or archbishops) could perform, such as confirmation, tonsure, blessing of abbots, abbesses and nuns, or coronation of kings and queens. Pontificals also contain the words of services for laying foundation stones, consecrating churches, altars and chalices, and such texts as excommunication and absolution thereof, not found in an ordinary sacramentary or missal. Since bishops also give special blessings (*benedictiones* in Latin), pontificals contain these too.

No early Anglo-Saxon pontificals survive.[31] The first extant pontifical, an import from the Continent, dates from the late ninth/early tenth century, namely Oxford, Bodleian Library, Bodley 579, which was written in Saint-Vaast, Arras and was in England as early as about 920, and which has already been mentioned among sacramentaries. In the tenth century,

---

[31] On pontificals, see also Gneuss, 'Liturgical books', pp. 131–3.

the Anglo-Saxons wrote their own pontificals, such as Paris, Bibliothèque Nationale, lat. 943 (s. x$^{3/4}$) and lat. 10575 (s. x med or x^2). The youngest surviving pontificals are CCCC 44 (s. xi$^{2/4}$ or xi med) and BL, Cotton Claudius A. iii, fols 9–18 and 87–105 (s. xi 2/4 or xi med).

In contrast to sacramentaries, surprisingly large numbers of pre-Conquest pontificals are complete. Of the seventeen Gneuss lists, only four are fragmentary.[32] Two described as 'incomplete' are nonetheless quite sizeable: London, BL, Cotton Claudius A. iii occupies 29 folios and Cotton Vitellius A. vii, fols 1–112 falls little short of a 'complete' pontifical. These texts, possibly because they were at episcopal centres, seem to have been treated more respectfully than every-day sacramentaries and missals – not only by Anglo-Saxons, but also subsequently.

> 'Whereas the Bible provided the foundations of the Christian faith for the Anglo-Saxons, liturgical books provided the means by which the God of the Bible would be worshipped.'

Pontificals, unless fragmentary, are never found alone, but always survive in the company of other texts. The most frequent pairing is that of pontifical plus benedictional, that is a corpus of special blessings which only a bishop had the right to confer.[33] Such a pairing of pontifical and benedictional occurs in, for example, London, BL, Additional 28188 (s. x$^{3/4}$); London, BL, Cotton Claudius A. iii, fols 31–86 and 106–50 (s. x/xi); Oxford, Bodleian Library, Bodley 579 (s. ix/x); and Paris, BN, lat. 943. The close connection between pontificals and blessings is also borne out by London, BL, Cotton Vitellius E. xii, a pontifical written in the first quarter of the eleventh century in Germany (possibly Cologne), to which benedictions and other texts were added after 1068 in Exeter, as though a pontifical without texts for special blessings was abnormal.

Integral to most Masses is the homily or sermon. On a saint's day, the officiating priest might read the saint's life or *passio* instead of delivering a homily or sermon. Priests had to remain within the accepted interpretations of the Church, and would be grateful for pre-written homilies from which they could draw inspiration and guidance. They could consult several sources: the first, and most obvious, would be a collection of Old English homilies such as can be found among Ælfric's works. The more conventional/conservative priest might draw on a Latin homiliary in which homilies, by both named and anonymous authors, are arranged in the same order as other liturgical books. A third source, less conveniently arranged, would

---

[32] These are Cambridge, Trinity College B.1.30A plus *membrum disiectum* (s. x med); Manchester, John Rylands University Library, Lat. Fragm. 11 (s. x); Oslo, Universitetsbiblioteket, Lat. fragm. 16 (s. xi); and Stockholm, Riksarkivet Lösa Pergamentsomslag s. 9 (s. x/xi).

[33] On benedictionals, see also Gneuss, 'Liturgical books', pp. 133–4.

be collected homilies by authors such as Bede, Gregory the Great, Paul the Deacon, or Haimo of Auxerre, or collected sermons by authors such as St Augustine, pseudo-Augustine, Caesarius of Arles, or Fulbert of Chartres. The fourth source would require some research on the part of the priest: he could look up the thoughts of a known exegete on a gospel passage or a section of the epistles which formed the liturgy of the day. Thus, if the gospel of the day were a passage from Luke, the priest could consult Ambrose's exegesis of that passage in his *In Evangelium Lucae*, or, if the epistle were by Paul, he could find inspiration in Hrabanus Maurus's *In epistolas Pauli*. We might add a fifth source: individual sermons or homilies that can be found among other quite diverse material in manuscripts, which probably owe their presence to a particular priest's predilection for them.

In the last category, Gneuss's index lists six pre-Conquest manuscripts containing 'homilies and sermons in Latin, anonymous or not identified'. Sometimes homilies and sermons appear with saints' lives or exegetical works, thus suggesting saints' lives and exegetical works could also be used as sources for sermons. In Avranches, Bibliothèque Municipale 29 (s. x/xi), for instance, fifty-five anonymous homilies are accompanied by material relating to St Martin: Sulpicius Severus's *Vita S. Martini*, excerpts from Gregory of Tours's *Historia Francorum*, and excerpts from the *De virtutibus Sancti Martini*. In Boulogne-sur-Mer, Bibliothèque Municipale 106, fols 1–92, 119–71 (s. x/xi) seven anonymous homilies appear next to the *Vita S. Walarici*, the *Vita S. Philiberti*, the *Vita S. Aichardi*, the *Vita S. Bavonis*, and Felix's *Vita S. Guthlaci*. London, BL, Harley 213 (s. ix$^{3/3}$) juxtaposes two anonymous homilies to Alcuin's exegetical texts *In Ecclesiasten* and *In Canticum canticorum*. The connection of sermons/homilies to other texts in the manuscript is not always apparent: Cambridge, Trinity College O.2.30 (s. x med), for instance, contains four anonymous sermons not obviously associated with the *Regula Benedicti*, the manuscript's primary text.

Individual sermons by named authors also appear among a variety of texts: Caesarius of Arles's *sermo* 100, for instance, appears with a metrical calendar, a horologium, various alphabets, a benedictional, pseudo-Jerome's *Breviarium in psalmos* and other works in Vatican City, Biblioteca Apostolica Vaticana Reg. lat. 338, fols 64–126 (s. x/xi); Bede's homily on Benedict Biscop appears in London, BL, Harley 3020 (s. x/xi) appropriately next to Bede's *Historia abbatum* and the anonymous life of another Jarrow/Monkwearmouth abbot, the *Vita Ceolfridi*.

Complete homiliaries with texts arranged according to the *circulus anni* are of greater benefit to the clergyman than individual sermons but evidence indicates that the Anglo-Saxons had few, if any, such homiliaries at their disposal. Of all the homily collections listed in Gneuss, only the homiliary by Paul the Deacon (*c.*725–799) is arranged this way. Though originally designed for use in the Night Office,[34] it would undoubtedly also have provided inspiration for sermons and homilies of the Mass, and is therefore included here. Most manuscripts containing Paul's homiliary are late eleventh-century, and hence too late for our purpose, but Canterbury, Cathedral Library and Archives Add. 127/1 (s. xi¹) and Saint-Omer, Bibliothèque Municipale 202 (s. ix²) show that the Anglo-Saxons knew at least some of Paul's homilies. The Canterbury manuscript is fragmentary, and it is impossible to decide whether it stems from a complete homiliary or a selection. The Saint-Omer manuscript was written in north-eastern France but seems to have arrived in England by the mid-eleventh century. It contains only thirty-five homilies of Paul's homiliary. The evidence suggests the Anglo-Saxons had only limited and relatively late access to Paul the Deacon's homiliary.

St Augustine's sermons do not fare much better. All surviving manuscripts listed by Gneuss as containing them date toward the end of the eleventh century, too late to have been used by Anglo-Saxon clergy before the Norman invasion. The homilies of Gregory the Great, by contrast, whom Bede called the 'apostle of England',[35] appear to have been there considerably earlier – at least if the manuscript evidence can be trusted. Gregory's *Homiliae in evangelia* and his *Homiliae in Ezechielem* are each preserved in three pre-Conquest manuscripts. The manuscripts containing the *Homiliae in evangelia* were written in the eighth century or at the turn of the eighth to ninth century. CCCC 69 (s. viii/ix), which contains homilies 21–40 of book ii, is the most extensive early witness for the Anglo-Saxons' knowledge of Gregory's homilies. The palimpsest Edinburgh, National Library of Scotland, Advocates 18.7.8 (s. viii ex) contains traces of the *Homiliae in evangelia* on the lower script of folios 26 and 33, and Boulogne-sur-Mer, BM 106 (s. viii/ix) contains short sections from them on its binding strip. Similarly, the manuscripts containing Gregory's *Homiliae in Ezechielem* are all eighth-century, and would seem to indicate that these texts were known in eighth-century Anglo-Saxon England, though the manuscripts are now on the Continent: Karlsruhe, Badische Landesbibliothek Aug. perg. 221, fols 54–107 (s. viii med.); Rome, Vatican City, Biblioteca Apostolica Vaticana, Pal. lat. 259 (s. viii–ix); and Würzburg, Universitätsbibliothek, M.p.th.f.43 (s. viii med.). The early date of these manuscripts and the lack of any manuscripts for the ninth, tenth, and early eleventh centuries does raise the question whether the Anglo-Saxons continued to read Gregory's homilies.

---

[34] Gneuss, 'Liturgical books', p. 122. For homiliaries in general, see *ibid.* pp. 122–5.

[35] *Quem recte nostrum appellare possumus et debemus apostolum*; Bede, *Historia Ecclesiastica*, II.1; Colgrave and Mynors, *Bede's Ecclesiastical History*, p. 122.

Anglo-Saxon clergy had a range of homilies and sermons to draw on, even though the number of pre-Conquest manuscripts containing collections of homilies and sermons is relatively small.[36] Other continental writers to whom they had access are Abbo of Saint-Germain-des-Prés, Ambrosius Autpertus, Basil the Great, Caesarius of Arles, Haimo of Auxerre, and Origines.

Only two Anglo-Saxon writers of Latin homilies survive in manuscripts, Bede and Wulfstan. The manuscript containing Bede's homily on Benedict Biscop (=*Homiliae in Evangelia* I.13) has already been mentioned. Surprisingly, only one further manuscript containing his homilies can be traced to Anglo-Saxon England: Lincoln, Cathedral Library 182 (s. x/xi) plus *membrum disiectum*. Wulfstan fares better, with four Anglo-Saxon manuscripts containing some of his sermons, though unlike Bede's homilies, which are a collection, Wulfstan's sermons seem to have circulated individually. CCCC 190 (s. xi¹), pp. 1–294 contains homily VIIIa as does CCCC 265 (s. xi med), pp. 1–268; London, BL, Cotton Vespasian D. ii (s. xi/xii) contains homily Ia, and Copenhagen, Kongelige Bibliotek, G.K.S.1595 (c.1002–1023) Ia and VIIIa.[37] These appear among a multiplicity of texts, including sermons by other writers such as Abbo of Saint-Germain (whose *sermones* 6–13, for instance, can also be found in the Copenhagen manuscript).

Martyrologies and legendaries also provided material for sermons. No pre-Conquest Latin legendaries survive,[38] but one martyrology exists,[39] in CCCC 57 (s. x/xi) alongside other texts such as the *Regula S. Benedicti*, the *Capitulare monasticum*, and Smaragdus's *Diadema monachorum*. The assemblage indicates the manuscript was in possession of monks and its texts were primarily intended for use in the Office (and of course, saints' lives might also have been read privately) though, as suggested, they might also serve as the basis for a sermon during Mass.

The scarcity of legendaries and martyrologies is probably best explained by texts such as Aldhelm's *De virginitate*, which provides short synopses of saints' lives and by the large number of individual saints' lives which were written by named writers. The available texts are listed in Table 2.

---

[36] The Norman invasion, it seems, brought an increased supply of manuscripts with Latin homilies and sermons: of the twelve manuscripts listed in Gneuss as containing sermons of Caesarius of Arles, for instance, as many are extant from the second half of the eleventh century as from the three centuries before.

[37] For sermons Ia and VIIIa, see Dorothy Bethurum, ed. *The Homilies of Wulfstan*, Oxford, Clarendon Press, 1957, pp. 113–15, 169–71.

[38] On legendaries, see also Gneuss, 'Liturgical books', pp. 125–7.

[39] On martyrologies, see also Gneuss, 'Liturgical books', pp. 128–9.

Table 2 Saints' lives by named writers.	Numbers in parentheses indicate the number of manuscripts in which each text appears. Asterisked numbers indicate the number of post-Conquest manuscripts of Anglo-Saxon saints or of saints important to the Anglo-Saxons such as Aidan.

Abbo of Fleury, *Vita S. Eadmundi* (4*)

Adelard of Ghent, *Vita S. Dunstani* (1*)

Adrevald of Fleury, *Historia translationis et miracula S. Benedicti* (1)

Ælfric, *Vita S. Aethelwoldi* (1*)

Alcuin (?), *Vita S. Judoci* (1)

'B', *Vita S. Dunstani* (3)

Bede, excerpts from the *Ecclesiastical History* on Æthelthryth, called Etheldreda in Latin (1*), Aidan (1*), Birinus (2*), and Oswald (2*), as well as *Vita S. Cuthberti* (prose 4 + 3* and verse 9 + 2*)

Bili of Alet, *Vita S. Machuti* (1)

Byrhtferth of Ramsey, *Vita S. Ecgwini* (1*), *Vita S. Oswaldi* (1*)

Felix, *Vita S. Guthlaci* (6 + 1*)

Folcard of St. Bertin, *Vita S. Botulphi* (1*)

Frithegod of Canterbury, *Breviloquium Vitae Wilfridi* (4)

Goscelin of Canterbury, vitae of St Æthelburga (1*), Augustine of Canterbury (1*), Archbishop Deusdedit (2*), Abbot Hadrian (2*), Kenelm (1*), Archbishop Laurentius (2*), Letardus (2*), Archbishop Mellitus (1*), Mildred (3*), Archbishop Theodore (2*), and Wulfhilda (1*)

Gregory of Tours, *De virtutibus S. Martini* (2)

Hermannus Archidiaconus, *Miracula S. Eadmundi* (2*)

Jerome, *Vita S. Malchi* (1), *Vita S. Pauli Eremitae* (2)

Johannes Diaconus, *Vita S. Gregorii* (1)

Lantfred of Winchester, *Translatio et miracula S. Swithuni* (1 + 3*)

Pseudo-Linus, *Martyrium S. Petri et Pauli* (1)

Osbern of Canterbury, *Vita et translatio S. Alphegi* (1*), *Vita S. Dunstani* (2*)

Stephen of Ripon, *Vita S. Wilfridi* (1*)

Sulpicius Severus, *Vita S. Martini* (3)

Wulfstan, *Narratio metrica de S. Swithuno* (2*), *Vita S. Aethelwoldi* (1*).

The list in Table 2 omits anonymous saints' lives, for which Gneuss provides another twelve manuscripts. The popularity of the genre is indicated by the fact that the texts listed in the table are distributed in more than fifty manuscripts, many manuscripts containing more than one saint's life. Paris, BN, lat. 5362, fols 1–39 (s. xi/xii), for instance, contains Bede's prose *Vita S. Cuthberti*, Abbo of Fleury's *Vita S. Eadmundi*, Lantfred's *Translatio et miracula S. Swithuni*, Ælfric's *Vita S. Aethelwoldi*, and excerpts from Bede's

5.1 Liturgy: London, British Library, MS Cotton Vitellius E. xviii fol. 18r.

The beginning of an eleventh-century psalter in Caroline script with Old English glosses in insular script.

Ecclesiastical History focussing on the lives of Saints Cuthbert, Oswald, Birinus, and Æthelthryth. The late date of this manuscript provides testimony that the new Norman lords of England were keen to continue the veneration of Anglo-Saxon saints.

Not all manuscripts containing saints' lives are so late, however. The earliest, which contains Bede's verse *Vita S. Cuthberti*, seems to be the fragment Berlin, Staatsbibliothek Preussischer Kulturbesitz, Grimm 132,1 plus *membra disiecta* (s. viii^2 or viii/ix). Another very early example, also fragmentary, is London, BL, Royal 4 A. xiv, fols 107 and 108 (s. viii/ix or ix in), which contains Felix's *Vita S. Guthlaci*. Anglo-Saxons continued to produce manuscripts containing saints' lives during the ninth, tenth, and eleventh centuries. Of eleven manuscripts containing Bede's verse *Vita S. Cuthberti*, one is the early Berlin manuscript mentioned above, two were written in the ninth century, five in the tenth (or at the turn of the tenth to the eleventh century), one at the beginning, and two at the end of the eleventh century. Felix's *Vita S. Guthlaci*, as well as the early Royal manuscript, survives in CCCC 307 (s. x in); CCCC 389 (s. x^2 or x$^{3/4}$); London, BL, Royal 13 A. xv (s. x med); Arras, BM 1029 (s. x/xi); Boulogne-sur-Mer, BM 106, fols 1–92 and 119–71 (s. x/xi); and BL, Harley 3097 (s. xi/xii). While it is unsurprising that Anglo-Saxons would keep producing manuscripts of Anglo-Saxon authors celebrating Anglo-Saxon saints, there is evidence that the Anglo-Saxons were also interested in works by non-Anglo-Saxon authors celebrating non-Anglo-Saxon saints. The entire manuscript London, BL, Royal 13 A. x, fols 63–103 (s. x^2 or x/xi) was dedicated to the praise of the Welsh saint Machutus containing Bili of Alet's *Vita S. Machuti*, a hymn in honour of St Machutus and a homily for his feast day. Sulpicius Severus's *Vita S. Martini* is contained in two manuscripts written at the turn of the tenth to the eleventh century, and another written at the beginning of the eleventh century; Jerome's *Vita S. Pauli Eremitae* survives in two manuscripts, the first written in the second half of the eighth century, and the second in the tenth century. While the context of some (for example London, BL, Royal 13 A. x, above), strongly suggests that the saint's life may have been used to supplement or supplant a homily, the same argument cannot be made as easily for others. London, BL, Cotton Caligula A. xv, for instance, which contains Jerome's *Vita S. Pauli Eremitae*, also contains Isidore's *Etymologiae*, a text less likely to form the basis for a homily.

Exegetical or theological works can also provide material for a homily or a sermon. The overlap between exegetical works and homilies can be seen, for example, in Origenes's *Homiliae in Genesin*, *Homiliae in Exodum*, or *Homiliae in Leviticum*, where exegesis forms the basis for the homilies. Likewise, Gregory's *Homiliae in Evangelia* leave little doubt that exegesis and homilies are closely linked. A work such as Ambrose's *Exhortatio virginitatis* or Augustine's *De mendacio* might without difficulty be transformed into a sermon. Obviously theological and exegetical works could also be pondered in the privacy of the monk's cell, but since some manuscripts combine exegesis and homilies, they are included here. They include Würzburg, Universitätsbibliothek M.p.th.f.43 (s. viii med), with excerpts from Augustine's *In Psalmos* and Gregory's *Homiliae in Ezechielem* I, 8 and 9, and Brussels, Bibliothèque Royale 9850–52 (s. vii/viii), which contains Caesarius of Arles's sermons as well as a commentary on the Gospels.

More than seventy pre-Conquest manuscripts contain theological or exegetical works. Table 3 lists exegetical and theological texts surviving in manuscripts which were fairly certainly written in England or had come to England by 1066.

Some of the oldest manuscripts listed in Table 3 deserve special mention. Boulogne-sur-Mer, BM 32, which was written on the Continent, probably in Italy, as early as the first half of the sixth century, was in England by the eighth century. The circumstances of its importation are not known, whether it was brought by early missionaries or was among the many books Benedict Biscop brought from Italy to Northumbria. It is, however, one of the oldest manuscripts of any kind extant from Anglo-Saxon England. It contains only works by Ambrose (*De apologia prophetae David*, *De Joseph patriarcha*, *De patriarchis*, *De paenitentia*, *De excessu fratris*, and some of his letters), and is an important witness of the dispersal of Ambrose's works to Anglo-Saxon England. Other early English manuscripts containing exegetical and theological material were taken to the Continent, presumably by the Anglo-Saxon mission: Kassel, Gesamthochschulbibliothek 2°Ms.theol.21 (s. viii), with Ambrose's *De apologia prophetae David*; Würzburg, Universitätsbibliothek M.p.th.f.43 (s. viii med), with excerpts from Augustine's *In psalmos*; and Düsseldorf, Universitätsbibliothek Fragm. K16:Z.3/1 (s. viii[1]), with parts of Cassiodorus's *In psalmos*.

One might expect a large number of early Anglo-Saxon Latin manuscripts containing the works of Anglo-Saxon exegetes such as Alcuin and Bede, but this is not borne out; for instance, only one pre-Conquest manuscript contains Bede's *In Apocalypsin* (London, Lambeth Palace Library 149, fols 1–139; s. x^2; Fig. 5.2). Alcuin's situation differs in that he wrote most of his exegetical and theological work on the Continent; nonetheless, since he was in regular correspondence with England, the Anglo-Saxon clergy might well have appreciated the works of their compatriot. They clearly imported some. Oxford, Bodleian Library, Barlow 35 (s. x), for instance, which contains Alcuin's *Interrogationes Sigewulfi in Genesin* and was written on the Continent, had arrived in England by the beginning of the eleventh century. Likewise, Rouen, BM 26 (s. ix[1] or ix med), which contains excerpts from Alcuin's commentary on the *Canticum canticorum*, was imported from Northern

Table 3
Exegetical and theological texts in manuscripts probably written in England or in England by 1066.

The number in parentheses indicates the number of extant manuscripts.

Adalbert of Metz, *Speculum Gregorii* (an epitome of Gregory the Great's *Moralia in Job*) (2)

Alcuin, *In Canticum canticorum* (1), *De fide sanctae et individuae Trinitatis* (2), *De trinitate ad Fredegisum* (1), and *Interrogationes Sigewulfi in Genesin* (1)

Ambrose, *De apologia prophetae David* (2), *De excessu fratris* (1), *De Joseph patriarcha* (1), *De paenitentia* (1), *De patriarchis* (1), *Expositio de psalmo CXVIII* (1), *Hexameron* (1)

Anonymous, *In psalmos* (2), *In evangelia* (1), *In Matthaeum* (1), *In epistolam ad Colossenses* (1)

Apponius, *In Canticum canticorum* (1)

Augustine of Hippo, *De adulterinis coniugiis* (1), *De civitate Dei* (1), *De consensu Evangelistarum* (1), *De orando Deo* (1), *De Trinitate* (1), *De videndo Deo* (1), *In epistolam Johannis ad Parthos* (2), *In Psalmos* (2), *Quaestiones Evangeliorum* (1)

Pseudo-Augustine, *De symbolo* (1)

Beda, *In Apocalypsin* (1), *In epistolas catholicas* (1), *In Evangelium Lucae* (2), *In proverbia Salomonis* (1)

Pseudo-Beda, *Quaestionum super Genesin dialogus* (1)

Caesarius of Arles, *In Apocalypsin* (3)

Cassiodorus, *In psalmos* (4), *De anima* (1)

Cyprian, *Ad Quirinum testimonia* (2)

Cyprianus Gallus, *Pentateuchos* (1)

Gregory the Great, *Moralia in Job* (4)

Hrabanus Maurus, *In epistolas Pauli* (1), *In Hester* (1), *In Judith* (1), *In Matthaeum* (1)

Isidore of Seville, *Quaestiones in Vetus Testamentum* (3)

Jerome, *Altercatio Luciferani et Orthodoxi* (1), *In Danielem* (1), *In Ecclesiasten* (2), *In Evangelium Matthaei* (2), *In epistolas Pauli* (1), *Tractatus in Psalmos* (2)

Pseudo-Jerome, *Breviarium in Psalmos* (3)

Johannes Chrysostomus, excerpts from *De muliere Cananaea* (1), *De reparatione lapsi* (1), *De compunctione cordis* (1)

Johannes Constantinopolitanus, excerpts (1)

Laidcenn, *Egloga de Moralibus in Job* (1)

Paschasius Radbertus, *De corpore et sanguine Domini* (1)

Paterius, *De expositione Veteris et Novi Testamenti* (1)

Pelagius, *In epistolam Pauli ad Philippenses* (1)

Philippus Presbyter, *Commentarii in librum Job* (3)

Primasius, *In Apocalypsin* (1)

Theodore of Mopsuestia, *Commentarii in epistolas Pauli* (1)

5.2 Liturgy: London, Lambeth Palace Library MS 149, fol. 10r.

Bede's *In Apocalypsin* in a tenth-century manuscript with the Latin text in insular script.

France and can be assumed to have been in England by the tenth century because of additions made to the manuscript at that time. Neither manuscript, however, seems to have been copied; if they were, no copies survive. Barlow 35 is the only pre-Conquest manuscript containing Alcuin's *Interrogationes Sigewulfi*, and Rouen, BM 26 is the only pre-Conquest manuscript with Alcuin's *In canticum canticorum*. As far as the manuscript evidence shows, the Anglo-Saxons did not favour the exegetical and theological works of their compatriots over those of Continental scholars.

Some manuscripts such as Boulogne, Bibliothèque Municipale 32 contain several works by one author; others contain works by several authors. Thus, London, Lambeth Palace Library 149, fols 1–139 contains both Bede's *In Apocalypsin* (Fig. 5.2) and Augustine's *De adulterinis coniugiis*; Oxford, Bodleian Library, Bodley 516 (s. x, in England by s. xi in) contains Augustine's *De videndo Deo*, Cassiodorus's *De anima*, and excerpts from Augustine, from Johannes Chrysostomus's *De muliere Cananaea*, and from Johannes Constantinopolitanus; Cambridge, Trinity College B.4.27 (s. x ex) contains Isidore's *Quaestiones in Vetus Testamentum*, Adalbert of Metz's *Speculum Gregorii*, and Augustine's *In epistolam Johannis ad Parthos*. Most of these manuscripts are surprisingly uniform in their contents, mostly containing only theological and exegetical works. There are exceptions, such as Paris, Bibliothèque Sainte-Geneviève 2410 (s. x ex or xi in), which has an incomplete anonymous commentary on the Gospel of St Matthew next to Juvencus's *Libri Evangeliorum*, Israel the Grammarian's *De arte metrica*, Sedulius's *Carmen paschale* and other works, or Rouen, BM 26 which contains excerpts from Alcuin's commentary on the *Canticum canticorum* next to – among other items – a selection from Isidore's *Etymologiae*, computistical, astronomical, and other scientific treatises, Mass prayers, and Office antiphons and responsories. The mix of materials in these manuscripts demonstrates that exegetical material could be studied in conjunction with classroom material, and that texts for the Mass and the Daily Office were not as carefully separated as my division of them may suggest.

Daily Office

The antiphons and responsories, as contained in Rouen, BM 26, form a relatively small part of the daily round of prayers monks undertook at the canonical hours (matins, lauds, prime, terce, sext, nones, vespers, and compline). The larger part of the Daily Office was occupied by psalms, hymns, canticles, lessons, and collects. A manuscript containing all the texts of the Daily Office would be called a breviary, but despite the name it would have been anything but 'brief'. As Mass texts are spread out over sacramentaries, graduals, and lectionaries, so breviary texts are usually distributed over several categories of manuscripts such as psalters, hymnals, antiphonaries, or collectars, though most non-fragmentary manuscripts contain two or sometimes more of these texts. London, BL, Additional 37517 (s. x/xi), for instance, contains a psalter, a hymnal, a litany and prayers, and London, BL, Arundel 155, fols 1–135 and 171–91 (1012 × 1023) a psalter, canticles and prayers. A few Anglo-Saxon breviaries survive;[40] the earliest of these, unfortunately both fragmentary, date to the end of the tenth or the beginning of the eleventh century: London, BL, Royal 17 C. xvii, fols 2, 3, and 163–6 and London, BL, Additional 56488, fols i–iii, and 1–5. The manuscript most inclusive of all the Office texts, the so-called 'Portiforium of St Wulstan', CCCC 391 (s. xi$^{3/4}$),[41] contains a psalter, a hymnal, monastic canticles, a collectar with Office chants plus other texts not pertaining to the Office, but despite its possible association with an Anglo-Saxon saint, the manuscript is dated post-Conquest. It is doubtful whether Anglo-Saxons ever collected all the texts of the Office between two covers.

Many psalters[42] contain additional material of the Office, such as canticles, collects, responsories, and litanies. Monks were supposed to memorize all the one hundred and fifty psalms, a reason why the psalms were collected in manuscripts separate from other biblical material and were often glossed in Old English. Likewise, monks had to memorize the hundred or so hymns that formed part of the daily Office. Six extant pre-Conquest hymnals[43] survive complete, all bound with other material such as calendars, psalters, canticles,

---

[40] On breviaries, see also Gneuss, 'Liturgical books', pp. 110–12.
[41] Published by Anselm Hughes, ed., *The Portiforium of St Wulstan*, Henry Bradshaw Society 89 and 90, Leighton Buzzard, Faith Press, 1958 and 1960.
[42] Discussed above with manuscripts containing biblical material, pp. 116–17.
[43] On hymnals, see also Gneuss, 'Liturgical books', pp. 118–19.

litanies, and even sermons. In contrast Ripon, Cathedral Library, MS frag. 2 (s. xi), survives only as binding strips of a printed book. Gneuss lists one very early manuscript, London, BL, Cotton Vespasian A. i (s. viii$^{2/4}$), as containing extracts from a hymnal, but it only contains three hymns. Except for this manuscript, all surviving hymnals are later. Rome, Vatican City, Biblioteca Apostolica Vaticana, Reg. lat. 338, fols 64–126 (s. x^2), which was written in Northern France or Germany, seems to have come to England by the beginning of the eleventh century, but the surviving Anglo-Saxon hymnals cannot derive from it since at least one, London, BL, Additional 37517 (s. x$^{3/4}$) was written before the Rome manuscript's arrival in England.

While several psalters are glossed in Old English, only one hymnal, Durham, Cathedral Library B.III.32 (s. xi$^{2/4}$) is so glossed. The special attention given to hymns, however, becomes apparent in a manuscript such as London, BL, Cotton Vespasian D. xii (s. xi med) which contains both a hymnal and an *expositio hymnorum*, a prose paraphrase of the hymns, added to help the monks comprehend the poetry. London, BL, Cotton Julius A. vi does not contain a hymnal but has an *expositio hymnorum*, bound with the monastic canticles as well as (in separate booklets) a metrical calendar, a *computus*, and various poems. Aids such as Old English glosses and the *expositio* were intended to promote the thorough understanding of hymns expected of monks.

Smaller parts of the Daily Office, other such as collects, antiphons, and canticles are also represented in manuscripts. Antiphonaries, manuscripts or sections of manuscripts with collections of antiphons, contain all those songs omitted from the breviary because they are sung by the choir, not intoned by the celebrant. Gneuss lists four pre-Conquest antiphonaries, all fragmentary and dating from the eleventh century, the earliest apparently London, BL, Burney 277, fols 69–72 (s. xi in or xi^1) or possibly Oxford, Bodleian Library, Selden supra 36* (s. xi^1) as well its *membra disiecta*. The manuscript evidence suggests that Anglo-Saxons used antiphonaries only from the beginning of the eleventh century.[44]

Canticles, also part of the breviary, never fill an entire manuscript. The canticle of the three children in the fiery furnace (Daniel 3:57 ff.) formed part of the Sunday Office, Moses's canticle (Exodus 15:1 ff.) formed part of the Thursday Office.[45] Canticles typically appear in psalters, but at least one fragment exists which contains only canticles: this is Cambridge, St John's

---

[44] For antiphonaries, see also Gneuss, 'Liturgical books', pp. 116–18.
[45] Bede wrote an exegesis of the song of Habacuc, which formed part of the Friday Office. Bede, 'In Canticum Habacuc' in J.E. Hudson, ed., *Bedae Venerabilis Opera, Pars I: Opera Exegetica*, Corpus christianorum. Series Latina 119B, Turnhout, Brepols, 1983, pp. 381–409.

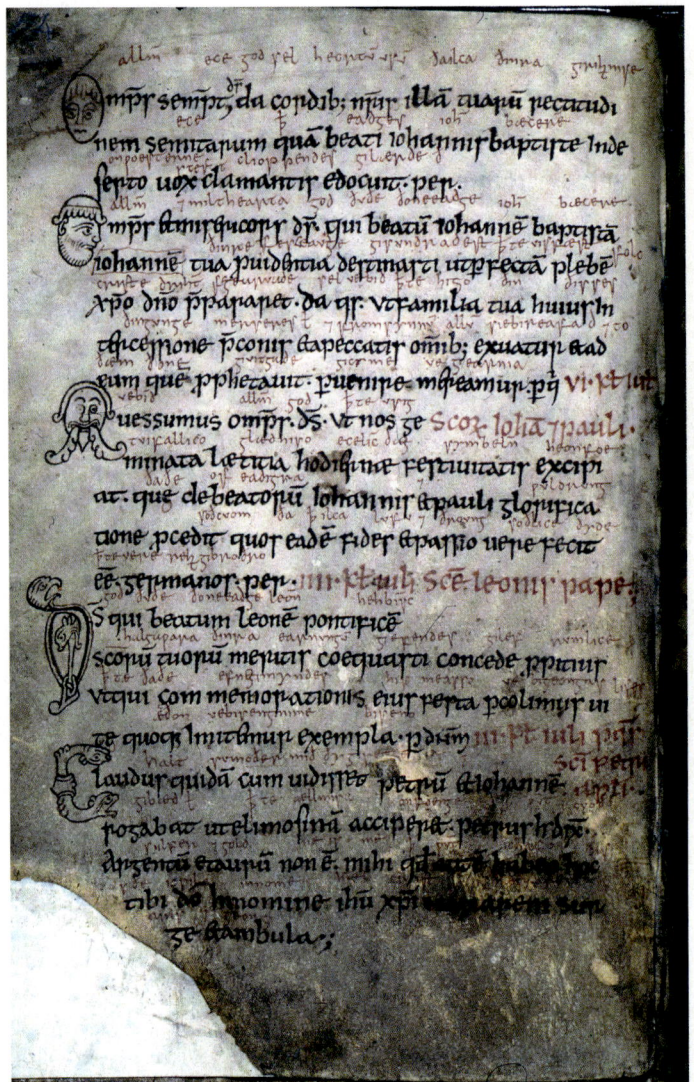

5.3 Liturgy: Durham, Cathedral Library MS A.IV.19, fol. 27v.

Even liturgical manuscripts, such as this ninth/tenth century collectar, were not devoid of humour. Both the Latin text and the Old English glosses are written in insular script.

RIGHT

5.4 London, British Library, MS Additional 37517 fol. 2r.

A tenth/eleventh-century Calendar, here for the months January to April.

College 82, fols 89–92 (s. x); even this probably belonged with a psalter originally.[46]

The collectar, again part of the breviary, is represented by three pre-Conquest examples.[47] Canterbury, Cathedral Library and Archives, Add. 172, fol. 189 (s. xi med), is fragmentary; Durham, Cathedral Library A.IV.19

[46] Psalters without canticles usually are either incomplete or fragmentary.
[47] On collectars, see also Gneuss, 'Liturgical books', pp. 112–13. Litanies will not be discussed here; see Michael Lapidge, *Anglo-Saxon Litanies of the Saints*, Henry Bradshaw Society 106, Woodbridge, Boydell, 1991.

Thomas Cantuarien

IANUARIUS

IANUARIUS SANCIT TROPICUS CAPRICORNUS
HABET DIES .XXXI. LUNA .XXX.

A			IAN.	Circumcisio dni nri ihu xpi
B	IIII	N		Sci isidori epi. Finit embolismus
C	III	N		Scae genouefe uirg
D	II	N		
E	NON			Sci simeonis monachi
F	VIII	ID		Epiphania dni nri
G	VII	ID		
H	VI	ID		Scoru luciani & iuliani
B	V	ID		Sci adriani abb. & sci furseuani
C	IIII	ID		Sci pauli primi heremite
D	III	ID		Depos sci benedicti abb
E	II	ID		Octauas epiphanie
IDUS				Sci felicis in pincis
G	XIX	kl	FEB	
A	XVIII	kl		Sci marcelli pape. & sci fursei prbi
B	XVII	kl		Sci antonii monachi
C	XVI	kl		Sci petri cathedr. Sol in aquario. Sci prisce uirg
D	XV	kl		
E	XIIII	kl		Scoru sebastiani & fabiani mart
F	XIII	kl		Passio scae agnetis uirg
G	XII	kl		Sci uincentii mar
A	XI	kl		
B	X	kl		Sci babille epi. & trium puerorum
C	IX	kl		Conuersio sci pauli apli
D	VIII	kl		
E	VII	kl		Octauas scae agnetis
F	VI	kl		Sci gilde sapientis
G	V	kl		Scae baltaldis reginae
A	IIII	kl		

Nox habet horas .xvi. Dies uero .viii.

FEBRUARIUS

HUME IN MEDIO SOLI DISTAT SIDUS AQUARII
FEBRUARIUS HABET DIES .XXVIII. LUNAM .XXIX.

			FEB	Scae brigidae uirg
	IIII	N		Yppapanti dni. & sci laurentii archiepi
	III	N		Scae paepburge uirg
	II	N		
	NON			Scae agathae uirg
	VIII	ID		
	VII	ID		Uerni initium habet dies .xci.
	VI	ID		Ante istud locum non potest esse .xl. ma.
	V	ID		
	IIII	ID		S. scae scolasticae uir. & scae maeppirne
	III	ID		
	II	ID		Sci eulaliae uirg
	IDUS			Scae eormenhilde uirg
	XVI	kl	MAR	Scoru ualentini & uitalis
	XV	kl		Diabolus abno recessit. Sol in piscibus
	XIIII	kl		Scae iulianae uirg
	XIII	kl		
	XII	kl		
	XI	kl		
	X	kl		Sci didimi. & gagi
	IX	kl		
	VIII	kl		Cathedra sci petri apli in antiochia
	VII	kl		Scae mildburgae uirg
	VI	kl		Sci mathie apli
	V	kl		
	IIII	kl		
	III	kl		

Nox habet horas .xiiii. Dies uero .x.

memento qd anno bissextili lunae februarii .xxx. dies computes
et tamen luna martii .xxx. dies habeat sicut semper habet
sed paschalis lunae ratio uacillet.

MARTIUS

HABET DIES .XXXI. LUNAM .XXX.

A	VI	kl		Deposi sci ceadde epi
C	V	kl		Scoru decem mar
D	IIII	kl		Sci ambrosii
E	III	kl		
F	II	kl		
NON				Scae perpetuae & felicitatis
H	VIII	ID		
I	VII	ID		Passio scorum .xl. mar
K	VI	ID		
L	V	ID		
M	IIII	ID		Depos beati gregorii pape
N	III	ID		
O	II	ID		Sci leonis papae
IDUS				
Q	XVII	kl	APR	Scae eugeniae uirg
R	XVI	kl		
S	XV	kl		Ramus dies equal
T	XIIII	kl		
V	XIII	kl		Sci cuthberti presulis
X	XII	kl		Sci benedicti abbatis
Y	XI	kl		Sedes epactarum
Z	X	kl		Concurrentes
	IX	kl		Adnuntiatio scae mariae uirginis
	VIII	kl		
	VII	kl		Resurrectio dni prima
	VI	kl		
	V	kl		Ordinatio sci gregorii pape
	IIII	kl		Sci dominini
	III	kl		

Nox habet horas .xii. Dies uero .xii.

APRILIS

APRELIS ARIES TRINES KALENDAS
HABET DIES .XXX. LUNAM .XXIX.

			APR	
	IIII	N		Sci ualerici confes
	III	N		Scae theodosiae uirg
	II	N		Sci ambrosii
	NON			
	VIII	ID		
	VII	ID		
	VI	ID		Scoru succesi & solutoris
	V	ID		
	IIII	ID		
	III	ID		Sci cuthlaci anachoritae
	II	ID		
	IDUS			Scae eufemiae uirg
	XVIII	kl	MAI	Scoru tiburtii ualeriani & maximi
	XVII	kl		
	XVI	kl		Sci felicis. luciani
	XV	kl		
	XIIII	kl		
	XIII	kl		Sci gagi. & rufi
	XII	kl		Scoru marcelli. petri
	XI	kl		
	X	kl		Sci leonis epi
	IX	kl		Sci georgii mar
	VIII	kl		Sci melliti archiepi anglorum
	VII	kl		Sci marci euangeli. Letania maior
	VI	kl		Sci germani
	V	kl		Sci uitalis mar
	IIII	kl		Egressio noe de arca
	III	kl		

Nox habet horas .x. Dies uero .xiiii.

Arundel *Lumley*

(s. ix/x) and London, BL, Cotton Titus D. xxvi and xxvii, are bound with a multitude of texts. The Durham manuscript is the earliest example of a collectar. Its scribe's sense of humour is evident from some initials (Fig. 5.3).

So-called 'calendars' appear in many liturgical manuscripts, providing the feast days of saints as well as fixed feast days in chronological order, such as Epiphany on 6 January, the Purification of Mary on 2 February and St Benedict on 21 March. Through red letters, capitals, and/or lower case letters, calendars establish a hierarchy among the feast days and thus provide guidance whether a saint's day should be celebrated rather than a Sunday in ordinary time or whether the Sunday's Mass should be read instead of the saint's. Calendars appear in twenty-five pre-Conquest manuscripts, an indication of their importance. Unless fragmentary, calendars often appear in liturgical manuscripts, both those used for the Office, as in London, BL, Additional 37517 (s. x/xi; Fig. 5.4), and those used for the Mass such as in Oxford, Bodleian Library, Bodley 579 (979 × 987), which in part is a sacramentary. The earliest calendar survives in Paris, BN, lat. 10837, fols 34–41 and 44 (s. viii in), which has a Continental provenance.

Manuscripts containing monastic rules and related texts

Monastic rules, and commentaries on them, would not be read in church but in the chapter house or refectory. Pre-eminent among them is the *Rule* of St Benedict of Nursia, composed *c*.540, which helped shape early Anglo-Saxon monasticism and became the exclusive rule for Anglo-Saxon monasteries during the Benedictine Reform which began under Saints Dunstan, Æthelwold and Oswald around the middle of the tenth century. Every monastery would have possessed a copy of Benedict's *Rule*, and one might therefore expect large numbers to survive. There are in fact ten pre-Conquest manuscripts. Only one is early: Oxford, Bodleian Library, Hatton 48, is late seventh- or early eighth-century. The other nine were written between the late tenth and the mid-eleventh centuries, all slightly later than the heyday of the Benedictine Reform, formalized at the Synod of Winchester in the early 970s.[48]

That tenth- and eleventh-century Anglo-Saxons had great interest in the Benedictine Rule becomes apparent from the existence of an Old English interlinear gloss (London, BL, Cotton Tiberius A. iii; s. xi med) and several translations. CCCC 178 (s. xi^1), London, BL, Cotton Titus A. iv (s. xi med), Oxford, CCC 197 (s. x $^{4/4}$; Fig. 5.5), and the fragmentary Wells Cathedral

---

[48] On manuscripts containing the *Benedictine Rule*, see Gneuss, 'Liturgical books', pp. 129–31 and Mechthild Gretsch, *Die Regula Sancti Benedicti in England*, Texte und Untersuchungen zur Englischen Philologie 2, Munich, Wilhelm Fink, 1973, pp. 18–48.

5.5 Oxford, Corpus Christi College MS 197, fol. 28v.

This late tenth-century copy of the *Benedictine Rule* has alternate Latin and Old English texts, and a change in script from Caroline to insular. The Old English is in the middle of the page.

Library 7 (s. xi med) all contain the *Rule* in both Latin and Old English, not, as one might expect, as separate texts, but with each Latin chapter followed by an Old English version, an interweaving technique designed to ensure comprehension of the Latin by English monks.

In five of its ten manuscripts[49] the *Benedictine Rule* is the only text.

---

[49] Oxford, Hatton 48; CCCC 178; CCCC 368; Oxford, CCC 197; as well as the fragmentary Wells Cathedral Lib. 7.

In five it is bound with other texts. Both the *Memoriale qualiter* and the *Capitulare monasticum* seem to have been considered especially appropriate to accompany the *Rule*, appearing in four manuscripts.[50] The *Memoriale qualiter*, composed in the eighth century, constitutes a supplement to the *Rule*; the *Capitulare monasticum* records a synod held in 818/819 at Aachen (Aix-la-Chapelle) regulating monastic life on the Continent. In Anglo-Saxon England the *Capitulare* appears only in company with the *Rule*. The *Memoriale qualiter* survives in one other manuscript (Rouen, BM 1385), but its appearance with the *Rule* in four manuscripts shows the closeness of its association.

The *Regularis Concordia*, which attempted to create a uniform observance of the *Benedictine Rule* in late Anglo-Saxon England, is the most important text of the Benedictine Reform, so might be expected to survive in multiple copies and to be bound with the *Rule*. However, the complete text of the *Regularis Concordia* is extant in only two manuscripts; in BL, Cotton Tiberius A. iii, fols 2–173, it does indeed accompany the *Rule*, but in London, BL, Cotton Faustina B. iii, fols 158–9 plus *membrum disiectum* (s. xi med), it does not, being bound with some formula letters and of a list of Roman emperors. Excerpts from the *Regularis Concordia* appear in two additional manuscripts: CCCC 190, pp. iii–xii and 1–294 (s. xi^1), with letters, sermons, a penitential, Wulfstan's Canon Law Collection and other texts; and Rouen, BM 1382 (s. xi^1), with Wulfstan's Canon Law Collection, a sermon, and excerpts from several other texts.

Nor is Smaragdus's *Expositio in Regulam S. Benedicti* bound with the *Rule* in any extant Anglo-Saxon manuscripts. It survives in two, Cambridge, University Library Ee.2.4 plus *membrum disiectum* (s. x med) and Paris, BN, lat. 4210 (s. x/xi), both without any accompanying text. Smaragdus wrote another work concerned with monasticism, the *Diadema monachorum*, in which he reflects on monastic rules and praises the virtues attained by following them. This work is extant in two pre-Conquest manuscripts: in Cambridge, University Library Ff.4.43 (s. x$^{4/4}$), it is the sole text; in the above-mentioned CCCC 57, however, it accompanies the *Benedictine Rule* as well as the *Memoriale qualiter* and the *Capitulare monasticum*. Smaragdus himself suggested that just as a section of the *Benedictine Rule* was read at chapter every morning, so a section of his booklet should be read at chapter every evening.[51] The difference in the numbers of extant manuscripts for

---

[50] CCCC 57 (s. x/xi); BL, Cotton Tiberius A. iii, fols 2–173 (s. xi med); Cotton Titus A. iv (s. xi med); and BL, Harley 5431, fols 4–126 (s x/xi).

[51] J.-P. Migne, ed., *Smaragdi Abbatis Diadema Monachorum*, Patrologia Latina 102, Paris, 1851, reprinted Turnhout, Brepols, 1997, cc. 593–690 at c. 593: *Et quia mos est monachorum, ut regulam beati Benedicti ad capitulum legant quotidie matutinum: volumus ut iste libellus ad eorum capitulum quotidie legatur vespertinum.*

the *Benedictine Rule* and the *Diadema monachorum* and the late date for the earliest copy of the *Diadema* suggest the Anglo-Saxons started to follow Smaragdus's recommendation only after the Benedictine Reform and even then not in all monasteries.

The *Benedictine Rule* served, at least in part, as model for other rules as well such as Chrodegang of Metz's *Regula Canonicorum*, written for the canons of a cathedral. Only one pre-Conquest manuscript containing the Latin *Regula Canonicorum* survives (Brussels, Bibliothèque Royale 8558–63, fols 1–79; s. x[1]). Its translation into Old English (see Fig. 6.20), however, indicates a greater interest in this text than the manuscript evidence suggests.

Just as Chrodegang used Benedict's *Rule* as a model, so Benedict himself was aware of antecedents, among them Cassian's *De institutis monachorum* and the *Collationes*. Benedict was so enthusiastic about the latter that he mentioned them in his *Rule*,[52] but lack of manuscript evidence leaves considerable doubt that Anglo-Saxon monks shared Benedict's appreciation: only one extant pre-Conquest manuscript contains excerpts from the *Collationes*: London, Lambeth Palace Library 414, fols 1–80 (s. ix[1]). It is uncertain whether this manuscript, written at Saint-Amand, arrived in England before 1100. Evidence is clearer regarding the *De institutis monachorum*: two pre-Conquest manuscripts survive, both from the second half of the tenth century: Cambridge, St. John's College 101, fols 1–14 (book xii of the *De institutis*) and Oxford, Bodleian Library, Auctarium D infra 2.9, fols 1–110 (s. x[2]). Both written at Canterbury, they were almost certainly copied and used by Anglo-Saxons.

Historical manuscripts

Two periods for reading were set aside for monks in both winter and summer schedules according to the *Regularis Concordia*, though what should be read was not fully stipulated.[53] Along with exegetical or hagiographical texts, and texts conducive to meditation, historical texts may also have contributed to this private reading, especially since 'history' in the Anglo-Saxon period included salvation history: Bede's *Ecclesiastical History* and

---

[52] John Chamberlin, ed., *The Rule of St. Benedict: the Abingdon copy edited from Cambridge, Corpus Christi College Ms. 57*, Toronto Medieval Latin Texts 13, Toronto, Pontifical Institute of Medieval Studies, 1982, chapter 73, pp. 72–3: *Necnon et Conlationes patrum et Instituta uitae eorum, sed et Regula sancti patris nostri Basilii, quid aliud sunt nisi bene uiuentium et oboedientium monachorum instrumenta uirtutum.*

[53] See Thomas Symons, ed. and transl., *Regularis Concordia Anglicae Nationis Monachorum Sanctimonialiumque: The Monastic Agreement of the Monks and Nuns of the English Nation*, London, Thomas Nelson and Sons, 1953, pp. xliii and xliv.

Gregory of Tours's *History of the Franks* did not hesitate to mix genres now distinguished as 'hagiography' and 'history'.[54] Bede's *Ecclesiastical History* was apparently the most popular since the Latin text occurs in twenty manuscripts.[55] Several contain only selections: Oxford, Bodleian Library, Digby 39, fols 50–6 (s. xi²), for instance, contains only the section referring to St Birinus; Paris, BN, lat. 5362, fols 1–84 (s. xi/xii) excerpts relating to the lives of Saints Cuthbert, Oswald, Birinus and Æthelthryth. Several manuscripts are fragmentary, including very early ones such as Münster in Westfalen, Universitätsbibliothek Fragmentenkapsel 1 no. 3 (s. viii²) and New Haven, Yale University, Beinecke Library M 826 (s. viii ex), and later ones such as CCCC 270, fols 1 and 197 (s. ix ex). Ten manuscripts, ranging from eighth- to eleventh-century, contain the entire work, all but one written during the Anglo-Saxon period, and in every century of it.[56] Because of its length, the *Ecclesiastical History* is rarely bound with other texts. When it is, as in Winchester, Cathedral Library 1, these are brief: Æthelwulf's *De abbatibus*, excerpts from Jerome and Orosius's 'de situ Babylonis'.

World history was accessible in Orosius's *Historiae aduersus paganos*. Oxford, Bodleian Library, Bodley 163 (s. xi in), contains excerpts from it as well as Bede's *Ecclesiastical History*. The complete text is extant in the fragment Exeter, Cathedral, Dean and Chapter Library FMS/1,2,2a (s. x¹) and Düsseldorf, Nordrhein-Westfälisches Hauptstaatsarchiv Z11/1 (s. viii²), also fragmentary. Though both manuscripts fall solidly in the Anglo-Saxon period neither could have served as exemplars for the Alfredian translation:[57] Exeter post-dates the translation by several decades, interestingly showing there was still demand for the Latin text; Düsseldorf was probably already on the Continent by the time Orosius was translated into Old English.

Anglo-Saxon history is represented by two texts: Æthelweard's *Chronicon*, a translation of the *Anglo-Saxon Chronicle* into Latin, survives in a single manuscript, London, BL, Cotton Otho A. x plus *membrum disiectum* (s. xi in). The lack of more copies can be explained by the fact that the Latin text

---

[54] I interpret 'history' in its medieval rather than its modern sense.

[55] Bede's *Ecclesiastical History* was, of course, translated into Old English as part of Alfred's educational programme; six manuscripts containing the Old English version survive.

[56] Cambridge, University Library Kk.5.16 (c. or after 737); Cambridge, Trinity College R.7.5 (s. xi in); Durham, Cathedral Library B.II.35, fols 38–118 (s. xi ex, and so post-Conquest); London, BL, Cotton Tiberius A. xiv (s. viii med); London, BL, Cotton Tiberius C. ii (s. ix²/⁴); London, BL, Royal 13 C. v (s. x/xi); Oxford, Bodleian Library, Bodley 163, fols 1–227 and 250–1 (s. xi in); Oxford, Bodleian Library, Hatton 43 (s. xi in); Winchester, Cathedral Library 1 plus *membrum disiectum* (s. x/xi); and St Petersburg, Russian National Library Q.v.I.18 (731 × 746).

[57] The Old English translation survives in four manuscripts.

was produced for abbess Mathilda of Essen. Native Anglo-Saxons interested in their history had the *Chronicle* in their own language. The *Encomium Emmae reginae*, produced for Ælfgifu/Emma, queen to Æthelbert and Cnut, is preserved in a single manuscript, London, BL, Additional 33241 (s. xi med). It was written in Flanders, and may not have arrived in England before 1100, so, although an important historical source today, only a very restricted number of Anglo-Saxons could have known it.

Other histories in pre-Conquest manuscripts are Gildas's *De excidio Britanniae*, Gregory of Tours's *Historia Francorum*, Josephus Flavius's *De bello Judaico*, Justinus's epitome of Pompeius Trogus's *Historiae Philippicae*, Rufinus's *Historia monachorum*, and Abbo of Saint-Germain's *Bella Parisiacae urbis*, though some of these may not have remained in England long. London, BL, Cotton Vitellius A. vi (s. x med), which contains Gildas's *De excidio Britanniae*, was written in England and remained there; as did the fragmentary London, BL, Harley 5915, fol. 10 plus *membrum disiectum* (s. viii med), which contains Justinus's epitome of Pompeius Trogus's *Historiae Philippicae*, and Vatican City, Biblioteca Apostolica Vaticana Reg. lat. 489, fols 61–124 (s. xi^1), which contains excerpts from Gregory of Tours's *Historia Francorum*. Other historical manuscripts were more mobile. Avranches, BM 29 (s. x/xi) was penned in Anglo-Saxon England, but moved to Mont-Saint-Michel during the eleventh century. It contains excerpts from Gregory of Tours's *Historia Francorum*. Kassel, Gesamthochschulbibliothek 2°Ms.theol.65 (s. vi), which contains Josephus's *De bello Judaico*, the oldest manuscript preserving historical material, was imported to England from Italy in the eighth century and exported to Germany the same century, presumably by Anglo-Saxon missionaries. Worcester, Cathedral Library F.48 (s. xi^1), which contains Rufinus of Aquileia's *Historia monachorum*, was written on the Continent, and may have arrived in England before the Norman invasion.

Abbo of Saint-Germain-de-Prés's *Bella Parisiacae urbis* is a historical text – it concerns the Vikings' attack on Paris in 885 and 886 – but composed in an obscure and scholarly style of poetry identified today as 'hermeneutic'. The manuscript contexts in which Abbo's poem appears imply the Anglo-Saxons were more interested in the poetic diction than its historical content. Four pre-Conquest manuscripts contain book iii of the *Bella*: Cambridge, University Library Gg.5.35 (s. xi med); CCCC 326 (s. x/xi); London, BL, Harley 3271 (which has both prose and verse versions; s. xi^1); and London, BL, Harley 3826 (s. x/xi). In all of them, Abbo's *Bella* appears with other poetic texts or grammatical treatises. In BL, Harley 3826, for instance, the text is preceded by Bede's *De orthographia* and followed by Martianus Capella's *De nuptiis Philologiae et Mercurii*; and in BL, Harley 3271, the *Bella* is bound with grammatical notes, Ælfric's *Grammar*, and glossary material.

Classroom manuscripts: *trivium*

Grammars, glossaries, colloquies, treatises on orthography, on dialectic, on etymology, and on metrics, and poetic texts – by classical, early Christian, Carolingian and Anglo-Latin authors – were studied in the Anglo-Saxon classroom as part of the *trivium*, as well as hymns and psalms. The extent of surviving texts on grammar indicates the importance of this subject. Thirteen extant manuscripts contain the *Grammar* of abbot and homilist Ælfric (*c*.955–*c*.1020), nine of them from the first half of the eleventh century, and four from the post-Conquest period, an indication that his text continued to be valued even after the Norman invasion. Since Latin grammar was studied in every monastery, it is safe to assume that Ælfric's *Grammar* found wide distribution throughout Anglo-Saxon England. Five of the pre-Conquest manuscripts are complete.[58] They often pair Ælfric's *Grammar* with his *Glossary* (as in BL, Cotton Julius A. ii, Harley 107 and Oxford, St John's College 154) and two also contain Abbo's *Bella Parisiacae urbis* (BL, Harley 3271 and Oxford, St John's College 154), discussed above.

Before Ælfric, the standard grammars throughout the early Middle Ages had been those of Donatus and Priscian. Manuscript evidence shows their works were known among the Anglo-Saxons, but suggests either that they did not achieve the popularity of Ælfric's *Grammar*, or that they were largely supplanted by it. Only two manuscripts containing Donatus's *Ars maior* survive, namely London, BL, Cotton Cleopatra A. vi, fols 2–53 (s. x med) and Geneva, Bibliotheca Bodmeriana 175 (s. x^2), of which the London manuscript contains the complete text and the Geneva excerpts. Commentaries on Donatus appear in St Paul (Carinthia, Austria), Stiftsbibliothek 2^1 (25.2.16) (s. viii^1) and Antwerp, Plantin-Moretus Museum M.16.2 plus *membrum disiectum* (s. xi^1).

Priscian wrote the *Institutiones grammaticae* and an abridged version, the *Institutio de nomine, pronomine et uerbo*. His *Institutiones* were also extracted in the anonymous *Excerptiones de Prisciano*, one of the sources for Ælfric's *Grammar*. The *Excerptiones* is preserved in Antwerp, Plantin-Moretus M.16.2, which also contains a commentary on Donatus, and in Paris, BN, nouv. acq. lat. 586, fols 16–131 (s. x/xi). Priscian's *Institutiones grammaticae* survive in

---

[58] Durham, Cathedral Library B.III.32 (s. xi med); London, BL, Cotton Julius A. ii, fols 10–135 (s. xi med); London, BL, Harley 107 (s. xi med); London, BL, Harley 3271 (s. xi^1); Oxford, St. John's College 154 (s. xi in). The following manuscripts containing Ælfric's *Grammar* are fragmentary: London, BL, Harley 5915, fols 8 and 9 plus *membrum disiectum* (s. xi^1); London, BL, Royal 12 G. xii, fols 2–9 plus *membrum disiectum* (s. xi med); Paris, BN, anglais 67 (s. xi^1). CCCC 449, fols 42–96 (s. xi^1), is incomplete.

two pre-Conquest manuscripts, Canterbury, Cathedral Library and Archives Add. 127/19 plus *membrum disiectum* (s. ix/x) and Columbia, University of Missouri, Ellis Library, Fragmenta manuscripta F.M.2 (s. ix). The manuscript evidence suggests Priscian's *Institutio de nomine, pronomine et uerbo* found the greatest echo among the Anglo-Saxons: five surviving manuscripts contain this work, ranging from the eighth to the end of the tenth century.[59] They thus suggest Priscian's grammar was more popular than Donatus's, and that both were replaced by Ælfric's at the beginning of the eleventh century. A few manuscripts contain other grammars: Boniface's *Ars grammatica*, Eutyches's *Ars de uerbo* and anonymous grammatical treatises.

Two Anglo-Saxon authors, Bede and Alcuin, wrote works entitled *De orthographia*; among their predecessors were Agroecius, Caper, and Cassiodorus. CCCC 221 contains the *De orthographia* by all five authors, the Bede and Alcuin texts on fols 1–24 (s. xi) which were definitely written in England. The second part of this manuscript, fols 25–64 (s. ix), which contains the *De orthographia* by the other three authors, was not originally bound with the earlier folios and may have been written on the Continent; fols 25–64 were clearly in England by the tenth century. Agroecius's, Caper's, and Cassiodorus's *De orthographia* survive only in this manuscript. Alcuin's *De orthographia* survives in two manuscripts, and Bede's in three, in two of which, CCCC 221, fols 1–24 and London, BL, Harley 3826 (s. x/xi), the Alcuin and Bede texts are adjacent.

De orthographia (regardless of author), concerns vocabulary and distinguishing between near-homographs and homophones. To appreciate how the vocabulary was built up we must turn to glossaries and Isidore of Seville's *Etymologiae*.[60] Latin–Latin glossaries survive in eleven pre-Conquest manuscripts, and Latin–Old English glossaries in fourteen, of which two fall in the post-Conquest period. The manuscripts containing Latin–Latin glossaries range from the eighth century[61] to the beginning of the eleventh.[62] The oldest Latin–Old English glossary survives in a manuscript of the late seventh century (Épinal, BM 72 (2) fols 94–107), the youngest from the late eleventh/early twelfth century (London, BL, Cotton Domitian i, fols 2–55 and Oxford, Bodleian Library, Auctarium F.2.14). Most glossaries are bound with

---

[59] London, BL, Cotton Domitian i, fols 2–55 (s. x med); Worcester, Cathedral Library Q.5 (s. x ex); Columbia, Ellis Library F.M.2 (s. ix); Karlsruhe, Badische Landesbibliothek, Fragm. Aug. 122 plus *membra disiecta* (s. viii ex); and St Petersburg, Russian National Library O.v.XIV.1, fols 1–16 (s. x in).

[60] Ælfric's glossary has already been discussed at p. 144.

[61] London, BL, Cotton Domitian ix, fol. 8 (s. viii²) and Berlin, Staatsbibliothek Preussischer Kulturbesitz Grimm 132,2 (s. viii med).

[62] London, BL, Harley 3271 (s. xi¹); Antwerp, Plantin-Moretus Museum M.16.2 (s. xi¹); and Brussels, Bibliothèque Royale 1828–30, fols 36–109 (s. xi in).

Table 4
Classical authors and works in Anglo-Saxon manuscripts.

Numerals in parentheses indicate the number of manuscripts.

The addition of an 'e' to the number of manuscripts means that only excerpts are preserved in Anglo-Saxon manuscripts.

Cicero, *Aratea* (4), *Philippicae* (1), *Somnium Scipionis* (1), *Topica* (1)

Horace, *Carmina* (1e)

Juvenal, *Satirae* (2), Glosses on the *Satirae* (1)

Martial, *Epigrammata* (1e)

Optantius Porphyrius, *Carmina* (2e)

Ovid, *Amores* (1e), *Ars amatoria* (2e), *Metamorphoseos* (1e)

Persius, *Satirae* (3), Commentary on the *Satirae* (2)

Pliny the Elder, *Naturalis historia* (4e)

Statius, *Thebais* (3)

Terence, *Comediae* (1)

Virgil, *Aeneid* (5), Servius's commentary *In Aeneida* (2), *Bucolica* (1), *Georgica* (3)

---

other texts, but five manuscripts contain only Latin–Old English glossaries: CCCC 144 (s. xi¹); London, BL, Cotton Cleopatra A. iii (s. x med); London, BL, Cotton Otho E. i (s. x/xi); London, BL, Harley 3376 + *membra disiecta* (s. x/xi); and Épinal, BM 72 (2), fols 94–107 (s. vii ex).

Isidore of Seville, unlike compilers of glossary lists, explains the meaning of most of his *lemmata*, and traces them back to their purported origins, one reason for the evident popularity of his work: three extant pre-Conquest Anglo-Saxon manuscripts contain Isidore's entire *Etymologiae*,[63] there are four fragments of what were presumably complete texts[64] and six pre-Conquest manuscripts preserving excerpts.[65]

The Latin and Old English glosses found in manuscripts of hymns and psalms, as well as such texts as the *Expositio hymnorum*, leave little doubt that these monastic and clerical texts were also used in the classroom.

It is generally assumed that the Anglo-Saxons had access to classical authors, but the manuscript evidence (Table 4) shows the list is not as extensive as one might expect.

---

[63] London, BL, Royal 6 C. i (s. xi med); Oxford, Queen's College 320 (s. x med); and Paris, BN, 7585 (s. ix²ᐟ⁴).

[64] They range in date from the end of the seventh/beginning of the eighth century (Longleat House, Wiltshire, Library of the Marquess of Bath NMR 10589, flyleaves) to the mid-ninth century (Cambridge, St John's College Ii.12.29, flyleaves).

[65] The shortest (only XI, 1–2) in Rouen, BM 26 (s. ix med), and the longest (V:33 to IX.7) in Cambridge, Trinity College B.15.33 (s. x in).

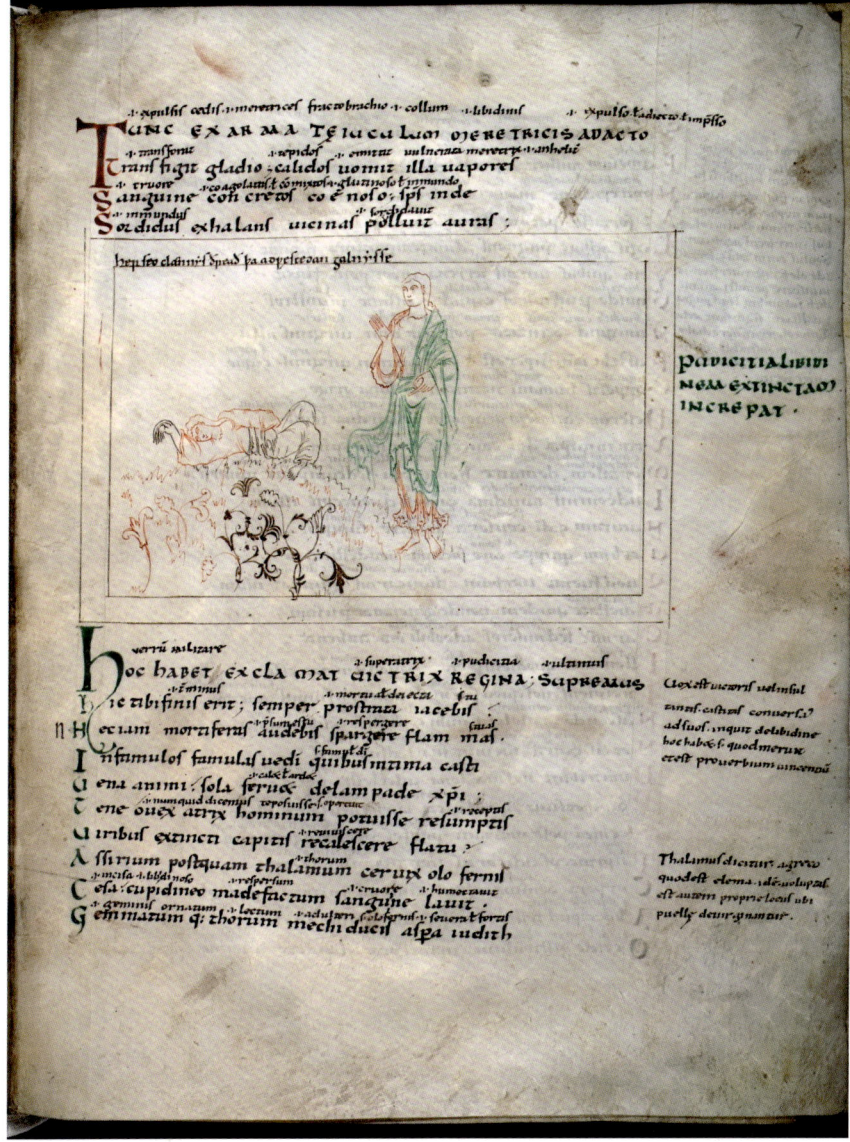

5.6 *Trivium*: Cambridge, Corpus Christi College MS 23, fol. 7r.

A late tenth-century copy of Prudentius's *Psychomachia* with an illustration (Chastity taunts Lechery) and Latin glosses.

Only twenty-five Anglo-Saxon manuscripts contain the works of classical authors,[66] several of them including more than one classical text. Vatican City, Biblioteca Apostolica Vaticana, Reg. Lat. 1671 (s. x/xi), for instance, contains Virgil's *Bucolica*, *Georgica* and *Aeneid*, interlinear glosses drawn from Servius's *In Aeneida* and a selection from Ovid's *Metamorphoses*.

---

[66] Cicero's *Aratea* is discussed in the survey of astronomical texts below (p. 154).

Cambridge, Trinity College O.4.10 (s. x[2/4]) contains Juvenal's *Satirae*, Persius's *Satirae*, and an epigram (I.xix) by Martial. In several instances manuscripts do not preserve entire texts, only excerpts. Ovid's *Ars amatoria*, for instance, survives in two manuscripts, namely Oxford, Auctarium F.4.32, fols 37–47 (s. ix/x) and Paris, Bibliothèque Sainte-Geneviève 2410 (s. x/xi), but the Paris manuscript contains only 2.279–80 and the Oxford manuscript only book 1 of the *Ars amatoria*.

Virgil's *Aeneid* was apparently read by the Anglo-Saxons, since Aldhelm, Bede, and Alcuin echo it in their works, but if this assumption is correct the total of five manuscripts or fragments is disappointingly low. The entire text survives only in the Vatican manuscript. Cambridge, University Library Gg.5.35 (s. xi med) contains only excerpts and the other manuscripts[67] are fragmentary, so it is not known how much text they originally contained.

However, the manuscript London, College of Arms, Arundel 30, fols 5–10 and 208 hints at a reason for the low number of survivals: the manuscript is a palimpsest and contains the *Aeneid* in its lower script. This shows at least one *Aeneid* manuscript was re-used. Perhaps, then, books containing the *Aeneid* were so heavily used that they eventually fell apart, which may account for the fragmentary state of three other manuscripts.

A relatively large number of pre-Conquest manuscripts contain the works of early Christian or late Antique authors (Table 5). Many are glossed, indicating they were used in the classroom.

Many manuscripts contain more than one early Christian or late Antique author. Of these, Cambridge, University Library Gg.5.35 (s. xi med), deserves to be singled out, since it contains just about all the important early Christian and late Antique authors studied in Anglo-Saxon and Continental schools: the *Disticha Catonis*, the works of Arator, Boethius, Juvencus, Lactantius, Prosper of Aquitaine, Sedulius, and Prudentius's *Dittochaeon*, *Psychomachia* plus an extract from his *Hamartigenia*. Only Prudentius has multiple works in Anglo-Saxon manuscripts. All, or almost all, of his writings are found in Cambridge, Corpus Christi College 223 (s. ix[3/4], in England by s. x[1]); Durham, Cathedral Library B.IV.9 (s. x med); Oxford, Bodleian Library, Auctarium F.3.6 (s. xi[1]); and Paris, BN, lat. 8085, fols 2–82 (s. ix med, in England by s. x/xi). Uniquely among school texts, Prudentius's *Psychomachia* is sometimes illustrated (Figs 5.6, 6.8).[68]

---

[67] London, BL, Royal 8 F. xiv, fols 3 and 4; London, College of Arms, Arundel 30, fols 5–10 and 208 (s. x[2/4]); and Oxford, Bodleian Library, Lat.class.c.2, fol. 18 plus *membra disiecta* (s. ix[2/3]).

[68] Cycles of drawings occur in four Anglo-Saxon manuscripts: Cambridge, Corpus Christi College MS 23 (s. x ex; Figs 5.6, 6.8 in this book); London, BL, Additional 24199 (s. x ex); London, BL, Cotton Cleopatra C viii (s. x/xi); and Munich,

Table 5
Early Christian and late Antique authors in Anglo-Saxon manuscripts.

Numerals in parentheses indicate the number of manuscripts.

Arator, *Historia apostolica* (6)

Boethius, *De consolatione philosophiae* (14)

Pseudo-Cato, *Disticha Catonis* (3)

Juvencus, *Libri Evangeliorum* (6)

Lactantius, *De ave phoenice* (2)

Martianus Capella, *De nuptiis Philologiae et Mercurii* (7)

Proba, *Cento Vergilianus* (1)

Prosper of Aquitaine, *Epigrammata* (5)

Prudentius, *Apotheosis* (4), *Cathemerinon* (6), *Contra Symmachum* (8), *Dittochaeon* (10), *Hamartigenia* (6), *Peristephanon* (8), *Psychomachia* (11)

Sedulius, *Carmen Paschale* (8)

Venantius Fortunatus, *Carmina* (4)

Boethius's *De consolatione philosophiae* appears most frequently, though not always complete: London, BL, Egerton 267, fol. 37 (s. x ex), for instance, is a fragment, and London, BL, Cotton Vespasian D. xiv, fols 170–224 (s. x in) contains only a few excerpts. CUL Gg.5.35, however, contains the full text of and glosses to the *De consolatione*, and in a different section, the so-called 'Cambridge Songs', excerpts from Boethius's metres. Manuscript evidence suggests the *De consolatione* was not studied in England before the end of the ninth century, roughly when Alfred had it translated. The oldest manuscript, Vatican City, Biblioteca Apostolica Vaticana, lat. 3363 (s. ix¹), written in the Loire region, possibly came to south west England by the end of the ninth century. Manuscripts written in England are all tenth- or eleventh-century, suggesting Alfred's translation did not arise from interest in the Latin original, but created it.

Traces of the oldest manuscript containing an early Christian author are found in Oxford, Bodleian Library, e Mus 66 (Fig. 1.5). Imprints of writing in the glue from pastedowns once inside both bookcovers testify that sheets from a late sixth- or early seventh-century manuscript containing sections from Arator's *Historia apostolica* were re-used when the book was bound, probably in the late twelfth century.

Martianus Capella's *De nuptiis* appears in seven different manuscripts, though only one, CCCC 153 (s. ix/x; in England by s. x¹), contains the entire

---

Bayerische Staatsbibliothek clm 29336(1 (s. xi in). There are two different versions of the illustrations.

text. The other manuscripts preserve only excerpts, book iv of the *De nuptiis* surviving in CCCC 206 (s. x[1]) and in London, BL, Harley 3826 (s. x/xi), and book viii in Cambridge, Trinity College R.15.32 (s. xi[1]) and London, BL, Harley 2506 (s. x/xi). Extracts were carefully selected: book iv, which deals with dialectics, appears with Alcuin's and Bede's *De orthographia* and glossaries; book viii, which deals with astronomy, alongside astronomical texts.

Among Anglo-Latin works included in the school curriculum[69] are the prose and verse of Aldhelm's *De virginitate*. The prose version survives in twelve manuscripts,[70] the verse in five. One early manuscript of the prose version survives (New Haven, Yale University, Beinecke Library 401 plus *membra disiecta*; s. viii/ix), and the others spread fairly evenly over the tenth and eleventh centuries; the poetic manuscripts range from the end of the ninth century to the mid-eleventh, the earliest, Oxford, Bodleian Library, Rawlinson C. 697 (s. ix[3/4]) being written in Northern France and arriving in England by the mid-tenth century. Six manuscripts preserve Aldhelm's riddles (*Aenigmata*), including two early ones apparently exported soon after being written. St Petersburg, Russian National Library Q.v.I.15 (s. viii[2]), written in south west England, was at Corbie by the end of the eighth century. Miskolc, Levay Jozsef Library s.n. (s. viii) was also written in southern England; its fragmentary nature does not provide much information as to its path to Hungary. The pattern of eighth-century English Aldhelm manuscripts ending up on the Continent, of ninth-century Continental manuscripts being imported to England, and of tenth- and eleventh-century manuscripts being written in England suggests that eighth- and ninth-century manuscripts of both the verse *De virginitate* and the *Aenigmata* became scarce in England and that Aldhelm's works needed to be re-imported from the Continent at the beginning of the tenth century. The number of surviving manuscripts and the amount of glossing in them (see pp. 167–8) testify to the heavy use of Aldhelm's writings.

CUL Gg.5.35, which preserves Aldhelm's poetic *De virginitate* and *Aenigmata*, also contains the riddles of Boniface, Eusebius (Hwætberht), and Tatwine. Boniface's riddles also appear in Aberystwyth, National Library of Wales 735C (s. xi[1]), a manuscript written in France and imported to England or Wales later in the eleventh century. Those of Eusebius and Tatwine are also in London, BL, Royal 12 C. xxiii (s. x[2] or x/xi), with both glosses and *scholia*, which reinforce the likelihood that the texts were used in the schoolroom.

---

[69] Exegetical, hagiographical and historical works by Anglo-Latin authors Bede and Alcuin (discussed here at pp. 131–3, 141–2, 148) may also have been read in school.

[70] Including one post-Conquest manuscript (London, BL, Royal 6 B. vii – s. xi ex).

Bede's *De die iudicii* also appears in contexts that suggest that it may have been read as part of the curriculum, occurring in CUL Gg.5.35; Cambridge, Trinity College O.2.31 (s. x/xi); London, BL, Additional 11034 (s. x); London, BL, Cotton Domitian i, fols 2–55 (s. x med); and Paris, BN, lat. 8092 (s. xi$^{2/4}$) with texts such as Arator's *Historia apostolica* (Paris and London Additional manuscripts), *Disticha Catonis* (Cambridge manuscripts), and Priscian's *Institutio de nomine, pronomine et verbo* (Cotton manuscript).

Carolingian authors seem to have contributed to the Anglo-Saxon curriculum primarily as commentators, chief among them Remigius of Auxerre who wrote commentaries on Boethius's *De consolatione philosophiae*, the *Disticha Catonis*, Martianus Capella's *De nuptiis*, Sedulius's *Carmen paschale*, and Donatus's *Ars minor*. Frequently, Remigius's material is added in margins or between the lines of the relevant text, but a few manuscripts preserve the commentaries separately: Cambridge, Gonville and Caius College 144/194 (s. x^1) contains Remigius's commentaries on Sedulius's *Carmen paschale*, on Sedulius's hymns, and on the *Disticha Catonis*; Salisbury, Cathedral Library 134 (s. x ex) his commentaries on the *Carmen paschale* and Sedulius's hymns; and London, BL, Royal 15 A. xxxiii (s. ix/x), which has a mid-tenth-century English provenance, preserves Remigius's commentary on Martianus Capella, correcting the impression given by surviving manuscripts of Martianus Capella's *De nuptiis*, that the Anglo-Saxons studied primarily books iv and viii rather than the whole text (see pp. 149–50).

Abbo of Saint-Germain's *Bella Parisiacae urbis* consistently appears in the company of texts that suggest inclusion in the Anglo-Saxon curriculum, especially in CUL Gg.5.35, a manuscript replete with school authors. Hrabanus Maurus's *De laudibus sanctae crucis*, which also appears in CUL Gg.5.35, might also have been used in the classroom, though its other manuscript contexts do not support this possibility: Cambridge, Trinity College B.16.3 (s. x med) does not contain any other school texts and accompanying texts in Rouen, BM 26 (s. x^2) indicate liturgical rather than pedagogical use.

Classroom manuscripts: *quadrivium*

According to Martianus Capella, the disciplines belonging to the *quadrivium* are arithmetic, geometry, music, and astronomy. *Computus*[71] is applied arithmetic concerning the calculations necessary to arrive at the correct date for Easter in any given year. Calculations for a larger number of years are presented as 'Easter Tables'. Easter is a pivotal date in the liturgical calendar

---

[71] See also p. 157.

5.7 *Quadrivium*: London, British Library, MS Cotton Tiberius B. v, fol. 34r.

An illustration of the constellation Perseus in an eleventh-century copy of Cicero's *Aratea*, an astronomical text.

since all Sundays after Easter up to Advent are counted from it.[72] Bede records the confusion that could occur when there was no uniform calculation for the date of Easter, describing the court of King Oswy and Queen Eanflæd,[73] in which some members were still fasting for Lent while others were already indulging in an Easter banquet. After the Synod of Whitby (664), Easter fell on 'the first Sunday which occurs after the first full moon (or more accurately after the first fourteenth day of the moon) following the 21st of March'.[74] Calculations were necessary to determine the beginning of the lunar month. Considering the importance of the matter, it is not surprising to encounter *computus* material in thirty pre-Conquest manuscripts, two eighth-century,[75] most of the others tenth- and eleventh-century. The *computus* is a relatively short text, which usually appears as prefatory material to other – mostly liturgical – texts, for example in psalter manuscripts such as London, BL, Arundel 155 (1012 × 1023), London, BL, Cotton Galba A. xviii (s. x in) and Salisbury, Cathedral Library 150 (s. x^2). In London, BL, Harley 5431 (s. x/xi) the *computus* material precedes the *Benedictine Rule*. The manuscript Oxford, Bodleian Library, Digby 63 (s. ix^2) is entirely dedicated to the paschal question, containing the *computus* material, a calendar, episcopal letters and writing about the dating of Easter including Dionysius Exiguus's *Epistola de ratione paschali*.

At least two manuscripts reflect the scientific aspect of the *computus*. In Cambridge, Trinity College R.15.32 (s. xi^1), the *computus* is surrounded by texts such as Cicero's *Aratea*, Abbo of Fleury's *De differentia circuli et sphaerae*, Hyginus's *Astronomica*, Helperic of Auxerre's *De computo*, and book viii of Martianus Capella's *De nuptiis*, which, as we have seen, concerns stars. London, BL, Cotton Tiberius B. v (s. xi$^{2/4}$; Fig. 5.7), unites *computus* material with Bede's *De temporibus*, Ælfric's *De temporibus anni*, Cicero's *Aratea*, and excerpts from Pliny's *Naturalis historia*.

Some *computus* material can be ascribed to specific authors. The Trinity College manuscript includes Helperic of Auxerre's *De computo*, the only pre-Conquest manuscript containing this. Hrabanus Maurus's *De computo* also

---

[72] To be exact, the liturgical calendar counts six Sundays after Easter. The seventh Sunday, which is the fiftieth day, is Pentecost. All subsequent Sundays up to Advent are counted as 'Sundays after Pentecost', but since the date of Pentecost is dependent on the date of Easter, Easter is indeed the pivotal date.

[73] Bede, *Historia Ecclesiastica*, III. 25; Colgrave and Mynors, *Bede's Ecclesiastical History*, p. 296.

[74] Charles G. Hebermann, ed., *The Catholic Encyclopedia*, vol. 5, New York, Robert Appleton, 1909, p. 230 under 'Easter'.

[75] The oldest, Paris, BN, lat. 10837, fols 34–41 and 44 (s. viii in), cannot be attributed unambiguously to England; it may have been written in Echternach. London, BL, Cotton Caligula A. xv (s. viii^2) was written in France and came to England by the end of the ninth century.

survives in only one pre-Conquest manuscript, Exeter, Cathedral Library 3507 (s. x²), here in the company of Isidore's *De natura rerum*. Similarly Cassiodorus's *De computo paschali*, found in London, BL, Cotton Caligula A. xv (s. viii²) among other computistical material and, uncharacteristically, alongside texts not usually associated with the *quadrivium* such as Jerome's *De viris illustribus*, Cyprian's *Ad Quirinum testimonia*, and selections from Isidore's *Etymologiae*.

Bede's *De temporum ratione*, albeit concerned with much more than the correct calculation of Easter, might also be categorized as 'applied arithmetic'. Patterns of manuscript survival suggest that, like Aldhelm's work (p. 150), Bede's *De temporum ratione* disappeared from England during the ninth century and had to be re-imported from the Continent.[76] The tenth-century Paris, BN, nouv. acq. lat 586, fols 16–131 is intriguing since excerpts from Bede's *De temporum ratione* appear in conjunction with excerpts from Priscian's grammar, seemingly indicating that one schoolroom text attracts another.

Major authors on astronomy are Aratus of Soli, Cicero, Germanicus, Hyginus, and Martianus Capella. Aratus's *Phainomena*, originally written in Greek, was translated into Latin by Cicero and Germanicus and both honoured Aratus by giving the title *Aratea* to their translations. Hyginus independently wrote a text with the title *Astronomica*, and Martianus Capella devoted book viii of his *De nuptiis* to astronomy. In addition there are anonymous treatises on astronomy, and the poem by Pseudo-Priscian entitled *Carmen de sideribus*. Four manuscripts are noteworthy for their concentration on astronomy: Aberystwyth, National Library of Wales 735C (s. xi), written in France and imported to England (or Wales?) soon after, contains astronomical drawings, Germanicus's *Aratea* and, by a different hand, Hyginus's *Astronomica*.[77] Cambridge, Trinity College R.15.32 (s. xi¹) contains Cicero's *Aratea*, an extract from Aratus, Martianus Capella's *De nuptiis* book viii, Hyginus's *Astronomica*, and an extract from Hyginus compiled by Abbo of Fleury. London, BL, Harley 2506 (s. x/xi) includes Cicero's *Aratea*, Hyginus's *Astronomica*, Pseudo-Priscian's *Carmen de sideribus*, an anonymous text entitled *De nominibus stellarum* and Martianus Capella's *De nuptiis* book viii, as well as Remigius's commentary on it. London, BL, Harley 647 (s. ix²/⁴), an import from the Continent, which reached England by the tenth to eleventh century, contains the *De nominibus stellarum*, Cicero's *Aratea*, an excerpt from Hyginus's *Astronomica*, and an excerpt from Martianus Capella.

Astronomical material occurs intermittently elsewhere: for example, Cicero's *Aratea* and short anonymous texts represent astronomy in the miscellany that is BL, Cotton Tiberius B. v (s. xi²/⁴; Fig. 5.7); Pseudo-Priscian's *Carmen*

---

[76] Two eighth-century fragments include this text: Darmstadt, Hessische Landes- und Hochschulbibliothek 4262 and Münster in Westfalen, Staatsarchiv MSC.I.243, fols 1,2, 11 and 12. The ninth-century manuscripts containing the *De temporum ratione* were all written on the Continent. Only one, London, BL, Cotton Vespasian B. vi, can be shown to have been in England prior to the Conquest.

[77] Despite the fact that it contains Cicero's *Invectivae* and his *Somnium Scipionis*, it does not contain his *Aratea*.

de sideribus appears in London, BL, Additional 11034 (s. x), but was perhaps included for its poetic qualities rather than astronomical content since none of the other texts (Bede's *De die iudicii*; Arator's *Historia apostolica*; Modoin of Autun's *Ecloga*) are concerned with astronomy.

Only two surviving pre-Conquest manuscripts contain geometrical treatises: Oxford, Bodleian Library, Douce 125 (s. x/xi), which preserves Pseudo-Boethius's *Geometria*, books i–iv of the *Euclides latinus*, and the *Altercatio duorum geometricorum*; and Paris, BN, lat. 6401 (s. x/xi), which contains 'Letters on geometry' written by Radulf of Liège and Ragimbold of Cologne, along with Boethius's *De consolatione philosophiae* and his *De institutione arithmetica*. Here, clearly, texts of the *trivium* and the *quadrivium* are combined.

CCCC 260 (s. x^2) is entirely dedicated to musical texts presenting part of Boethius's *De institutione musica*, the *Musica Enchiriadis*, the *Scolica Enchiriadis*, and the *Commemoratio brevis de tonis*. CUL Gg.5.35, among many texts relating to the trivium, preserves Hucbald of Saint-Amand's *De harmonica instituone*. Avranches, BM 236 (s. x/xi) contains Boethius's *De institutione musica*, the only text in the manuscript concerned with music.

Practical works: geographical and medical texts

The major geographical texts available to the Anglo-Saxons were Aethicus Ister's *Cosmographia* which survives in two pre-Conquest manuscripts[78] and Priscian's *Periegesis* which occurs in three,[79] one of which, BL, Cotton Tiberius B. v, exhibits some interest in geography, also containing a map of the world, the itinerary of Archbishop Sigeric's journey to Rome and *The Wonders of the East*. There is, of course, other evidence of the Anglo-Saxons' awareness of geography, such as the geographical excursus at the beginning of Bede's *Ecclesiastical History* and the insertion of the voyages of Ohthere and Wulfstan into the Old English version of Orosius's *Historiae adversos paganos*.

Medicine, as that topic was understood in the early Middle Ages, was dealt with exclusively in a manuscript destroyed in the second World War, Herrnstein near Siegburg, Bibliothek der Grafen Nesselrode 192, fols 1–20 (s. ix/x), which contained Antonius Musa's *De herba vettonica*, Pseudo-Apuleius's *Herbarius* and *De taxone liber*, as well as Sextus Placitus's *Liber medicinae ex animalibus*. The fragment Munich, Bayerische Staatsbibliothek,

---

[78] London, BL, Cotton Vespasian B. x, fols 31–124 (s. x/xi) and Leiden, Bibliotheek der Rijksuniversiteit, Scaliger 69 (s. x^2).

[79] London, BL, Cotton Tiberius B. v (s. $xi^{2/4}$); Karlsruhe, Badische Landesbibliothek, Fragm. Aug. 122 (s. x^1); and Paris, BN, lat. 4839 (s. x/xi).

clm 29698(2 (s. xi), which contains a section from the 'Petrocellus', may have been part of a medical manuscript, but that cannot be proven. Quintus Serenus's *Liber medicinalis* seems to be the only complete Latin medical text surviving from the Anglo-Saxon period, apart from a few recipes: it occurs in Paris, BN, lat. 4839 (s. x/xi) in the company of Priscian's *Periegesis* and Nemesianus's *Cynegetica*, texts dealing with geography and hunting. Various Latin medical recipes survive in Cambridge, University Library Gg.5.35 (s. xi med), CCCC 223 (s. x), and CCCC 356, pt. iii (s. xi), but none of these manuscripts concentrate on medicine.[80]

Script and the attribution of Latin manuscripts

Types of script are considered elsewhere in this book (pp. 38–51) and will only be discussed in connection with the problems of attributing Latin manuscripts to Anglo-Saxon England. The Anglo-Saxons used Insular script for Latin texts well into the tenth century, and began using Caroline script for Latin texts progressively from the tenth century onwards. Thus, for example, Bede's *In Apocalypsin* of London, Lambeth Palace Library 149 (s. x^2 Fig. 5.2) is written in Insular script while the scribe of Prudentius's *Psychomachia* of CCCC 23, who writes at approximately the same time (s. x^2 or x ex), already employs Caroline script (Figs 5.6, 6.8). Manuscripts that have alternate Latin and Old English texts, such as the *Benedictine Rule* in Oxford, CCC 197 (s. $x^{4/4}$; Fig. 5.5), differentiate between the two languages by using the Caroline script for the Latin and the Insular script for the Old English. The co-existence of Caroline and Insular script in the late Anglo-Saxon period poses some problems since it is not always certain whether a Caroline script was written by an Anglo-Saxon or a Continental scribe. Occasional lapses into Insular letter forms by Anglo-Saxon scribes writing Caroline script, help to locate scribes in England rather than the Continent. Problems in unambiguously ascribing manuscripts to Anglo-Saxons also exist for the early Anglo-Saxon period: since Iro-Scottish missionaries helped to convert the Anglo-Saxons to Christianity and taught them to write in the Insular style, it is not always easy to differentiate between manuscripts written by Iro-Scottish masters and those penned by their Anglo-Saxon students. Equally difficult is differentiation between the hands of Anglo-Saxon missionaries to the Continent and those of their Continental students.

---

[80] There are, of course, vernacular medical texts such as 'Bald's *Leechbook*' in London, BL, Royal 12 D. xvii.

Conclusions

About nine hundred pre-Conquest manuscripts still survive. The majority by far are biblical and liturgical manuscripts (about 340 all together). For the sake of this chapter, manuscripts have been subdivided into major categories, and this might create the false impression that what have, for example, been classified as liturgical manuscripts were never read in the classroom, or that historical manuscripts, that were usually read in the refectory or in the monk's cell, had nothing to do with either liturgy or the classroom. These subdivisions are not rigid. Biblical manuscripts were used in the liturgy; the glosses and the *expositio hymnorum* suggest that psalters and hymnaries served not only in the liturgy but also in the classroom; the fact that a sacramentary was copied into an Old English version of the *Ecclesiastical History* allows the conclusion that historical and liturgical manuscripts were not always strictly separated; nor were historical and classroom manuscripts, as Abbo's *Bella Parisiacae urbis* demonstrates; manuscripts with exegetical texts could be read by a monk in his cell, but parts could just as easily find their way into a homily for either the Mass or the Office; while the *computus* texts are in essence arithmetical, the arithmetic here stands in the service of the liturgy; and finally, classroom texts such as Arator's *Historia apostolica* can form the basis of exegesis and hence of homilies. Latin manuscripts, in other words, tend to be predominantly exegetical, liturgical, historical, or pedagogic, but each of the categories can easily overlap with any of the others. The same can be said about Old English manuscripts: if they are translations of the Latin, they attempt to present the Latin material in a different medium; but even if they are original texts, much of their content is undoubtedly influenced by, fuses with, and complements the material preserved in the Latin manuscripts. To understand the Anglo-Saxons, we need to study both the Latin and Old English manuscripts they have produced.

Finally, important as manuscript evidence is, it has its limitations. While the presence of a text in a manuscript either written or owned in Anglo-Saxon England proves that the Anglo-Saxons could have known the work, it cannot prove that they actually read and studied it. A manuscript may reflect the personal interests of one reader, or the collective interest of a monastery or a cathedral. A pristine manuscript with no annotations allows practically no determination of how it was used. Moreover, many manuscripts were destroyed either during the Anglo-Saxon period or in the centuries afterwards. Their destruction and their disappearance will never allow a full reconstruction of the holdings of Anglo-Saxon libraries and of the texts available to the Anglo-Saxons. Any look at the Anglo-Saxon past will at best be 'through a glass darkly'.

Introduction to Chapter 6

The abhorrence of despoiling a book by writing upon it is a modern sensitivity (not shared by all, even today). Throughout medieval and early modern times, owners and other readers of manuscripts often wrote their own thoughts and discoveries directly onto the parchment. This chapter focuses on a matter already apparent from earlier discussions in this book: that many of the manuscripts that survive today continued to develop long after their primary texts were inscribed. Some of the additions, especially interlinear translations and illustrations, were part of the original conception of the manuscript. Other annotations were added later in the Anglo-Saxon period and still more were inserted in the later Middle Ages and Renaissance times.

Glosses – whether continuous or of individual words – usually aimed to translate or explain the text. Individual glosses to words were first inserted, one can assume, when a reader experienced difficulty understanding a text on first reading; and thus served as a useful reminder when the text was revisited for study or teaching. Subsequent readers might add to existing glosses, providing alternatives and expansions, and glossing other words. Some manuscripts have 'layers' of glosses testifying to heavy use. The earliest surviving glosses were to help English speakers with Latin vocabulary, especially that of hermeneutic poetry which deliberately used obscure and archaic language; and with the grammar and word order of Latin, which differed from Old English, a germanic language. Subsequent annotators, striving to read Anglo-Saxon manuscripts in the thirteenth century and again in the sixteenth and seventeenth, were more familiar with Latin than Old English and sometimes used Latin versions of the same texts to help them understand a form of their own language that had become incomprehensible.

Glosses and glossaries anticipate scholarly practices and tools found today in printed books and electronic resources. The Old English glossary arranged according to alphabetical principles is the forerunner of today's dictionary, and the subject-order glossary is an embryonic thesaurus. Pioneering habits of Renaissance scholars anticipated modern editorial practices: transcribing the text; identifying and collating different manuscripts of the same text; recognizing and recording sources; adding explanatory endnotes; writing indexes; and emending the text in the belief that the editor's version was more 'correct' than the manuscript, the latter a hostage to fortune to be commended or condemned by any other scholar conscientious enough to compare edited text with manuscript.

6

Glosses and notes in Anglo-Saxon manuscripts

Timothy Graham

Any student who has the opportunity to work with Anglo-Saxon manuscripts, whether at first hand or in photographic reproduction, rapidly discovers that many of them include glossatorial activity: that is, they have text entered between the lines or in the margins. Any entry of script the purpose of which is to help explicate the original text of the manuscript may be called a gloss. Glosses in Anglo-Saxon manuscripts were sometimes the work of the scribe of the main text or a collaborator who was a fellow member of the scriptorium that produced the manuscript, and in such cases were therefore a planned component of the manuscript from the outset. Frequently, however, the glosses were the work of later readers encountering the manuscript either within Anglo-Saxon times or during some later era. These later glosses can tell us much about the reception of Anglo-Saxon material in subsequent historical periods. There is, moreover, a striking difference between the type of manuscript that tended to attract glosses from Anglo-Saxons and the type of manuscript that was glossed at a later date, whether within the Middle Ages or during the early modern period. The Anglo-Saxons tended to gloss manuscripts that were written in Latin, their glosses to the Latin texts being variously in Old English and in Latin. For Anglo-Saxon readers, in other words, it was the Latin manuscripts that required supplementary explanations of various kinds. Later readers, however, tended to gloss manuscripts written in Old English. Their glosses were typically in Latin, although occasionally such glossators would use the form of the English vernacular appropriate for their time. The primary interest of such readers was to understand the Anglo-Saxon language and to investigate the content of texts written in Old English.

Manuscripts with full interlinear gloss

The most extensive glossing activity in Anglo-Saxon manuscripts comprises complete interlinear Old English translations of Latin texts. The texts that tended to attract such translations fall into a small number of categories, being variously biblical, liturgical, monastic, or pedagogical. This, of course, reflects the fact that those who produced and used books during the Anglo-Saxon period were for the most part monks and ecclesiastics. The glossing in these manuscripts attests to the need of such individuals for help in understanding Latin texts and reminds us that there were times during the Anglo-Saxon period when the knowledge of Latin was imperilled.

Ten Anglo-Saxon copies of the book of Psalms include a complete interlinear translation.[1] This is a much higher number than for any other text – not surprising in view of the centrality of the psalms in the daily monastic worship: Benedictine monks recited the complete set of 150 psalms each week during the Divine Office, that is, the cycle of services (not including the Mass) in which they participated at the eight different 'Hours' of the day (Matins, Lauds, Prime, Terce, Sext, None, Vespers, and Compline). The earliest of the manuscripts with a full psalter gloss – and the only one dating before the Viking attacks on Anglo-Saxon England – is the *Vespasian Psalter* (London, British Library, MS Cotton Vespasian A. i; Figs 6.1, 7.8). One of the greatest manuscripts of the early Anglo-Saxon period, distinguished for its elegant Uncial script and for its historiated initials which are the earliest in any surviving manuscript, the *Vespasian Psalter* was produced in southern England, probably at St Augustine's Abbey, Canterbury, in the 720s. It was glossed more than one hundred years later, around the middle of the ninth century, and this may remind us of King Alfred's comment, in his preface to his translation of Pope Gregory's *Pastoral Care*, that knowledge of Latin had practically died out in southern England even before the major Viking attacks of the second half of the ninth century. The gloss is written in the Mercian dialect – shown, in Fig. 6.1, by such forms as *scuan* ('shadow'; above *umbra* in line 4) and *ic cleopiu* ('I cry out'; above *Clamabo* in line 6) – but this

---

[1] The manuscripts are Cambridge, University Library MS Ff.1.23; London, British Library, MSS Arundel 60, Cotton Tiberius C. vi, Cotton Vespasian A. i, Cotton Vitellius E. xviii, Royal 2 B. v, and Stowe 2; London, Lambeth Palace Library MS 427; Oxford, Bodleian Library, MS Junius 27; and Salisbury, Cathedral Library MS 150. An eleventh manuscript, the *Eadwine Psalter* (Cambridge, Trinity College MS R.17.1), was made nearly one hundred years after the Norman Conquest; it includes a full Old English gloss between the lines of one of its three Latin versions of the psalms (see below). In the late tenth-century *Bosworth Psalter* (London, British Library, MS Additional 37517), there is an interlinear gloss to just twenty-five of the psalms and to parts of four other psalms and six canticles.

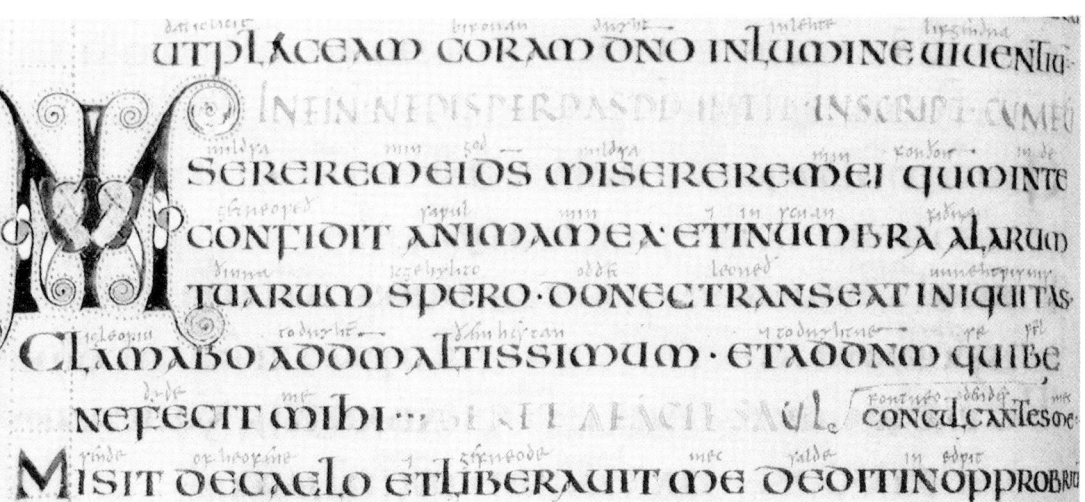

6.1 London, British Library, MS Cotton Vespasian A. i, fol. 55v, with the opening of Psalm 56.

need not mean that the manuscript had moved to Mercia; rather, the gloss reflects the Mercian dominance of Kent in the late eighth and early ninth centuries. The interlinear gloss of the *Vespasian Psalter* has the distinction of being the earliest extant translation of any portion of the Bible into the English language.

The interlinear glosses in the other glossed psalters range in date from the first half of the tenth century to the middle of the twelfth, with most of them belonging to the eleventh century. Several of these psalter manuscripts are associated with Canterbury and Winchester, the two major centres of the Anglo-Saxon Church's southern province. In all but two of these manuscripts, the gloss was entered contemporaneously with the main text and in some cases even by the same hand, but it is distinguished from the main text by being written in a smaller script (the result of the glossing scribe using a more finely cut quill), as glosses often were.[2] An exception to this pattern is Cambridge, University Library MS Ff.1.23 (Fig. 6.2), produced in the mid-eleventh century probably in Winchcombe, an important monastic centre in the west of England founded by St Oswald in the 960s. Here, the gloss is accorded a status equal to that of the main text by being written on ruled lines in script of the same size as the main text; it is also privileged by being entered in red, whereas the main text is written in regular

---

[2] The two manuscripts that do not have a gloss contemporaneous with the main text are Lambeth 427 (the gloss, dating from the first half of the eleventh century, appears to be a little later than the main text); and Salisbury 150 (gloss of the late eleventh or early twelfth century added to a manuscript of the second half of the tenth century).

6.2 Cambridge, University Library MS Ff.1.23, fol. 5r, with the opening of Psalm 1.

Unusually, throughout this manuscript the Old English gloss is written in red in script of the same size as the Latin text.

ink.[3] The latest of the psalters with a complete interlinear Old English gloss is the *Eadwine Psalter*, made at Christ Church, Canterbury, c.1155–60. This is a manuscript of particular complexity that is a masterpiece of book design. It includes three different Latin versions of the psalms, greater emphasis being given to the 'Gallican' version – the version used in Benedictine monasteries in northern Europe – by the greater width of the column in which it is entered. While this version has Latin explanatory glosses between its lines, the two others have interlinear translations, one in Anglo-Norman (the language of the aristocracy following the Norman Conquest), the other in Old English. This continuous Old English gloss is one of the latest pieces of written Old English that we have. A further distinguishing feature of this outstanding manuscript is that each psalm is preceded by a colored line-drawing based on the pictures of the *Utrecht Psalter*, a major Carolingian manuscript that had made its way from northern France to Canterbury by about the year 1000, giving rise there to a sequence of three fully illustrated psalters produced between the early eleventh and the late twelfth centuries.

---

[3] Another manuscript of similar design, with the gloss entered in red and on ruled lines by the original scribe, is London, British Library, MS Cotton Vespasian D. xii, a mid-eleventh-century manuscript from Christ Church, Canterbury, that contains an extensive collection of hymns and canticles.

From the evidence of surviving manuscripts, the psalter was apparently the only Old Testament text to receive a full vernacular gloss in Anglo-Saxon England;[4] as noted above, this reflects the importance of the book of Psalms in the life of the Church, while the psalter also had instructional value in developing students' knowledge of Latin. Of the twenty-seven books of the New Testament, it was only the four gospels that received a complete gloss, and only in two surviving manuscripts, each of which was glossed long after its original production. These were the *Lindisfarne Gospels* (London, British Library, MS Cotton Nero D. iv) and the *Macregol Gospels* (Oxford, Bodleian Library, MS Auct. D.2.19; also known as the *Rushworth Gospels* from the name of its mid-seventeenth-century owner, John Rushworth, deputy clerk to the House of Commons). The *Lindisfarne Gospels*, made at the great monastery off the north-east coast of Northumbria in the late seventh or early eighth century, travelled with the members of the monastic community when, after repeated Viking attacks, they abandoned Lindisfarne in 875. In 883 the community settled at Chester-le-Street in County Durham, and it was there that in the third quarter of the tenth century, one Aldred, priest and provost of the community, provided the text of all four gospels with a complete interlinear gloss. We know this because Aldred himself informs us of the fact in an inscription that he added following the end of St John's gospel, where he also proffers the information that it was Eadfrith (bishop of Lindisfarne, 698–721) who wrote the manuscript, that Ethilwald (Eadfrith's successor as bishop) provided it with its binding, and that the hermit Billfrith adorned the binding with precious metals and gemstones. Although one historian has recently questioned the reliability of this information, it seems likely enough that Aldred was committing to writing a tradition about the origins of the *Lindisfarne Gospels* that had been preserved orally by the members of the community.[5]

As with all the full Old English interlinear glosses, Aldred's translation follows the original Latin word by word, placing an Old English equivalent directly above each Latin word. What results is therefore not so much a fluent

---

[4] The copy of the book of Proverbs on fols 2–37 of London, British Library, MS Cotton Vespasian D. vi has numerous glosses but these do not amount to a complete interlinear gloss.

[5] See David N. Dumville, *A Palaeographer's Review: the Insular system of scripts in the early Middle Ages*, Osaka, Institute of Oriental and Occidental Studies, Kansai University, 1999, pp. 76–80, for scepticism about the reliability of Aldred's colophon. See also the interesting speculation that elements of Aldred's colophon could have been derived from six lines of Old English verse in Jane Roberts, 'Aldred signs off from glossing the Lindisfarne Gospels' in Alexander R. Rumble, ed., *Writing and Texts in Anglo-Saxon England*, Cambridge and Rochester, NY, D. S. Brewer, 2006, pp. 28–43, at pp. 39–40.

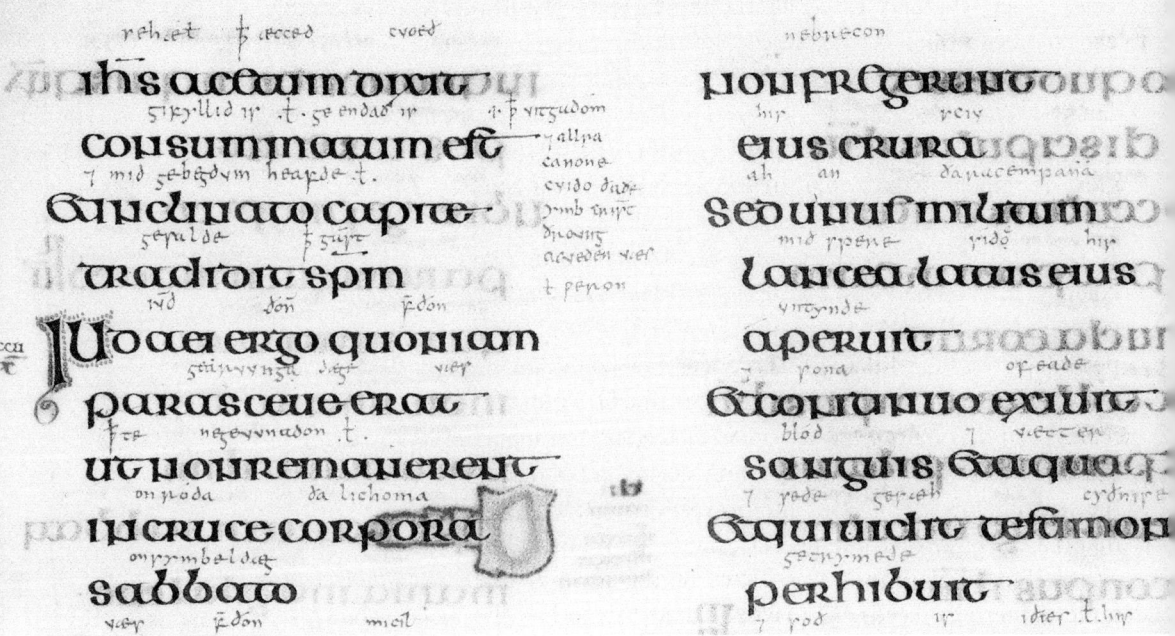

6.3 London, British Library, MS Cotton Nero D. iv, fol. 255r, with text from John 19 glossed by Aldred.

vernacular translation of the gospel text as a vocabulary key to the Latin. The extent to which Aldred's gloss differs from a fluent translation can be gauged by comparing his gloss to John 19:34 with the text of the same verse in the vernacular translation known as the *West Saxon Gospels*, which is found in four manuscripts of the eleventh century and two of the twelfth, and which was intended to stand as an independent translation, unaccompanied by the Latin on which it was based. Aldred's word-for-word version in the *Lindisfarne Gospels* reads: *ah an ðara cempa*[6] *mid spere sidu*[7] *his untynde (and) sona ofeude blod (and) uætter* ('but one of the soldiers with spear side his opened and immediately outwent blood and water'; see lines 3–7 of the right-hand column in Fig. 6.3). The version of the *West Saxon Gospels* uses a more natural word order: *Ac an þære cempena geopenede his sidan mid spere and hrædlice þar fleow blod ut and wæter* ('But one of the soldiers opened his side with a spear and immediately there flowed blood out and water').[8] Aldred used regular ink for most of his interlinear gloss in the *Lindisfarne*

---

[6] Corrected from *cempana*: the dots above the *n* and *a* indicate that these letters should be ignored.
[7] Corrected from *sido*.
[8] See R.M. Liuzza, ed., *The Old English Version of the Gospels*, vol. 1, Early English Text Society, original series, 304, Oxford, Oxford University Press for the Early English Text Society, 1994, p. 198.

Gospels but switched to red for the last forty leaves of the manuscript (fols 220–59), beginning at John 5:10.

Aldred added his gloss some two hundred and fifty years after the *Lindisfarne Gospels* was first made. The *Macregol Gospels*, originally written in Ireland in the late eighth or early ninth century, received its interlinear gloss during the second half of the tenth, by which time the manuscript had evidently reached England. The gloss is the work of two scribes, who are identified in two colophons. Farmon, who was responsible for glossing the gospel of Matthew, the opening of Mark, and a small portion of John, names himself in a colophon following the end of Matthew, where he uses the rune ᛗ, known as *mon* ('man'), to represent the second element of his name. The colophon that follows St John's gospel both names the second glossator, Owun, and provides the information that Farmon was 'priest at Harewood', a reference to either Harewood near Ross-on-Wye or the town of the same name near Leeds. The colophons at the end of the *Lindisfarne* and *Macregol Gospels* offer unique examples of Anglo-Saxon glossators identifying themselves by name.

Aldred, the *Lindisfarne* glossator, was also responsible for entering the continuous gloss in a manuscript known as the *Durham Ritual* (Durham, Cathedral Library MS A.IV.19; Fig. 5.3), a service book containing collects and scriptural readings for the Hours of the Divine Office throughout the liturgical year. The manuscript originated in southern England but by Aldred's time had evidently reached the displaced Lindisfarne community at Chester-le-Street; it was probably among the numerous gifts bestowed upon the community by King Athelstan (924–39) when he marched north in 934 to do battle with the Scots, stopping en route to offer prayers at the tomb of St Cuthbert, whose relics the members of the community had carried with them when they abandoned Lindisfarne. To help distinguish his gloss from the main text, Aldred used red ink for all his glossatorial activity in the *Durham Ritual*.

A few other Latin texts received a complete interlinear translation during the Anglo-Saxon period. Among them were three copies of the basic hymn collection of the Anglo-Saxon church: Durham, Cathedral Library MS B.III.32, and London, British Library, MSS Cotton Julius A. vi and Cotton Vespasian D. xii, all of which are eleventh-century, their glosses being contemporary with the main text and apparently entered by the same hand. The *Liber scintillarum* (Book of Sparks), a popular collection of extracts from the Bible and the Church Fathers first compiled in the late seventh

> 'Glosses in Anglo-Saxon manuscripts were sometimes the work of the scribe of the main text or a collaborator who was a fellow member of the scriptorium that produced the manuscript, and in such cases were therefore a planned component of the manuscript from the outset. Frequently, however, the glosses were the work of later readers encountering the manuscript either within Anglo-Saxon times or during some later era.'

century by Defensor, a monk of Ligugé (near Poitiers), received a complete interlinear translation in one eleventh-century manuscript that belonged to Christ Church, Canterbury (London, British Library, MS Royal 7 C. iv). The *Rule of St Benedict*, a text of central importance in Anglo-Saxon England during and after the Benedictine Reform of the third quarter of the tenth century, is accompanied by a complete interlinear translation in one manuscript made at Canterbury in the mid-eleventh century (London, British Library, MS Cotton Tiberius A. iii). This gloss differs from the Old English translation of the *Rule of St Benedict* made by Æthelwold, bishop of Winchester (963–84), one of the architects of the reform movement; the manuscripts containing Æthelwold's translation adopt a different form of layout, placing Æthelwold's Old English version of each chapter of the *Rule* after the original Latin version of the chapter. Tiberius A. iii also offers a complete interlinear gloss to the *Regularis Concordia*, the primary document of the tenth-century monastic reform movement. Composed probably by Æthelwold, the *Regularis Concordia* prescribes liturgical practice and other aspects of the religious life to be observed in monasteries and nunneries throughout England.[9]

All the texts mentioned so far were of a type central to Christian worship and the monastic life. That they received continuous interlinear translations indicates the importance attached to the correct understanding of these texts. One other text that received a complete interlinear gloss (again in Tiberius A. iii) was of a rather different nature, its purpose being to develop young students' knowledge of Latin. This was the *Colloquy* by Ælfric, the great homilist and educator of late Anglo-Saxon England. Taking the form of imaginary conversations between a teacher and the members of his class, Ælfric's *Colloquy* was designed to develop young monks' ability to converse with one another in Latin, a practice that was frequently required by monastic legislation. It is somewhat ironic, therefore, that this text too received a complete vernacular gloss.

---

[9] One interesting aspect of Anglo-Saxon glossatorial activity not covered here is the effort, evidently initiated by Æthelwold, to establish particular Old English words as the appropriate translations of specific Latin *lemmata* within certain semantic contexts (such as the liturgy). This effort can be detected in texts glossed at Winchester in the late tenth and early eleventh centuries, and seems to have spread from there to Canterbury. Glossing thus played a part in what Mechthild Gretsch has called 'an active forging and regularizing of the English language'. See Mechthild Gretsch, 'Winchester vocabulary and standard Old English: the vernacular in late Anglo-Saxon England', *Bulletin of the John Rylands University Library of Manchester*, 83, 2001, pp. 41–87, especially pp. 44–68 (the phrase quoted occurs on p. 46).

Other glossed manuscripts

Many other Anglo-Saxon manuscripts were glossed besides those that carry full interlinear translations. The density of the glossing in these other manuscripts varies considerably, from a few interlinear notes entered more or less capriciously to heavy concentrations of interlinear and marginal comments that explicate both individual words of the main text and ideas and concepts within the text. It is important to realize that in many cases the glosses in Anglo-Saxon manuscripts were not individual readers' spontaneous responses to the text but were themselves copied from another manuscript. In several manuscripts, glossing is heavy on the first pages but then tails off or even ceases completely, evidently because the scribe decided not to continue copying the glosses of the exemplar (or because those glosses likewise tailed off).

The glossing in manuscripts that do not have full interlinear translations may be in either Latin or Old English, but Latin glossing is more common. The texts that tended to attract most glossing included those (many of them poetic) produced by Christian authors in the late Antique period: because the Latin of these texts was quite correct, while the content was Christian (in contrast to the pagan content of great classical authors such as Virgil and Cicero), these texts were used extensively for the teaching of Latin, in Anglo-Saxon England as elsewhere in western Europe; their use is recommended by such great Anglo-Saxon pedagogues as Bede and Alcuin. These Christian-Latin texts included *Evangelium libri quattuor*, a harmony of the four gospels in more than three thousand lines of hexameter verse composed c.330 by Juvencus, a Spanish priest; *De actibus apostolorum*, a verse rendition of the Acts of the Apostles composed by Arator and first delivered before Pope Vigilius in Rome in 544; *Paschale carmen* and *Paschale opus*, respectively a verse and a prose account of the miraculous events of Christ's life, and the Old Testament events that prefigured them, written early in the fifth century by the Italian author, Sedulius; the *Psychomachia*, an allegorical portrayal of the battle between the virtues and vices for the possession of the individual human soul by the early fifth-century Spanish poet, Prudentius; and the *Epigrammata* of Prosper of Aquitaine, a collection of verse epigrams based on statements of St Augustine that Prosper compiled while serving as secretary to Pope Leo I in the mid-fifth century. *The Consolation of Philosophy*, a work that was not overtly Christian in content but that had been written by the Christian author Boethius while awaiting execution at Pavia in the early 520s, was another popular work of which several glossed copies survive. The work of one Anglo-Saxon author, Aldhelm – in particular, the verse and prose versions of his *De virginitate* – attracted extensive glossing, hardly surprising in view of the difficulty of his Latin vocabulary and style. Indeed, there

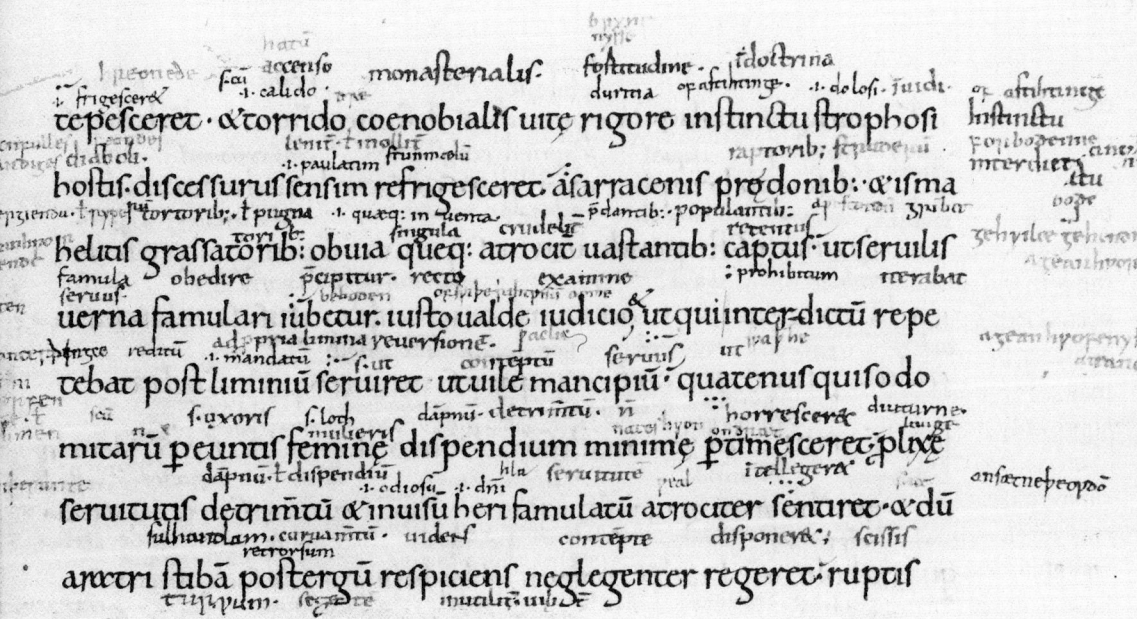

6.4 Brussels, Bibliothèque Royale de Belgique MS 1650 (Aldhelm, prose *De virginitate*), fol. 25r.

The glosses to this manuscript were entered in stages.

survive more glossed copies of Aldhelm's *De virginitate* than of any of the other works just mentioned, and the Aldhelm manuscripts are also glossed more densely (with well over five thousand glosses in two manuscripts: Brussels, Bibliothèque Royale MS 1650 (see Fig. 6.4), and Oxford, Bodleian Library, MS Digby 146). We can learn much about Anglo-Saxon habits of glossing by looking at pages from copies of some of these works.

Much of the glossing consists of the entering of one or more synonyms above a word in the main text the meaning of which might not be clear to readers. Modern scholars refer to this type of glossatorial activity as 'lexical glossing'. The correct term to refer to the word glossed is *lemma* (plural *lemmata*), while the explanatory gloss is the *interpretamentum* (plural *interpretamenta*). *Interpretamenta* in Anglo-Saxon manuscripts may be in Latin or Old English, or a combination of the two. Often more than one *interpretamentum* glosses a single *lemma*. An *interpretamentum* may stand alone above its *lemma* or may be preceded by the abbreviation .*i*., standing for *id est* ('that is'; see, for example, the gloss .*i. frigesceret* above *tepesceret* in line 1 of Fig. 6.4). Sometimes two or more *interpretamenta* are entered over a *lemma*; in such cases, the *interpretamenta* are normally separated by the abbreviation *l̄* (an *l* with a slash through it), standing for *vel* ('or'; see *lenit(er) (ve)l mollit(er)* above *sensim* in line 2 of Fig. 6.4). Old English *interpretamenta* were sometimes written in abbreviated form; the Brussels Aldhelm manuscript includes over two hundred examples of this practice, such as *fagernyss* ('beauty') shortened to *fager* and *dælnimung* ('participation') reduced to *dælni*.[10] Scholars refer to such abbreviated forms as 'merographs'.

Another type of brief interlinear gloss does not provide a synonym or translation of a *lemma* but rather completes the meaning of a sentence or clause by supplying a word or words not present in the original text. Such glosses are known as 'suppletive glosses'. For example, in Latin it is frequently possible to omit the verb 'to be' from a clause; a suppletive gloss may provide the verb in the appropriate inflection. Again, suppletive glosses may clarify the referent of the Latin demonstrative pronouns ('this', 'these', 'that', 'those'), personal pronouns ('I', 'you', 'he', 'she', etc.), or relative pronouns ('who', 'which') by specifying the person or thing referred to. Suppletive glosses may serve other clarificatory purposes. They are typically preceded by the abbreviation s., standing for *scilicet* ('namely'). In Fig. 6.4 the suppletive gloss *s. ut* stands above the verb *seruiret* in line 5 to show that the verb is in the subjunctive mood because it falls within the *ut* clause beginning in line 4; two additional suppletive glosses appear in the line below, clarifying that the text's *p(er)euntis feminę* is a reference to Lot's wife. Figure 6.4, also shows how a manuscript could attract glosses over an extended period of time: the manuscript was initially glossed early in the eleventh century, not long after the main text was written, but includes glosses in at least four different hands working at different times during the first half of the eleventh century. In such cases where a manuscript has been glossed over a prolonged period, the chronological sequence of the glossatorial activity will be implicit in the placing of the glosses upon the page, with earlier glosses standing neatly above the *lemmata* to which they apply, and with later glosses squeezed in wherever there is room for them. The placement of the Old English glosses above lines 1 and 2 of Fig. 6.4 shows that they were entered on the page after the Latin glosses above which they stand.

Both lexical and suppletive glosses typically consisted of single words (or sets of single words) entered above the *lemmata* to which they applied. Another type of glossing activity consisted in providing a more extended explanation of a word or idea found within the main text. Such a gloss may be called a *scholion* or *scholium* (the plural is *scholia* in both cases). Because *scholia* were longer than simple lexical or suppletive glosses, there often was insufficient room for them in the interline and they were therefore entered in one of the margins of the page, commonly the outer margin. Because the

---

[10] See Louis Goossens, *The Old English Glosses of MS. Brussels, Royal Library, 1650 (Aldhelm's De Laudibus Virginitatis)*, Brussels, Paleis der Acadamiën, 1974, pp. 29, 187 (no. 611), and 198 (no. 773). For a discussion of the merographs in London, British Library, MS Cotton Tiberius A. iii, see Lucia Kornexl, ed., *Die 'Regularis Concordia' und ihre altenglische Interlinearversion*, Munich, W. Fink, 1993, pp. ccxx–ccxxi.

scholion now did not stand in direct juxtaposition to the word or idea to which it related, the glossator would often use a pair of matching symbols to link the one to the other, placing one symbol above the point in the text to which the *scholion* related and the other at the beginning of the *scholion*. Such pairs of marks are termed *signes-de-renvoi* by modern scholars. Anglo-Saxon glossators could be inventive and even artistic in the design of these marks, as may be seen in a glossed copy of an important mathematical text, Boethius's *De institutione arithmetica* (Fig. 6.5). This manuscript (Cambridge, Corpus Christi College MS 352) was prepared at St Augustine's Abbey, Canterbury, in the third quarter of the tenth century, with glosses entered on the first five leaves by the scribe of the main text. On the page illustrated, the pairs of *signes-de-renvoi* used to link text and gloss include a fish, a lion's head, a circular symbol with a central dot and with a diagonal line extending from the circle (so that the whole somewhat resembles a frying pan with an egg in it), and a vegetal motif. An especially elegant touch is the way the two fish and the two heads face one another, as it were to signify how the glosses address the text.

Much glossing in Anglo-Saxon manuscripts reflects the difficulty experienced by Anglo-Saxons – whose own language was not directly related to Latin as were the vernaculars of Italy, France, and Spain – when they attempted to read Latin texts. A major barrier to their understanding was the use by Latin authors, especially poets, of a word order quite different from that which was natural in the English vernacular. Some Anglo-Saxon readers therefore adopted the practice of 'syntactical glossing', which may first have been used by Irish glossators of Latin manuscripts and which aimed to make it easier for the reader to construe the Latin.[11] There existed two rather different methods of syntactical glossing, both of them used by Anglo-Saxons. One consisted of picking out the major elements in a sentence while the other provided a means to put the Latin words into an order that the reader would find more natural and easy to understand. Glossators achieved the latter aim by entering a letter of the alphabet over each word of the Latin text. (Modern scholars have sometimes used the term 'paving letters' to refer to the alphabetical sequence.) The reader should take first the word that had the first letter of the alphabet entered above it, then the word with the next letter above it, and so on. In some manuscripts – such as the copy of Boethius's *Consolation of Philosophy* in Cambridge, Corpus Christi College MS 214, or the verse version of Bede's *Life of St Cuthbert*

---

[11] The classic account of Anglo-Saxon syntactical glossing is that of Fred C. Robinson, 'Syntactical glosses in Latin manuscripts of Anglo-Saxon provenance', *Speculum*, 48, 1973, pp. 443–75. See also Michael Korhammer, 'Mittelalterliche Konstruktionshilfen und altenglische Wortstellung', *Scriptorium*, 34, 1980, pp. 18–58.

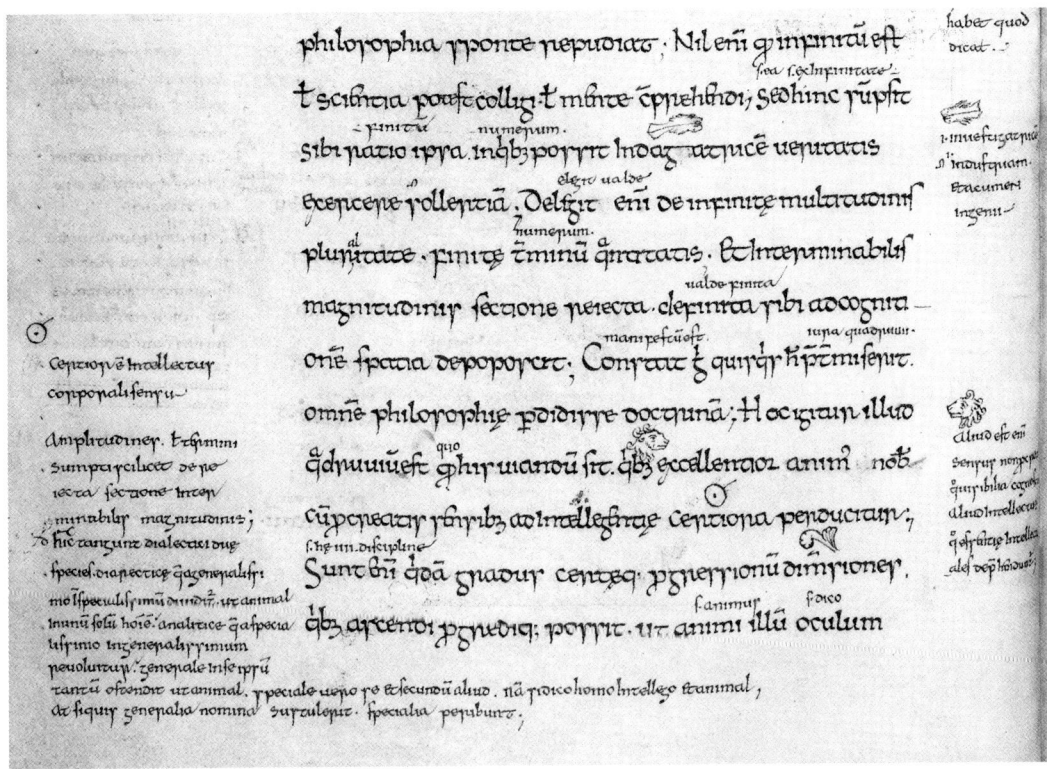

6.5 Cambridge, Corpus Christi College MS 352 (Boethius, *De institutione arithmetica*), fol. 4v.

Here, marginal *scholia* are linked to the text to which they relate by pairs of matching *signes-de-renvoi*.

in Paris, Bibliothèque nationale de France, MS lat. 2825 – lengthy passages of text have been glossed in this way. In others – for example, a copy of Sedulius's *Paschale carmen* (Cambridge, Corpus Christi College MS 173, Part II) – only a few short passages have received such treatment. In Boulogne-sur-Mer, Bibliothèque municipale MS 189, a single three-line passage of Prudentius's *Cathemerinon* has alphabetical syntactical glossing. Here, an instruction entered in the margin – *signa hic constructionem* ('mark the construction here') – suggests that the letters were entered by a pupil at the command of a teacher.

The example illustrated (Fig. 6.6) comes from the copy of Boethius's *Consolation of Philosophy* in Corpus Christi College 214, prepared in Canterbury, perhaps at Christ Church, in the second half of the tenth century. The severely damaged edges of this and all other leaves result from the manuscript's having been attacked by rodents at some point in the early modern period. Letters of the alphabet have been entered above every single word on the page. The glossator included in his alphabetical sequence the special Anglo-Saxon letters *wynn* (ƿ), *thorn* (þ), *aesc* (æ), and *eth* (ð), as well as the Tironian symbol for the word *and* (7), all of which he added on at the end of the alphabet (see the examples of these forms in

6.6 Cambridge, Corpus Christi College MS 214 (Boethius, *Consolation of Philosophy*), fol. 107r.

Letters of the alphabet have been entered above the words of the Latin text to produce a word order that would be more easily understood by an Anglo-Saxon reader.

lines 5, 8–9, and 14–15). When he had finished one alphabetical sequence, he distinguished the next one by placing dots after each letter, so that there would be no confusion between two consecutive sequences (see the transition from an undotted to a dotted sequence in lines 5 and 14, and from a dotted to an undotted sequence in line 9). Lines 11–13, carrying the sentence *Auferetur igit(ur) … depraecandi* (*Consolation of Philosophy*, Book V.iii), show well how the system works. If one takes the words in the order indicated by the alphabetical sequence, one gets: *igitur auferetur illud unicum commercium scilicet sperandi ac depraecandi inter homines deumque*.[12] Translating word for word, one arrives at a statement that makes perfect sense in Modern English and would also have done so in Old English: 'Therefore there will be taken away that sole intercourse – namely of hoping and of praying – between men and God.'

The practice of entering alphabetical 'paving letters' above the words of a Latin text offered a sure method for correctly construing the Latin – provided the right letter was entered over each word (mistakes did occur, for example in the copy of Sedulius's *Paschale carmen* mentioned above, where a passage about Judas's suicide includes an error in the sequencing of

---

[12] Note that *deumque*, in line 12, has two letters of the alphabet (*y* and *x*) entered over it, indicating that one should take first the enclitic *-que* (meaning 'and'), then *deum*.

6.7 London, British Library, MS Cotton Vitellius A. xix (Bede, *Life of St Cuthbert*), fol. 32r.

This example has syntactical glossing consisting of symbols entered below or above key elements of sentences of the Latin text.

the alphabetical letters).[13] Another, more sophisticated method of syntactical glossing consisted of entering symbols or 'construe marks' below or above certain words of the Latin text. The purpose of these marks was to pick out the most important words in the sentence – those that signified its basic structure – as well as to link together associated words (such as a noun and its adjective or a verb and its subject) that might be separated in the text by intervening words. This system of glossing thus aimed to help readers understand the Latin syntax rather than to provide a foolproof method of rearranging the Latin into a more easily understood word order. Among the manuscripts using the system is a copy of Bede's *Life of St Cuthbert* made probably at St Augustine's Abbey, Canterbury, around the middle of the tenth century (London, British Library, MS Cotton Vitellius A. xix). The symbols employed consist of combinations of dots and dashes entered variously below or above words of the Latin text; typically, when a particular symbol is used more than once to link elements within a sentence, the first one or more occurrences are entered below the line, but the final occurrence is entered

---

[13] In another of the six passages of this manuscript that include alphabetical glossing, the letters were entered first in drypoint, then in ink, as if the glossator first made a trial run and inked the letters in only when he was sure they were right. In the case of the passage describing the woman taken in adultery, some of the letters were erased and then rewritten, as if the glossator changed his mind about how to construe the passage.

above the line, to show that the sequence has achieved its resolution. The glossator of the Vitellius manuscript employed this system quite sparingly, merely to pick out key elements that reveal the syntax. In the example illustrated here (Fig. 6.7), a symbol consisting of two dots aligned horizontally is entered under both *At* (the conjunction beginning the sentence) and the following word, *ego* (the first word of the compound subject, *ego et mei similes*); the same mark is then entered in the next line both above an adverb (*quidem*) modifying the verb of which *ego et mei similes* is the subject, and above the verb itself (*sumus*). Another symbol, consisting of a dot and a comma-shaped mark aligned horizontally, is entered below the adjective *certi* and, three words further on, below the conjunction *quia*, which introduces the clause of which the meaning flows from that adjective. Five lines further down the page, three dots arranged in triangular formation are entered below the relative pronoun, *quę*, that opens a subordinate clause; the same symbol is used three lines further on, this time above *inpendat*, the verb of which *quę* is the subject. Construe marks of the same kind may also be seen in Fig. 6.4: note the matching symbols placed below *ut* and above *seruiret* in lines 4–5, and another matching set below *quatenus* and above *sentiret* in lines 5 and 7. In both cases, the marks link the conjunction that introduces a clause with the subjunctive verb governed by that conjunction.

As already noted, the glossing of a manuscript was often planned from the outset, and in such cases, the glosses themselves were often copied from an exemplar, just as was the main text. The glosses were, necessarily, entered onto the page after the main text had been written; it is likely that the entire main text of the manuscript would be written first and the glosses entered only once the copying of the main text was complete. The glossing scribe would cut his quill more finely than that of the text scribe, so that the glosses would be in a smaller script than the main text. For those glosses that were written in the margin, the glossing scribe might rule lines on which to enter the gloss; within the Anglo-Saxon period, such marginal ruling was done in drypoint (that is, with a metal or bone stylus that left a furrow in the parchment), just like the rulings for the main text. It would seem that, in cases where a manuscript also included a significant programme of illustrations, the glossing scribe would complete his work before the manuscript was turned over to the artist. Persuasive evidence for this comes from a magnificent illustrated copy of Prudentius's *Psychomachia* that was made in southern England, perhaps at Canterbury or a south-western centre, in the late tenth or early eleventh century (Cambridge, Corpus Christi College MS 23). The codex includes eighty-nine pictures in coloured outline illustrating the various conflicts between individual virtues and vices described by Prudentius. In several places, the ink of the simple frames of the illustrations lies on top of glosses that are entered above the first line of text immediately following

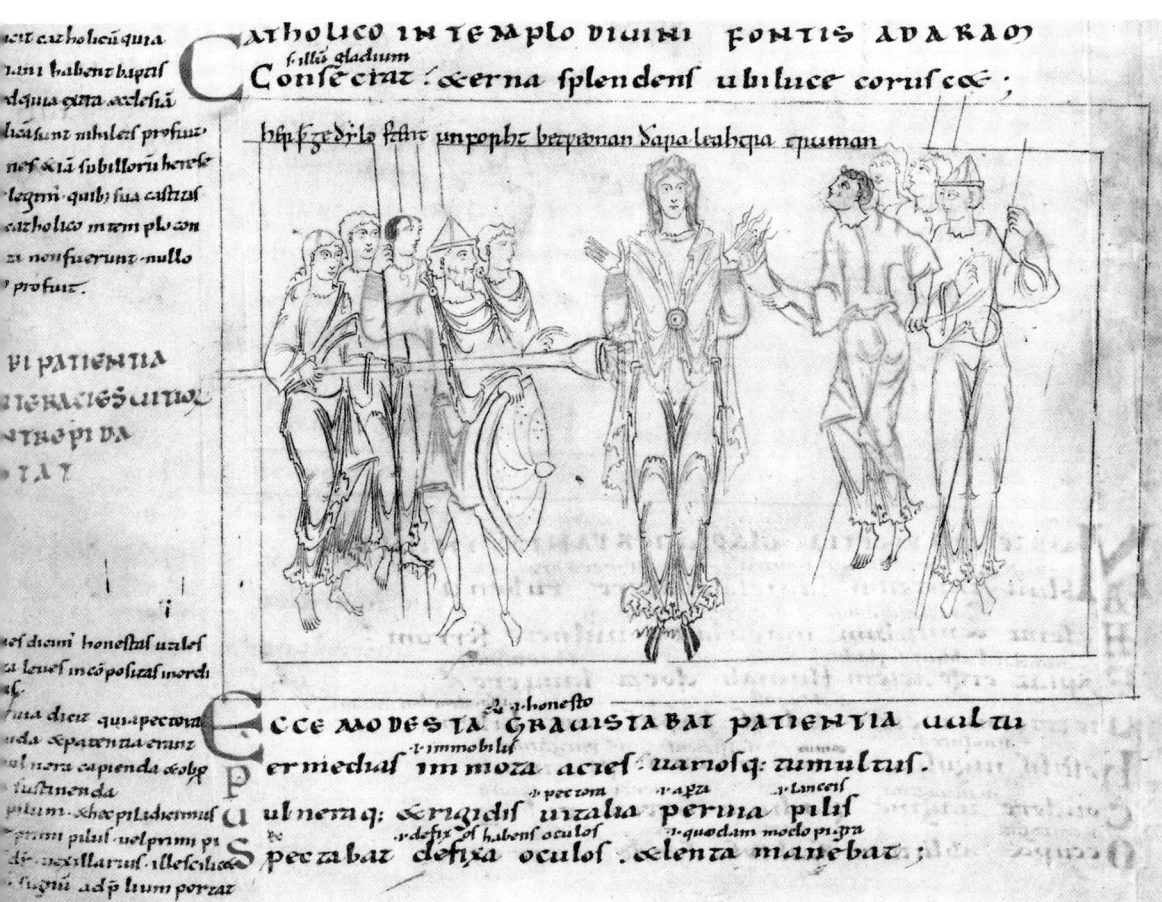

6.8 Cambridge, Corpus Christi College MS 23 (Prudentius, *Psychomachia*), fol. 8v.

Note that at the bottom of the picture, the outer line of the frame has been divided to either side of the gloss *.i. honesto*, showing that the gloss was entered on the page before the frame.

an illustration, showing that the frames were drawn only after the glosses were already on the page; and in several other instances (see Fig. 6.8 for an example), the artist interrupted the course of the frame of a picture in order to avoid a gloss.

If the Anglo-Saxon period yields many examples of manuscripts of which the glosses were copied from an exemplar – particularly when the glossing was part of the original process of production of the manuscript – there also exist cases where glosses were not copied, but represent the responses of individual Anglo-Saxon readers to the text. A manuscript that demonstrates this well is the copy of Sedulius's *Paschale carmen* already mentioned (Cambridge, Corpus Christi College MS 173, Part II). Made in southern England in the second half of the eighth century, by the late ninth it was apparently at Winchester, where, after it had suffered quite extensive damage by liquid, blurred or effaced portions of the text were carefully restored by the scribe who wrote the annals up to the year 891 in the earliest of the seven surviving

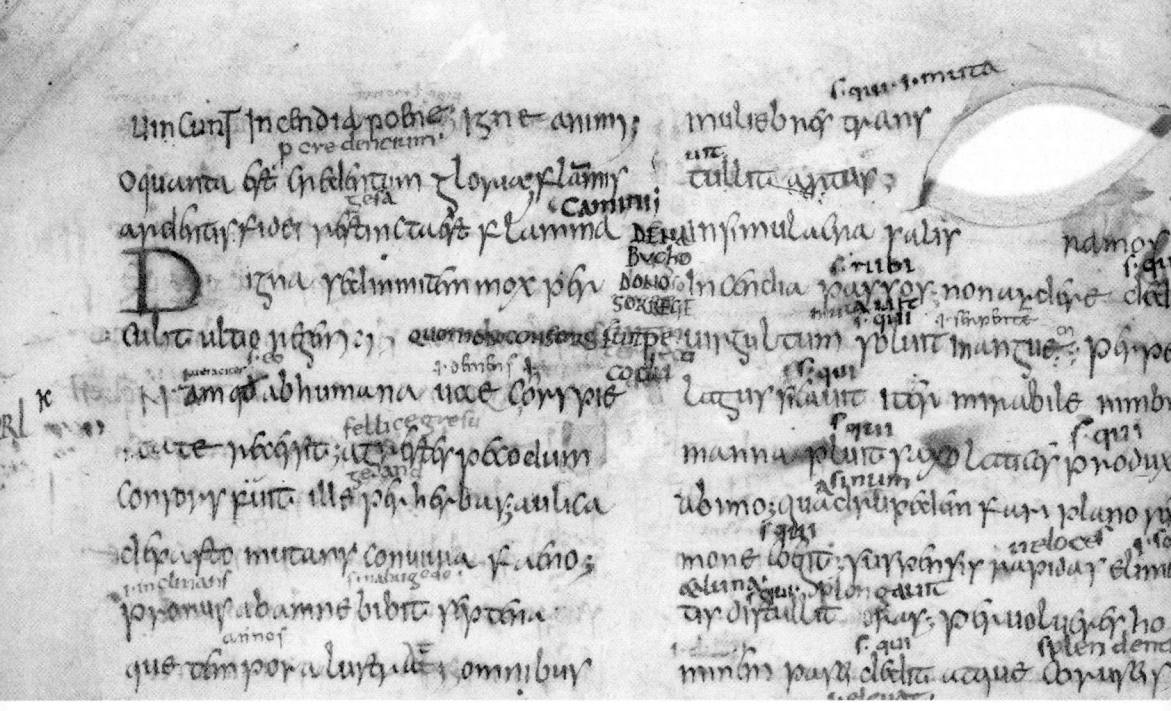

6.9 Cambridge, Corpus Christi College MS 173, Part II (Sedulius, *Paschale carmen*), fol. 61v.

In this manuscript, glosses are entered in a variety of different hands, some of them inexpert.

copies of the *Anglo-Saxon Chronicle* (Cambridge, Corpus Christi College MS 173, Part I); the 'Friðestan diaconus' whose name is entered at the top of the first leaf of the Sedulius manuscript is almost certainly the Frithestan who became bishop of Winchester in 909. The *Corpus Sedulius*, as the manuscript is known, contains glosses in a variety of hands that seem to date from the tenth and perhaps also the eleventh centuries. Many of these hands are unskilled, while some of the glosses are erroneous (for example, in the page illustrated (Fig. 6.9), the gloss *fellice gresu* above *agrestes* in line 7 of the left-hand column is both incorrect and misspelled). These characteristics have led some scholars to suggest that the manuscript was by this time being used by students. It may, indeed, be the best example we have of an Anglo-Saxon 'classbook', for many of the manuscripts that have been identified as classbooks (most of these being glossed copies of the Christian-Latin authors mentioned above) are in too pristine a condition to suggest that they ever saw extensive use by students.[14]

---

[14] The controversy over which Anglo-Saxon manuscripts may legitimately be classified as classbooks has been aired in a series of articles. See, for example, Michael Lapidge, 'The study of Latin texts in late Anglo-Saxon England [1]: the evidence of Latin glosses' in Nicholas Brooks, ed., *Latin and the Vernacular Languages in Early*

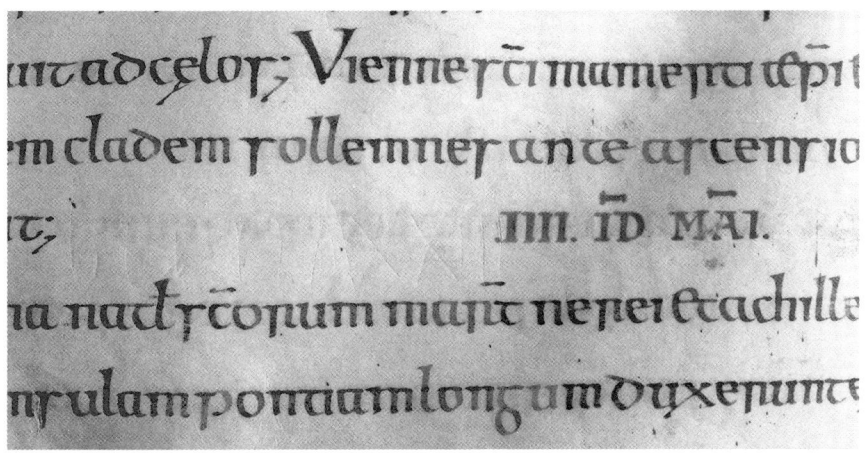

6.10 Cambridge, Corpus Christi College MS 57, fol. 58v.

Here, the gloss *luna XXIII* has been scratched in drypoint at the head of the entry for 12 May in a *Martyrology* used at St Mary's Abbey, Abingdon. The photograph was taken under cold fibre-optic light.

Many of the glosses in the *Corpus Sedulius* were not written with pen and ink, but were scratched onto the page with a stylus, that is, the implement of metal or bone that might also be used to write on wax tablets and to make the rulings on a leaf of parchment. Such glosses are known as 'scratched glosses' or 'drypoint glosses'. Scratched glosses have been found in numerous Anglo-Saxon manuscripts, and more are no doubt awaiting discovery, for, until one knows they are there, they can be extremely difficult to detect. Often it is the chance fall of light onto a page at a particular angle that first reveals a scratched gloss in a manuscript; once one has been found, several more may present themselves to the scholar's searching eye. Given the difficulty of detecting and deciphering such glosses, it is not easy to understand why Anglo-Saxon readers sometimes chose to gloss in drypoint. Possibly the drypoint glossator sought to avoid having the gloss interfere with or distract attention from the main text, as an ink gloss might. It is even conceivable that drypoint glosses were sometimes entered by instructors who were not keen for their pupils to know that they were using such 'teaching aids'. The best way for the modern scholar to search for scratched glosses in a manuscript is to use a fibre-optic cold light source of the kind that is often available in the manuscripts departments of major research libraries. The fibre-optic tubes may be bent to send light raking across the page at any desired angle, and because the light emitted from the ends of the tubes has no heat, the light source may be brought as close to

Medieval Britain, Leicester, University Press, 1982, pp. 99–140; Gernot R. Wieland, 'The glossed manuscript: classbook or library book?' *Anglo-Saxon England*, 14, 1985, pp. 153–73; and Gernot R. Wieland, 'Gloss and illustration: two means to the same end?' in Phillip Pulsiano and Elaine M. Treharne, ed., *Anglo-Saxon Manuscripts and their Heritage*, Aldershot, Ashgate, 1998, pp. 1–20.

the surface of the page as desired without any risk of damaging the ink or parchment. Figure 6.10 shows an example of a scratched gloss photographed using fibre-optic cold light. In this case, the gloss, *luna XXIII*, was discreetly entered next to the entry for 12 May in a *Martyrology* (a manuscript listing the saints who died on each day of the year) by an eleventh-century monk at Abingdon Abbey who was anticipating having to read out loud from the manuscript. In Benedictine monasteries, it was customary practice for one of the community to read each day's entry from the *Martyrology* when the monks met in chapter each morning; and since Carolingian times it had been prescribed that, upon getting up to read, the lector must first say not only what day of the year it was, but also how old the moon was on that day. The glossator in this manuscript had evidently done his homework beforehand and had entered this gloss as a prompt for himself.

Glossae collectae and glossaries

Glosses originally entered over the *lemmata* to which they related might subsequently be pooled together into lists that included all the *lemmata* and *interpretamenta* for a particular text or section of text. Such compilations of glosses are called *glossae collectae*. In England, the oldest sets of *glossae collectae* were probably drawn up in the important school established at Canterbury by the learned Theodore, the Cilician monk who in 668, at the age of 66, was despatched from Rome to head the English Church; arriving in England in 669, Theodore served as archbishop of Canterbury until his death in 690, and was aided in his educational initiatives by Hadrian, a North African monk who assumed the abbacy of St Augustine's Abbey, Canterbury, in 670, continuing in the post until 709 or 710. None of the original sets of *glossae collectae* drawn up in the school of Theodore and Hadrian survive, but they were later re-copied into such manuscripts as the *Leiden Glossary* (Leiden, Bibliotheek der Rijksuniversiteit, MS Voss. Lat. Q. 69), compiled at the abbey of St Gallen, Switzerland, around the year 800.

When first drawn up, sets of *glossae collectae* may have been entered on individual sheets of parchment or, alternatively, scribbled into available blank areas of a manuscript containing the text to which the glosses related. Examples of both of these practices survive. Three pages in London, British Library, MS Cotton Domitian A. i (fols 37v–38v) contain a set of *glossae collectae* for Book III of the *Bella Parisiacae urbis* of Abbo of Saint-Germain-des-Prés, a work that describes the Viking siege of Paris in 885–87. Abbo's text was much studied for its unusual vocabulary; the glosses collected in Domitian A. i were compiled in the late eleventh century from the interlinear glosses entered in the copy of Abbo's work in Cambridge, University Library MS Gg.5.35 (both Domitian A. i and Gg.5.35 are from St Augustine's Abbey,

Canterbury). A ninth-century copy of Bede's *Ecclesiastical History* (London, British Library, MS Cotton Tiberius C. ii) presents a case of collected glosses for a text being entered in available blank areas of a manuscript containing that text: here, sets of *lemmata* and *interpretamenta* for chapters 10–22 of Book I of Bede's work – these chapters describe the Pelagian heresy, the arrival of the Anglo-Saxons in Britain, their battles with the native British, and the mission of St Germanus to combat Pelagianism – were entered during the ninth century in blank areas following the chapter lists of Books I, II, and III and at the end of Book IV.

Once a set of *glossae collectae* for a particular work had been compiled, it might be combined with the actual text in subsequent manuscripts of the work. Certain manuscripts of the *Rule of St Benedict*, for example, follow each of the seventy-two chapters of the *Rule* with a set of glosses for that chapter; one of these manuscripts (Cambridge, Trinity College MS O.2.30, fols 129–72) is Anglo-Saxon, having been copied at St Augustine's Abbey in the mid-tenth century. Alternatively, a complete set of glosses for a work might be written at the beginning of a copy of that work, as a kind of preface, as has happened on fols 70r–71r of Cambridge, Corpus Christi College MS 183 (Fig. 6.11). Here, the scribe who copied the text of Bede's poetic version of his *Life of St Cuthbert* prefaced the text with a set of fifty-one *lemmata* and *interpretamenta* for the work. The list is headed with the title *Hæc sunt quæ in libello sequenti caraxata sunt atq(ue) archana* ('These are the things written in the following little book that are mysterious'). While most of the *interpretamenta* are in Latin, several are in Old English; the first two of these, visible in Fig. 6.11, are the definition of *face* as *ðæcela* and *crisostomus* as *gylden muþa*.

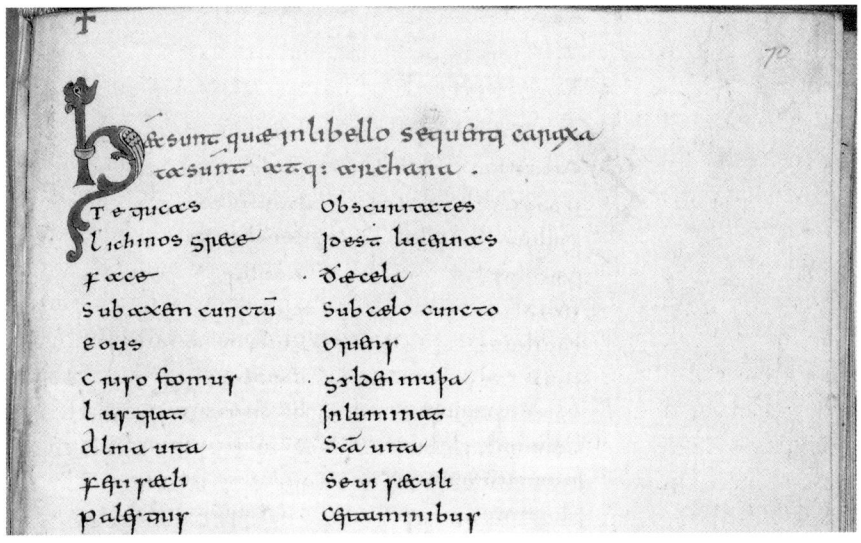

6.11
Cambridge, Corpus Christi College MS 183, fol. 70r.

This page carries the opening of a set of fifty-one *glossae collectae* for Bede's verse *Life of St Cuthbert*.

In a subsequent phase, *glossae collectae* for a particular work might be combined with *glossae collectae* for other works, in extensive glossary manuscripts that have been called 'England's oldest dictionaries'. In some of these glossaries, there was no attempt to integrate the *glossae collectae* derived from different sources; instead, all the *glossae collectae* from one source – say, Aldhelm's *De virginitate* – were followed by all those from another source – say, Orosius's *Histories against the Pagans*. The *Leiden Glossary* (Leiden, Bibliotheek der Rijksuniversiteit, MS Voss. lat. Q. 69 – a continental copy of an Anglo-Saxon exemplar) is of this kind, consisting of forty-eight sections each of which comprises *glossae collectae* from one particular source (canons and papal decretals, the *Rule of St Benedict*, individual books of the Old and New Testaments, and so on). Within each section, the words are not listed in alphabetical order, but in the order in which they occur in the original source.

In other manuscripts, however, some attempt was made to integrate the glosses from different sources and to arrange them alphabetically. In some cases, the alphabetization was by first letter only; that is, all words beginning with *a* were grouped together, then all letters beginning with *b*, and so on, but within the group of words beginning with a particular letter there was no further attempt at alphabetization. In other cases, the alphabetization would be taken a step further, so that it was by the first two letters of each word; that is, all words beginning with the letters *ab* stand together, then all words beginning with *ac*, all words beginning with *ad*, and so on. The most notable Anglo-Saxon example of such a manuscript is the glossary on fols 4–64 of Cambridge, Corpus Christi College MS 144, made in southern

6.12 Cambridge, Corpus Christi College MS 144 (the *Corpus Glossary*), fol. 13v, with *bu*, *by*, and *ca* sections of the glossary.

England in the first half of the ninth century. Within each group of words beginning with the same two letters, the *Corpus Glossary* shows no further attempt at alphabetization. This can be seen in Fig. 6.12, where the left-hand column shows the beginning of the *Corpus Glossary*'s *bu* section, while the right-hand column has the *by* section and the opening of *ca*. The sequence of words at the beginning of the *bu* set runs *bulla, butio, busticeta, busta, busticeta* (again), *bullae, bubo*.

Glossaries ordered only by the first letter of each word are described by modern scholars as being in *a*-order, whereas those ordered by the first two letters are said to be in *ab*-order. Within each alphabetical block, the glosses derived from a particular source may continue to be grouped together. For example, near the beginning of the *ab* section that opens the *Corpus Glossary*, six entries derived from Orosius's *Histories against the Pagans* stand together; the *ac* section includes a block of three consecutive entries from the same source.[15] In all of these glossaries, *lemmata* typically appear in the inflected form that they have in the source from which they ultimately derive. Nouns, in other words, are not cited in their nominative singular form, nor do verbs appear in the first person singular of the present tense, unless those happen to be the forms they have in the source. While the appearance of the words in their inflected forms can help the modern scholar greatly in ascertaining the sources that lie behind the Anglo-Saxon glossaries, this practice distinguished the glossaries from a true dictionary.

Medieval glosses post-dating the Anglo-Saxon period

During the Anglo-Saxon period, it was manuscripts written in Latin that attracted the attention of glossators – whose glosses might be in Latin or the vernacular, as we have seen. For several decades after the Norman Conquest of 1066, glosses continued to be entered in Old English in some Latin manuscripts; the most notable case of a post-Conquest Latin manuscript with an Old English gloss is the *Eadwine Psalter*, mentioned above. From the late twelfth century onwards, however, if Anglo-Saxon manuscripts attracted the attention of glossators, it was typically manuscripts written in Old English, not those in Latin, into which the glosses were entered. The reason for this was that the very language in which these vernacular Anglo-Saxon manuscripts were written had now become a point of interest for certain readers, although those readers were few in number. Old English had by this time evolved into Middle English, which differed from it considerably

---

[15] See W.M. Lindsay, ed., *The Corpus Glossary*, Cambridge, Cambridge University Press, 1921, pp. 1, 4.

in vocabulary and in points of morphology, to the extent that for most, the language of the Anglo-Saxons had become largely incomprehensible.[16]

Apart from manuscripts that belonged to Worcester Cathedral, which form a special case discussed below, very few manuscripts written in Old English attracted any glossatorial attention between the late twelfth and the mid-sixteenth century. Neil Ker lists eight in his great *Catalogue of Manuscripts Containing Anglo-Saxon* (pp. xlix–l). These manuscripts belonged to cathedral or monastic libraries at Canterbury, Ely, Exeter, Rochester, Thorney, and Winchester. The glosses added to these manuscripts are usually in a single hand and often very few in number – for example, just two glosses, dating to the late thirteenth or early fourteenth century, in Cambridge, Corpus Christi College MS 303 (within a homily on the seven deadly sins). In Oxford, Bodleian Library, MS Bodley 343 – a homiliary that seems to have been made somewhere in the West Midlands – one homily (on a passage of St Mark's gospel) attracted a concentrated spate of about one hundred glosses, all in Middle English, by a glossator of the fifteenth century whose knowledge of Old English was remarkably good; but he did not gloss any other part of the manuscript. It is difficult to fathom the exact motivation that lay behind the work of these later medieval glossators, but their entries do at least demonstrate that manuscripts written in Old English attracted interest in certain places and at certain times during the last centuries of the Middle Ages. And it is clear that some individuals succeeded quite well in understanding certain texts written in the ancient English vernacular.

The manuscripts that belonged to the library of Worcester Cathedral form a special, and most interesting, case. Here, a single hand, datable to the first half of the thirteenth century, entered glosses – in most cases, a large number of glosses – in sixteen manuscripts written in Old English. These manuscripts variously contained homilies, a penitential, a range of ecclesiastical texts, the Old English translation of the *Rule of St Benedict*, and three translations associated with King Alfred and those who assisted him in his effort to render into English 'certain books that are the most necessary for all men to know': the *Pastoral Care* and the *Dialogues* of Pope Gregory the Great, and Bede's *Ecclesiastical History*. The script of the Worcester glossator has an unsteady, quivery quality, and for this reason

---

[16] Thus it was that at Ely around the year 1300, a manuscript in Old English could be described as *non apreciatum propter ydioma ignota* ('not valued on account of the unknown language'), while at Glastonbury in the mid-thirteenth century, several Old English manuscripts could be designated *vetusta et inutilia* ('old and useless'). See N.R. Ker, *Catalogue of Manuscripts Containing Anglo-Saxon*, Oxford, Clarendon Press, 1957, p. xlix.

scholars have dubbed him the 'Tremulous Hand of Worcester'.[17] He seems to have suffered from a nervous impairment of some kind – such as congenital tremor – which evidently worsened as he aged, for some of his glosses are much more 'tremulous' than others, and these variations in the quality of his script make it possible to establish an approximate chronology of his glossatorial activity.

The Tremulous Hand clearly had difficulty understanding Old English – yet was determined to do so. While the grammar of the language seems not to have presented him with major difficulties, its vocabulary evidently did; this was a testimony to the degree of change that had occurred in the lexis of the English vernacular between the Anglo-Saxon and early Middle English periods. It is also clear that his knowledge of Old English improved as he persisted in his work, and that it was his habit to keep returning to and re-reading the manuscripts that interested him: there are several cases where he has entered more than one gloss to an Old English word and where the later gloss – that is, the one in more tremulous script – is more accurate.

> 'For Anglo-Saxon readers it was the Latin manuscripts that required supplementary explanations of various kinds. Later readers, however, tended to gloss manuscripts written in Old English.'

The Tremulous Hand usually glossed in Latin though sometimes in Middle English (there is more Middle English in his earlier work). His typical practice was to enter one or more Latin equivalents above certain words of an Old English text. When the text itself was a translation of a Latin original – as with the translations that had been produced at King Alfred's court, and the Old English version of the *Rule of St Benedict* – he could compare it with a copy of the Latin and take many of his glosses from the original. He used this technique when glossing copies of the Alfredian versions of Pope Gregory's *Pastoral Care* and *Dialogues*, the Old English *Rule of St Benedict*, and the Old English translation of Bede's *Ecclesiastical History*. But several of the texts that he glossed – for example, King Alfred's famous *Preface* to the Old English *Pastoral Care* – did not have Latin originals, and here he was on his own. The uncertainties he might experience in identifying the correct meaning of a word or phrase can be seen when he made multiple attempts at glossing it. Figure 6.13 shows a page of King Alfred's *Pastoral Care Preface* in Cambridge, Corpus Christi College MS 12, a manuscript extensively glossed by the Tremulous Hand. His glosses to the preface fall into at least two phases, an earlier one in which his hand was small and relatively neat and a later one in which the writing was larger and shakier. In line 1, his initial gloss to *furður* was *post*, but he

---

[17] The fullest analysis of his work is that by Christine Franzen, *The Tremulous Hand of Worcester: a study of Old English in the thirteenth century*, Oxford, Clarendon Press, 1991.

6.13

Cambridge, Corpus Christi College MS 12, fol. 3r.

The page shows a portion of King Alfred's *Pastoral Care Preface* glossed by the Tremulous Hand of Worcester.

later preferred *ult(e)ri(us)*. Five lines further down the page, he first glossed *oð* with *usq(ue) m(od)o*, then added *usq(ue) n(un)c* in the inner margin after his script had deteriorated. In this case, both glosses are wrong: *oð* is not here the preposition meaning 'until'/'as far as', but is merely the prefix of the past participle *oðfeallen*, 'declined'. The Tremulous Hand's glosses offer a fascinating insight into the progression of his understanding of Old English and the difficulties he encountered.

As well as providing straight lexical equivalents, the Tremulous Hand looked to resolve potential ambiguities in the Old English text. He regularly sought to distinguish the prefix *ge-* from the personal pronoun *ge* ('you'). The potential for confusion between the two different usages was exacerbated by the vagaries of word separation in Anglo-Saxon manuscripts: the prefix was often separated from the word to which it belonged, while the pronoun was occasionally written without a space between it and the next word. The Tremulous Hand's method for distinguishing between the two usages was to write *i* above the prefix – thus giving it the form it had in Middle English (see, for example, the *i* entered above the prefix of *gewrit* at the end line 7 in Fig. 6.13) – and to enter either the letter *yogh* (ȝ) or the Latin word *vos*, meaning 'you', above the pronoun. Figure 6.13 includes no occurrences of the pronoun, but there is a comparable example in line 7 where he has entered a *yogh* over the *g* of *monege*, thus establishing that the *ge* sequence belongs to the end of that word and is not a prefix to the immediately following verb, *cuðon*. Again, to distinguish between Old English dative singular and dative plural *him* ('to him'/'to them'), when the word was plural he would enter *a* above the *i*, thereby altering the word into its Middle English form, *ham*. He sometimes sought to clarify word separation by entering a straight vertical line between two words that were not separated in the manuscript – see the vertical line separating *siððan* from *furður* in line 1 of Fig. 6.13 – or by entering linking strokes between elements of a single word that included a gap between two of its letters – see the linking strokes erroneously placed between *lar* and *læden* in line 5 of Fig. 6.13. He also occasionally made adjustments to punctuation.

It is not easy to deduce exactly why the Tremulous Hand devoted so much time and effort to reading and understanding Old English texts, but it is possible to hazard some conjectures. On the mere level of linguistic proficiency, he certainly seems to have set himself the goal of learning the Old English language to the fullest extent that he could. It was in line with this that he made his own complete copy of Ælfric's *Grammar and Glossary* (Worcester, Cathedral Library MS F.174). Ælfric's work was intended to serve as a grammar of Latin but in addressing this topic it revealed much about the grammar of Old English; the glossary appended to it, consisting of more than twelve hundred Latin terms (organized by categories) and their Old English equivalents, provided a useful repository of Old English vocabulary. Beyond this interest in grammar and vocabulary, the Tremulous Hand seems to have studied Old English texts in search of material that he could use in teaching and/or preaching. Annotations that he entered in the margins of the manuscripts that he studied indicate his interest in such basic theological topics as the nature of Christ and the Trinity as well as in the sacraments and the duties of priests and bishops.[18] These preoccupations are in line with points of doctrine emphasized at the Fourth Lateran Council presided over by Pope Innocent III in 1215 and may well reflect the influence in England of the canons issued by the council, which also sought to promote the use of the vernacular for teaching the general populace the major points of the Christian faith. It has been plausibly suggested that the Tremulous Hand's main goal in studying Anglo-Saxon manuscripts was to mine them for vernacular material which, suitably updated, could be used for instructional purposes and that it may have been his responsibility to train those who were candidates for holy orders, preparing them for work in the parishes of the Worcester diocese.[19] Whatever his exact purposes, one fact is clear: the attention that

---

[18] See Wendy E.J. Collier, 'A thirteenth-century user of Anglo-Saxon manuscripts', *Bulletin of the John Rylands University Library of Manchester*, 79, 1997, pp. 149–65, at pp. 151–2.

[19] Collier, 'A thirteenth-century user', pp. 160–2.

the Tremulous Hand paid to Anglo-Saxon manuscripts was unique in the period between the demise of Old English as a living language and the renewed interest in the language that sprang up in the sixteenth century.

Early modern glosses and annotations

From about the middle of the sixteenth century, Anglo-Saxon manuscripts – particularly those written in the Old English language – began to attract renewed interest. Several factors were at play here. Henry VIII's dissolution of all English monasteries in the later 1530s had led to the dispersal of the contents of the monastic libraries, with the result that in the ensuing years medieval manuscripts came into the hands of private owners. A developing interest in England's past, coupled with a growing national self-awareness, were characteristics that manifested themselves strongly in sixteenth-century literary circles; and such interests were among the motives that led the new owners of manuscripts to examine their contents in detail. Anglo-Saxon manuscripts often elicited the greatest attention because they were the earliest written records of England's past. They contained, for example, the earliest known forms of many English place names – the study of which assumed a prominent place in sixteenth-century descriptions of England such as that planned but never completed by John Leland (c.1503–1552) and William Camden's magnificent *Britannia* of 1586. Further, from the 1560s powerful ecclesiastical figures came to realize that Anglo-Saxon manuscripts had much to reveal about the early practices of the Church in England; they perceived what to them were striking parallels between these practices and those of the sixteenth-century English Church that had now broken away from Rome, and they believed that these early practices provided historical justification for the Church of England's current practices where they differed from those of Rome.

Of course, in order to make use of manuscripts written in Old English, sixteenth-century scholars had first to apply themselves to recovering the knowledge of the ancient vernacular. One of their principal methods of achieving this was to study manuscripts with Latin texts glossed in Old English, or manuscripts containing Old English texts that had been translated from Latin originals; by comparing Old English glosses with their *lemmata*, and Old English translations with the Latin texts on which they were based, they could develop their knowledge of Old English vocabulary, morphology, and syntax.

Most of the scholars known to have immersed themselves in the study of Anglo-Saxon manuscripts between the mid-sixteenth and the mid-seventeenth centuries have left substantial traces of their work in the form of glosses and annotations that they entered in the manuscripts themselves. At first impression it may seem astonishing that these scholars should have taken such liberties with precious codices that would fetch huge prices if sold at auction today and that are now guarded so jealously in their libraries. Attitudes in the early modern period were, however, rather different. Indeed, one of the most assiduous annotators of Anglo-Saxon manuscripts, Abraham Wheelock (1593–1653), was from 1629 the librarian of Cambridge University (as well as its first lecturer in Arabic and Anglo-Saxon, from 1632 and 1639 respectively); he saw no contradiction between his responsibility for the care of the books and his proclivity for annotating them. And there are resulting benefits for modern students and scholars, for the glosses and notes entered by early modern Anglo-Saxonists – for the most part in hands that are easily recognizable – reveal much about these scholars' interests and their methods of work.

The first individual known to have paid significant attention to manuscripts written in Old English was Robert Talbot (c.1505–1558), a prebendary of Norwich Cathedral who developed strong antiquarian interests. It was probably during the latter part of his life that some ten Anglo-Saxon manuscripts passed into his hands. They included the famous illustrated copy of the *Old English Hexateuch* (now London, British Library, MS Cotton Claudius B. iv), as well as copies of the *West Saxon Gospels*, the Old English versions of Bede's *Ecclesiastical History* and Orosius's *Histories against the Pagans*, Ælfric's *Grammar and Glossary*, and collections of Anglo-Saxon laws, homilies, and ecclesiastical institutes. Talbot's glosses and notes may be found in all of these manuscripts, in his characteristic right-sloping, vigorous, somewhat angular script. Several of the Old English texts of which he possessed copies were based on Latin originals, and it was clearly Talbot's practice to compare the vernacular and Latin versions; he would then enter the occasional Latin gloss over words in the Old English text, as he has done on a few pages of his copy of the *West Saxon Gospels*, now Oxford, Bodleian Library, MS Bodley 441. He would have learned much about the structure and morphology of the Old English language by studying his copy of Ælfric's *Grammar and Glossary* (Cambridge, University Library MS Hh.1.10), in which he has entered numerous marginal notes. The manuscript that he annotated most copiously was the miscellaneous collection of ecclesiastical institutes and laws, variously in Latin and Old English, that is now London, British Library, MS Cotton Nero A. i, fols 70–177. His comments may be seen in the margins of numerous leaves of this manuscript that has strong connections with Wulfstan, the great Anglo-Saxon homilist.[20]

---

[20] See the complete facsimile of the manuscript: Henry R. Loyn, ed., *A Wulfstan Manuscript Containing Institutes, Laws and Homilies: British Museum Cotton Nero A. I*, Early English Manuscripts in Facsimile 17, Copenhagen, Rosenkilde & Bagger, 1971.

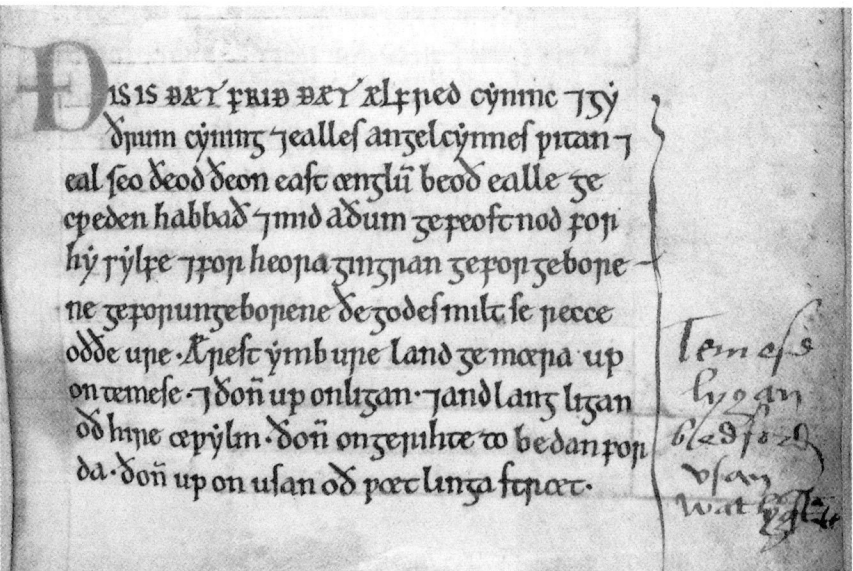

6.14
Cambridge,
Corpus Christi
College MS 383,
fol. 57r.

The outer margin carries Robert Talbot's annotations to the opening of the treaty between Alfred and Guthrum.

It emerges strikingly from Talbot's annotations that he had a special interest in any occurrences of Anglo-Saxon forms of English place names. The study of the early forms of place names was a prominent component of sixteenth-century antiquarian research. Talbot's typical habit when coming upon an Anglo-Saxon place name was to make a note of the term in the margin, in either its original Anglo-Saxon or its sixteenth-century form. Figure 6.14 shows his notes to the opening of a copy of the treaty drawn up between King Alfred and the Viking leader Guthrum in or soon after 886. The treaty's first clause establishes the extent of the territories ruled over by each by describing the boundaries between them. Talbot has bracketed the whole passage with a vertical line and has noted in the margin the references to the Rivers Thames, Lea, and Ouse (*Temese, Lygan, Usan*), the town of Bedford, and the ancient Roman road known as Watling Street.

Laurence Nowell (1530–*c*.1569) applied himself assiduously to the study of Anglo-Saxon manuscripts in connection with his wider interest in England's medieval history. His work with Old English texts was conducted principally during a five-year period from 1562 to 1567, when he was serving as tutor within the household of Sir William Cecil, Queen Elizabeth's Secretary of State; in 1567 Nowell departed England for the Continent – a journey from which he never returned – and left his papers in the hands of his scholarly collaborator William Lambarde (1536–1601). During his years in Cecil's household, Nowell was extremely productive, making transcripts from several copies of the *Anglo-Saxon Chronicle*, compiling an extensive dictionary of Old English, and projecting an edition of the Anglo-Saxon laws which was

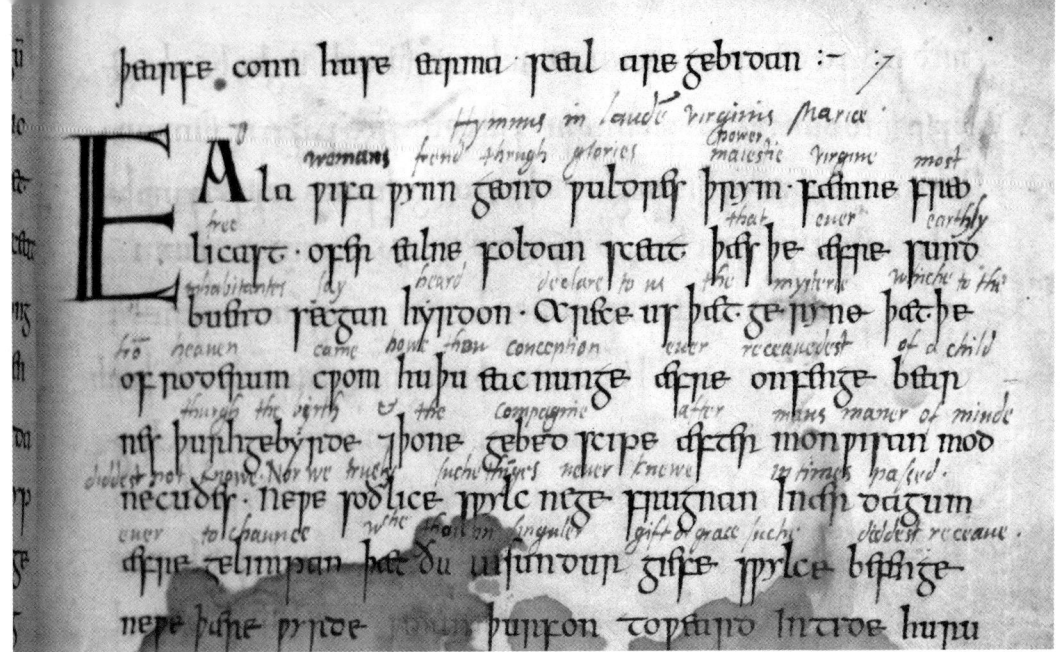

6.15 Exeter, Cathedral, Dean and Chapter Library MS 3501, fol. 9r.

The page includes Laurence Nowell's interlinear gloss to a portion of Christ I.

brought to completion and published by Lambarde in 1568.[21] Nowell also has the distinction of being the first known owner of the *Beowulf Manuscript* (London, British Library, MS Cotton Vitellius A. xv, fols 94–209). The medieval home of the manuscript is unknown; but in the upper margin of its first page, Nowell has written his name and the date '1563'. Neither Nowell nor Lambarde glossed or annotated the Anglo-Saxon manuscripts they studied as freely as did other scholars of their era. However, a single sixteenth-century gloss written on the first page of the *Beowulf* poem ('feared' above *egsode*, fol. 132r, line 6; see Fig. 4.4) appears to be in Nowell's hand.

Nowell also entered an interlinear English gloss above the first seven lines of the hymn to the Virgin Mary that occurs near the beginning of the poem *Christ I* on fol. 9r of the great *Exeter Book* of Old English poetry (Exeter, Cathedral, Dean and Chapter Library MS 3501; see Fig. 6.15). Here, the sloping, somewhat elongated character of the letter forms is easily recognizable as Nowell's through comparison with the script of the facing-page translations with which he provided several of his Old English transcripts, such as his translation of the laws of King Alfred in London, British Library, Henry Davis Collection, no. 59. Nowell's gloss includes some errors, for example the rendition of *sundbuend* ('sea-dwellers') as 'earthly inhabitants', and he did not

---

21 For Nowell's *Anglo-Saxon Chronicle* transcripts, see Angelika Lutz, 'Das Studium der angelsächsischen Chronik im 16. Jahrhundert: Nowell und Joscelyn', *Anglia*, 100, 1982, pp. 301–56. Nowell's dictionary was published in 1952 under the editorship of Albert H. Marckwardt as *Laurence Nowell's 'Vocabularium Saxonicum'*, Ann Arbor and London, University of Michigan Press and Oxford University Press. The edition of the Anglo-Saxon laws was published in Lambarde's name under the title *Archaionomia, sive de priscis Anglorum legibus libri*, London, ex officina Joannis Daij, 1568.

attempt a translation of *ofer ealne foldan sceat* ('over all the surface of the earth'). What is especially interesting about his gloss in the *Exeter Book* is that it offers about the only evidence we have that the sixteenth-century scholars had any interest whatever in Old English poetic texts; even *Beowulf* itself seems to have attracted little sustained interest until the eighteenth century.

During the years in which Nowell was at work in Cecil's household, the Archbishop of Canterbury's residence at Lambeth on the other side of the Thames was a veritable hive of bibliographic activity. Matthew Parker, archbishop from 1559 until 1575, set himself the task of rescuing as many manuscripts as possible from the threat of loss, destruction, or abuse that had hung over them ever since the dissolution of the monasteries. By the time of his death in 1575 he had accumulated over five hundred manuscripts, most of which he bequeathed to Corpus Christi College, Cambridge, of which he had been Master from 1544 to 1553; he also gave twenty-five manuscripts to Cambridge University Library in 1574 and assigned others to members of his family. While the manuscripts were in his hands, Parker and those who worked in his household studied them attentively, the fruits of their studies being embodied in a series of publications appearing between 1566 and 1574, including the earliest editions of several Old English texts. Anglo-Saxon manuscripts held special interest for Parker because of what they could tell him about the early practices of the English Church; in his publications he repeatedly drew upon the evidence of the manuscripts to make polemical points against the Roman Catholic Church. The member of Parker's circle who developed special expertise in Old English was his chaplain and secretary John Joscelyn (1529–1603). Joscelyn was by far the most copious sixteenth-century annotator of Anglo-Saxon manuscripts. His glosses and comments may be found in several dozen manuscripts; usually entered in Joscelyn's small, somewhat cramped informal italic hand, they reveal a great deal about his scholarly methods.

Much of Joscelyn's work was connected with a mammoth lexicographical project the final outcome of which was intended to be the publication of a full-scale dictionary that would serve as a tool for all who sought to understand texts written in Old English. Joscelyn's efforts towards the production of such a dictionary fell into several stages, the first of which was his intensive study of Anglo-Saxon manuscripts and his identification of words of lexicographical interest. He used various methods to signal such words. He might merely underline them as he read through a manuscript: the underlining of several Old English words on the page of the *Corpus Glossary* illustrated in Fig. 6.12 is by Joscelyn and similar underlinings are to be found in other manuscripts that he studied. Frequently, he would enter a gloss – typically in Latin but occasionally in sixteenth-century English – above an Old English term that interested him. His Latin glosses were in many cases drawn from the original

Latin text on which the Old English was based. Sometimes, indeed, he could find the Latin within the very same manuscript: for example, in entering glosses to the Old English version of the *Rule for Canons* by Chrodegang of Metz in Cambridge, Corpus Christi College MS 191, he consulted the Latin version of the text in the same manuscript, in which each Latin chapter is followed by its Old English translation (see Fig. 6.20, where the underlinings within both the Latin and the Old English text are by Joscelyn). In one manuscript that he glossed, Joscelyn made use of the work of the Tremulous Hand: in entering Latin equivalents above numerous words of King Alfred's *Pastoral Care Preface* in Oxford, Bodleian Library, MS Hatton 20 (the copy that Alfred despatched to Worcester), Joscelyn simply transcribed the Tremulous Hand's glosses to the preface in Cambridge, Corpus Christi College MS 12, which also belonged to Worcester. A third practice of Joscelyn's was to enter numbers above Old English words that interested him. He did this in just a few manuscripts, including Oxford, Bodleian Library, MS Junius 121 (a miscellany of ecclesiastical texts), Cambridge, Corpus Christi College MS 198 (a homiliary), and London, British Library, MS Cotton Tiberius B. iv (the D version of the *Anglo-Saxon Chronicle*). In Junius 121, for example, he used a new sequence of numbers for each text that he marked in this way: he entered numbers from 1 to 33 over words within the text *Be ðeodwitan* on fols 11r–12v and a new sequence of numbers from 1 to 25 over words in the next text, *Item de episcopis*, on fols 12v–13v.

Having marked words of lexicographical interest in these various ways, Joscelyn then went through the manuscripts again, compiling his own lists of such words and assigning each word a definition. A collection of his lists, compiled from about twenty manuscripts, survives in his notebook, London, Lambeth Palace Library MS 692, but it is clear that there must have been further lists that have not survived. The word lists represent an intermediate stage in his lexicographical activity, which culminated in a two-volume handwritten dictionary produced by Joscelyn in collaboration with Matthew Parker's son John (1548–1619). This was the dictionary that Joscelyn evidently wished to publish, although he never succeeded in doing so. The line of continuity between the different stages of Joscelyn's lexicographical work is clear: words that he underlined or glossed in the earliest phase of the work reappear in the dictionary, and the arabic numerals that he entered in certain manuscripts are there used as a referencing system.[22]

---

[22] For a fuller account of Joscelyn's lexicographical activity and the manuscript evidence attesting to it, see Timothy Graham, 'John Joscelyn, pioneer of Old English lexicography' in Timothy Graham, ed., *The Recovery of Old English: Anglo-Saxon studies in the sixteenth and seventeenth centuries*, Kalamazoo, MI, Medieval Institute Publications, 2000, pp. 83–140.

RIGHT

6.16 London, British Library, MS Cotton Tiberius B. iv (*Anglo-Saxon Chronicle*, MS D), fol. 20r.

The page has been extensively annotated by John Joscelyn.

Joscelyn's interest in Anglo-Saxon manuscripts, however, extended far beyond the merely lexicographical. His many entries reveal the close attention with which he studied Old English texts and the depth of his familiarity with the content of a broad range of manuscripts. Part of his work for Parker involved his scouting for material of ecclesiastical significance that the Archbishop could use in his publications; Joscelyn would often underline or otherwise signal such passages when he came upon them. In the course of his studies he evidently developed a consuming interest in Anglo-Saxon history along with a fascination with the different copies of the *Anglo-Saxon Chronicle* and the discrepancies between those copies. He became familiar with five of the seven surviving copies of the work – those to which modern scholars have assigned the sigla A, B, C, D, and E. He entered interlinear and marginal notes in four of these (all but MS E). His typical practice was to record variant readings by adding to a passage within one manuscript the variant text found in one or more of the others. He annotated MS D (London, British Library, MS Cotton Tiberius B. iv), the copy from Worcester, far more heavily than any of the others and it seems likely that he was himself the owner of the manuscript before it passed into the hands of Sir Robert Cotton early in the seventeenth century. Figure 6.16 shows fol. 20r of MS D and provides a representative sample of the nature of Joscelyn's annotations in this manuscript.

In twenty-one places on the page, Joscelyn has noted variant spellings of particular words within the text of D by underlining the part of the word affected and entering the variant letters in the interline. All his variants accord with the spellings to be found in MS A (Cambridge, Corpus Christi College MS 173, Part I), the copy of the *Chronicle* that belonged to Parker; it is thus clear that Joscelyn conducted an extensive comparison of A and D. In two places on the page he has provided Latin glosses to Old English terms: *vir* to *wer* in line 18, and *ecclesiastica(m) tonsura(m)* (a phrase which he notes he has derived from Bede) to *sancte petres scære* in line 20.[23] In two other places he has specifically identified the manuscripts with which he has compared D. At the end of the annal for 910, he first noted (below line 3) that the material of this annal was also to be found *in hist(oria) Sax(onica) Petroburg(ensi)* ('in the Saxon history of Peterborough' – a reference to MS E (Oxford, Bodleian Library, MS Laud Misc. 636), compiled at Peterborough;

---

[23] Joscelyn presumably found the phrase in the chronological summary that Bede included at the end of his *Ecclesiastical History of the English People* (Book V, chapter 24). There, under the year 716, Bede notes that *uir Domini Ecgberct Hiienses monachos ad catholicum pascha et ecclesiasticam correxit tonsuram* ('Egbert, the man of God, converted the monks of Iona to the catholic Easter and corrected their ecclesiastical tonsure'); see Bertram Colgrave and R.A.B. Mynors, ed., *Bede's Ecclesiastical History of the English People*, Oxford, Clarendon Press, 1969, pp. 566–7.

man wið peohtas. betwux hæþe. 7 cære. 7 me
7 nun his mæg gefultron wið gewende peala
cyninge. 7 þam ylcan geare man sloh sigbald.

An̄. dccxi.

Aā. dccxii.

Aā. dccxiii.

Aā. dccxiiii. her gewende guðlac se halga.

Aā. dccxv. her ine 7 ceolred gefuhton
æt woðnes beorge.

Aā. dccxvi. her osred norþan hymbra
cyning weard ofslagen beruðan gemære. 7 se
hæfde . viii. wintra æfter ealo ferde. þa feng cen
red to rice. 7 heold . ii. gear. þa os ric. 7 heold. xi.
7 eac on þam ylcan geare ceolred myrcna
cyning forð ferde. 7 his lic resteð on licet felda.
7 æþelred wendinges on beardan igge. 7 þa
feng æþel bald to rice on myrcum. 7 heold. xli.
wintra. 7 ecgberht se arwurða wer ge cyrde
se hwam to fuhtum ceastrum. 7 to sancte
petres rære.

Aā. dccxvii.

Aā. dccxviii. her ingild forð ferde ines
broþor. 7 heora sweostra wæron cwen burh. 7
cuþ burh. 7 seo cuþ burh þlif æt winburnan

he then added the words *et Eccl(es)iæ Chr(ist)i Cant(uariensis)* ('and of Christ Church, Canterbury' – a reference to MS A, which had belonged to Christ Church). The sequence of these annotations establishes that he compared D with E before he compared it with A. To the annal for 716, he has added material about the genealogy of King Æthelbald of Mercia and about the introduction at the monastery of Iona, by the Anglo-Saxon missionary Egbert, of correct practice concerning the calculation of the date of Easter and the form of the monastic tonsure. He found this material in MS A, again identified as *hist(oria) Sax(onica) eccl(es)ię Chr(ist)i Cant(uariensis)*. Because this was a longer entry, he has placed it in the inner margin, sideways, linking it to the appropriate point in the text with a pair of alpha-shaped *signes-de-renvoi*. He has also entered A's version of the text about the tonsure in the interline above lines 19–20, directly above the equivalent text of MS D. In his work on MS D and other *Chronicle* manuscripts, Joscelyn was in many ways acting like a modern scholar preparing a critical edition, except that he has entered his observations of textual variants directly on the pages of the original manuscripts themselves. This practice, although now entirely unacceptable, has left us precious evidence of the manner in which this major early scholar of Anglo-Saxon texts went about his work.

Following Joscelyn's death in 1603, the most assiduous student of Anglo-Saxon manuscripts in the early seventeenth century was William L'Isle (c.1569–1637), one-time Fellow of King's College, Cambridge, who lived at Wilbraham, just outside Cambridge. L'Isle collected a few manuscripts of his own – including MS E of the *Anglo-Saxon Chronicle* – and also borrowed manuscripts from the great library that his contemporary Sir Robert Cotton was in the process of assembling. Cotton's own records, and a series of letters that L'Isle wrote to the collector, reveal that L'Isle was able to borrow MS G of the *Anglo-Saxon Chronicle* (London, British Library, MS Cotton Otho B. xi, which also contained a copy of the Old English translation of Bede's *Ecclesiastical History*), the illustrated copy of the *Old English Hexateuch* (London, British Library, MS Cotton Claudius B. iv), and a second, unillustrated copy of the *Hexateuch* accompanied by Ælfric's homily on the book of Judges (Oxford, Bodleian Library, MS Laud Misc. 509).[24] L'Isle had not returned this latter manuscript by the time of Cotton's death in 1631, which explains why it is now in the Bodleian and not the British Library: on L'Isle's own death in 1637, the manuscripts that were in his possession passed to Archbishop William Laud, who gave them

---

[24] See Timothy Graham, 'William L'Isle's letters to Sir Robert Cotton' in *Early Medieval English Texts and Interpretations: studies presented to Donald G. Scragg*, ed. Elaine Treharne and Susan Rosser, Tempe, AZ, Arizona Center for Medieval and Renaissance Studies, 2002, pp. 353–79.

to the Bodleian in 1639. Until recently, L'Isle has been known to Anglo-Saxonists primarily for his *A Saxon Treatise Concerning the Old and New Testament*, published in 1623, which contains his edition of Ælfric's letter to ealdorman Sigeweard on the contents of the various books of the Bible; L'Isle prepared the edition from the only surviving copy of the work, found at the end of Bodleian MS Laud Misc. 509, the second of the two *Hexateuch* manuscripts that he borrowed from Cotton. Research on L'Isle conducted since the mid-1990s has established that he intended to follow up his edition of the letter to Sigeweard with further publications devoted to the *Anglo-Saxon Chronicle* and to the Old English translations of parts of the Old and New Testaments. Although these projects never reached final fruition, they are amply attested by the marks and annotations that L'Isle has left in numerous manuscripts.

Evidence for L'Isle's *Chronicle* project survives principally in MS E, which he owned. L'Isle has in fact significantly altered the physical state in which this manuscript has come down to us by placing between each of its original parchment *bifolia* a sheet of paper of larger dimensions than the parchment – something he could only have accomplished with the manuscript disbound. He then entered in the outer area of the paper leaves, as well as on available blank areas of the original parchment leaves, the fruits of his collation of MS E against two other copies of the Chronicle, MS A (which was available to him in Cambridge) and MS G (which Cotton lent him). All the notes that L'Isle entered on the original leaves may be seen in the facsimile of MS E that was published in 1954.[25] The facsimile, however, does not show any part of the inserted paper sheets, with the result that it provides only an incomplete record of L'Isle's work in the manuscript and leaves the reader puzzled: L'Isle linked several of his entries on the paper sheets to the point on the original leaf to which they relate by drawing an ink line leading from the one to the other, but in the facsimile, given the absence of the paper inserts, these lines appear to lead nowhere. Figure 6.17 shows a page of MS E with the associated paper leaf. On the original manuscript page, next to E's blank entry for the year 894 (which is followed by six more blank entries for the years 895–900), L'Isle has entered the comment, *Liber Cottonian(us) et Benet multa habe(n)t de hoc Anno et reliquis* ('The Cottonian and Benet books have many things concerning this year and the others'). The 'Cottonian book' was MS G; 'Benet' was MS A, L'Isle's appellation resulting from the name 'Benet College', by which Corpus Christi College was often known in the early modern period (because the church next to the college was dedicated to St Benedict). That

---

[25] Dorothy Whitelock, ed., *The Peterborough Chronicle (the Bodleian Manuscript Laud Misc. 636)*, Early English Manuscripts in Facsimile 4, Copenhagen, Rosenkilde & Bagger, 1954.

a° 892.
Benet. ⁊ þy ilcan geare ofer
eastron ymbe gang dagas
oððe ær æteowde se steorra
þe mon on boclæden hat co-
meta ſume men cweðaþ on
englisc þ hit ſie feaxede steorra forðan þær ſtent
lang leoma of hwilum on
ane healfe on hwilum on
ælce healfe.

✠ þas words are added
on of Benet. who w alſo ſa
hend of þa kinges reigne þt
yppeared but otherwyſe ſhewes to
wyt a yeare elder than other
hiſtory wryters.

902. þa gwad æþelwald his fæderan
ſunu þone ham æt winburnan ⁊ æt
tweoxn eam butan þes cyniſ leafe
⁊ his witena. þa gwad ſe cyng mid fyrd
⁊ he gepicod æt badanbyrig pið winburnan. ⁊ æþelwald ſæt binnan þæm ham
mid þæm monn þe him to gebugon
⁊ hæfde eall his geatu fpopoſtet into him
⁊ ſæd þ he wold oððer ðæn þær libban
oððe þer licgan. þa under þæm þa
beſtal ne hime on riht upper ⁊
ſoht þone here on norþhymbre.
⁊ ſe cyng het pidan æfter ⁊ þa ne
miht hine mon ofridan. þa berad
mon þæt pif þæt he hæfde ær ge
numen butan cynges leafe ⁊ ofer þa
biſcopa gbod. forðan he hepay ær to
nunnan ghalgod. ⁊ on þy ilcan geare
forþferde æþered ſe paſ on defene
ealdormon feoper puct ær elfred
cyning.
903. her gefo aþulf ealdormon
ealfpide bropor ⁊ vinzilius abbud
of scotta ⁊ grimbald maſſe preost.
viii idus iulii.
904. her co æþelwald hider ofer ſæ
mid þam flotan þe he mid pæs on eaſtſexe
þa æt ſeton ða centiſcan þær boxtan ofer his bebod ⁊ ſpa ofer engla nacan he him hæfd to ægeð.
hie twæn ⁊ tuhto. ⁊ ðæn pearð ſigulf ealdormon ofſlægen
breht ſigulfes ſunu ⁊ eadpald acca ſunuf. ⁊ monige eac mid ic þa ðunge ſeð
of ſægæ eohrric hira cyng ⁊ æþelwald æþeling þe hine to þæm unfriðe
iſpahold ⁊ ofcytehold ⁊ ſpide monige eac him þe ge nu gene mæne magð.

up heora ſcipa oððone pald .iiii. mila fra þam mu-
þan utan peardū ⁊ þæp abyacon an ge peope inne on
dam fenne fæton forpa cyrilice men on ⁊ þær fam
poſiht. þa sona æfter þam com hæren mid .lxxx. ſcipa up inne tæmeſe muþe ⁊ porhte him ge peopc æt
middel tune. ⁊ ſeo oðen hepe æt apuldre. Hic obiit
pulfhepe norðan hymbroru arc epſ.

Ā. ñ. dccc. xciii.
Ā. ñ. dccc. xciiii.   et Benet
                        Liber Cottonian ⁊ multa habet
                        de hoc Anno et reliquis.
Ā. ñ. dccc. xv.
Ā. ñ. dccc. xcvi.
Ā. ñ. dccc. xcvii.
Ā. ñ. dccc. xcviii.
Ā. ñ. dccc. xc ix.
Ā. ñ. dccc.
Ā. ñ. dccci.   ✠ Þis mihtū ær calpa haligra mæſſan
                    her gefor ælfred cyning .vii.
                    kl̄ Novēb. ⁊ he heold þæt pice .xxviii. pintra ⁊ healf
                    geap. ⁊ þa fens eadpard his ſunu pice.
Ā. ñ. dccc ii.   Se paſ cyning ofer eall angel cyn
                    butan þæm dæle þe under dena
                    onpald pæſ.
Ā. ñ. dccc iii.
Ā. ñ. dccc iiii.
Ā. ñ. dccc v.
Ā. ñ. dccc vi.   Her ge fertnode eadpard cyng
                    fori neode frið ægðer ge pið eaſt engla here. ge
✠ Benet.   pið norðhymbre. ⁊ alfred ⁊ fop ſe pæſ æt baðum ⁊ þefa.
Ā. ñ. dccc vii.
Ā. ñ. dccc viii.
✠ B. Ā. ñ. dccc ix. her ge for denuſ biſcop on pinte ceaſt re.
Ā. ñ. dccc x.   her engle here ⁊ ðere ge fuh-
                    ton æt teotan heale. ⁊ æþered myrcena ealdor forð

905. her aſſon æþelwald þone here on eaſt englit to unfride. ⁊ hie heryodo
ofer mercena land oð hie como to creccagelade. ⁊ for no her ofer temere
⁊ namo egðer ⁊ on bradene ⁊ þæp ymbutan eall. ⁊ hie ⁊ henton mehton
pendon þa æſt ham peard. þa for eadpard cyning æfter ſpa he paðoſt mehte
nov̄ þa he þa eft ſonan ut faran polde. þa het he beodan ofer ealle baſypod þæt hie
foran calle æt ſomne...

L'Isle has here added the words *et Benet* above the line, with a caret marking the insertion, suggests that he compared this portion of E with G first, then with A. Further down the page, within E's entry for 901 noting the death of King Alfred, L'Isle records A's alternative wording for the date of Alfred's demise and its statement about the extent of his dominion in England; he then adds the following note alongside, on his inserted paper leaf, using Secretary script as he is now writing in his own vernacular language: 'Thes[e] word(es) are added out of Benet, where also the tyme of this kings raigne is the same but otherwise expressed, viz. a yeare & halfe lesse then thirty winters.' L'Isle ties this comment to his addition within the text with a pair of crosses. Toward the bottom of the original page, he rounds off E's annal for 906 by adding A's statement about the death of Alfred, reeve of Bath, and he fills out E's barren annal for 909 with A's record of the death of Denewulf, bishop of Winchester. What is most striking, though, is the mass of additional Old English material he has entered on his inserted paper leaf. In the upper left area, he has transcribed the reference to the appearance of a comet that occurs in A's annal for 892 but is not in E; and in the lower half of the added leaf he has compensated for E's lack of information for the years 902–905 by entering the complete text of A's annals for these years – ending the annal for 905 at the bottom of the adjacent paper leaf. L'Isle's paper inserts have much to reveal about the assiduity with which he studied the three different manuscripts of the *Anglo-Saxon Chronicle* that were known to him.

L'Isle announced his intention to publish an edition of the Old English version of the Scriptures in his introduction to the 1623 *Saxon Treatise*. From this introduction it emerges that he believed, erroneously, that a complete vernacular translation of the Bible had been produced by the Anglo-Saxons: he thought that the Old English versions of the *Hexateuch*, the book of Psalms, and the gospels were remnants of this full translation and that the many scriptural texts that were quoted in the vernacular in Old English homilies also derived from it. The work that L'Isle completed in connection with this project included his full collation of the two *Hexateuch* manuscripts against one another, his collation of four manuscripts containing the Old English translation of the book of Psalms, and his detailed examination of nine Old English homiliaries as well as a manuscript of the early Middle English *Ancrene Wisse*.

Both of the *Hexateuch* manuscripts include extensive evidence of his activity in the form of interlinear and marginal entries in his hand. For example, when the two manuscripts displayed variant readings for a particular word or phrase, L'Isle would often underline that word or phrase, then record in the margin the variant reading from the other manuscript. In each manuscript, phrases of the *Hexateuch* text were occasionally omitted in error by the original scribes; on numerous occasions, having spotted

LEFT

6.17 Oxford, Bodleian Library, MS Laud Misc. 636 (*Anglo-Saxon Chronicle*, MS E), fol. 34v.

The annotations are by William L'Isle.

such an omission in one manuscript, L'Isle made it good by copying the missing text from the other manuscript. It is also clear that as he collated one manuscript against the other, he compared the Old English with the Latin of the Vulgate, for in several places he has entered the Vulgate reading above a word or phrase of the Old English. In one remarkable instance where the Old English failed to provide a translation of a phrase of the Latin text of Exodus 22:15, L'Isle composed a translation of his own and inserted it between the lines of fol. 58v of MS Laud Misc. 509. Equally striking is the entry that occurs in the lower margin of fol. 24r and the upper margin of fol. 24v of the Laud manuscript (Fig. 6.18). Here, L'Isle has entered an extended Old English passage describing how Shechem raped Jacob's daughter Dinah and how Jacob's sons subsequently deceived and slew the Shechemites (Genesis 33:18–34:31). This passage was originally omitted from the Old English version, presumably because its content was deemed too lurid (Ælfric, in his preface to the Old English translation of Genesis, had commented upon how the common people might misinterpret certain of the Old Testament narratives). In the late twelfth century, a summary of the incident was added, in a very late form of Old English, on fol. 51rv of the illustrated copy of the *Hexateuch*, MS Claudius B. iv. It was this summary that L'Isle transcribed into MS Laud Misc. 509; but as he did so, he altered the spellings of Claudius B. iv in an attempt to make the language appear more like 'pure' Old English. Thus, in line 3 of his entry (see Fig. 6.18), L'Isle's *dohtor* represents Claudius B. iv's

6.18 Oxford, Bodleian Library, MS Laud Misc. 509, fol. 24r.

The lower margin carries a passage transcribed (with alterations) by William L'Isle from the other *Hexateuch* manuscript, London, British Library, MS Cotton Claudius B. iv.

6.19
Cambridge,
Corpus Christi
College MS 162
(Homiliary),
p. 531.

The underlinings of biblical quotations within the text and the crosses in the margin are attributable to William L'Isle.

docter; two lines below, he has transcribed *muculum* as *miclum*, and in the last line on fol. 24r, he has altered Claudius's *herde* to *herigde* – thereby creating a form that does not occur in the surviving corpus of Old English.

In his efforts to recover as much as he could of the Old English text of the Bible, L'Isle subjected nine collections of Old English homilies to intense scrutiny.[26] When he came upon a passage of Scripture quoted in the vernacular within a homily, he would often mark it – either by underlining it or by entering a cross in the margin or, very occasionally, by noting in the margin the biblical book that was the source of the quotation (see Fig. 6.19). Only recently have scholars recognized that these marks within the manuscripts are L'Isle's work. They can be attributed to him because he subsequently transcribed these very same passages into a notebook, now Oxford, Bodleian Library, MS Laud Misc. 381, in which he compiled as many scriptural quotations in Old English as he could find, with the ultimate intention of publishing them as 'Saxon-English Remains' of the Bible.[27] L'Isle

---

[26] The manuscripts are Cambridge, University Library MS Gg.3.28; Cambridge, Corpus Christi College MSS 162, 178, 188, 198, 303, 419, and 421; and Cambridge, Trinity College MS B.15.34.

[27] For fuller discussion of this aspect of L'Isle's work with Anglo-Saxon manuscripts, see Stuart Lee, 'Oxford, Bodleian Library, MS Laud Misc. 381: William L'Isle, Ælfric, and the *Ancrene Wisse*' in Graham, *The Recovery of Old English*, pp. 207–42, at pp. 217–42; and Timothy Graham, 'Early modern users of Claudius B. iv: Robert Talbot and William L'Isle' in Rebecca Barnhouse and Benjamin C. Withers, ed., *The Old English Hexateuch: aspects and approaches*, Kalamazoo, MI, Medieval Institute Publications, 2000, pp. 271–316, at pp. 303–13.

also studied the version of the Middle English rule for nuns, the *Ancrene Wisse*, in Cambridge, Corpus Christi College MS 402. Here too, he underlined or otherwise marked those passages of Scripture quoted in the vernacular. He apparently thought that these early Middle English passages ultimately derived from the full Old English version of the Bible that he believed had once existed, and when he copied them into his notebook, he made alterations to the orthography and vocabulary so that the texts would more closely resemble Old English – just as he had done with the passage about the Shechemites that he added to MS Laud Misc. 509.

The last early modern scholar whose hand occurs frequently in the interlines and margins of Anglo-Saxon manuscripts is Abraham Wheelock (1593–1653). Appointed librarian of Cambridge University in 1629, in the mid-1630s Wheelock was recruited by Sir Henry Spelman to examine Anglo-Saxon manuscripts in Cambridge in search of materials Spelman could use in his monumental survey of the customs and laws of the English Church, published in 1639 as *Concilia, decreta, leges, constitutiones, in re ecclesiarum orbis Britannici*. In 1639, thanks to an endowment by Spelman, Wheelock was appointed lecturer in Anglo-Saxon at Cambridge, thereby becoming the first person ever to hold a university post in Anglo-Saxon studies. Wheelock combed large numbers of manuscripts in Cambridge University Library and at Corpus Christi College and Trinity College as he worked on Spelman's behalf, the record of his efforts being preserved in their correspondence.[28] But Wheelock also set in motion a major project of his own, an edition of the Latin and Old English versions of Bede's *Ecclesiastical History* – accompanied by the first ever edition of the *Anglo-Saxon Chronicle* – which he published in 1643. For the Old English text of his Bede edition, Wheelock collated three manuscripts: Cambridge, University Library MS Kk.3.18, Cambridge, Corpus Christi College MS 41, and London, British Library, MS Cotton Otho B. xi. His edition also included many detailed notes (placed at the end of chapters) in which he commented at length on points within Bede's text and quoted material illustrative of the practices of the early English Church that he garnered from a wide range of manuscripts, principally homiliaries.

Entries in Wheelock's hand may be found in many of the Anglo-Saxon manuscripts in Cambridge, and these entries provide fascinating insights into his methods and practices as a scholar of Old English. For example, his marginal notes in Cambridge, University Library MS Hh.1.10 (Ælfric, *Grammar and Glossary*), show him utilizing this text to teach himself Old English grammar, commenting, for example, on the correspondences between

---

[28] Spelman's letters to Wheelock are preserved in Cambridge, University Library MS Dd.3.12; Wheelock's to Spelman are in London, British Library, MSS Add. 34600 and 34601.

Latin and Old English verb tenses. At the front of this manuscript, he also entered an *ex-libris* inscription that preserves the record of an episode in the book's history that would otherwise be unknown: *Sum Academiæ Cantabrigiensis, quem olim fraude abreptum e Bibliotheca Publica restitui curavit Abrahamus Whelocus* ('I belong to the University of Cambridge; after I had been stealthily removed from the University Library, Abraham Wheelock succeeded in restoring me'). Throughout the University Library's copy of King Alfred's translation of Pope Gregory's *Pastoral Care* (MS Ii.2.4), he entered marginal notes providing page references to the equivalent chapters of the Latin version, and he entered in the interlines Latin glosses deriving from Gregory's original text: in other words, he was developing his knowledge of Old English by directly comparing the vernacular translation with its Latin source text. At the beginning of the codex he entered this informative note about his reading practices: *cœpi legere librum hunc tertio die Septembris 1638, perfeci Julii 17 1639. A.W.* ('I began to read this book on the third day of September 1638 and finished it on 17 July 1639. A.W.'). Perhaps reflecting that anyone who subsequently read this might feel that thirteen and a half months was an inordinately long time to spend reading a single book, he then added the words *per otium* ('during my leisure time') to the beginning of the note.

In manuscripts in which portions of the original text had become difficult to read – for example, where the red lead pigment of rubricated titles had corroded and darkened – Wheelock developed the habit of transcribing the affected passage in the interline or the adjacent margin, as he has done with the opening title of Ælfric's *Catholic Homilies* in Cambridge, University Library MS Gg.3.28 and with several of the chapter titles of the Old English version of the *Rule for Canons* by Chrodegang of Metz in Cambridge, Corpus Christi College MS 191 (Fig. 6.20). He also liked to compile indexes of the contents of manuscripts on blank endleaves at their beginning and end.

6.20
Cambridge, Corpus Christi College MS 191 (*Rule for Canons* by Chrodegang of Metz, in Latin and Old English), p. 95.

The interlinear transcription of the faded chapter title is by Abraham Wheelock.

Within these indexes, after he had noted down the number of the page on which mention of a particular topic occurred, he would often add a symbol, entering the same symbol on the page itself, alongside the passage that had attracted his interest; the symbols thus functioned as reference markers, drawing the eye immediately to the relevant part of the page. Manuscripts containing Wheelock's indexes include Cambridge, University Library MS Hh.1.10 (Ælfric's *Grammar and Glossary*) and Cambridge, Corpus Christi College MSS 162, 188, and 419 (all homiliaries) and MS 201 (a collection of ecclesiastical and other texts associated with Wulfstan). The passages to which Wheelock's index entries refer typically relate to ecclesiastical customs and practices – the very issues that he discussed in his notes to his edition of Bede. The indexes thus bear witness to his efforts to gather material for those notes.

It is the manuscripts that Wheelock used for the Old English text of his Bede edition that bear the fullest record of his work – in particular, the University Library copy, MS Kk.3.18, which (as he reveals in the preface to the edition) provided him with his base text, and which he annotated on almost every page. Throughout the manuscript, he has entered marginal references to the equivalent page numbers, not only in the other Cambridge manuscript of the Old English Bede (Corpus Christi 41), but also in the edition of Bede's Latin text published at Cologne in 1612. In a note at the front of MS Kk.3.18, he says he has done this *ut Saxonica cum Latinis facile conferas* ('so that you may easily compare the Saxon with the Latin'). He used the Cologne edition as the source for the numerous interlinear Latin glosses that he entered in MS Kk.3.18; curiously, most of these glosses were subsequently erased, leaving just sufficient traces of ink to enable the identification of the hand as Wheelock's.[29] He also noted significant discrepancies between the Old English and Latin versions, as well as between his three different manuscripts of the Old English text. For example, he commented on the omission in both MS Kk.3.18 and the Cottonian manuscript of Bede's narrative of St Fursey's vision of the afterlife; and he provided references to the pages on which this episode occurs both in the Cologne edition and in the Old English version of Corpus Christi 41 (Fig. 6.21). In places where his Old English manuscripts displayed variant readings for a particular word or phrase, he would note down the variants on the manuscript pages themselves. In other words, as Joscelyn and L'Isle had also done, he recorded within the manuscripts the kinds of information now

---

[29] If, as seems likely, these are the glosses described by Humfrey Wanley in his account of MS Kk.3.18 as being present *quamplurimis in locis* ('in very many places'), then their erasure postdates Wanley's examination of the manuscript during his visit to Cambridge in 1699. See Humfrey Wanley, *Librorum vett. septentrionalium … catalogus historico-criticus*, Oxford, e theatro Sheldoniano, 1705, p. 153.

typically included in the critical apparatus of a printed edition. To conduct his extensive work on Bede's text, he must have been able to place his sources side by side. That he did this at the Cambridge University Library is not only indicated by correspondence recording his success in borrowing manuscripts from Sir Thomas Cotton but also strongly implied by the *ex-libris* inscription that he entered at the front of Corpus Christi 41: *Collegii Corp. Christi Cantabr. sum incola* ('I am a resident of Corpus Christi College, Cambridge'). Of the many Anglo-Saxon manuscripts at Corpus Christi studied by Wheelock, this is the only one in which he entered an *ex-libris* inscription, evidently because – quite against the stringent provisions of Matthew Parker's bequest of his manuscripts to the College – Wheelock was permitted to remove the manuscript from the college in order to study it at his leisure.[30]

It may seem extraordinary from our present perspective that a university librarian should have permitted himself such liberties in annotating and glossing the books in his custody. Indeed, different attitudes soon came to prevail, for the scholars who were to dominate the field of Anglo-Saxon studies in the decades following Wheelock's death were much more reticent about leaving traces of their work within the manuscripts they examined. Yet in many ways it is our good fortune that Wheelock and those who came before him have left us such a generous record of their activity: much more can thereby be learned of the efforts of these first Anglo-Saxonists than may be gleaned from the printed record of their work alone. Through a process of detective work that is never less than intriguing – and always rewarding – we may uncover their successes and failures, their methods and preoccupations, and thus greatly enrich our understanding of the history of Anglo-Saxon scholarship. Just as the manuscripts are our primary witnesses for the Anglo-Saxon period itself, so they serve to illumine a key epoch in Anglo-Saxon studies.

6.21 Cambridge, University Library MS Kk.3.18 (Old English Bede), fol. 41r.

The marginal note by Abraham Wheelock comments on the absence of St Fursey's vision of the afterlife in this and the Cottonian manuscript of the Old English Bede.

---

[30] For further discussion of this issue, see Timothy Graham, 'Abraham Wheelock's use of CCCC MS 41 (Old English Bede) and the borrowing of manuscripts from the library of Corpus Christi College', *Cambridge Bibliographical Society Newsletter*, Summer 1997, pp. 10–16.

Introduction to Chapter 7

Present-day scholars often study selected manuscript art in some wider historical context: Insular manuscripts, for example, are related to 'The Golden Age of Northumbria', and considered along with near-contemporary sculpture and remains of domestic and ecclesiastical buildings in relation to Bede's accounts of the dynastic and missionary activity of seventh- and eighth-century Northumbria. Manuscripts in the Winchester style are related to the Benedictine Reform, to King Edgar and Saints Dunstan, Oswold and Æthelwold, to similarly dated metalwork, carving and embroidery, and to the importance of Winchester and the intellectual milieu of that royal Wessex city. Most medieval art was based on older models and some scholars direct their work to tracking the influences, direct and indirect. Late Antique, Carolingian and Ottonian sources can be found in Anglo-Saxon art, but influences could go the other way too, since missionaries, scholars and brides with their entourages moved to the Continent. Some recent research involves 'combing out' the material of older models in an attempt to identify contemporary items such as tools, drinking vessels, furnishings, dress, ships and buildings in the illustrated pages of narrative texts. Whatever the present-day reader's purpose in studying Anglo-Saxon manuscript art, it is important to remember that this is the art of the book, and that books were confined to the privileged few: the literate, the ecclesiastical and the wealthy secular. Those few might study the books and their illustrations intensely and at length, not merely glancing, but learning, contemplating and remembering for life.

What we call 'Anglo-Saxon manuscript art' varies from a decorated initial designed to indicate the opening of a new passage of text to sequences of full-page, elaborately coloured illumination. It may be executed in outline with ink, sometimes in contrasting colours, or it may be painted with subtle contours and highlights. It may be geometric, abstract, naturalistic or fantastic. It may be simply decorative, or illustrate accompanying text, or it may be redolent with complex theological symbolism. At its most splendid, manuscript art exhibits an extreme form of conspicuous consumption: precious vellum, laboriously produced, is decorated with pigments, some of them rare, and sometimes with precious gold. Like all pre-modern art, it also reflects an enormous investment of time, in the long-term training of the craftsmen/women as well as in the immediate work on the surviving artefact. This elaborate work was carried out primarily for the glory of God, but also reflected the generosity of the patron, and the prestige of the church, monastery or individual who owned the manuscript. The surviving examples testify to the immense riches of church and royalty in Anglo-Saxon England.

7

Manuscript art

Catherine E. Karkov

One of the most important things to bear in mind when dealing with any medieval manuscript is that there is an enormous difference between the purpose and function of medieval illumination and illustration in the modern sense of the word. The Latin verb *illuminare* means 'to light up', suggesting that the different forms of decoration found in manuscripts were literally understood as bringing light to, or shining light on the book itself. What sort of light they brought to a manuscript could vary dramatically according to the type of manuscript, its intended audience, or the status or interests of its patron. Miniatures in some Anglo-Saxon manuscripts, the *c.*1000 *Harley Psalter* (London, British Library, Harley 603; Fig. 1.3) for example, are seemingly literal illustrations of the accompanying text, but when examined in detail, it becomes clear that they interpret the text by drawing particular attention to certain verses, or words, or ways of understanding the individual psalms. They also provide a dramatic and visually entertaining pictorial narrative that would have served, at least in part, a mnemonic function – that is, they would have aided in the memorization of the psalms themselves. They are thus every bit as important to the function of the manuscript as the text. In other manuscripts, such as the *c.*800 *Book of Kells* (Dublin, Trinity College Library MS 58), illumination functions as a complex visual gloss designed to bring out the exegetical and liturgical meaning of the gospels, as well as to create an intervisual programme that unites the different parts of the book to each other, and to other images and texts.[1] There is no norm when it comes to Anglo-Saxon manuscript illumination, and it is therefore essential that each decorative or pictorial cycle be treated as a unique set of images, even if it is a copy of an earlier manuscript, as the *Harley Psalter* is a copy

---

[1] The *Book of Kells* is an Insular rather than an Anglo-Saxon manuscript. See below on the difference between Insular and Anglo-Saxon.

of the c.800 Carolingian *Utrecht Psalter* (Utrecht, Universiteitsbibliotheek 32, Script. eccl. 484).[2]

Anther important thing to remember about medieval manuscripts, especially Anglo-Saxon manuscripts, is that they were often treated as 'works in progress' rather than finished objects. Oxford, Bodleian Library, Junius 11, or the *Galba Psalter* (London, British Library, Cotton Galba A. xviii), are excellent examples of manuscripts in which this can be seen to be the case. The poems in the unfinished Junius 11 manuscript were composed at different dates, but brought together, rewritten, and illustrated by two successive artists at some point in the late tenth or early eleventh century. Layers of time, style and meaning are evident throughout this manuscript.[3] The ninth-century *Galba Psalter* was produced in the region of Liège, but given additional textual material and illuminated (almost certainly by more than one artist) in Winchester after reaching England in the early tenth century. Inscriptions in the manuscript indicate that it was a gift, and would thus clearly have been considered a high-status manuscript in its original state, but that did not preclude its expansion and illustration, perhaps even its Anglicization.

RIGHT
7.1 London, British Library, MS Cotton Nero D. iv (The *Lindisfarne Gospels*), fol. 29r. Chi-Rho (or XPI) page.

Time, place and styles

The art of early medieval England has by tradition been divided into two phases based on chronology and style. The term 'Insular' or 'Hiberno-Saxon' art refers to the art of the British Isles and Ireland between roughly the sixth and ninth centuries. It is characterized by an interest in abstract and geometric ornament, colour and pattern, and the survival of motifs that can be traced back to the native Celtic or pre-Christian tradition. The animal ornament, spirals, and geometric patterns of the carpet pages and great Chi-rho page of the *Lindisfarne Gospels* (Fig. 7.1), for example, may reflect the influence of earlier Irish and Anglo-Saxon metal- and enamel-work.[4] 'Anglo-Saxon' art is often used to refer more narrowly to the art of England between roughly the years 900 and 1066–1100. The art of this period is heavily influenced by that

---

[2] On the ways in which the *Harley Psalter* differs from its exemplar see William Noel, *The Harley Psalter*, Cambridge Studies in Palaeography and Codicology, No. 4, Cambridge, Cambridge University Press, 1995.

[3] See the discussion of the manuscript below; see also Catherine E. Karkov, *Text and Picture in Anglo-Saxon England: narrative strategies in the Junius 11 Manuscript*, Cambridge Studies in Anglo-Saxon England, 31, Cambridge, Cambridge University Press, 2001.

[4] For examples of Insular metalwork see Susan Youngs, ed., *'The Work of Angels' Masterpieces of Celtic Metalwork, 6th–9th Centuries AD*, London, British Museum Press in association with the National Museum of Ireland and the National Museums of Scotland, 1989.

7.2 Stockholm, Royal Library MS A. 135 (*Codex Aureus*), fol. 150v. The evangelist John.

of the Continent, especially by the art of the Carolingians, and to a lesser extent by that of the Ottonians (itself heavily influenced by Carolingian and Anglo-Saxon art), and Byzantines. The figure style and inhabited vine-scroll borders of the dedication page of Cambridge, Corpus Christi College 183, for example, show a new classicism, a new interest in the figure, and a new naturalistic plant and animal ornament that does seem to have developed in the wake of the reforms and Continental interests of King Alfred and his immediate successors. The distinction between the two periods can, however, be misleading. The eighth-century Ruthwell cross is far more classicizing than the style of the CCCC 183 dedication page, and the source of the figure style of the early eighth-century *Lindisfarne Gospels* and *Codex Amiatinus* lies equally in Italy and Northumbria. Moreover, manuscripts such as *Lindisfarne*

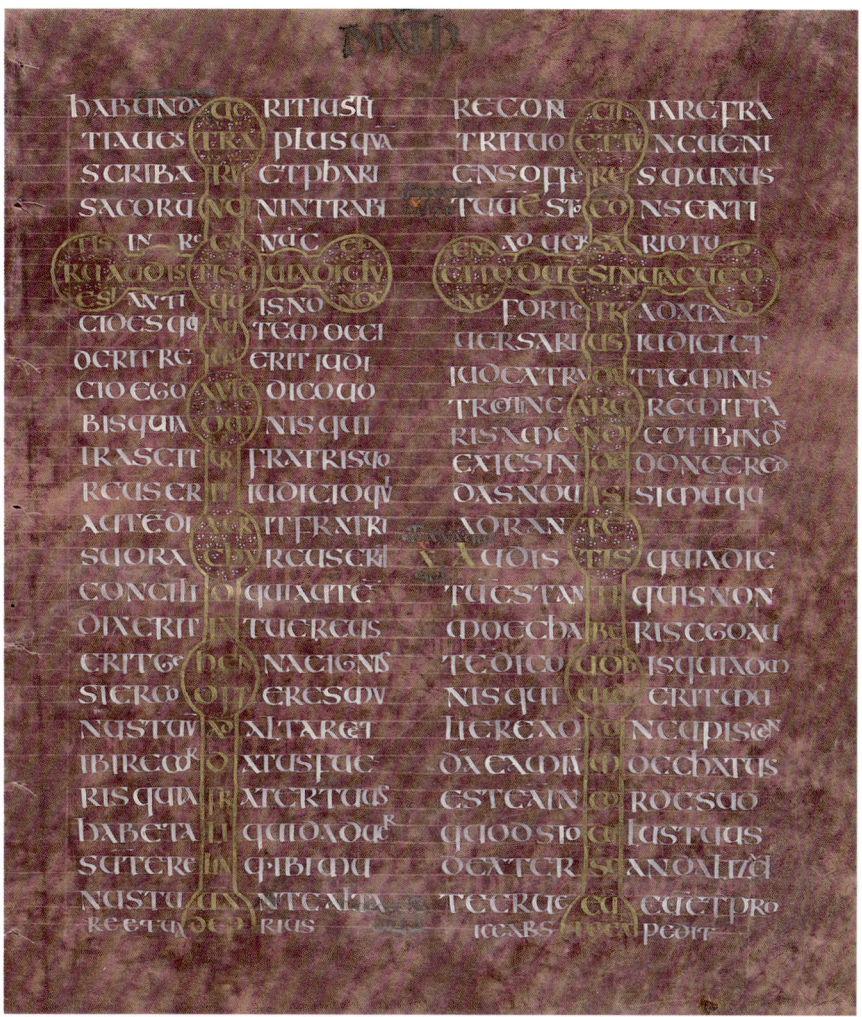

7.3 Stockholm, Royal Library MS A. 135 (*Codex Aureus*), fol. 16r.

Purple text page with embedded crosses.

and *Amiatinus* have been classified as both Insular and Anglo-Saxon. The difficulties with such classifications have not been resolved, and the debate over terminology lingers on.

It is true, however, that style did vary across time as well as by region, or even monastery. The *Lindisfarne Gospels*, for example, contains many more Celtic elements than does the *Codex Amiatinus*, even though they were both produced in Northumbria at about the same date. The difference most likely reflects *Lindisfarne*'s origins in Irish monasticism, and Wearmouth-Jarrow's Romanizing interests respectively. It may also be possible that the producers of the *Lindisfarne Gospels* desired to create a manuscript in which Celtic motifs such as we see on the *Chi-Rho* page were deliberately adapted to make these pages look like precious metalwork as a way of signalling the precious nature of the book itself. This was not a book to be read, but a display manuscript symbolically enshrined by its ornament. Wearmouth-Jarrow, on the other hand, was copying manuscripts of ultimately Italian origin and, in the case of *Amiatinus*, ultimately for an Italian audience.

The art of Southumbrian monasteries (that is, the monasteries of Mercia and Kent) in the same period remained closely tied to Mediterranean models, a stylistic feature generally linked to the mission of St Augustine and the foundation of Canterbury. The evangelist portraits of the mid-eighth-century Stockholm *Codex Aureus* (Stockholm, Royal Library A.135) are treated more

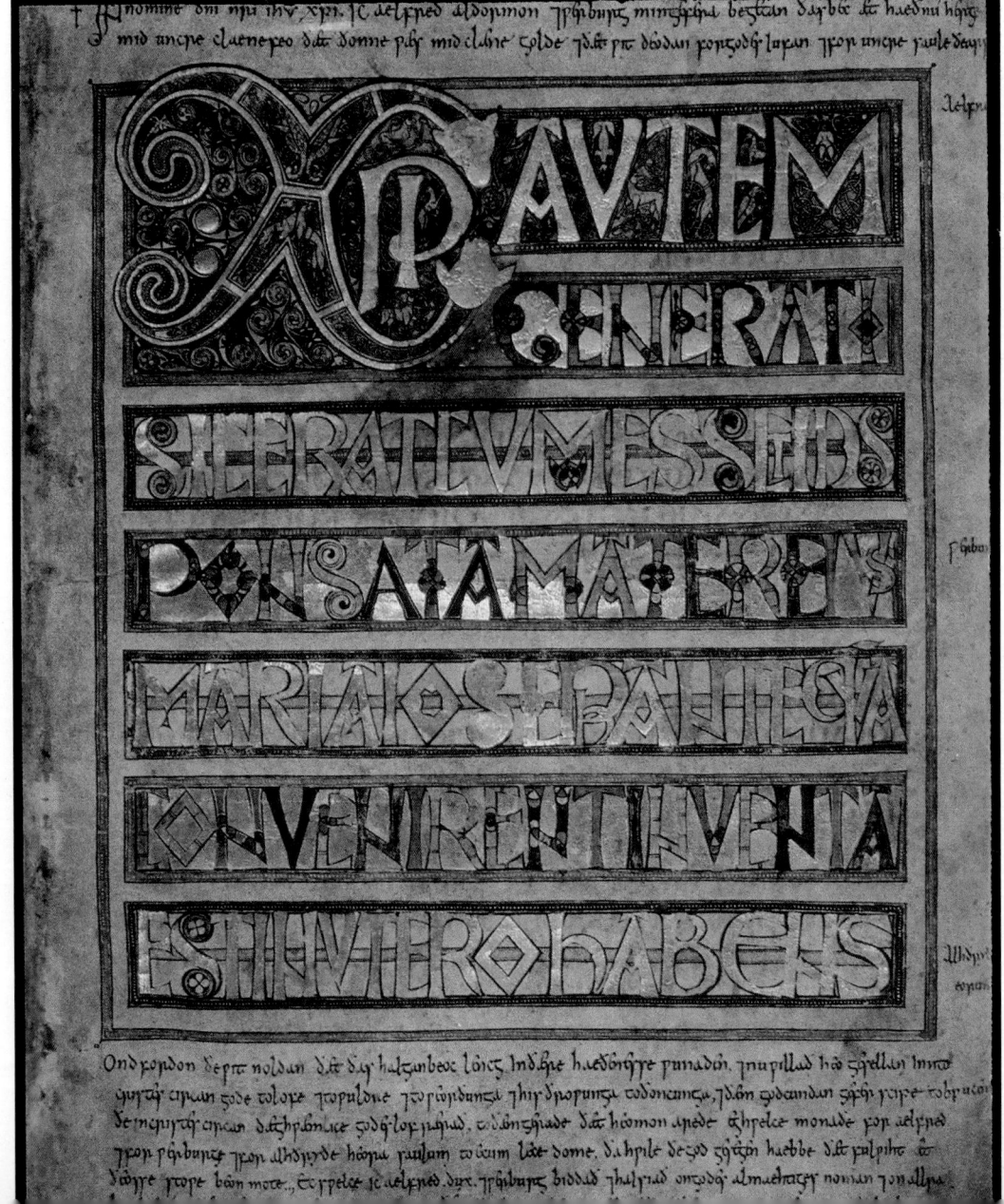

7.4 Stockholm, Royal Library MS A. 135 (*Codex Aureus*), fol. 11r.

Chi-Rho (or XPI) page.

three-dimensionally than their Northumbrian counterparts, and are placed within architectural settings that convey a sense of space (Fig. 7.2). The text is written on alternating pages of purple and undyed parchment, with the purple pages emulating the purple-dyed manuscripts of Early Christian Rome. They are written in a combination of gold, silver and white ink, and cross-patterns reminiscent of late Antique or Early Christian *carmina figurata* have been worked into the text of the more elaborate pages (Fig. 7.3). Insular style and motifs are, however, evident in the spiral patterns of the roundels above the columns of the arch under which John sits, as well as in the enlarged *Chi-Rho* and the decoration in which it is set (Fig. 7.4). Traditionally believed to have been made in Canterbury, it has recently been suggested that the manuscript may in fact have been produced by the nuns of Minster-in-Thanet, although it must be admitted that the evidence for this is completely circumstantial.[5] The manuscript was rescued from the Vikings by Ealdorman Alfred and his wife Werburgh, who presented it to Christ Church, Canterbury, an event commemorated in the margins of the *Chi-Rho* page.

Michelle Brown has argued that linking so many of the Southumbrian manuscripts to Canterbury has led to the neglect of other known or possible centres of production, like Minster-in-Thanet, Lichfield, or Worcester, and especially to the neglect of the kingdom of Mercia and the Mercian contribution to manuscript culture. The *Book of Cerne* (Cambridge, University Library MS Ll.1.10), dated 820–840, is one such manuscript. Likely to have been produced in Worcester, or possibly Lichfield, for private devotional use, the manuscript contains gospel extracts, prayers, hymns, a litany and a breviate psalter (as well as later additions).[6] In the John miniature (Fig. 7.5) we see something of the interest in classically derived figure style and the use of drapery to suggest three-dimensional form, but the influence of Northumbria is still present in the patterning of the dot motifs and the formalized curls of the drapery above John's right shoulder. The composition of the *Cerne* portraits with their full-length symbols and busts of the evangelists is unique. One of the purposes of the *Cerne* evangelist portraits is to bring out the relationship between the evangelists and their symbols, and this is made particularly clear in the inscription that surrounds the eagle. There are other new and

---

[5] See Michelle P. Brown, 'Female book-ownership and production in Anglo-Saxon England: the evidence of the ninth-century prayerbooks' in Christian J. Kay and Louise M. Sylvester, ed., *Lexis and Texts in Early English, Studies presented to Jane Roberts*, Costerus new series 133, Amsterdam, Rodopi, 2001, pp. 45–67; Michelle P. Brown, ed., *In the Beginning: Bibles before the year 1000*, Washington, DC, The Smithsonian Institution, 2006, p. 184.

[6] See further Michelle P. Brown, *The Book of Cerne: prayer, patronage and power in ninth-century England*, London, British Library; Toronto, Buffalo, University of Toronto Press, 1996.

distinctive elements to this manuscript, such as the beast masks that flank John's eagle symbol. In fact *Cerne*, like other Mercian manuscripts, uses masks and fanciful beast ornament to bring many of the pages of the book to life. The masks that bite at the border of the decorative panel of the John *incipit*, and the serpentine beasts that form the letters within the panel (Fig. 7.6) add a visual dynamism that is mirrored in the pointed minuscule of the text below. Of course, the repetition of the mask motif also helps to unite the image of John and his symbol with the words of the text. The manuscript's text pages (Fig. 7.7) are alive with little worm-like creatures, some of which are used for the purely practical function of indicating run-over text. As Brown notes, these beasts seem friendly, even comical, in comparison to their toothy Insular counterparts.

The last century and a half of Anglo-Saxon manuscript illumination is renowned especially for the development of two co-existing 'styles', as well as for the development of narrative illustration. A style of outline drawing often incorporating energetic lines and sometimes executed in multiple

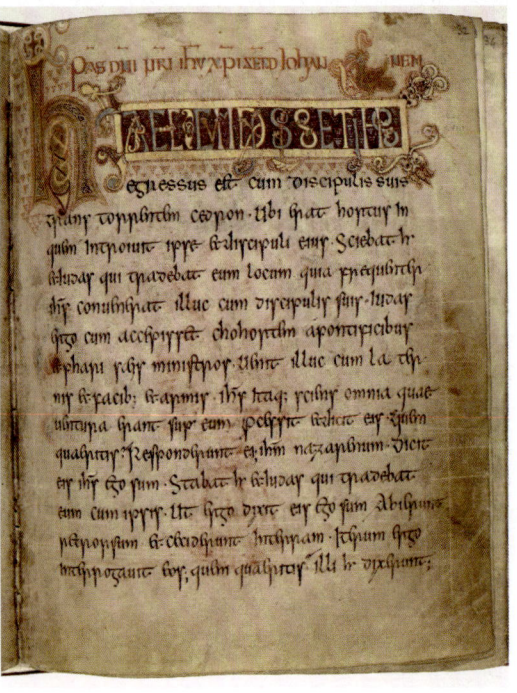

LEFT

7.5 Cambridge, University Library MS Ll.1.10 (The *Book of Cerne*), fol. 31 v.

The evangelist John.

RIGHT

7.6 Cambridge, University Library MS Ll.1.10 (The *Book of Cerne*), fol. 32r.

Incipit to the gospel of John.

7.7 Cambridge, University Library MS Ll.1.10 (The *Book of Cerne*), fol. 56r

Text page containing a prayer, with decorated beast-head initial.

coloured inks (as for example in the *Harley Psalter* Fig. 1.3), was at one time attributed to Canterbury, but is now recognized as being common across Anglo-Saxon England. It is sometimes referred to as the 'Utrecht Psalter' or 'second' style. It co-existed with the 'Winchester Style', a style characterized by the overlay of rich colour washes, by frames composed of a golden trellis wrapped in lush acanthus ornament, and by the unified treatment of figures, settings and frames (as in the *Benedictional of Æthelwold*, London, British Library, MS Additional 49598, Figs 7.19–7.21).[7] While this style does appear

---

[7] For a discussion of the frame as not only integral to, but also determinate of the composition of Winchester Style manuscripts see Robert Deshman, *The Benedictional of Æthelwold*, Princeton, NJ, Chichester, Princeton University Press, 1995, pp. 219–24.

to have originated in Winchester with works such as the portrait of King Athelstan in CCCC 183 and the embroidered Cuthbert stole and maniple, it also quickly became popular throughout the country and was the dominant style of manuscript illumination throughout the eleventh century, eventually influencing the art of Continental houses in northern France and Flanders that maintained contacts with England. The *Benedictional of Æthelwold* and the New Minster Charter (London, British Library, Cotton Vespasian A. viii, Fig. 7.27) are the two classical Winchester Style manuscripts. Both manifest an interest in the representation of fully modelled sculptural figures, often in elaborate architectural settings, or landscapes enlivened by dynamic linear patterns of coloured ink. There is a sense of weight to the bodies, achieved through both the depth of the colours used and the delineation of anatomical details beneath the rich folds of the draperies. This is balanced by the weightlessness of draperies that blow out and hover about the figures, and by the decorative contours of clouds and groundlines. Elements of the style, such as the classicizing figures, 'wind-blown' draperies, animated use of line and acanthus ornament show the influence of Carolingian art, especially that of the Rheims and Metz regions, but have their ultimate origins in Early Christian and Byzantine art. Byzantine influence is also evident in the iconic, static treatment of figures such as the Benedictional's St Swithun (Fig. 7.19). The imperial associations of all these styles, plus their ultimately Roman origins, made them perfectly suited to the united concerns of king and church in the period of the Benedictine Reform.

'There is an enormous difference between the purpose and function of medieval illumination and illustration in the modern sense of the word.'

The Reform period has also been seen as ushering in a new emphasis on kingship in art via such manuscripts as the New Minster Charter and *Benedictional of Æthelwold*, but in fact this is something that goes back at least to the reign of King Athelstan (924/5–39). Athelstan was not only a great collector of books (many think that the *Galba Psalter* was one of his manuscripts), but established enduring dynastic links with other courts of Europe through the marriages of his half-sisters, most importantly that of Eadgifu to King Charles the Simple of Francia, and Edith to Emperor Otto I. His portrait in the *c.*934 CCCC 183 is the first surviving Anglo-Saxon ruler portrait outside of coinage, and its iconography and style both show the influence of Carolingian royal portraiture. It demonstrates a new interest in the display of kingship that would remain a part of English art from this period forward. Anglo-Saxon royal portraiture in particular would continue to reflect the interaction between Anglo-Saxon and Ottonian art initiated during Athelstan's reign.

While both the major styles of late Anglo-Saxon illumination were heavily influenced by developments in the Carolingian and Ottonian empires, the love of colour and surface pattern they exhibit may also be understood as a transformation of stylistic elements already present in the earliest Anglo-Saxon manuscript art. Moreover, style alone is not enough to establish origin or provenance. Artists travelled and, as we shall see, may also have manipulated style as deemed appropriate for certain types of manuscripts or motifs.

Image and text

One of the things that characterizes the manuscript art of Anglo-Saxon England from its earliest phases through to the Conquest is that it was highly literate, showing a sustained interest in writing, the book, and the unity of word and image that does not appear to have been quite as highly developed (or at least manifested itself differently) elsewhere in the early medieval world. One of the earliest and clearest examples of this interest is the Anglo-Saxon development of the historiated initial, which is at once both word and image. Important initial letters had been picked out with various forms of ornamentation for centuries, and inhabited initials (initials composed of or containing one or more creatures) were common in early medieval illumination. A historiated initial, however, contains an abbreviated

7.8 London, British Library, MS Cotton Vespasian A. i (The *Vespasian Psalter*), fol. 53r.

Historiated initial showing David rescuing the lamb.

narrative scene that relates directly to the text in which it is found. Michelle Brown has aptly described it as the 'most intimate symbiosis of text and image'.[8] The earliest surviving historiated initials are found in the eighth-century *Vespasian Psalter* (London, British Library, MS Cotton Vespasian A. i) and *St Petersburg Bede* (St Petersburg, National Library, Q.v.I.18). A depiction of David rescuing the lamb appears in the initial *d* of Psalm 52 of the *Vespasian Psalter* (Fig. 7.8), while in the *St Petersburg Bede*, a portrait of Pope Gregory the Great prefaces Bede's account of the year 605, the year in which Gregory died.[9]

In general, decorated initials were used to mark divisions between texts or internal divisions (chapters, verses, fitts) within a text. In most manuscripts there is a hierarchy of initials just as there is a hierarchy of illustration, so just as the most important texts or parts of texts received the largest or most elaborate miniatures, so the most important textual divisions are marked by particularly grand initials. Such a hierarchy is already evident in the earliest Insular manuscripts such as the early seventh-century *Cathach of St Columba* (Dublin, Royal Irish Academy s.n.) and the mid-seventh-century gospel book Durham, Cathedral Library MS A.II.10. The introduction of the great *Chi-Rho* (XPI), the abbreviation for the name of Christ that marks the beginning of Matthew 1.18 ('Christi autem generatio' / 'Now the generation of Christ') is a development of this tradition (Figs 7.1, 7.4). While most clearly and consistently used in luxury manuscripts, the use of decorated initials to emphasize specific passages is also evident in less grand books such as the Junius 11 poetic manuscript. In addition to guiding the reader through the text, such initials also helped to bring the word and the book to life.

Towards the end of the Anglo-Saxon period even more complex combinations of image and word were developed. One example is the Preface to the Canon of the Mass in the *c*.1021 *Red Book of Darley* (Cambridge, Corpus Christi College MS 422),[10] which begins with an image of Christ in Majesty surrounded by angels *and* the opening words of the Preface (Fig. 7.9). The image is quite literally incorporated into the text. The words *vere dignum et iustum est equum et salutare* are written in small capitals within Christ's mandorla, physically surrounding him with the words of praise that would have been read or sung by the reader. Beginning with the word *nos*, they spread out around the lower bodies of the angels and flow seamlessly into

---

[8] Michelle P. Brown, *The Lindisfarne Gospels: society, spirituality and the scribe*, British Museum Studies in medieval culture, London, British Library, 2003, p. 76. See also J.J.G. Alexander, *The Decorated Letter*, New York, Braziller, 1978.

[9] A later hand has mistakenly written *Augustinus* in Gregory's halo.

[10] The manuscript also contains a tenth-century copy of the *Dialogues of Solomon and Saturn*.

the regular lines of the text written at the bottom of the page.[11] The image is absolutely unique. We find quite the opposite combination of word and image in a *c.*1062 gospel book (Rheims, Bibliothèque Municipale MS 9) in which the evangelists are each depicted on a recto writing the opening words of their respective gospels (Fig. 7.10). The gospel texts continue on the verso without repetition of the words being written within the miniatures. Here the text

7.9 Cambridge, Corpus Christi College MS 422 (The *Red Book of Darley*), p. 52.

Historiated preface to the Mass.

---

[11] See further Catherine E. Karkov, 'Text and image in the Red Book of Darley' in Alistair Minnis and Jane Roberts ed., *Text and Image: studies in Anglo-Saxon literature in honour of Éamonn Ó Carragáin*, Turnhout, Brepols, 2007; Mildred Budny, *Insular, Anglo-Saxon, and Early Anglo-Norman Manuscript Art at Corpus Christi College, Cambridge: an illustrated catalogue*, Kalamazoo, MI and Cambridge, Medieval Institute Publications in association with Research Group on Manuscript Evidence, the Parker Library, Corpus Christi College, 1997, cat. no. 44.

7.10 Rheims, Bibliotheque Municipale MS 9 (Gospels), fol. 23r. The evangelist Matthew writing his gospel.

has been incorporated into the image, an inverse arrangement from that of the historiated initial.

Evangelist portraits are a type of scribal or author portrait, and they have their ultimate origins in the author portraits of late antiquity; however, as with so many other aspects of Anglo-Saxon culture, certain elements of Anglo-Saxon evangelist portraits have their origins in the age of Bede. I do not mean simply that the earliest Anglo-Saxon evangelist portraits to survive are from this period, but rather that it is in manuscripts of this era that we can see the image of the author that would become so popular in later Anglo-Saxon manuscripts (like the Rheims gospel book) first taking shape. It was in the early eighth-century *Lindisfarne Gospels* that the iconography of the evangelist scribe seems to have made its first appearance in northern Europe.[12] The *Lindisfarne* evangelists (Fig. 7.11) are complex images, with

---

[12] Brown, *Lindisfarne Gospels*, p. 349.

Manuscript art 219

LEFT

7.11 London, British Library, MS Cotton Nero D. iv (The *Lindisfarne Gospels*), fol. 25v.

Portrait of the evangelist Matthew.

RIGHT

7.12 London, British Library, MS Cotton Nero D. iv (The *Lindisfarne Gospels*), fol. 27r.

Incipit to the gospel of Matthew.

their combination of Greek and Latin, writing evangelist and inspirational symbol, imagery suggesting the production and transmission of texts, and the movement from the act of writing depicted in the first three evangelist portraits to the state of having written in the fourth. John is differentiated from the other three evangelists by being shown frontally displaying his text rather than in profile and writing, a differentiation which draws our attention to the process of textual production. The transmission and translation of texts are suggested by the relationship between the words and languages used in the evangelist portraits and those used for the inscriptions at the top of the incipit pages. For example, in the Matthew portrait the evangelist's symbol is labelled in Latin *imago hominum*, and the evangelist himself with the Greek formula *HAGIOS MATTHEUS*. The inscriptions are then combined at the top of the *incipit* page (Fig. 7.12), where, after the cross and monogram of Christ, is written *Matheus homo*, a sign that the actual gospel text is the product

ABOVE LEFT

7.13 Hanover, Kestner Museum, Hs. W.M. XXIa 36 (The *Eadwig Gospels*), fol. 9v. Canon table with the Hand of God holding the tools of Creation.

ABOVE RIGHT

7.14 Hanover, Kestner Museum, Hs. W.M. XXIa 36 (The *Eadwig Gospels*), fol. 10r. Canon table with the head of Christ *Logos*.

of both the human evangelist and the divine inspiration represented by the symbol. Details such as this are easy to overlook if one is focusing solely on a single page or image, so it is important always to familiarize yourself with how the whole of an opening works. Finally, all these aspects of the *Gospels* are taken up again in the famous colophon added to the manuscript in the tenth century by Aldred the glossator, but part of which is thought to reflect an eighth-century original.[13] In the colophon the four men credited with producing the manuscript (Eadfrith, Ethilwald, Billfrith and Aldred) are portrayed as the successors to the four evangelists who produced the original gospel texts. This type of scribal genealogy has its source in the patristic tradition as outlined by Cassiodorus in his *Institutiones* and his commentary on Psalm 44:2, in which he explains that the Holy Spirit present in the biblical authors is also present in those who preserve their words through copying, translation, or glossing. The colophon also provides an excellent example of the way in which books were perceived as living things that could change and grow over the course of centuries rather than as static objects.

[13] See Jane Roberts, 'Aldred signs off from glossing the Lindisfarne Gospels' in Alexander R. Rumble, ed., *Writing and Texts in Anglo-Saxon England*, Woodbridge, Cambridge and Rochester, NY, D. S. Brewer, 2006, pp. 28–43; see also Brown, *Lindisfarne Gospels*.

The focus on the process of textual production in the *Lindisfarne Gospels* sets it apart from virtually all other Insular gospel books and unites it with the later Anglo-Saxon tradition. The power of books, writing and reading are central themes in Anglo-Saxon prose and poetry from Bede's focus on texts in the *Historia ecclesiastica* to King Alfred's much studied writing of the kingdom, to the prominence of books in the lives and portraits of later Anglo-Saxon kings and queens.[14] In terms of art, the best example of the culmination of the tradition begun with *Lindisfarne* is the *Eadwig* (or *Hanover*) *Gospels* (Hanover, Kestner Museum, W.M. XXIa 36) written and possibly illuminated at Christ Church, Canterbury *c.*1020 by the famous scribe Eadwig Basan. The program of illustration in the *Eadwig Gospels* begins with the opening canon tables, the tympana of which depict the Hand of God holding a divider and scales, and the head of Christ *Logos*, symbolizing Creation and the *Logos* eternally present in and before Creation respectively (Figs 7.13–7.14). Read together, the four evangelist portraits then depict four sequential steps in the process of creating the book. Matthew

ABOVE LEFT

7.15 Hanover, Kestner Museum, Hs. W.M. XXIa 36 (The *Eadwig Gospels*), fol. 17v.

The evangelist Matthew with scribe's tools.

ABOVE RIGHT

7.16 Hanover, Kestner Museum, Hs. W.M. XXIa 36 (The *Eadwig Gospels*), fol. 65v.

The evangelist Mark sharpening his pen.

---

[14] See Catherine E. Karkov, *The Ruler Portraits of Anglo-Saxon England*, Woodbridge and Rochester, NY, Boydell, 2004.

(Fig. 7.15) sits at the start of the sequence with the tools of scribal creation – a pen, penknife and open book – which we can relate back to the tools of Creation held by the Hand of God at the opening of the manuscript. Mark (Fig. 7.16) sharpens his pen, preparing to write, while Luke (Fig. 7.17) puts pen to page. John (Fig. 7.18) displays the final product, the written word, as well as its triumph. The opening words of John's gospel *In principio erat Verbum et Verbum erat apud D(e)um et De(us) erat Verbum. Hoc erat in principio* skewer the heretic Arius who lies beneath John's feet and holds a scroll inscribed with his heretical belief that *erat tempus quando non erat* ('there was a time when he was not'). This portrait relates back to the image on the second page of the canon tables, the eternal *Logos*. The evangelists thus take their place in a cycle of creation that moves from the divine, to the human authors of the biblical texts, to the producers of this book in the eleventh century. As in the *Lindisfarne Gospels*, a brief colophon at the end of John's gospel extends the cycle down to Eadwig himself (Fig. 2.11). If Eadwig was the illuminator as well as the scribe of the manuscript, the book's pictorial programme shows his keen understanding of the interrelated roles of author and artist; if he was not the artist, the programme demonstrates how closely scribes and artists worked together in bringing out the meaning and function of the book.

BELOW LEFT

7.17 Hanover, Kestner Museum, Hs. W.M. XXIa 36 (The *Eadwig Gospels*), fol. 96v.

The evangelist Luke writing.

BELOW RIGHT

7.18 Hanover, Kestner Museum, Hs. W.M. XXIa 36 (The *Eadwig Gospels*), fol. 147v.

The evangelist John displays the written word and triumphs over the heretic Arius.

Illuminated scriptural and liturgical books

I have begun this chapter with a consideration of gospel books because, if we can trust the evidence of their rate of survival, they were far and away the most common type of illuminated book produced – both in the early and later periods. This is hardly surprising as gospel books served multiple functions, all of which were central to the mission of the Christian Church. Most importantly, they contained the word of God. The gospel was also an evangelizing book, crucial to the process of christianization; it was used in the celebration of the sacraments; it was an instructional text used for the training of clerics and catechumens (candidates for baptism); and it could be a luxurious display object signifying wealth and status as much as piety. Its special status in the Insular world is demonstrated by the fact that over half of all surviving gospel books from before the year 800 are associated with Insular monastic houses.[15] Art was of course central to all of a gospel book's functions.[16] The earliest extant English gospel book was written in Northumbria by an Irish or Irish-trained scribe in the mid-seventh century, and survives as the fragments Durham, Cathedral Library MSS A.II.10, C.III.13 and C.III.20. As noted above, it already displays the hierarchy of decorated initials that would become so prominent in later manuscripts. It also displays the diminuendo characteristic of Insular gospel books, whereby a text opens with a very large initial followed by a line or two of enlarged but progressively smaller letters. Also distinctly Insular was the introduction of the great cross carpet pages in manuscripts such as the *Books of Durrow* and *Kells* and the *Lindisfarne Gospels*. While their meaning is debated – they have been interpreted as symbolic crucifixions, painted prayer mats, labyrinths and painted book covers – functionally they not only helped to mark the beginning of each gospel, but also to stress their unity and precious nature.[17] They were not, however, to survive into the later Anglo-Saxon period.

The ninth century is problematic for the history and development of Anglo-Saxon manuscripts as so little can be assigned to it with any certainty.

---

[15] George Henderson, *From Durrow to Kells: the Insular gospel-books, 650–800*, London, Thames & Hudson, 1987, p. 15.

[16] For studies focusing on this aspect of the book see especially Henderson, *From Durrow to Kells*; Carol Farr, *The Book of Kells, its Function and Audience*, The British Library studies in medieval culture, London, British Library and University of Toronto Press, 1997; Jennifer O'Reilly, 'Patristic and Insular traditions of the evangelists: exegesis and iconography' in A.M. Luiselli Fadda and É. Ó'Carragáin, *Le Isole Britanniche e Roma in Età Romanobarbarica*, Rome, Herder Editrice e Libraria, 1988, pp. 49–94; Brown, *Lindisfarne Gospels*.

[17] On the various possible meanings of the carpet pages of the *Lindisfarne Gospels* see Brown, *The Lindisfarne Gospels*, pp. 312–31.

There are manuscripts from the first half of the ninth century, such as the *c*.820–40 *Royal Bible* (London, British Library, MS Royal 1 E. vi), which show the strengthening influence of both Carolingian and Byzantine art; but there is nothing from the second half of the century. This is generally thought to be the result of the devastation and turmoil caused by the Viking invasions, but it is also possible that this idea has become so accepted among scholars that we automatically assume a manuscript cannot be of late ninth-century date. It seems reasonable to assume that the connections made between the Anglo-Saxons and Carolingians via such figures as Alcuin of York, who became one of Charlemagne's top scholars, and abbot of Tours, or Judith, daughter of Charles the Bald, who married Æthelwulf, king of the West Saxons, in 856, could only have strengthened the influences apparent in the *Royal Bible*.

> 'One of the things that characterizes the manuscript art of Anglo-Saxon England ... is that it was highly literate, showing a sustained interest in writing, the book, and the unity of word and image.'

A very strong Carolingian influence is clear in the many illuminated gospel books produced from the period of the Benedictine Reform through to the Norman Conquest and beyond, not only in the style of the miniatures (see the 'Winchester Style' and 'Utrecht Psalter' style discussed above) and their naturalistic settings, but also in more architectural canon tables, and the use of scripts such as Caroline minuscule and Rustic capitals. Many of the gospel books of the later period can be related to each other either through scribes such as Eadwig Basan at Canterbury, or through patrons such as Judith of Flanders (see below) or Margaret of Scotland.

Other types of illuminated scriptural or liturgical books in use in Anglo-Saxon England included bibles, evangelaries, sacramentaries, lectionaries, benedictionals, pontificals, psalters, collectars, tropers, prayerbooks, hymnals, and homiliaries – although some types of manuscript, homiliaries and collectars, for example, were embellished only with decorated initials.[18] The most lavishly decorated of the service books were those made either for display or for particularly wealthy patrons. The *Benedictional of Æthelwold* (London, BL, Add. 49598; Figs 7.19–7.21), the *Benedictional of Archbishop Robert* (Rouen, Bibliothèque Municipale, Y.7) and the *Sacramentary of Robert of Jumièges* (Rouen, Bibliothèque Municipale, Y.6) are perhaps the best known of this group.

---

[18] See, e.g., Elżbieta Temple, *Anglo-Saxon Manuscripts 900–1066*, A Survey of Manuscripts Illuminated in the British Isles, 2, London, Harvey Miller, 1976, nos 3 and 30. See Richard W. Pfaff, ed., *The Liturgical Books of Anglo-Saxon England*, Old English Newsletter Subsidia 23, Kalamazoo, MI, Medieval Institute Publications 1995 for liturgical manuscripts in use in Anglo-Saxon England. Opinions as to what type of book can be described accurately as a service or liturgical book differ among scholars.

7.19 London, British Library, MS Additional 49598 (The *Benedictional of Æthelwold*), fol. 97v.

St Swithun.

The Benedictional of Æthelwold

While all three are magnificent manuscripts, the *Benedictional of Æthelwold* is particularly noteworthy because of its introduction of new iconographic types, and because of the way in which it has clearly been produced with the needs and wishes of its patron, Bishop Æthelwold of Winchester, in mind.

Architectural metaphors and models were an important part of the Benedictine Reform as promulgated by Æthelwold. Architectural motifs in the art historical record became visual propaganda for the Reform and beg to be understood in relation to its history, its texts, and its material building

repleri . ut cum ei[s] caelestis sponsi thalamum ualeatis ingredi . quod ipse

campaign. They figure prominently in the texts of the *New Minster Charter*, the *Regularis Concordia*, and the text known as 'Edgar's Establishment of Monasteries'.[19] They figure equally prominently in the art of Reform-era Winchester. Two of the miniatures in the *Benedictional* that merit special attention in this regard are the portrait of St Swithun (Fig. 7.19) and the miniature accompanying the blessing for the dedication of a church (Fig. 7.20). Swithun was the patron saint of Winchester Old Minster, and an active part of Æthelwold's narrative of the cleansing and refoundation of the monastery.[20] The Old Minster itself was expanded over the years to include first a western annexe and finally an impressive westwork as a home for the translated body of the saint. In the *Benedictional* portrait, Swithun has literally been portrayed as a part of the architecture; he is both a human figure and an architectural pillar. His feet are placed upon a column base, while arches springing from the flanking columns of the border rest on his haloed head. The fact that he has been placed before an arch may further reflect the location of his relics at the entrance to the church with the westwork rising above him.

LEFT

7.20 London, British Library, MS Additional 495958 (The *Benedictional of Æthelwold*), fol. 118v.

Bishop dedicating a church.

The church is also intimately connected with the living bodies it houses in the miniature that accompanies the blessing for the dedication of a church (Fig. 7.20). Here the use of outline drawing for both the church's architecture and congregation suggest their unity. The bishop (Æthelwold?) is set apart by the use of full-colour, perhaps indicative of his exalted position – something of which Æthelwold would have been acutely aware; but the artist (or patron) may also have been making a connection between Æthelwold and Swithun. Both stand in similar poses beneath arches, both are dressed in similar colours, and both are shown holding a book in one hand and making the sign of blessing with the other – although there is a difference in that the bishop is shown reading from an open book held by an acolyte.

---

[19] See further Mercedes Salvador, 'Architectural metaphors and christological imagery in the Advent Lyrics: Benedictine propaganda in the Exeter Book?' in Catherine E. Karkov and Nicholas Howe, ed., *Conversion and Colonization in Anglo-Saxon England*, Essays in Anglo-Saxon Studies, Tempe, AZ, Centre for Medieval and Renaissance Studies, 2006, pp. 169–211; Catherine E. Karkov, 'The frontispiece to the New Minster Charter and the King's two bodies' in Donald Scragg, ed., *Edgar, King of the English 959–975: new interpretations*, Woodbridge, Boydell, 2008, pp. 224–41.

[20] On this aspect of Swithun and the reform see the text of the charter in Sean Miller, ed., *Charters of the New Minster, Winchester*, Oxford, British Academy by Oxford University Press, 2001; Alexander R. Rumble, *Property and Piety in Early Medieval Winchester: documents relating to the topography of the Anglo-Saxon and Norman city and its minsters*, Oxford and New York, Clarendon Press, 2002; on Swithun see also Michael Lapidge, *The Cult of St Swithun*, Winchester Studies 4.ii, Oxford, Clarendon Press, 2003.

7.21 London, British Library, MS Additional 49598 (The *Benedictional of Æthelwold*), fol. 102v.

The Dormition (with Coronation) of the Virgin.

The Dormition, or Death and Coronation of the Virgin (Fig. 7.21), seems likely to have introduced another new iconographic type. It is the first depiction of the Virgin being crowned as Queen of Heaven to survive in a western manuscript. It has been connected with two facets of the Benedictine Reform as it was popularized at Winchester: the growth of the cult of the Virgin Mary, and the rising importance of the Anglo-Saxon queen as a visible presence in both the court and Church. What is perhaps the earliest evidence for the coronation of Anglo-Saxon queens is associated with the Winchester of Æthelwold and Edgar,[21] and the *Regularis Concordia* made the queen the overseer of women's religious houses, a role that paralleled her directly with Mary. It is also at this time that Mary may have been added to the dedication of the New Minster.[22]

Ælfwine's Prayerbook

Anglo-Saxon manuscript illumination of the late tenth and eleventh centuries provides abundant evidence that the cult of the Virgin continued to grow in importance, and Winchester remained one of its centres. An excellent example of continued Marian interest is provided by *Ælfwine's Prayerbook* (London, British Library, Cotton Titus D. xxvi and xxvii). This is a very small manuscript (only 128 × 93mm) produced for Ælfwine between 1023 and 1031 while he was deacon at the New Minster. Mary has a prominent place in two of the manuscript's three miniatures, as well as in a number of its prayers.[23] While the *Benedictional* is a large and lavish manuscript which was no doubt intended as much for display as for use by the bishop, *Ælfwine's Prayerbook* is small and intended for personal use, and its understated ink drawings are a telling contrast to the gold and rich colours of the *Benedictional*. It has been speculated that Ælfwine was the artist and one of the scribes of the manuscript,[24] but that remains no more than speculation. Nevertheless, the contents of the drawings address Ælfwine the reader as closely as they do the texts of the prayers, and are rich and complex in their iconography. For example, the miniature of the Crucifixion (Fig. 7.22) introduces a series of twenty-one prayers to the Holy Cross, but also reaches out to the reader through the inscription flanking the cross at the top of the page; 'Hec crux consignet Ælfwinum corpore mente. In qua suspendens tra(xit) and d(eu)s omnia secum' ('This cross signs Ælfwine in body and mind on which the hanging God drew all things to him'). There is an emphasis on living figures and active gestures that helps to make this particular crucifixion scene more about life than about death. Christ is alive and smiles down at Mary, and she

---

[21] See Janet Nelson, 'The second English Ordo' in her *Politics and Ritual in Early Medieval Europe*, History Series 42, London, Hambledon, 1986, pp. 361–74, but see also Karkov, *Anglo-Saxon Ruler Portraits*, pp. 111–12.

[22] See Miller, *Charters of the New Minster*, p. 39.

[23] See B. Günzel, ed., *Ælfwine's Prayerbook*, Henry Bradshaw Society 108, Woodbridge, Henry Bradshaw Society by Boydell, 1993; Catherine E. Karkov, 'Judgement and salvation in the New Minster Liber Vitae' in Kathryn Powell and Donald Scragg, ed., *Apocryphal Texts and Traditions in Anglo-Saxon England*, Cambridge, D.S. Brewer, 2003, pp. 151–63.

[24] For a summary of the different arguments see Simon Keynes, ed., *The Liber Vitae of the New Minster and Hyde Abbey Winchester*, Early English Manuscripts in Facsimile 26, Copenhagen, Rosenkilde & Bagger, 1996, pp. 111, 112–13.

7.22 London, British Library, MS Cotton Titus D. xxvii (*Ælfwine's Prayerbook*), fol. 65v.

Crucifixion with text; *Sol, Luna* and the Hand of God above, Mary and John below.

and John smile back at him, rather than turning away; the personifications of the sun and moon look towards each other, while the moon gestures down at the scene below; and the hand of God reaches into the space of the drawing from above. These details all serve to draw attention to the triumphant and salvific nature of the Crucifixion, and to focus Ælfwine's attention on Christ (everyone points in one manner or another to him), but, along with the inscription, they also help to unite Ælfwine with the scene, to make him seem an active participant in the events depicted. Ælfwine is present in body and mind before the cross. Further, the amount of writing on the page helps visually to enact the movement from reader to drawing to the texts of the prayers that follow.

Psalters

More psalters survive from Anglo-Saxon England than from anywhere else in the early medieval world. Psalters could be used as liturgical books (for example, the late tenth-century *Ramsey Psalter*, London, British Library, MS Harley 2904) because reading of the psalter (the text of the book of Psalms) could be augmented with canticles, prayers and so forth. However, far fewer psalters were produced for liturgical use than were produced for private devotional reading or educational purposes. In the Middle Ages people grew up chanting the psalms, learning to read from the psalter, and regarding it as their most important source of prayer, both as part of the liturgy and as part of private study. For devout Christians both within and without the monastery, the psalter also structured the day. Ideally all one hundred and fifty psalms were recited daily, though for the vast majority such a level of devotion was impractical. The Benedictine Rule (composed in the sixth century) divided the psalms over the eight daily canonical hours of Matins, Lauds, Prime, Terce, Sext, None, Vespers and Compline, and this division was followed by most of Western Europe from the ninth century on. Clergy were required to know the psalter by heart, though not all were able to meet this requirement. The psalms were also used in penance, especially the penitential psalms, but the recitation of different numbers of psalms was mandated for different offences.

The psalter's illustrative programme could take on a wide variety of forms depending on the intended function or patron of the book. Because the psalms were attributed to King David, early psalters were decorated with scenes from his life, as in the *Vespasian Psalter* discussed above (Fig. 7.8), but fully illustrated psalters do not appear until the ninth century. The Carolingian *Utrecht Psalter* was illuminated with pictorial translations of each of the psalms, but this type of decoration does not seem to have had a major influence on Anglo-Saxon illumination until the manuscript was brought to England some time before the year 1000. The text of the *Utrecht Psalter* does, however, show the influence of Alcuin of York and of early Insular manuscripts, along with that of the Carolingian Court School.[25] Byzantium provided another source of influence; however, the most important influence on the development of the Anglo-Saxon psalter was the Insular tradition of typological illustration used to mark the major divisions and important psalms of the book: Psalms 1, 51, 101, and 109. The ninth-century *Galba Psalter*, a Carolingian manuscript, which, as we have seen, was augmented with Anglo-Saxon miniatures upon its arrival in England, is the

---

[25] Koert van der Horst, William Noel and Wilhelmina C.M. Wüstefeld, ed., *The Utrecht Psalter in Medieval Art, picturing the psalms of David*, Tuurdijk and London, HES in conjunction with Harvey Miller, 1996, p. 38.

7.23 London, British Library, MS Cotton Galba A. xviii (The *Galba Psalter*), fol. 21r.

Christ enthroned, surrounded by choirs of martyrs, confessors and virgins.

earliest surviving example of the Anglo-Saxon adaptation of this tradition.[26] Its calendar indicates that it was intended for private devotional use. The page illustrated here (Fig. 7.23) depicts Christ enthroned with choirs of martyrs,

---

[26] On the Insular tradition of psalter illustration see Kathleen M. Openshaw, 'The symbolic illustration of the psalter: an Insular tradition', *Arte Medievale* 2, ser. 6, 1992, pp. 41–60. On the *Galba Psalter* see Robert Deshman, 'The Galba Psalter: pictures, texts and context in an early medieval prayerbook', *Anglo-Saxon England*, 26, 1997, pp. 109–38.

confessors and virgins. It is part of the manuscript's introductory material, which also includes prayers to the cross, archangels, Mary, John, martyrs, confessors and virgins. Only three of the original full-page miniatures remain in the book, the other two being Christ enthroned with angels and prophets on folio 2v, and the Ascension of Christ preceding Psalm 101 on folio 120v. Psalm 51 was preceded by a miniature of the Crucifixion; the Nativity, which originally preceded Psalm 1, became detached from the manuscript and is now Oxford, Bodleian Library, Rawlinson B.484, folio 85. This is an instance of a pictorial programme that cannot be understood in full without first reconstructing its original contents. It is also one that absolutely must be seen in the original rather than via reproductions. It is tiny (128 × 88mm) and the first two of its full-page miniatures (the two showing Christ enthroned) are exceptionally finely painted, with delicate details and lines that appear thick and clumsy when enlarged, as they inevitably are in almost all published pictures. In the page illustrated, for example, the artist has placed tiny orange dots at the outside of each of Christ's eyes, which serve to draw attention to his powerful stare and thus add to the impression of power and majesty. In reproductions these appear as heavy orange blobs. Unfortunately, the *Galba Psalter* is extremely fragile and thus enormously difficult to gain access to unless you are already an established scholar in the field with specific reasons for needing to see the original.[27] In terms of style and iconography, the miniatures reflect a combination of Insular, Continental and Byzantine sources, but the style also looks forward to the development of the Winchester Style (discussed above), while the inclusion of Christ's wounds and the instruments of the Passion in the prefatory miniatures look forward to later eleventh- and twelfth-century developments.

The *Tiberius Psalter* (London, British Library, Cotton Tiberius C. vi) of c.1060 is a lavish manuscript which includes two fully painted miniatures, twenty-four pages of line drawings, and eleven decorated initials, all painted in the 'Winchester Style'. The psalms are divided in the Insular tradition discussed above. Important innovations of this manuscript include a clear hierarchy of decoration,[28] the introduction of a decorated initial page at the opening of the *Psalter*'s prefatory texts, and the fact that it is the first surviving psalter to contain a typological cycle of Old and New Testament miniatures (meaning that the miniatures draw out the theological connections between

---

[27] Many libraries will encourage readers to consult facsimiles rather than original manuscripts, but persevere if you do need to see the original. Remember also that microfilm or microfiche facsimiles are absolutely useless for the study of miniatures and other forms of decoration.

[28] See Kathleen M. Openshaw, 'Weapons in the daily battle: images of the conquest of evil in the early medieval Psalter', *Art Bulletin*, 75, 1993, pp. 17–38.

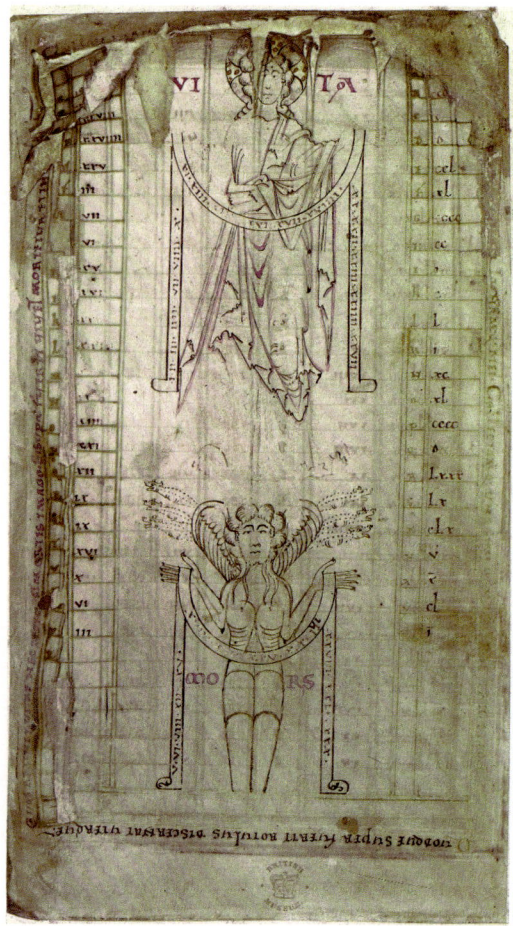

LEFT

7.24 London, British Library, MS Cotton Tiberius C. vi (The *Tiberius Psalter*), fol. 6v.

Opening of prefatory cycle showing *Vita* (Life) triumphing over *Mors* (Death).

RIGHT

7.25 London, British Library, MS Cotton Tiberius C. vi (The *Tiberius Psalter*), fol. 14r.

Christ's Harrowing of Hell.

the Old and New Testament episodes depicted). Both its quality and its clear yet complex programme of illustration suggest that it was produced for the private devotional use of a member of the Church. The prefatory cycle opens with a drawing of *Vita* (Life; manifested as Christ) triumphing over *Mors* (Death; Fig. 7.24) that introduces the theme of spiritual battle and the conquest of evil, an area in which the psalter generally provided guidance for everyday life in the world.[29] The drawing introduces a series of computistical tables, and the numbers on the scrolls held by the two figures

---

[29] See further Openshaw, 'Weapons in the daily battle'.

are for calculating the chances of recovery or death from illness. The theme of battle and victory continues throughout the Christological cycle, but is brought out especially clearly in the drawing of the Harrowing of Hell on folio 14 (Fig. 7.25), in which an enormous figure of Christ, so large that he must stoop to be contained within the frame of the miniature, tramples on the much smaller bound Satan, while rescuing a group of Old Testament figures from Hell. Note that the frame of the miniature is broken by a sunburst containing a cross that is connected to Christ's halo by a thin yellow fillet with red dots. The detail serves to emphasize the theme of triumph, as well as to unite the episode to that of the Crucifixion depicted on folio 13 (i.e. in the previous opening). It is also a good example of the late Anglo-Saxon interest in suggesting a space outside the borders of the miniature that could be used to gloss, comment on, or add to the meaning of the central image. Details such as this look forward to the full-blown use of border space in post-Conquest works such as the Bayeux Tapestry.

The *Bury Psalter* (Vatican City, Biblioteca Apostolica, MS reg. lat. 12), produced at Christ Church, Canterbury for Bury St Edmunds Abbey in the second quarter of the eleventh century, provides a second and rather different example of the innovative use of border space. The fifty-three coloured outline drawings of this manuscript are arranged around the margins of the text. For the most part, the subject matter of the drawings provides literal illustrations of the accompanying psalm texts in the tradition of the Carolingian *Utrecht Psalter*, but the drawings also include a New Testament cycle of illustrations that, while derived from the Insular tradition, is iconographically innovative. Psalm 67:19, for example, is illustrated with a depiction of the Ascension of Christ of a typically Anglo-Saxon type.[30] This is the 'disappearing' Christ, an iconographic invention of the Anglo-Saxons, in which Christ vanishes into heaven with only his feet and the hem of his robe remaining within the space of the page. A pair of angels, Mary and the twelve apostles witness the event from the margins of the page. A balance is achieved here between the downward motion of our eyes as we read the words of the psalm, and the upward motion of the visual narrative that is reminiscent of the layout of earlier Anglo-Saxon monuments such as the Ruthwell cross, on which the upward growing vine-scroll is balanced by the descending arrangement of the vernacular poem. Elsewhere, the decoration is arranged to be read across the central text of the page, or even across an opening. The lively style of the drawings not only adds visual interest to the manuscript, but may also have served as a mnemonic aid.

---

[30] A complete set of illustrations of the *Bury Psalter* can be found in Thomas H. Ohlgren, ed., *Anglo-Saxon Textual Illustration: photographs of sixteen manuscripts with descriptions and index*, Kalamazoo, MI, Medieval Institute Publications, 1992.

The New Minster Liber Vitae

While not liturgical books proper, *libri vitae* were an important element of liturgical commemoration, in that the names recorded in them would have been remembered as part of daily services. The *New Minster Liber Vitae* (London, British Library, Stowe 944) has the distinction of being the only surviving example of an early medieval *liber vitae* to include figural miniatures. It opens with a series of three drawings depicting Queen Ælfgifu/Emma and King Cnut donating a gold altar cross to the New Minster while Christ, Mary, Peter, and the abbey's community look on (Fig. 7.26); a depiction of saints and the special dead waiting to enter heaven; and a scene

7.26 London, British Library, MS Stowe 944 (The *Liber Vitae* of New Minster and Hyde Abbey), fol. 6r.

Ælfgifu/Emma and Cnut donating a golden altar cross to the New Minster, Winchester.

of judgement in three registers that shows St Peter welcoming the dead to Heaven, Peter using his key to save a soul, and, in the lowest register, the damned being locked in Hell. The meaning of the individual pages has been much discussed, but the drawings are also important for the way in which they work together to provide a visual summary of the function of the book. Ælfgifu and Cnut have given to the community and therefore will be commemorated in its prayers. Both the donation and the prayers help to ensure that they will join the patron saints of the Minster (Mary and Peter), in Heaven. Turning the page we see the start of the procession that will lead them into Heaven, and the fate of those whose future is less assured. The illustration also serves as a reminder of the close interaction between Church and court, especially at the royal centre of Winchester, and of the way in which art could function as a focal point for the coming together of the secular and clerical realms of society. The *New Minster Liber Vitae* is also a historical manuscript. Along with the lists of historical names it preserves, it also contains the will of King Alfred, regnal lists, charters, and a text on the founding of the New Minster (along with religious items); it is therefore perfectly appropriate that its miniatures should reflect these interrelated concerns.

Non-liturgical illuminated manuscripts

The New Minster Charter

A charter, at least in function if not entirely in language, is a secular manuscript containing a historical text, and usually devoid of illustrations. The *New Minster Charter* (London, British Library, Cotton Vespasian A. viii) is a notable exception, which tells us immediately that this is a very special manuscript and that its artwork was designed to be displayed and noticed. The *Charter* is written entirely in gold and decorated with one full-page miniature (Fig. 7.27), two framed pages containing an elegiac couplet and opening rubric, and a framed page containing the *Charter*'s enlarged 'pictorial invocation' (the monogram of Christ with which the prologue of the *Charter* begins), all worked in gold and rich colour washes. The portrait of Edgar donating the *Charter* is even painted against a 'purple' background reminiscent of Carolingian and Early Christian imperial manuscripts. This is a royal manuscript *par excellence*, but its decoration, along with the fact that it was originally displayed on the altar of the church, assimilate the manuscript to a gospel book. The purpose of the decorated pages was to invoke the joint authority of Edgar and Christ as rulers, and as rulers associated with the foundation of the New Minster and the Christian Church respectively. The frontispiece also portrays Edgar as a pious and generous ruler whose actions will assure him a place in the heavenly kingdom. It is no doubt for this reason

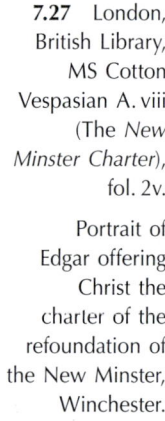

7.27 London, British Library, MS Cotton Vespasian A. viii (The *New Minster Charter*), fol. 2v.

Portrait of Edgar offering Christ the charter of the refoundation of the New Minster, Winchester.

that the composition of the frontispiece of the *New Minster Liber Vitae* was modelled on that of the *Charter*, and the two books were likely to have been displayed together on the altar.

Calendars

While all Anglo-Saxon illumination has something to tell us about the Anglo-Saxons' attitudes towards their world, some illustrations may be more revealing than others. Calendar illustrations for example, while derived ultimately from late Antique models, do reveal something of contemporary perceptions of time, labour, and landscape. London, British Library, Cotton Julius A. vi, an early eleventh-century manuscript, contains the earliest surviving depictions of the labours of the months. It represents a break with

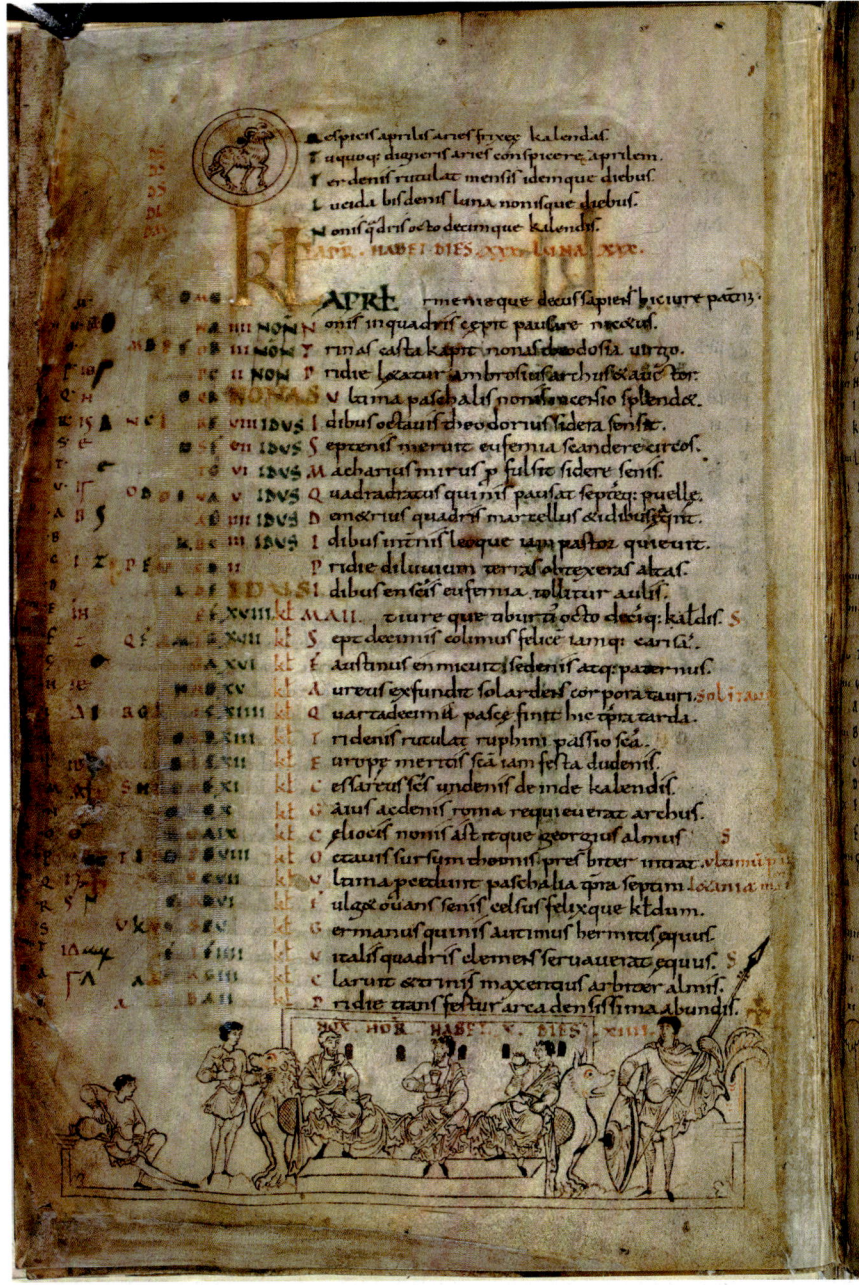

7.28 London, British Library, MS Cotton Julius A. vi (Calendar), fol. 4v.

April page with sign of the zodiac at the top and feasting, the labour for the month, at the bottom.

the earlier tradition of symbolizing the months with single figures holding tools or other attributes, and the introduction of a visual narrative of human labour. The calendar itself is written in metrical verse and illustrated with drawings of the labours at the bottom of each page (Figs 7.28–7.29), and

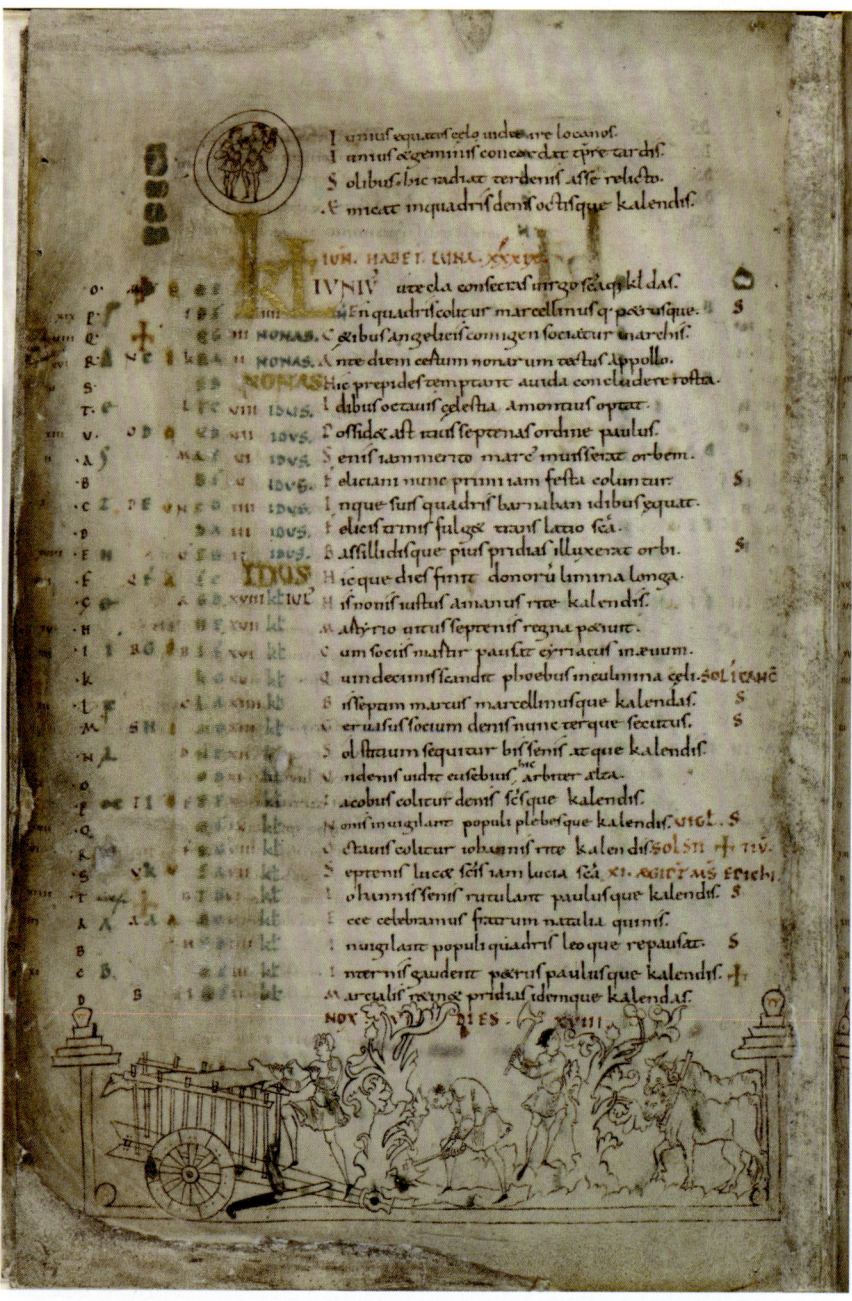

7.29 London, British Library, MS Cotton Julius A. vi (Calendar), fol. 5v.

June page with sign of the zodiac at the top and cutting wood, the labour for the month, at the bottom.

signs of the zodiac at the top. The arrangement of the page was standard and designed to show the harmony of the celestial and human year. The arrangement of each image, with the signs of the zodiac within roundels and the drawings of the labours within horizontal panels may also be significant, with the circular forms suggesting celestial spheres, and the horizontal panels suggesting the linear progression of the earthly year and the cycle of human labour. Calendars were used for maintaining a record of the commemoration of saints, religious occasions and individuals that were important to a given religious house or secular patron. Calendar illustration is conventionally linked with the Christian conception of time and the divine order imposed on humanity and the natural world at the time of the Fall. Labour, particularly the working of the soil, was an ever-present reminder of the Lord's order that Adam live by the sweat of his brow, but it was also a reminder of the rewards of Heaven. Yet calendar images are not exclusively religious images. The pictorial year was divided rather unequally between aristocratic and peasant labour, and the individual labours for each month could vary, often, but not always, according to the geographical area and climate in which each manuscript was produced. The labours in the Julius A. vi calendar do not always accord with the months in which they would actually have taken place, so the artist may have been privileging his model(s) over his experience. In this case it is known that the immediate exemplar was also Anglo-Saxon, as the metrical texts for October and December contain integral references to the deaths of King Alfred (d. 899) and his wife Ealhswith (d. 902). It is also possible that there was a specific reason for this particular arrangement of the labours. In this calendar the labour for April is feasting, and the illustration combines the aristocratic activity of feasting with the more menial labour of the peasants serving the food and drink. The scene remains relatively close to its classical origins, with the diners arranged sitting or reclining on a great beast-ended couch. This particular detail has close iconographic parallels in the Carolingian *Utrecht Psalter*. The labour for June is cutting wood, and the representation of the landscape, with its stylized yet dynamic trees and yoked oxen, is thoroughly Anglo-Saxon. This and other of the agricultural scenes suggest a lush and vibrant natural world in which any tendency toward unruliness is kept in check by man. There is much work that remains to be done on the varied iconography of calendar illustrations, so this is an area ripe for research.

The unknown world

The unknown world was, of course, far more threatening than the known one, and the artists who depicted it had to be capable of conveying simultaneously its danger and the idea that distance helped to keep that danger in check. One of the most famous of surviving texts dealing with the strange and exotic is the *Wonders* (or *Marvels*) *of the East*, which survives in two Anglo-Saxon manuscripts.[31] The earlier of the two is London, British Library, Cotton Vespasian A. xv, folios 98v–106v. This is the famous *Beowulf Manuscript*, a composite volume brought together by Sir Robert Cotton, and again it is very difficult to gain access to the original manuscript. This is particularly unfortunate for anyone interested in the *Wonders*, the only illustrated section of the manuscript, as they have been reproduced slightly out of focus in the otherwise excellent digital facsimile of the manuscript.[32] One of the more fascinating of the creatures in the *Wonders* is the *Donestre* (Fig. 7.30), a half-human creature that lives on an island in the Red Sea. It understands all human languages, and when it encounters strangers it seduces them with false words and, feigning friendship, renames them with a familiar name. It then eats all but the stranger's head, over which it weeps in sorrow. In the Vitellius manuscript the *Donestre* is shown as a naked beast-headed creature, a sign of its bestial nature, and has clearly defined male genitals. He confronts a female victim. In the other Anglo-Saxon illustrated cycle, that of London, British Library, Tiberius B. v, the victim is male.[33] The Vitellius cycle of illustrations is clearly derived from a different model than that of Tiberius, but is that enough to explain the many differences in the two drawings? In Vitellius the *Donestre* is marked as the male aggressor, but he is also marked as foreign (to the Anglo-Saxons), uncivilized, and unchristian. The woman, on the other hand, might be the powerless victim, but her clothing also marks her as civilized and probably also to be understood as Christian. The scene destabilizes some of our notions of the traditional binary divisions that equate the female with the monstrous, bestial, and/or heathen. Is this simply the result of a different model, or might it be connected with contemporary events – the Viking invasions, perhaps? Or might it be connected with other stories, the seduction of Eve by false language in the Junius 11 *Genesis*, for example? As Susan Kim has noted, the illustration is not as closely keyed to

---

[31] On the *Wonders of the East* in general see Asa Simon Mittman, *Maps and Monsters in Medieval England*, Studies in Medieval History and Culture, New York, Routledge, 2006. Also still of interest is Rudolf Wittkower, 'Marvels of the East: a study in the history of monsters', *Journal of the Warburg and Courtauld Institutes* 5 (1942), 159–97; reprinted as chapter three in his *Allegory and the Migration of Symbols*, The Collected Essays of Rudolf Wittkower, 3, London, Thames & Hudson, 1977.

[32] Kevin Kiernan, ed., *The Electronic Beowulf*, London, British Library, 2003.

[33] On issues of gender see Susan M. Kim, 'The Donestre and the Person of both sexes' in Benjamin C. Withers and Jonathan Wilcox, ed., *Naked Before God: Uncovering the body in Anglo-Saxon England*, Morgantown, WV, West Virginia University Press, 2003, pp. 162–80; John Block Friedman, *The Monstrous Races in Medieval Art and Thought*, Syracuse, NY, Syracuse University Press, 1981, pp. 31–2.

the words of the text as are the rest of the drawings.³⁴ The *Donestre* seems to be threatening his victim with a severed leg rather than befriending her, and he is not shown weeping over his victim's head. The perhaps deliberately crude style of the drawings³⁵ and the breaking of the frame by both the monster and his victim add to the sense of threat. Both style and frame can be understood as devices that separate the image from its audience,³⁶ but the breaking of the frame is also a sign of the possibility of the intrusion of the foreign into the viewer's world.

London, British Library, Cotton Tiberius B. v is a mid-eleventh-century composite manuscript of uncertain origins. Three of its sections seem to have been illustrated by one artist, and may have been intended to accompany each other from the start: (1) a calendar, *computus* and metrical tables (fols 2–19); (2) Cicero's *Aratea* (fols 32v–49v); (3) the *Wonders of the East* (fols 78v–87v). The sections are thematically related in that they all deal with material conveying knowledge of the physical world. Unlike the Vitellius *Wonders*, the drawings in this manuscript are all neatly framed, convey closely the content of the accompanying text, and are of a very high quality. One of the best known of its drawings is that of the *Blemmyae* (Fig. 7.31), headless creatures eight feet tall and eight feet wide whose eyes and mouths are in their chests. In fact, so appealing is this drawing that it was chosen as the cover illustration of Andy Orchard's *Pride and Prodigies: Studies in the Monsters of the* Beowulf *Manuscript* (Cambridge, 1995), even

7.30 London, British Library, MS Cotton Vitellius A. xv (The *Beowulf Manuscript*), fol. 103v, detail.

The *Donestre* from the *Wonders* (or *Marvels*) of the *East*.

---

³⁴ Kim, 'The Donestre', 172.

³⁵ Paul Gibb, '"Wonders of the East": a critical edition and commentary', unpublished Ph.D. dissertation, Duke University, 1977, p. 5; for a possible sculptural parallel see Catherine E. Karkov 'Sheela-na-gigs and other unruly women: images of land and gender in medieval Ireland' in Colum Hourihane, ed., *From Ireland Coming: Irish art from the Early Christian to the late Gothic period and its European Context*, Index of Christian Art, Princeton, NJ, Department of Art and Archaeology, Princeton University in association with Princeton University Press, 2001, pp. 313–31.

³⁶ On the frame see Friedman, *Monstrous Races*, p. 144.

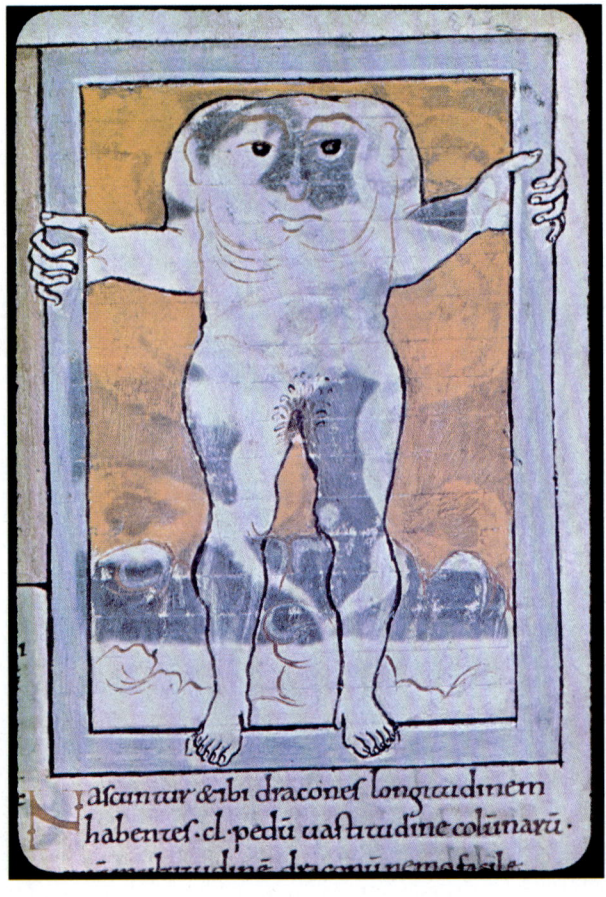

7.31 London, British Library, MS Cotton Tiberius B. v, fol. 82r.

The *Blemmyae* from the *Wonders* (or *Marvels*) of the East.

though it does not belong to that manuscript. One aspect of the miniature that has elicited much scholarly comment is the way in which this monster confronts us with his headless stare while seeming to shake the confining bars of the frame.[37] The idea conveyed is again that of a threat contained, at least for the moment, but the way in which the creature looks directly at us with its displaced face suggests a likeness with us at the same time that it conveys difference: that headless face has a very human appearance. Indeed, a number of the illustrations in the Tiberius *Wonders of the East* have a psychological depth unrivalled in other illustrated cycles, Anglo-Saxon or otherwise, that merits further attention.[38] This is a manuscript that could benefit from future research from perspectives as divergent as traditional source study and contemporary theoretical practice.

RIGHT

7.32 London, British Library, MS Cotton Claudius B. iv (The *Old English Hexateuch*), fol. 26r.

Above, Abraham and the Lord; below, Abraham scaring birds.

---

[37] See further Friedman, *Monstrous Races*.

[38] As noted by Jeffrey Jerome Cohen, *On Giants*, Minneapolis, University of Minnesota Press, 1999, pp. 1–2.

ıerosolıma. et tande p sıncopam. ıerosolıma·

cƿæð þa toȝode· Mın drıhten god. hu ƿæst ıc þ ıc hyt aȝan sceal
God cƿæþ to hı. ȝeof me þa mettolæce· anþrıƿıntre hryðer. ⁊ ane
þrıƿıntre ȝat. ⁊ ane þrıƿıntre ȝat. ⁊ ane turtlan. ⁊ ane culfran·

He dyde þa ſƿa ⁊ todælde hı onƿeȝ buton þa fuȝelaſ he ne todælde
þa coman oðre fuȝelaſ þ.....tu to þam holde. ⁊ hıa aflıȝde fram þam
flæſce ealle:⁊

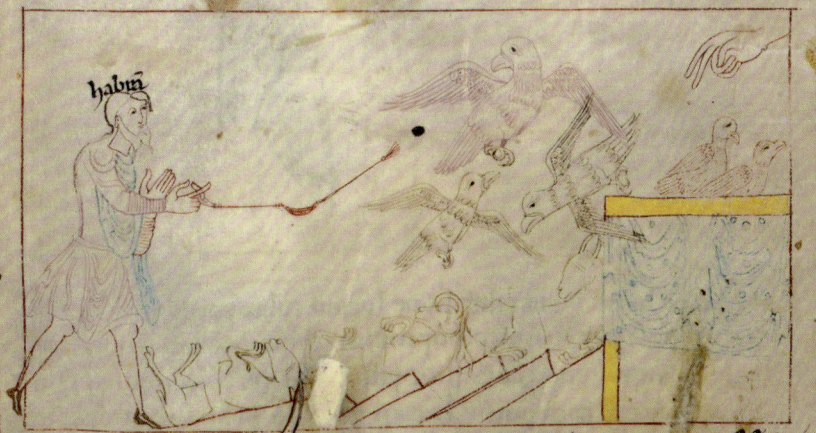

Et ab anno naṫıuıtatıſ yſaac uſq; ad annū egſſıonıſ ab egıpto nūaṫ· cccc·v· annoſ· S; ſcrıp
tura ſubıcıet dnŝ· ꝗ legıt ıntellıȝ&· ſeme ṫuū peꝑınū erıṫ· cccc annıſ· ſıue ın ṫerra capaan· ſıue ın egıpto
peꝑınī fuıṫ· donec huıṫ heredıtaṫē ex pmıſſıone deı· qd̄ aū dıcıt· ſedū ı bū ſacerdotale ıntellıȝendū
ē· leuı ꝗ ȝenuıṫ· cahaṫ· ꝗ ȝenuıṫ. amrā· ꝗ ȝenuıṫ aaron· ꝗ ȝenuıṫ· eleazar· ꝗ cū aaron egreſſuſ eſṫ· Nō duaſ· iiij· ȝenera
ṫıoneſ pſonalı ſ; ſucceſſıoneſ· uṫ coſ ſınṫ ȝeneratıoneſ· ꝗens ıbı leȝıṫ ȝenuıṫ· QZ alıa ıṫa ht̄. quıa ſedm̄

Literary texts

One final category of manuscript that remains to be considered is that of literary texts. Two examples will suffice, the first a prose manuscript, the *Old English Hexateuch* (London, British Library, Cotton Claudius B. iv), and the second the only illustrated Anglo-Saxon poetic manuscript, Oxford, Bodleian Library, Junius 11. Both manuscripts may of course also be considered biblical manuscripts of a type, but both are original retellings of the biblical stories. More to the point, the style and function of their illustrations is very different.

The Old English Hexateuch

Claudius B. iv contains a paraphrase of the first six books of the Old Testament illustrated with over four hundred miniatures (Fig. 7.32), many of them unfinished. Because so many of the pictures are incomplete it provides us with some knowledge of Anglo-Saxon techniques of illumination. They seem to have been produced in five stages: (1) the under drawings were sketched out, (2) the text was added, (3) areas of flat colour were blocked in, (4) facial details were added, (5) details of drapery, shading and highlighting were added. The miniatures themselves are narrative in both composition (meaning that many are laid out in continuous narrative format), and style (meaning that figures are portrayed in active poses and with exaggerated gestures so that they visually convey the story), and follow the text of the manuscript quite closely. The clarity of its pictorial program is generally linked to the probability that the manuscript was produced for a lay patron. The *Hexateuch*'s illustrations are also believed to have been an important source for many of the scenes and details in the Bayeux Tapestry.

The Junius Manuscript

Junius 11 is a poetic manuscript illustrated with line drawings rather than fully painted miniatures. It too was left unfinished, with drawings completed only as far as Abraham's approach into Egypt on page 88.[39] As with Claudius B. iv, the Junius 11 illustrations provide a visual narrative, but the way in which that narrative relates to the poetic text is quite different. In fact, rather than illustrating the text, most of the Junius 11 images gloss the text, that is,

---

[39] Excellent images of all pages are available on the Bodleian website (http:image.ox.ac.uk/show?collection=bodleian&manuscript=msjunius11) and indeed, the complete manuscript has been published as a CD-ROM, yet digital images and facsimiles will still not give you a real sense of the way the manuscript works. Only sitting down and turning the actual pages will allow you to understand exactly how the images move the story forward and help to direct your movement through the book.

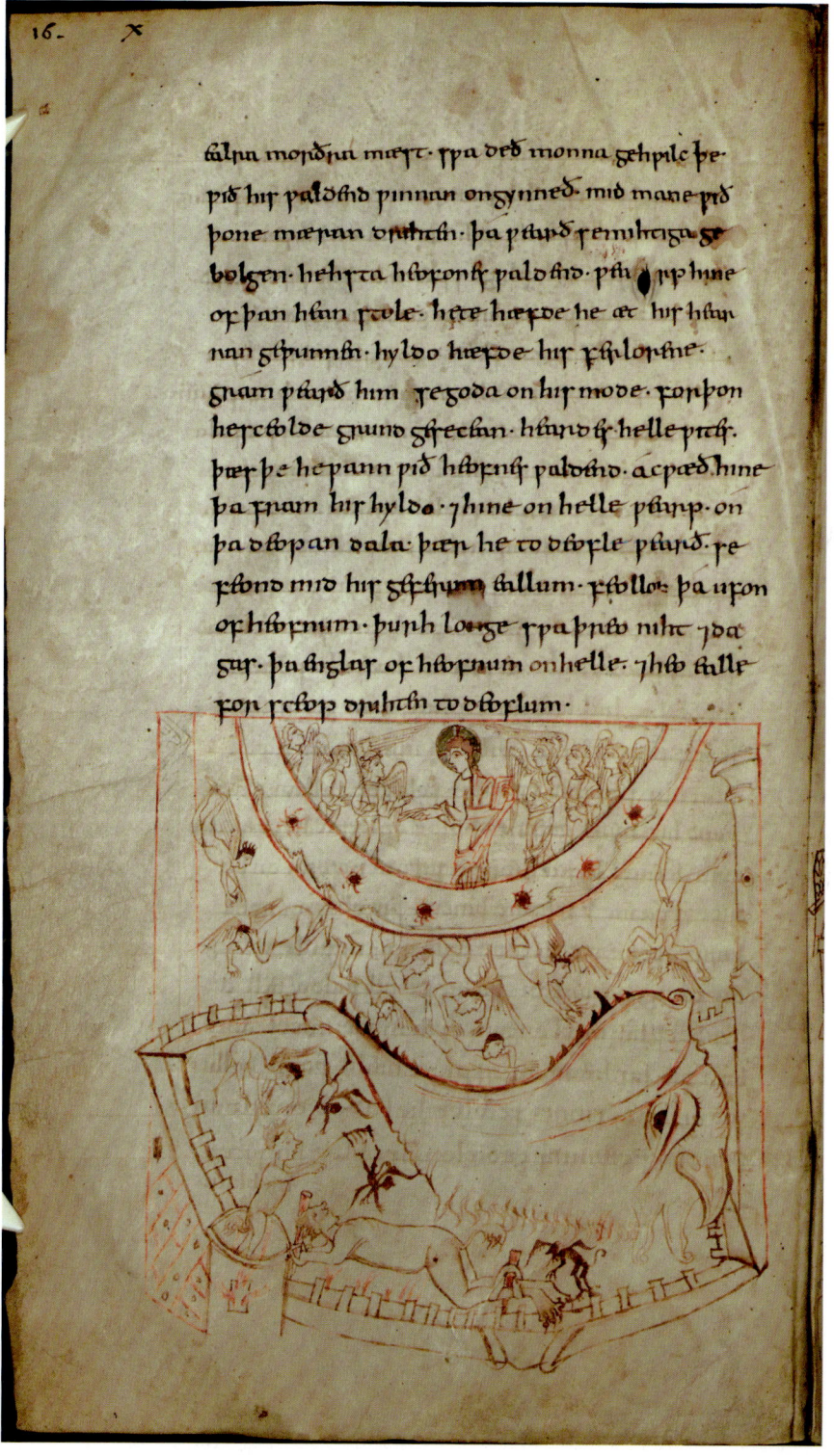

7.33 Oxford, Bodleian Library, MS Junius 11 (The *Junius Manuscript*), p. 16.

The fall of the angels from *Genesis*.

7.34 Oxford, Bodleian Library, MS Junius 11 (The *Junius Manuscript*), p. 47.

The birth of Abel from *Genesis*.

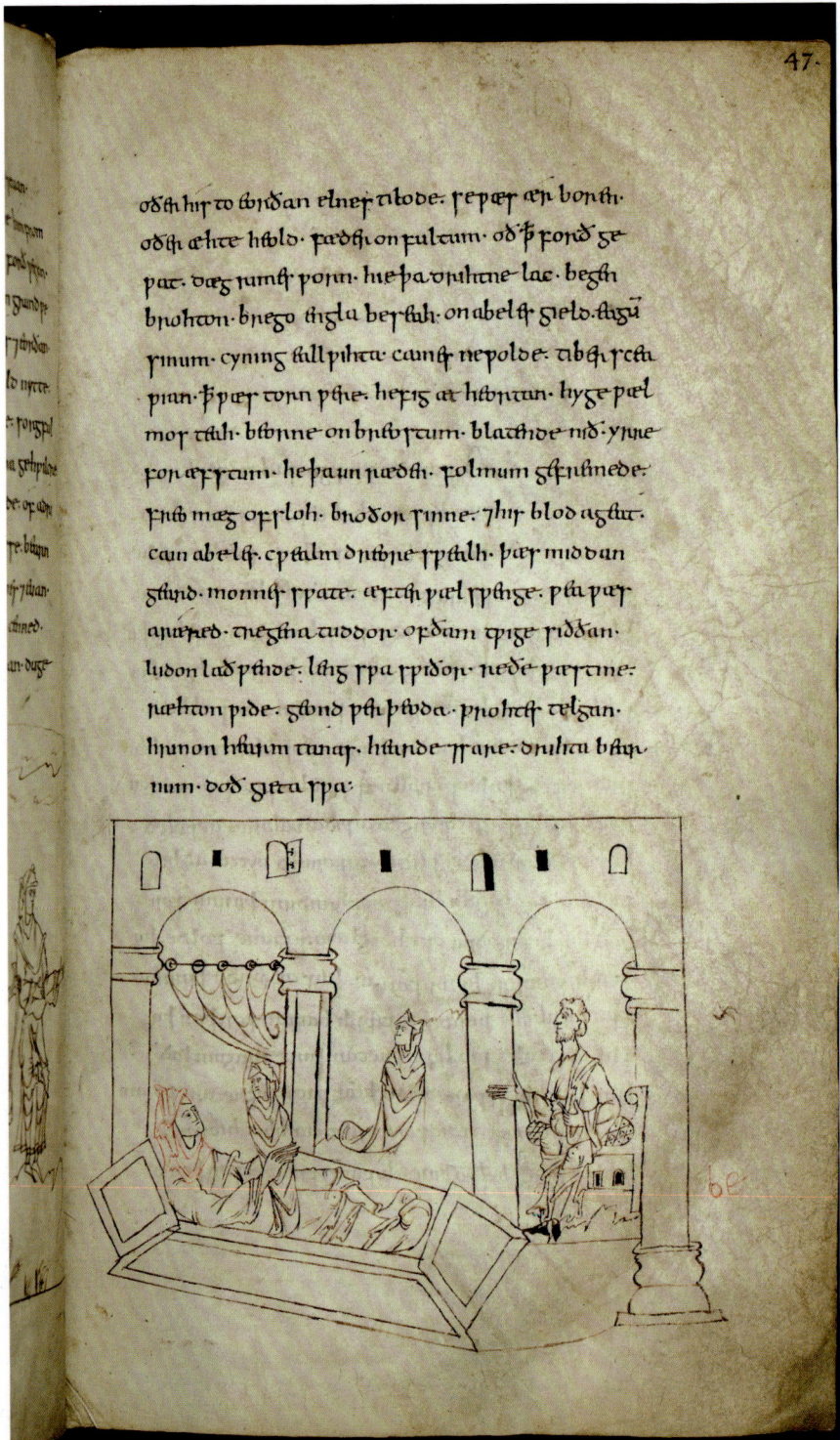

they provide additional layers of meaning to the verse. This is a manuscript in which it is absolutely essential to read text and image together if one is to understand the full picture. One area in which the drawings bring out additional layers of meaning is that of gender. There are, for example, two depictions of the fall of the rebel angels, the first on page 3 and the second (Fig. 7.33) on page 16. In the first, the focus is on Heaven (two-thirds of the drawing is devoted to it), but in the second the focus is on the descent of the angels and their entry into Hell. Most unusually for early medieval depictions of the scene, several of the angels in this second drawing receive male genitalia, suggesting that the fall from genderless angelic bodies is also a fall into gendered human bodies. This second fall of the angels precedes the account of the fall of Adam and Eve, and thus reminds us of the relationship between the two episodes, as well as providing a male precedent to and balance for Eve's role in the fall of man.

Of equal interest is the prominence of women in the drawings illustrating the birth of Abel (Fig. 7.34) and the descendents of Adam and Eve. In the illustration of the birth of Abel, Eve is depicted giving birth within a comfortable interior in a composition that is most likely modelled on that of the Nativity.[40] Adam too has been elevated from his usual depiction as an agricultural labourer to that of an enthroned head of the household. The reasons for these iconographic innovations are likely to be complex, but they do raise questions about the patronage and intended audience of this manuscript. Might it have been intended for a courtly or aristocratic audience? Might it have been commissioned by or for a woman?

Illuminated manuscripts and Anglo-Saxon society

The Junius 11 drawings bring us finally to questions of what manuscript illumination can tell us about the society that produced and used these manuscripts. Clearly, unfinished manuscripts have much to reveal about methods of production, and clearly the types of manuscripts produced, and innovations in style and iconography can help us to gain an understanding of the changing concerns of those who produced them and the development of contacts with foreign courts, churches, artists or styles. In other areas, patronage for example, what is or is not revealed is not always as straightforward as one might think. The Crucifixion miniature in New York, Pierpont Morgan Library 709, for example (Fig. 7.35), includes a small female

---

[40] See Karkov, *Text and Picture in Anglo-Saxon England*, pp. 81–8; Catherine E. Karkov, 'The Anglo-Saxon Genesis: text, illustration and audience' in Rebecca Barnhouse and Benjamin C. Withers, ed., *The Old English Hexateuch: aspects and approaches*, Kalamazoo, MI, Medieval Institute Publications, 2000, pp. 187–223.

figure embracing the foot of the cross. It is just possible that the figure was intended to represent Mary Magdalene, but if so, there are problems with the discrepancy of scale; moreover, this would be the earliest representation of the Magdalene at the foot of the cross. It thus seems more reasonable to assume that she represents the woman by or for whom the gospel book was commissioned. The pose suggests that she was, or at least wished to be perceived as, a very pious woman. The portrait cannot, however, be safely interpreted as a portrait of Judith of Flanders, wife of Earl Tostig of Northumbria, despite the manuscript's known association with her. While there is little doubt that Judith once owned the manuscript, it is not clear whether it was made specifically for her or acquired by her at some time after its production.[41] It does seem to be clear that she donated the book to the Weingarten Abbey library in 1094, but the possibility remains that the woman in the miniature may represent someone other than Judith. We may not be able to be certain as to who is depicted, but we can be certain that the style of the miniature reveals something about the time in which it was produced. The emotional gestures and poses of all the figures depicted are symptomatic of the increased emotional content of later Anglo-Saxon art in general. They also reveal an increasingly personal expression of piety and devotion which says something about changing religious attitudes. It should also be born in mind that no matter who the woman at the foot of the cross may be, she is a sign of the growing number of female book owners beginning to appear in the documentary record. For the most part, all images are open to interpretation as it is a very rare thing indeed for an artist (or patron) to explain to us exactly what he or she was trying to achieve, yet they do provide us with some idea of the ways in which the Anglo-Saxons responded to the material world in which they lived as well as to the spiritual and intellectual worlds created in the texts they chose to illustrate.

LEFT

7.35 New York, Pierpont Morgan Library MS 709 (The *Judith Gospels*), fol. 1v.

Crucifixion with *Sol, Luna* and the Hand of God above, Mary, John and donor portrait below.

---

41 See Patrick McGurk and Jane Rosenthal, 'The Anglo-Saxon gospelbooks of Judith, Countess of Flanders: their text, make-up and function', *Anglo-Saxon England*, 24, 1995, pp. 251–308; Jane Rosenthal and Patrick McGurk, 'Author, symbol and word: the inspired evangelists in Judith of Flanders's Anglo-Saxon gospel books' in Susan L'Engle and Gerald B. Guest, ed., *Tributes to Jonathan J.G. Alexander, The making and meaning of illuminated medieval and Renaissance manuscripts, Art & Architecture*, Turnhout and London, Harvey Miller, 2006, pp. 185–201.

Introduction to Chapter 8

Students of the Anglo-Saxon period now make extensive use of electronic resources in order to aid their understanding and research. The following chapter explains techniques of digitization in simple terms and considers both the advantages and the potential drawbacks inherent in the technology.

Digitization of manuscripts not only makes readily available images of sufficiently high quality to satisfy most scholars; it also offers enhanced research possibilities, since details can be enlarged, disparate parts can be laid together for comparison, damage can be stripped out to reveal previously obscured original material and new information gained by viewing under special lighting conditions can be permanently recorded.

However, since photographing a page from a codex or a detail of a folio potentially divorces that image from its manuscript, the need for a responsible approach, linking images to meaningful contexts, is essential, and the authors accordingly examine methods used in recent digitization projects that successfully address this issue. One project simulates the manuscript experience by 'binding together' individual images so that each folio is viewed as a page in a codex; another presents images as one aspect of producing an edition of the text, so that visual representations of the manuscripts are linked to textual and bibliographic context.

Crucial early decisions in any digitization project involve prioritizing the features of manuscripts that are to be marked and how they are to be captured. Data may include details of codicology, presentation and scribal history, collations with other manuscripts and diplomatic transcription. The usefulness of a digitized text is dependent on this pre-planning and the sophistication of its structural mark-up language. The authors of this chapter survey this fast-developing field covering the advantages and drawbacks of using XML (eXtensible Mark-up Language), devising one's own mark-up language, or exploiting the TEI (Text Encoding Initiative), which has published guidelines containing a standard mark-up language for use by encoders of historical and scholarly documents.

The process of information acquisition is not very different from the research collected by traditional text editors in the pre-digital age. The results however, are far more sophisticated, offering the scholar desktop access to complex, digested information on individual manuscripts or simultaneously on multiple comparable texts.

8

From manuscript to computer

Stuart D. Lee and Daniel Paul O'Donnell

As every Anglo-Saxonist knows, one of the greatest catastrophes to afflict the discipline occurred in 1731 with the fire at Ashburnham House. The great collection of medieval manuscripts assembled by Sir Robert Cotton was ravaged, and the scenes as the flames raged through the library bordered on the chaotic as people attempted to salvage as many of the great codices as they could. As Prescott suggests, the aftermath was equally bad:

> The morning after the fire, Little Dean's Yard must have been a sad sight, littered with fragments of burnt manuscripts, which the boys of Westminster School picked up and kept as souvenirs.[1]

Thus began the painstaking process of reassembling the remains of the manuscripts and over the subsequent decades and centuries scholars have had to contend with the disastrous consequences of that day. Not only that, but they have also had to overcome mistakes in the rebinding of some of the manuscripts originally held in the Ashburnham collection, and misguided attempts to use chemicals to read the burnt fragments.

Nevertheless many manuscripts and fragments did survive the disaster, and together with the major collections held in Oxford and Cambridge, they represent one of the largest collections of western vernacular early medieval literature in existence. Over the centuries scholars have sought these out in the great libraries, and pored over their content.

The fire in Ashburnham House illustrates the great weakness of manuscript culture: each object is unique and (literally) irreplaceable. While it is true that the production of some very popular medieval texts was such that the loss of a single exemplar posed no real threat to our knowledge of the period, many other texts – especially, perhaps, those from the Anglo-Saxon period – were produced in such small numbers that the loss of

---

[1] A. Prescott. 'The Electronic Beowulf and digital restoration', *Literary and Linguistic Computing*, 12.3, 1997, pp. 185–96.

even relatively undistinguished copies of individual items diminished our knowledge considerably. For example, approximately twenty-five Anglo-Saxon vernacular poems and fragments (representing about 2% of the entire verse corpus) are known from more than one manuscript copy[2] and only two of these – *Bede's Death Song* and *Cædmon's Hymn* – are known from more than four. Even texts we know to have been extremely popular – such as the Old English translation of the psalms or Bede's *Historia ecclesiastica* – have large gaps in their early textual histories caused by the loss of primary manuscript sources.

> 'The great weakness of manuscript culture [is that] each object is unique and (literally) irreplaceable ... Making high-quality digital images available should mean less handling of the manuscript, and consequently, better preservation.'

Despite the fragility of the evidence, scholars must, of necessity, work closely with the primary sources. As Fred Robinson long ago demonstrated with Anglo-Saxon vernacular poetry, texts in a manuscript acquire rich layers of meaning when we 'consider the source' in which they are found.[3] Reading texts without paying attention to their immediate physical context can easily lead to questionable interpretations. While not all Anglo-Saxonists have easy access to the great manuscript libraries, few can afford to carry out their research without detailed knowledge of these libraries' holdings.

Print-age scholars developed a number of partial solutions to this problem. Hand-drawn, typed, and later, photographic facsimiles of manuscripts, texts or individual pages were used to attempt to convey to researchers a sense of the original documents' physical appearance. Diplomatic transcriptions and (particularly in Anglo-Saxon studies) a long tradition of conservative best- or sole-text critical editions reproduced the textual content of individual manuscripts, very often with transcriptions of relevant corrections, deletions, additions, marginalia and other aspects of the scribal performance.

Such tools were useful to scholars in the initial stages of their research, particularly those who lacked easy access to the great manuscript collections. But they were rarely more than rough substitutes, and rarely able to capture

---

[2] Daniel Paul O'Donnell, 'Manuscript variation in multiple-recension Old English poetic texts: the technical problem and poetical art', unpublished Ph.D. dissertation, Yale University, 1996, Appendix A (Available online at http://people.uleth.ca/%7Edaniel.odonnell/offPrints/dissertation.pdf).

[3] Fred C. Robinson, 'Consider the source: medieval texts and medieval manuscripts' in *Medieval Perspectives: papers from the twelfth annual conference of the Southeastern Medieval Association*, ed. Merritt Blakeslee, William Provost and Katharina Wilson, Richmond: Eastern Kentucky University, 1987, title and *passim*.

the type of detail concerning ink, *mise-en-page*, or scribal performance upon which the scholars themselves increasingly began to focus.

The rapid integration of advanced digital technology has, over the past twenty years or so, greatly improved our ability to represent manuscripts in ways useful to contemporary scholarship. This has contributed greatly to the study of medieval literature by making primary source material more accessible to the average scholar, and providing new analytical tools and processes to allow easier research of the primary evidence. At the same time, however, it is easy to be too sanguine about what it is now possible to do with a computer. While we can represent manuscripts with a far higher degree of fidelity than was ever possible before, this ability brings with it a greater responsibility of care and documentation. What we want to avoid is replicating in digital form the chaos of the Ashburnham House fire and the often ill-fated, if well meaning, attempts to preserve what was left of a large portion of Great Britain's manuscript heritage.

What is digitization?

We should begin by defining 'digitization'. In formal terms, digitization is the conversion of an analogue signal or code to a digital signal or code. This sounds daunting but can easily be explained by the now common handheld digital camera. This simply takes the analogue signals and converts them internally into a digital file which is usually stored on a removable memory card in the camera. The file itself is like any computer file: it can be copied (usually from the camera to a desktop machine), saved, or deleted.

Digitization is not restricted to the production of photographs; it is common to digitize audio and video, for example (time-based media). However, with reference to the main focus of this book – the manuscript – taking things to the next level entails providing a text that can utilise the power of the computer's searching capability. For manuscripts, what one commonly does is to provide a machine-readable transcription which can be searched or used in other applications (such as concordance or collation software). Here we use what is called 'plain text' where all the formatting has been stripped out (for example, we remove bold, italics, underlines, or the position of the word on the page).

There are several reasons why people choose to use plain text for transcriptions of manuscripts and electronic texts in general (as opposed to Word documents, or something produced by a desktop publishing package). First, most of the analysis engines one would subsequently use require plain text. Second, plain text is future-proofed in that it does not require a proprietary piece of software to read it (such as Microsoft Word). Third, we may want to do something more advanced with the text that simple formatting (such as bold and italics) will not allow, that is to say, we may wish to insert information into the text about key features.

This article will discuss both aspects of the digitization of manuscripts. It will begin with a discussion of digital photography, particularly as this is practised by manuscript libraries and museums. In the second half, the article will review approaches to the mark-up of textual content, focussing particularly on how this can be accomplished within the current scholarly standard for such projects – the guidelines of the Text Encoding Initiative (TEI).

Digitizing the manuscript

The basic processes involved in digital photography, as we have seen, are straightforward enough: there is an object (for example, the folio of a manuscript), a digital camera is pointed at it, and a picture is taken, or more correctly a digital file is created that records all the information about the image in a machine-readable manner. Yet the story is more complicated and interesting than that.

First of all we should distinguish between two types of digitization – contact and non-contact. The former will be familiar to many people and involves such everyday equipment as the flat-bed scanner. Here the document is laid face down on a plate of glass and a beam (called a 'charge coupled device' or CCD) moves beneath the glass, bouncing light off the document and recording in digital form the information it receives. This is termed 'contact scanning' because something actually comes into contact with the surface of the document (i.e. the plate of glass).

'Non-contact scanning' involves, for example, using a digital camera. Again,

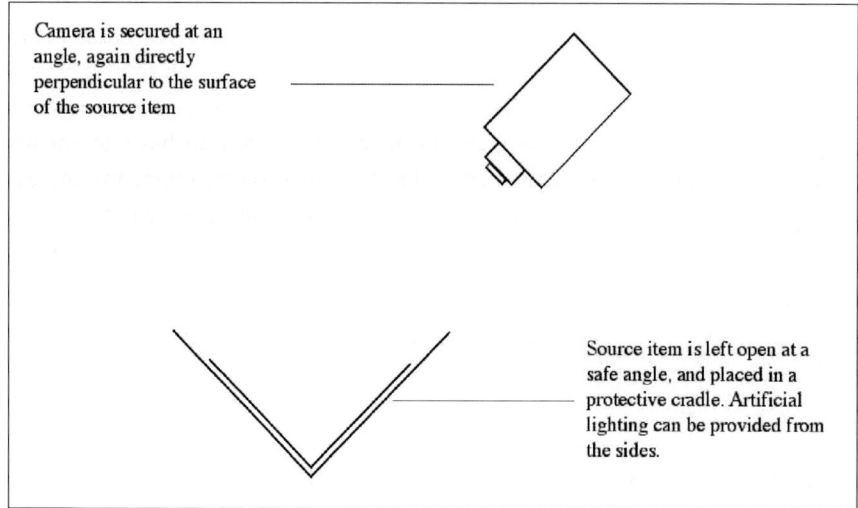

8.1 A possible positioning of a camera to avoid too much pressure on the binding of the manuscript.

Camera is secured at an angle, again directly perpendicular to the surface of the source item

Source item is left open at a safe angle, and placed in a protective cradle. Artificial lighting can be provided from the sides.

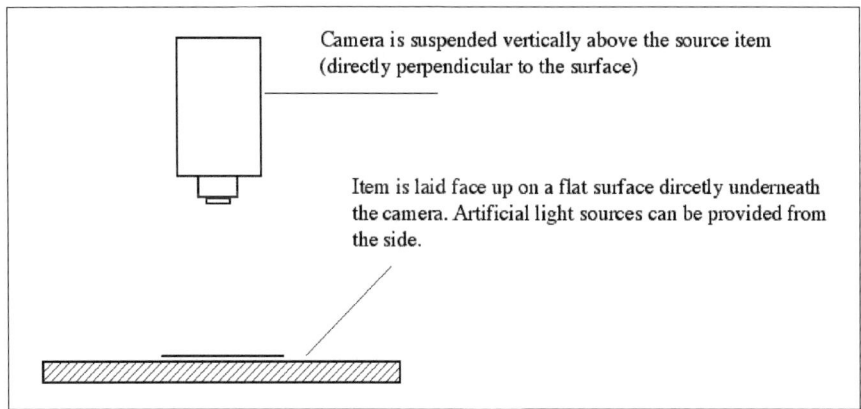

8.2 Overhead positioning of a camera, useful for single-sheet flat digitization.

though it is not as obvious, this receives the light reflection from the object via a CCD and creates a digital file of the information. The key point here, though, is that there is no physical contact between camera and document.

In Figures 8.1 and 8.2, two standard approaches to non-contact digitization are shown. In the first, the book or manuscript is held in an angled cradle to avoid putting too much pressure on the binding. The camera is positioned and fastened perpendicular to the surface of the folio or page in question. Suitable lighting (that won't damage the object) is positioned around the cradle. In Fig. 8.2 we can see overhead scanning, where the object, a single flat sheet (for example, a single photograph or painting) is laid flat. Here there are no issues of tight bindings to concern the digitizer.[4]

This type of digitization has been extremely common in the major projects involving medieval manuscripts undertaken by libraries over the past fifteen years. As there is no contact with the surface of the manuscript and conservation concerns about binding and damage from lighting can be addressed, such set-ups are usually preferred. Of course, the cameras employed are more expensive than the consumer-level equipment available in the High Street, and the cradles and lights are specialised.

It should also be noted that it is not always necessary to have access to the primary source material to run a digitization project. Often initiatives have digitized surrogates of the object, such as photographs, 35mm slides, or microfilms in the case of manuscripts. Here, as long as the surrogate is

---

[4] A good example of bindings causing problems is the digitization of *The Exeter Book*. See N. Pickwoad, 'Report on the preparation of Exeter D&C MS 3501 for digitisation' (1996) in B.J. Muir, *The Exeter DVD: The Exeter Anthology of Old English Poetry*, Exeter, University of Exeter Press, 2006. For a full analysis of the digitization process see Stuart D. Lee, *Digital Imaging: a practical handbook*, New York, Neal-Schuman Publishers in association with Library Association Publishing, 2000.

not rare or unique, one can utilise contact scanning, and specialised high-throughput slide and microfilm scanners are regularly employed and produce highly effective results, although the quality will always depend upon the quality of the surrogate.[5]

The aim of digitization is to produce a digital file that contains all the information about the image. This file can then be opened and displayed, processed, or altered, using software applications. To understand this further, however, we must get to grips with the main features of a digital image.

The first feature is relatively obvious – namely whether an image is colour, greyscale (shades between black and white), or simply black and white. Most users would not find this too problematic. However, this is complicated further when we talk about the number of colours or the number of 'shades' of grey an image contains. The term utilised here is 'bit-depth' or 'colour-depth'. Without going into the complexities of 'bits', the higher the number, the more colours can be displayed; so a 1-bit image would display two colours (black and white usually), a 2-bit image four colours, ranging up to what is occasionally called 'true colour' at 24-bit which can represent 16,777,216 mixed colours. Users of flat-bed scanners may already have come across this feature when looking at the preferences of the scanning software they use. The higher the bit-depth, the better the range of colours that can be represented; so most high-quality scanning by libraries of rare manuscripts occurs at 24-bit. The problem, though, is that the higher the bit-depth, the bigger the size of the file, which will have implications for storage. Thus a 24-bit image of a folio at a high resolution (see below) will regularly occupy well in excess of a 100Mb.

The second feature can be termed the 'density' of the image. A computer screen is made up of picture elements or pixels, and everything that is displayed on the screen will occupy these pixels. A computer image will have been scanned at a certain resolution, called 'pixels per inch' or ppi. (The term 'dpi' or 'dots per inch' is used to mean the same thing, though strictly speaking this should be reserved for printing.) The higher the ppi, the better the resolution of the image. A 300ppi image is an image sampled at 300 pixels × 300 pixels per inch. The easiest way to witness the limits of an image's resolution is to open up a digital image file and, using a piece of

---

[5] Surrogates, sometimes created years ago, are also used if the original is deemed to be put at risk by further photography. In O'Donnell's edition of *Cædmon's Hymn*, for example, Paris, Bibliothèque Nationale, fonds latin 5237 is represented by a scan of a black-and-white photograph of the original (and fragile) manuscript (see Daniel Paul O'Donnell, *Cædmon's Hymn: A multimedia study, edition and archive*, Society for Early English and Norse Electronic Texts A.7, Cambridge, D.S. Brewer, 2005). In Martin K. Foys, *The Bayeux Tapestry Digital Edition*, Leicester, Scholarly Digital Editions, 2003, the edition is based on scanned images from a print facsimile.

image analysis software, 'zoom in'. Gradually the image will begin to appear 'pixelated', degenerating into small squares or blocks with no gradation in tone or colour between them. In other words, one is seeing the individual pixels, and the lower the resolution of the image the quicker this will become evident as the image is magnified. The standard process when digitizing rare items such as medieval manuscripts is to take the original at the highest possible resolution and colour-depth and save this as the master file (for example, 600ppi at 24-bit colour).

A further set of considerations involve file formats. There are numerous file formats available for digital images; the most common being TIFF (.tif), JPEG (.jpg) and GIF (.gif). These represent different methods of coding an image as a computer file. To the user this will often be irrelevant, as most applications can open all these files, but to the 'digitizer' and the scholar it is important. TIFF is the file format of choice for master images. It is an open standard (that is, it is not owned by any one company), can be viewed by nearly all image analysis software, and most importantly is by default lossless in its compression. What this means is that it does not throw away information (such as gradations in colour) in order to make the file size (in terms of kilobytes) smaller. From these TIFFs one can then create 'derivatives', copies of the master image in other file formats more suitable for distribution. Thus it is common for derivative JPEG images to be created from the master TIFF image. JPEGs are almost the default image format for the web; they open seamlessly in web browsers and handle colour particularly well. However they do lose some of the original information (such as colour gradation) to allow for reduced file size. It is important to be aware of this, as when one is viewing a JPEG image of a manuscript, 'pixelation' (as described above) can occur quickly when zooming in (the resolution of the JPEG being lower than the TIFF), and the colour information may not be as accurate as that of the original master image. If this is the case, then the scholar should see if it is possible to request a copy of the original TIFF image.

The benefits of digital images

There are many benefits to digitization that we should highlight before considering the pitfalls. First, a digital file can be copied endlessly without any degradation to its quality. It is also extremely cheap to do this and disseminate the copy, more often than not via the web, which makes the image much more accessible. If we consider the alternatives (expensive facsimiles, expensive microfilms and readers or other surrogates, or requesting permission to actually see the manuscript itself) it is easy to justify the claim that digitization is a democratizing process by virtue of the way it provides access to rare items.

There is also the preservation issue. Making high-quality digital images available should mean less handling of the manuscript, and consequently, better preservation. But conversely, the increased awareness of the manuscript resulting from the availability of digital images may lead to more requests to see it. The preservation of digital files is also problematic. Some people argue that a digital file of high enough quality is, itself, a preservation copy. However, problems in the past with technology becoming obsolete and file formats becoming unreadable still suggest that a preservation copy made using an analogue process (e.g. microfilm) is safer.

Finally, there are the benefits of the file's flexibility once it has been created. As well as the potential for creating derivatives, or disseminating the file as part of a bundled package (see below), image enhancement facilities available through reasonably inexpensive or free pieces of software (such as Adobe's proprietary Photoshop[6] or the open source GIMP[7]) open up a range of possibilities. Simple examples include the ability to magnify sections of the manuscript, or cut out portions and overlay them next to different folios for comparison. Even more exciting opportunities arise when we consider restoration. Craig-McFeely and Lock illustrate the potential for digital restoration in their work with the Digital Image Archive of Medieval Music manuscripts (DIAMM).[8] Through the use of filters and layers in Photoshop they present a series of examples of the process of digitally restoring damaged or obscure manuscript originals. A master image is acquired, and then the tools of the software are applied to this master image. The aim, as they note, is 'to retrieve information rather than attempt to re-create the look of the original'. Importantly this is information that is already there but is obscured by the surrounding 'noise'. Image analysis software, for example, can quickly alter colour hues and contrasts, stripping out superfluous information that may be hiding the desired text, or accentuating important factors.

Once we have the image we can treat it like any other computer-file: cut, paste, organise, and search. Arianna Ciula has outlined work in the field of digital palaeography.[9] Here, using the System for Palaeographical Inspections (SPI), individually segmented characters are taken from a digital image and stored in a central knowledge base (using shape recognition processes) thus

---

[6] http://www.adobe.com/products/photoshop

[7] http://www.gimp.org/

[8] J. Craig-McFeely and A. Lock, *Digital Restoration Workbook*, Oxford, Oxford Select Specialist Catalogue Publications, 2006. http://www.diamm.ac.uk/

[9] Arianna Ciula, 'Digital Palaeography: using the digital representation of medieval script to support palaeographical analysis', *Digital Medievalist*, 1.1, 2005. (http://www.digitalmedievalist.org/article.cfm?RecID=2).

allowing automatic retrieval of similar shapes, comparisons, and computer-generated attempts to group together scribal similarities and produce an idealised representation of the core features of an individual scribe's hand.

Digitization does not always have to take place under 'normal' conditions. Special lighting can be used – such as ultra-violet (UV) – in the actual capturing process. It is true that facilities to view damaged manuscripts under UV conditions are often available in libraries holding the manuscripts, but the amount of time one is allowed to use the UV facility is often limited for safety reasons. Therefore digitizing a manuscript under such conditions can provide a permanent UV record for consultation. In the eBoethius project [10] Kevin Kiernan demonstrates the benefits of placing a UV image alongside a standard image of the damaged manuscript London, British Library, Cotton Otho A. vi. Below, in Fig. 8.3 using the Edition Production Technology software, one can see the UV image overlaid on the 'normal' original. This allows, as Kiernan suggests, 'for testing hypotheses for conjectural restorations'. Importantly it enables the scholar to look at both the original and the UV image, without altering the former.

Even more interesting is the application of advanced image techniques utilised in other disciplines and not commonly associated with codicology or palaeography. In the Archimedes Palimpsest project [11] work is under way using a variety of imaging techniques to display a hidden copy of Archimedes' work under a thirteenth-century palimpsest. Two techniques are being investigated here that show immense promise: multispectral and X-ray fluorescence imaging. In the former, a series of photographs are taken of the same page but at different light wavelengths (UV, for example, is one such 'wavelength') which reveal different information. By combining these, the full characteristics of the manuscript, and in this case the 'under text' of the palimpsest, can be revealed. X-ray fluorescence imaging builds on the fact that different atoms give out different X-rays under certain conditions. Thus the atoms of one pigment or ink yield different X-rays from a different pigment or ink. If these can be isolated and mapped, again, the 'under text', which would have used different pigments from the 'over text', can be revealed.[12]

---

[10] http://beowulf.engl.uky.edu/~kiernan/eBoethius/inlad.htm, but see especially http://beowulf.engl.uky.edu/~kiernan/eBoethius/edit.htm for a description of the capturing and editing process.

[11] http://www.archimedespalimpsest.org

[12] For further applications of this see K.L. Brown and R.J.H. Clark, 'Analysis of key Anglo-Saxon manuscripts (8–11th centuries) in the British Library: pigment identification by Raman Microscopy', *Journal of Raman Spectroscopy*, 35.3, March 2004, pp. 181–9 (available online at http://www3.interscience.wiley.com/cgi-bin/abstract/107632977/ABSTRACT.

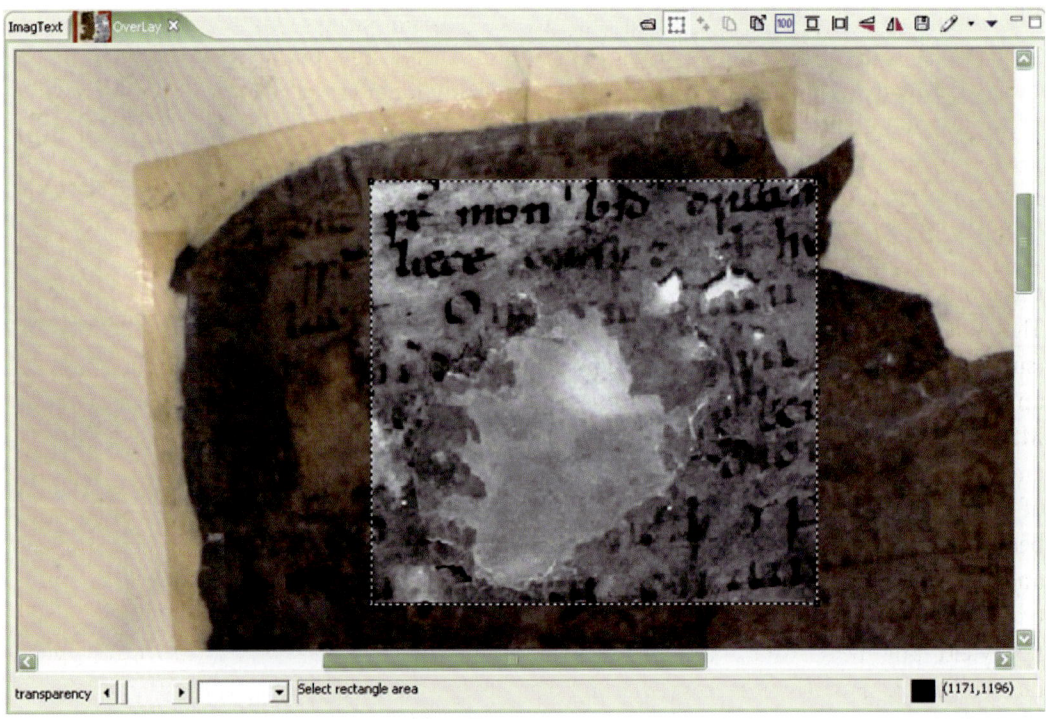

8.3 The eBoethius Project's EPT software showing a UV image overlaid onto the original.

The drawbacks of digitization

Although there are clear benefits to digitization, it could be said (albeit contentiously) that digitization 'destroys' the codex. This it is not to suggest the manuscript comes to any physical harm, rather, it is the notion that digitization destroys the concept of the codex, in terms of its existence as an integrated whole: a collection of parchment sheets bound into a single volume.

As we noted earlier, the digital process produces digital files (in this case, images), and it does so by creating one for each folio or 'opening' that the camera 'photographs'. In other words, what one will be left with after 'digitizing' a manuscript is a collection of individual files each representing a single image. Importantly, therefore, what is produced by default is not a single integrated file with all the images collected together. It is true that one could collect all of these individual images together into the same folder on a computer, but that is hardly a permanent or robust referencing system. Moreover, each file will probably yield only very basic information such as:

- file name (which may be representative but more often than not will simply say 'f1v.jpg' or similar);

- folder name (again this may indicate the manuscript, but this can easily be renamed or files may be moved in and out of folders);
- automatically generated data such as date of creation and image file format.

Why might this be a problem? An example of the issues that might arise from this occurred on the ANSAX email discussion list recently. In a posting dated 29 June 2006 a scholar asked, 'I wonder if anybody can help me ID the following image: http://z.about.com/d/historymedren/1/0/M/A/bede.jpg'. This was a perfectly legitimate question and, as it transpired, the answer (supplied by a list member who recognised the image) was that this was an illustration from Cambridge, Corpus Christi College MS 389. Yet, the original email clearly illustrated an emerging problem that is arising from the proliferation of digitization, namely that the digital image can quickly become disassociated from its cataloguing information and become 'free-floating'. In the above example, even truncating the URL (the web address of the image) did not yield any page where the image was listed with its shelfmark. Furthermore, opening up the image in Photoshop and viewing the information about the file also yielded no information. In short, to all intents and purposes this was an image adrift on the internet that could only be identified through prior knowledge. The filename itself was also unhelpful as it was probably incorrect: the iconography of the actual picture suggests that it is more likely a depiction of St Jerome.

'Not only can the complete [digitized] image become detached from its metadata and thus untraceable, but parts of it may be disseminated, or even worse distorted, cropped, rotated or collated with other images, creating further problems for people attempting to locate its original source.'

It is easy to over-labour such drawbacks, and one must remember the alternatives: reduced access to images of manuscripts via expensive printed facsimiles or visits. Moreover, there are also examples of paper-copied images that have somehow become detached from any information about their source.[13] However, what we are beginning to witness is a magnification of the problems experienced in the old analogue world, as a result of poor cataloguing, and the ease with which copying and distribution via the web are carried out. In these circumstances, tracing provenance can be a very problematic business.

How, then, have people set about addressing the issue of providing meaningful context, and how might they do so in the future? Considering the main 'medieval' digital imaging projects one can discern three main approaches: the 'catalogue', the 'simulation', and the 'edition'.

---

[13] See for instance Owen-Crocker's anecdote on p. 9.

Cataloguing

The simplest approach is to catalogue or list the image files relating to the folios of the manuscript. Here one might describe each image in turn, with the individual catalogue entry mapping to the individual image (in this case its folio or page). Catalogues and finding aids can be searched and once the appropriate entry has been found there is a direct link to the image. A catalogue could be a simple browsable web page as in the example taken from the Bodleian Library's digitization project (Fig. 8.4).

Usually, however, catalogues provide more sophisticated functionality and take the form of files marked up using agreed standards, which are searched using text analysis software. Database systems can also be used, or, in the case of the *Electronic Beowulf* CD-ROM, folders and sub-folders. For example, if one chooses to take the direct route to the images in the *Beowulf* CD, browsing via the folder structure is meaningful, affording codex-centred navigation (Fig. 8.5).

8.4
A browsable image catalogue from the Bodleian Library's digitization project (http://image.ox.ac.uk/)

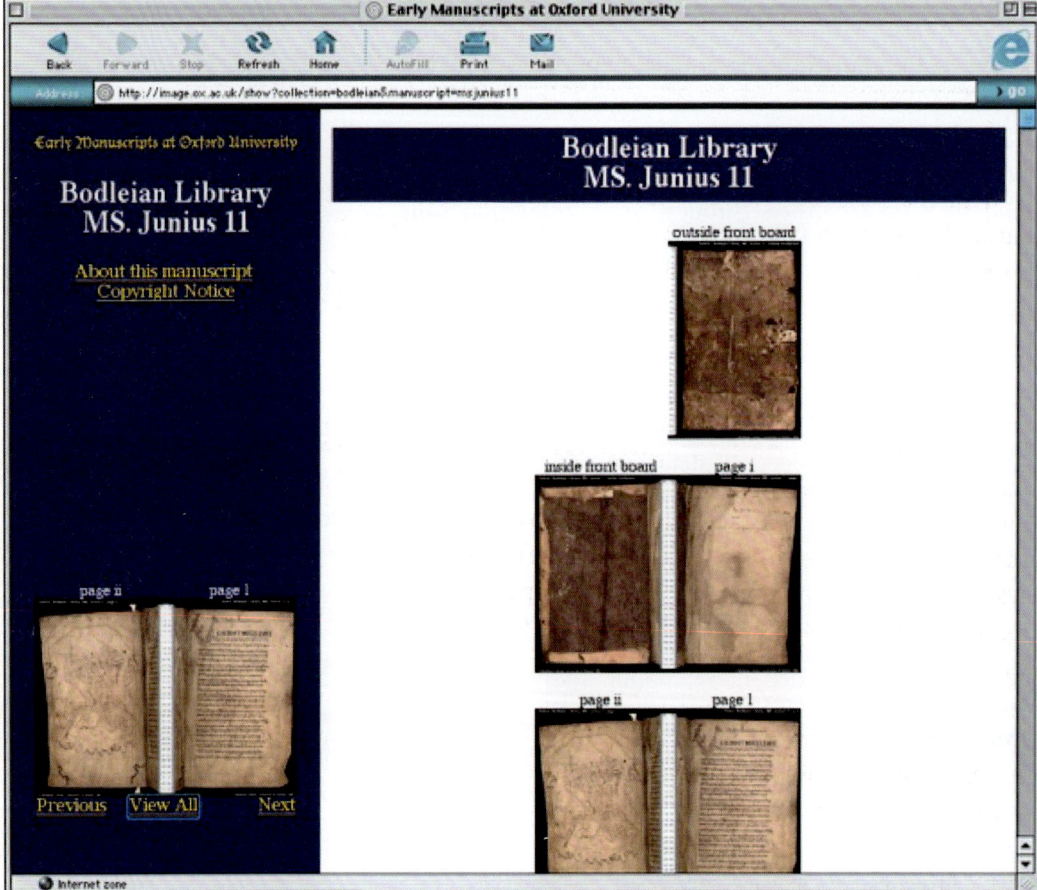

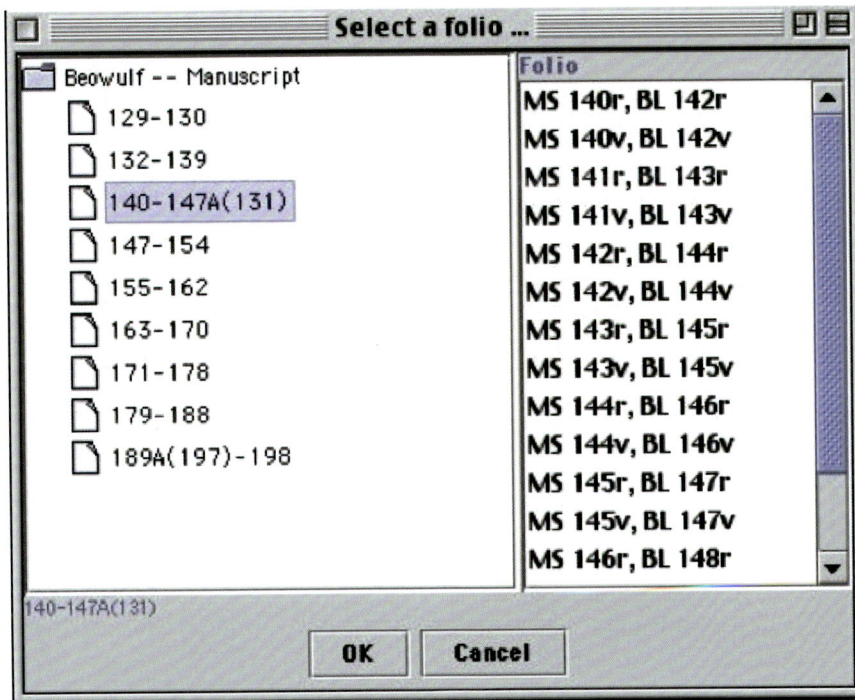

8.5 File names and folders in the *Electronic Beowulf* CD-ROM.

With the Bodleian project one is also presented with a further minor but useful function (Fig. 8.6). Here one can see a 'thumbnail' image of the opening, and move from one folio to another in order by clicking on the 'previous' and 'next' links. This leads us neatly to the second approach for presenting manuscript images, the 'simulation' model.

The simulation model

Projects that fit this model involve some form of interactive experience that simulates the idea of reading the original manuscript. Commonly the individual image files are bound together into a single package using tools like Macromedia Flash or similar. A good example of this is the 'Turning the Pages' system developed by the British Library (http://www.bl.uk/onlinegallery/ttp/ttpbooks.html). In Fig. 8.7 we can see the presentation of the *Lindisfarne Gospels* (British Library, Cotton Nero D. iv). The user is presented with an opening of the manuscript and can 'turn the page' by dragging the mouse from right to left (and *vice versa*), and then zoom in on particular aspects. A similar model is used by the electronic publication (on DVD) of the *Book of Kells* (Dublin, Trinity College MS 58; formerly A I 16).[14]

---

[14] http://www.bookofkells.com

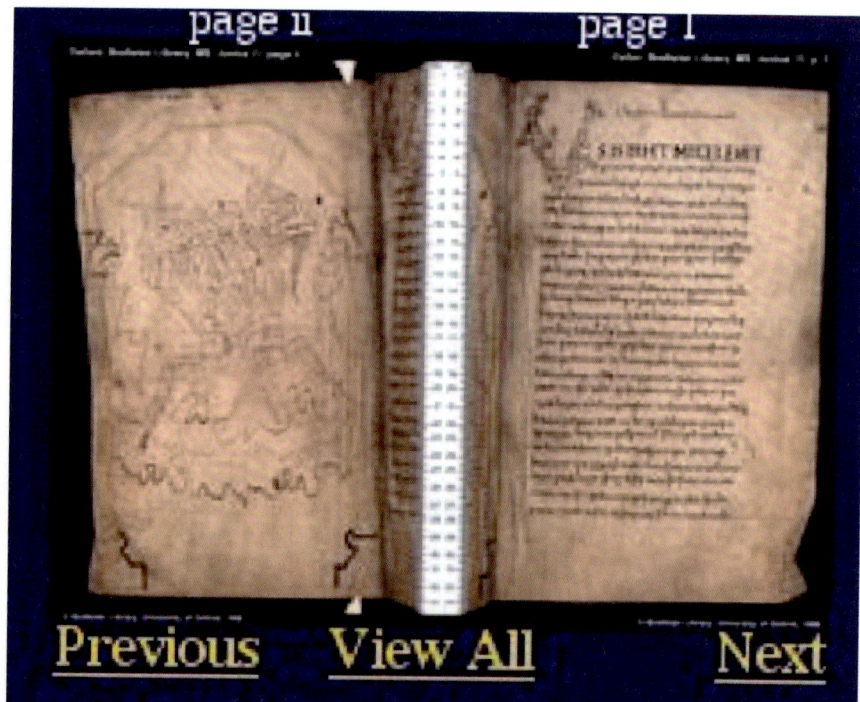

RIGHT

8.6 'Page-turning' in the Bodleian's digital images website.

BELOW

8.7 The *Lindisfarne Gospels* presented in the British Library's 'Turning the Pages' website.

There are clear advantages to this approach. From the users' perspective it simulates the act of engaging with the manuscript (to a degree) and presents a clear sense of a unified codex, with the pages in their correct order. From the perspective of overcoming the issues discussed above it retains the sense of a 'whole', and it is difficult to take a single image from the product and use it elsewhere. Yet there are also notable disadvantages. The fact that it is difficult to remove a single image (except through screen shots) may deter some people from using it: those, for example, who just wish to refer to a specific carpet page or to run a single image through other software packages. Moreover, unless the package is designed well it may not be easy to go directly to a particular folio.[15]

Currently, moreover, most projects of this nature rely on proprietary formats, such as Flash or Shockwave, rather than agreed international archival standards. The reliance on such formats has caused archival problems in the past and current opinion on the long term suitability of such proprietary formats is mixed.[16]

The edition model

The final approach is what may be termed the 'edition' model. Here the images are presented as individual files linked to an edition of the text in question. This promotes the centrality of the piece of literature, presenting the images as important, but in the context of the text itself. O'Donnell's edition of *Cædmon's Hymn*, for example, is a critical edition and archive based on a collection of transcriptions and digital facsimiles of all known manuscript copies of the poem. In this edition, images of individual pages from manuscripts are presented to readers in a textual and bibliographic context: users access images from a page containing diplomatic and semi-normalised texts of the individual witnesses (Fig. 8.8). This page is accessed either directly from the table of contents or by following links that appear every time a manuscript reading is cited in an introductory chapter, collation, or critical apparatus (Fig. 8.9).

Thus the core focus with most 'editions' is the text itself, with links directly to the images. Yet the nuances and idiosyncrasies of medieval texts require special handling, especially when attempting to describe palaeographical, codicological, or linguistic information and embed it within the text itself.

---

[15] For a review of several simulation projects see Daniel Paul O'Donnell, 'O Captain! My Captain! Using technology to guide readers through an electronic edition', *The Heroic Age*, 8 (http://www.heroicage.org/issues/8/em.html), 2005.

[16] See Richard Entlich, 'Flash in the pan or around for the long haul? Assessing Macromedia's Flash technology', *RLG DigiNews* 8.3. June 15, 2004 (http://www.rlg.org/en/page.php?Page_ID=17661#article3).

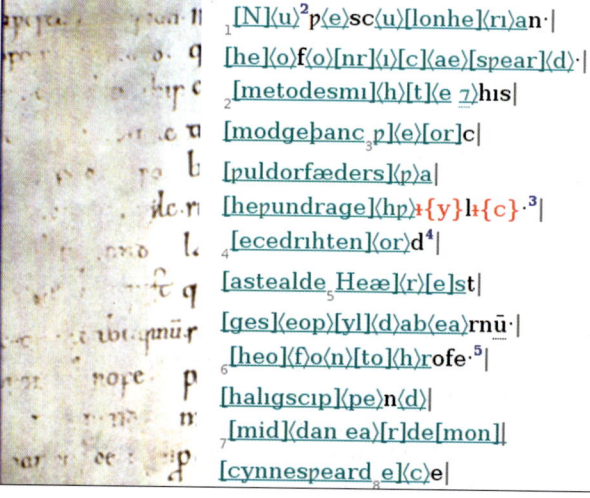

8.8 Parallel image-and-diplomatic transcription of Oxford, Bodleian Library, MS Bodley 163 from O'Donnell, *Cædmon's Hymn*.

Complicated 'mark-up'[17] systems have been developed over the years, most notably by the Text Encoding Initiative (TEI; discussed at greater length below).[18] This allows scholars to create highly complex editions that can be handled by advanced text analysis software.

The most recent example of this is the *Exeter Book* DVD.[19] This, though not as detailed as O'Donnell's edition of *Cædmon's Hymn* in terms of textual mark-up, links transcriptions and critical apparatus to facsimiles of the pages. It also retains some of the simulation method in terms of a 'page-turning' animation, and animated video files accompanied by audio of texts and translations. The folder structure on the DVD allows one to access directly individual image files (for example '/damaged3500/119r.jpg')

---

[17] So called because you mark up or encode certain sections to contain extra information such as parts of speech.

[18] http://www.tei-c.org/

[19] B. Muir, *The Exeter DVD: The Exeter Anthology of Old English Poetry*, Exeter, University of Exeter Press, 2006.

From manuscript to computer   269

1a **pe]** *pe* H *pe* W *p⟨e⟩* Bd *pe* Mg *pe* Ln *pe* Tr1 *pe* SanM.
1a **sculon]** *sculon* H *sculon* W *sc⟨u⟩[lon]* Bd *sculon* Mg *sculun* Ln *sceolon* Tr1 *sculon* SanM.
1a **herian]** *herian* H *heria⟨n⟩|~~heri~~* W *[hel⟨ri⟩an·|* Bd *herian* Mg *herian* Ln *herion* Tr1 *herian* SanM.   [Link to original reading in diplomatic transcription of this witness]
1b **heofonrices]** *heofon rices* H *heofon rices* W *[hel⟨o⟩f⟨o⟩[nr]⟨i⟩[c]⟨ae⟩[s]* Bd *heofon|rices* Mg *heofon rices* Ln *heofenrices·* Tr1 *heofo⟨n⟩|rices* SanM.
1b **peard]** *peard·* H *p⟨e⟩[ard]|* W *[pearl⟨d⟩·|* Bd *peard·* Mg *peard·* Ln *peard·* Tr1 *peard·* SanM.
2a **metudes]** *metudes* H *meto*d*des* W *[metodes]* Bd *metudes* Mg *metudes* Ln *metudes* Tr1 *mecudes* SanM.
2a **myhte]** *myhte·* H *mihte* W *[mi]⟨h⟩[t]⟨e⟩* Bd *mihte·|* Mg *michte·* Ln *mihte|* Tr1 *míhte|* SanM.
2b **ond]** 7 H 7 W ⟨7⟩ Bd 7 Mg 7 Ln 7 Tr1 æ SanM.
2b **his]** *his* H *h[is]|* W *his|* Bd *his* Mg *his* Ln *his* Tr1 *his* SanM.
2b **modgeþanc]** *mod ge þanc-|* H *mod ge þanc* W *[modgeþanc]* Bd *mod ge þanc·* Mg *mod⟨t{g}⟩e þanc·* Ln *modgeþanc·* Tr1 *mod ge þanc* SanM.
3a **purc]** *purc* H *peorc* W *[pl⟨e⟩[or]c|* Bd *purc|* Mg *peorc|* Ln *peorc* Tr1 *pure|* SanM.
3a **puldorfæder]** *puldu{a}r fæder·* H *p⟨u⟩[ll|dor fæder* W *[puldorfæder]* Bd *puldor fæder·* Mg *puldor fæder·* Ln *puldor feder·* Tr1 *puldor· fæder* SanM.
3b **spa]** *spa* H *spa* W *[s]⟨p⟩a|* Bd *spa* Mg *spa* Ln *spa* Tr1 *spa* SanM.
3b **he]** *he* H *he* W *[he]* Bd *he* Mg *he* Ln *he* Tr1 *he* SanM.
3b **nundra]** *nundra* H *nu[n]dra* W *[nundra]* Bd *nun-|dra* Mg *nundra* Ln

8.9 Link to a manuscript reading in Bodley 163 from the collation in the previous figure.

although no metadata or watermarks are contained within the image files themselves (see below). The next step may be a combination of all three models but expanded to include multimedia elements aimed at assisting in teaching (an approach also evident in the previously mentioned *Book of Kells* DVD).

Ongoing problems

How far do any of these models assist us in overcoming the issue noted earlier whereby a scholar located a free-floating image on the internet and could not identify it? The simulation model safeguards best against this happening, since images are usually packaged up into a single application, and it is very difficult to extract them beyond screen grabbing software.

Yet against this we must balance the issues of usability noted above. The edition model and the catalogue provide more flexible systems, and offer possibilities for more sophisticated scholarship (the mark-up can allow for far more information to be included, and for more advanced analyses to be undertaken than simply 'turning pages') but fundamentally these systems do not solve the problem of image and context disassociation. The metadata (the information about the digital object: in this case the image of the folio) is in one file and the images are separate. Therefore, *ab initio*, there is a gap between the image and the information about the image and as the digital facsimiles are free-standing it is very easy to copy them, move them, disseminate them, and in so doing widen this gap.

This problem can be exacerbated by the proliferation of image processing tools. Not only can the complete image become detached from its metadata and thus untraceable, but parts of it may be disseminated, or even worse distorted, cropped, rotated or collated with other images, creating further problems for people attempting to locate its original source. For example, below (Fig. 8.10) we can see four entirely 'valid' images all derived from a single source; but it is only with the last one that we can see the familiar 'h' of the opening *hwæt* of *Beowulf* (cf. Fig. 4.4). Using the naked eye it would be nigh on impossible to identify the other three with any certainty.

Solutions

Two solutions to this problem are emerging. The first is to include visible information in the image itself. The second is to include 'hidden' data in the information about the file.

The first is the easier to explain. Here, when taking the digital photograph, one also includes information about the image, such as its provenance, measurements and colour matching. This information cannot become disassociated from the image because it is part of the image to begin with unless deliberately 'cut' by a user. In Fig. 8.11, taken from p. 1 of Oxford,

8.10 Opening initial of *Beowulf* in various cropped forms.

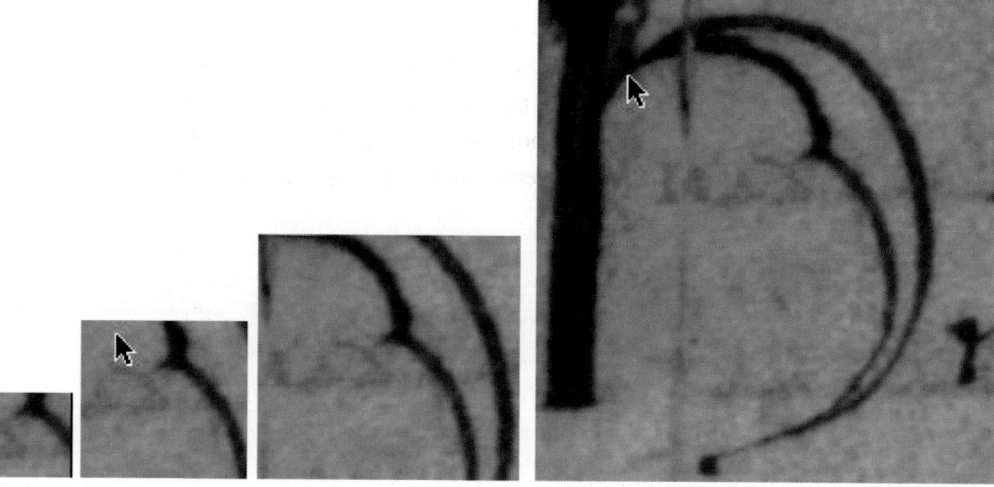

8.11 Top and bottom of one of Bodley's Junius 11 images, illustrating the inclusion of information within the image.

Bodleian Library, MS Junius 11, we have the 'header' and 'footer' of the image which give us its shelfmark, some indication of measurement (in cm), the date of the image creation, and copyright information.

The method of including 'hidden' information in the file involves using information not immediately obvious to the naked eye which can nevertheless be extracted by simple image analysis software. This is metadata concerning the image (cataloguing information, in other words) that is part of the image file, which means that when the image is opened in an appropriate piece of software, the information about the file can be retrieved. This is termed 'tagged image metadata'. Two common standards are in use for this. One is based on the long-standing International Press Telecommunications Council (IPTC) and is available for embedding in most image file formats. It generally contains information about the provenance of the image, as it has emerged from the interests of world press agencies. The second is Exif (Exchangeable image file format) which covers such things as date and time information, camera settings, locations (possibly derived from GPS), and a space for description and copyright information. Most of these (with the exception of description and copyright) can be automatically created by digital cameras nowadays and embedded in the file at the point of capture. The non-technical data, however, still requires manual intervention (cataloguing) after the image has been created.

It is true that this information could be removed by an individual, or that less sophisticated image processing packages (that are 'tag-unaware') may just strip out this data, but leaving those drawbacks aside, the potential benefit is immediately clear. Suddenly the divide between the metadata and the image file is non-existent; they are bundled into the same code. If the image file in our earlier anecdote was of this type, then the scholar's question could have been answered using the IPTC or Exif metadata.

Hidden information, especially that hidden through digital watermarking, also answers the age-old concern of the holders of manuscripts: 'how can I track its use?' (and, more importantly, its misuse). Digital watermarking allows the digitizer to embed data into an image relating to IPR (for example). Watermarks are not usually visible to the naked eye, but more importantly, they are indestructible; that is, even if the image is cropped or copied, the watermark will remain and can be read by standard image analysis packages. Watermarks can also be tracked across the web automatically to find out where the images are being used.[20] As a side-effect the watermark can be used to locate the image's original provenance in terms of the IPR statement, which will lead back to its shelfmark.

Capturing the text

Digitization produces a facsimile of the manuscript page with, hopefully, some information about provenance, ownership, and techniques used. As scholars, however, we usually want to do more than see the manuscript page: we are also, commonly, interested in its content. We may want to quote from the text, compare it to other texts, analyse its language or literary qualities, study the mistakes or changes made by its scribes. All of these require access to the words on the manuscript page.

As with digital photography, the basic processes involved in capturing a text for use with a computer are relatively straightforward. First the linguistic contents of the primary source are recorded, either by hand-keying (the usual solution for manuscripts, whether medieval or modern) or using Optical Character Recognition (OCR) software (more common with print sources). This basic content is then 'marked up' to include information about the text not immediately obvious from the bare transcription. In a print text this might involve elements of typography (such as use of italics, bold-face, or underlining) as well as layout and *mise-en-page* (paragraph division, textual alignment, indentations, or bulleted lists); in a manuscript, this might include similar details of presentation and script as well as other information about the manuscript's codicology or scribal history such as the contributions of individual scribes, recordings of corrections, additions, marginalia, or losses due to damage by fire or other causes. Finally, if this mark-up has been achieved using a recognised standard language such as the HyperText Mark-up Language (HTML) or its more flexible parent, the eXtensible Mark-up Language (XML), the captured text is ready for immediate publication or further processing, searching, or collection.

---

[20] For example, see MyPictureMarc by Digimarc (http://www.digimarc.com/watermark/mypicturemarc/).

As with our discussion of digital facsimiles above, however, this basic outline glosses over what can rapidly become a far more intellectually challenging process. This is particularly true in the case of manuscripts and other documents of historical or scholarly significance, where decisions made during the mark-up stage can have important theoretical, scholarly, or archival consequences. In such cases, deciding what features are going to be marked up and how they are to be captured can be among the most crucial early decisions those involved in a digitization project must make.

Mark-up languages

After the initial data capture, the next step in a digital text project involves the choice of mark-up language. This might seem to be relatively straightforward. All of us have written documents using WYSIWYG (What-You-See-Is-What-You-Get) word processors such as Microsoft Word or Open Office and all of us have viewed texts on the web that reproduce common typographical conventions. Those of us who have designed our own web pages know that such word processors can save documents in HTML for internet publication. We may already be familiar with the basic elements of HTML these word processors use to indicate the most common elements of typographical layout: <b> for bold faced text, <i> for italics, <u> for underline, <p> for paragraphs, and perhaps more specialised or unusual codes for features such as block quotations (<blockquote>) and bulleted lists (<ul>).

From the earliest days of the internet, web page designers have been faced with the problem of representing common features of layout on the screen or printer – multi-column texts, marginal annotations, changes in font or script. While not all these conventions are suitable for the transcription of manuscripts, and while not all aspects of manuscript transcription have directly corresponding HTML codes, it is certainly possible using the powerful formatting features available in most word processors to combine such elements in ways that allow us to produce quite reasonable on-screen type-facsimiles of most manuscript pages. Marginal annotation and multi-column layouts can be positioned using tables. Abbreviations, deletions, and corrections can often be mimicked using combinations of font effects such as strike-through, underlining, and super- and sub-script. Coloured fonts can be used to replicate rubrication and other forms of highlighting. Individual scripts can often be replicated using specially designed fonts. By typing out a manuscript text in a standard WYSIWYG word processor, taking advantage of the word processor's layout engine to ensure that the display on the screen matches the appearance of our manuscript as closely as possible, and saving the result as an HTML document, scholars with even quite a limited knowledge of modern technology can produce digital type facsimiles that reflect the general appearance of their source documents relatively quickly.

The case against WYSIWYG

In fact, and despite its familiarity and ease of implementation, this approach to textual encoding represents relatively poor digital practice. This is because it focuses on capturing the simple appearance of the text on the manuscript page – a task for which, as we have seen above, better technology already exists through digital photography – rather than the intellectual and rhetorical significance of this appearance to the human reader – features no computer can capture without explicit human assistance.

The nature of this problem can best be illustrated by an example. A serious problem in the early days of the world wide web involved replicating print layouts that contained relatively positioned elements such as columns and insets (places where the main text wraps around an illustration, photograph, or advertisement). The most common solution was to format these as HTML tables. Individual columns of text or inset photographs and advertisements could be placed in their own table cells and positioned absolutely on the screen. When the table borders were suppressed, the text would closely mimic the appearance of a print page (Fig. 8.12)

To a human reader who understands the conventions involved in ordering this text and who views the text in a graphical browser that reproduces the table correctly, the rhetorical organisation of this text is easy to understand: the headline (A) spans the two main columns of text and is found in the first row of the table; the main text (B) begins in the first cell of the table's second

8.12 Table-based web page layout (deprecated). In this design, table cells are used to position text absolutely on the screen. Intended reading order is indicated by capital letters A through F.

(A) Two Column Story		
(B) This is the first paragraph. It is in the first cell of the second table row. Rhetorically it follows the headline in row one and is followed by the first cell of the third row.	(C)  IMAGE	(E) This is the third paragraph. It appears in the third cell of the second row of this table, where it is preceded by a cell containing a paragraph of text and an image. The row above contains the headline for the story. Rhetorically, the contents of this cell follow the first cell in the third row of this table.
(D) This is the second paragraph. It is in the first cell of the third row in the table. It is preceded rhetorically by the text in the first cell of the second row in this table, and followed by the text in the third cell of the second row.		(F) This is the fourth paragraph. It appears in the second cell of the third row. Rhetorically, however, it follows on the content of the cell above it in the table, the third cell of the second row.

row and runs down the side of the image (C) contained in the second cell; the text continues in the first cell of the third row (D); the second column begins with the third cell of the second row (E) and concludes with the second cell of the third row (F).

Unfortunately, this rhetorical structure is only comprehensible to a human reader who is reading the text in a graphical environment. To a blind person reading this text in an aural browser or to a search engine attempting to index it automatically, the text will appeared to be ordered very differently. Because the HTML table model encodes text on a row-by-row basis, a computer in these cases will misunderstand the relationship among the various textual components: it will begin by reading the single cell of the first row (A); it will then go on to read the three cells in the second row, beginning with the first paragraph (B), moving on to the image (C), and then reading what rhetorically speaking should be the third paragraph (E); finally, it will move on to the third row, reading the second (D) and fourth (F) paragraphs in sequence (see Fig. 8.13).

Similar problems can arise with transcriptions of medieval manuscripts that concentrate on replicating appearance rather than rhetorical structure. Visual cues that make perfect sense on the computer screen to a trained human reader can easily become nonsensical when collected in a corpus, printed to a black and white printer, searched by scholars looking to collect

8.13 Order in which the text of the previous figure would read by an automatic indexer or aural screen browser.

(A) Two Column Story
(B) This is the first paragraph. It is in the first cell of the second table row. Rhetorically it follows the headline in row one and is followed by the first cell of the third row.

(E) This is the third paragraph. It appears in the third cell of the second row of this table, where it is preceded by a cell containing a paragraph of text and an image. The row above contains the headline for the story. Rhetorically, the contents of this cell follow the first cell in the third row of this table.
(D) This is the second paragraph. It is in the first cell of the third row in the table. It is preceded rhetorically by the text in the first cell of the second row in this table, and followed by the text in the third cell of the second row.
(F) This is the fourth paragraph. It appears in the second cell of the third row. Rhetorically, however, it follows on the content of the cell above it in the table, the third cell of the second row.

examples of specific features from multiple manuscripts, or read by students who do not understand the specific conventions involved. Thus, while it is a relatively easy matter to position marginal corrections or interlinear text (using an approach similar to that adopted by the early web designers in their attempts to produce multiple-column layouts) the significance of this layout may be lost on the non-specialist reader and give rise to more questions than it answers. These questions might include: Why does text appear in the margins of the manuscript? What is the significance of the alternating lines of Latin and the vernacular? Why are certain words reproduced in red or blue type, or surrounded by boxes? What does an Old English letter thorn with a bar through it mean? By concentrating on an imperfect representation of the physical appearance of a manuscript text, encoders can easily fail to take account of the considerable knowledge they bring to understanding the significance of the original's appearance.

Structural mark-up languages

The solution to these problems, both on the web and in the Digital Humanities, has been to separate the encoding of structure and form from the description of physical appearance.[21] While it is still possible to find web pages that use tables and other similar tricks to replicate print layout on the screen, developments in browser technology and the languages used by web designers over the last half-decade or so have rendered this approach largely obsolete. In contemporary web design, encoders first mark text up according to its intrinsic structural properties and function rather than its appearance: a given section of text is described as a textual division, a floating image, a paragraph, or a block quotation. They then describe how this content is to appear using a separate language to format the text for display, indicating, for example, that a floating image is supposed to appear inset within the paragraph to which it belongs, or that textual divisions such as columns are to be arranged side-by-side on the screen. This allows the text to be displayed for human users in much the same way as in Fig. 8.12 without misrepresenting the structure of the text to programmes that do not rely on human understanding of the graphical conventions involved in its layout. Moreover, because the physical appearance of the text

---

[21] This is not the place for a history of mark-up languages. It should be noted, however, that the use of tables for positioning and other layout-oriented techniques in early web-page design represented something of an aberration in their development. The mark-up language from which HTML is descended (Standard General Mark-up Language) was itself oriented towards representing structure rather than appearance.

is controlled by external codes, it is possible to reformat this same text for use in several different contexts: for use on a standard computer monitor; in less elaborate form for use on a cellphone or digital assistant; or, with the removal of interactive features such as hyperlinks, converted to PDF format for publication as a conventional book.[22]

HTML and XML as structural languages

Because it was designed primarily for the encoding and distribution of contemporary information, HTML employs a relatively limited set of structural elements. A website promoting a political party or explaining course requirements to incoming students makes relatively few structural distinctions: it will have some headers, some paragraphs, perhaps a list or a quotation or two, some hyperlinks, and, for emphasis, bold, italic, or underlined fonts.

However, encoders of historical documents and documents intended for use by professional researchers need access to a far broader set of structural distinctions. In HTML, for example, italic text is commonly represented using one of two elements: <i> (italics) or <emph> (emphasis). But italic type is used for a far wider range of purposes than simple rhetorical emphasis, including the titles of books, indicating examples of meta-linguistic usage, distinguishing passages in a foreign language from the main text, and to introduce technical terms or their definitions. In the course of their work, scholars might need to distinguish between these many uses: a librarian conducting a bibliometric survey might want to extract all monographic titles from a text; a linguist might be interested in identifying examples of quotations from foreign languages; an indexer might wish to identify all the examples of meta-linguistic discussion for an *index verborum*; a rhetorician or literary scholar might be interested in extracting all examples of rhetorical emphasis for a stylistic study.

The study of manuscripts in particular commonly involves drawing structural distinctions that have no equivalent in print or on the web. Changes in hand or ink, the representation of different types of correction or physical damage to the manuscript, gaps left for (never finished) rubrication or illumination all represent structural features found in manuscripts that are rarely if ever found in post-incunabula print sources. In a critical edition, further structural distinctions, unanticipated by the designers of HTML, rapidly appear: there can be distinctions between emended or normalised

---

[22] The website CSSZenGarden (http://www.csszengarden.com/) is a showcase for such design: all its pages are different layouts of the same sample HTML page. In O'Donnell's edition of *Cædmon's Hymn*, this approach was used to produce different versions of the text in print and on CD-ROM.

text and the original readings; there may be abbreviations to expand; line breaks (metrical or physical) may be of interest to the encoder; and there may be a textual apparatus with readings from other editions or witnesses. In an anthology of texts, encoders might want to include some kind of ontological information: means of recognising individuals, places, or dates despite differences in form, or methods for identifying occurrences of different metrical patterns or rhetorical figures, or for marking the recurrence of specific literary themes or tropes.

It is possible to create elements to make these distinctions. HTML contains a number of generic elements, including <span> (an arbitrary segment of text) and <div> (an arbitrary division), for such purposes; and these and all other elements in the language can also be qualified in order to express finer distinctions that are not explicitly delimited in the standard language. Thus the distinction between italics used to indicate the title of a monograph and italics used to indicate meta-linguistic usage might be distinguished by the use of <i> with attribute values such as 'monographic_title' and 'meta-linguistic_usage'. Different scribal contributions might similarly be enclosed by generic <span> tags with the class attribute used to identify individual scribes: <span class="Scribe_A"> vs. <span class="Scribe_B">.

The eXtensible Mark-up Language (XML), the language on which modern versions of HTML are built, provides a set of rules within which designers can build their own mark-up languages. An encoder who is not happy with customising HTML might decide to create a set of custom elements that more accurately describe the type of features he or she is trying to capture. In this language, one might begin with a <manuscript> tag, identify the main body using a <main_body> tag, and create different elements for things like <marginalia>, <illumination>, or, of course, <scribe>.

Neither of these solutions is entirely satisfactory. Customising HTML involves creating a number of essentially *ad hoc* distinctions that are open to misunderstanding by outsiders. In the absence of any agreed-upon standard, different projects might develop different customisations to describe identical phenomena: an erasure might be described as <span class="deletion"> by one project and <span class="erasure"> by another; scribes might be identified as 'scribe' in one text, and 'hand' in a second. Thus, the lack of standardisation involves extra work and, at the same time, may give rise to confusion.

Creating one's own mark-up language addresses some of these issues, since XML has mechanisms by which elements can be described in ways that allow others to understand their significance more easily. Creating such a language, however, is itself quite a demanding intellectual and technical task. Mark-up languages are, in a sense, grammars of text. Building them requires both a knowledge of the relevant computer syntaxes and an understanding of how the various parts of the intended document fit together. These are themselves research skills that take time and a knowledge of many different real-life examples to acquire. They are unlikely to be part of the skill-set of academics setting out on their first scholarly encoding project.

The Text Encoding Initiative (TEI)

Fortunately, a third option exists. For the last twenty years, the Text Encoding Initiative has published guidelines containing a standard mark-up language for use by encoders of documents of historical or scholarly interest. These guidelines – the fourth edition of which ran to over a thousand pages in print form – are intended to cover 'texts in any natural language, of any date, in any literary genre or text type, without restriction on form or content' and contain an 'inventory of features most often found useful for text processing'.[23] They identify and provide methods for encoding most of the distinctions required by researchers working with manuscripts and other types of scholarly or historical documents, and provide copious documentation and examples of usage, many of which are drawn from real research projects.[24]

This standard has two main advantages over other approaches to the digitization of manuscripts and similar texts. The first is that the guidelines have been written and reviewed by teams of scholars active in the field over a considerable period of time. This means that the system has been tested by encoders in a variety of different contexts at different stages of a project's life. Scholars can therefore benefit from this collective experience by avoiding the potential pitfalls of designing their own languages from scratch and consulting with the larger community of TEI users for advice in dealing with difficult encoding problems.

The second advantage of the TEI Guidelines over other approaches to scholarly textual encoding lies in the possibilities for interchange and aggregation. A custom-designed language, by definition, runs the risk of

---

[23] TEI Consortium, ed., *TEI P5: Guidelines for Electronic Text Encoding and Interchange*, Oxford, Providence, Charlottesville, Nancy, TEI Consortium, 2007. http://www.tei-c.org/Guidelines/P5/.

[24] The TEI guidelines are too complex and involve distinctions that are too refined to allow for the detailed discussion of the encoding of Anglo-Saxon manuscripts in this chapter. Many resources exist to help scholars as they begin their first projects. In addition to the guidelines themselves, workshops are offered annually at major medieval and digital humanities conferences, in summer schools, and online. There are also several communities upon which scholars can draw for help and advice, the most prominent of which include the Text Encoding Initiative's own mailing list (tei-l@tei-c.org) and the Digital Medievalist Community of Practice (http://www.digitalmedievalist.org/).

being more or less *sui generis*. The designer may introduce distinctions that are not observed by others in the field, occlude distinctions more commonly recognised as significant, or duplicate distinctions found in standard languages in ways that are not immediately recognisable to automatic indexers or other types of processors. By complying with standard guidelines such as the TEI, designers can ensure with relatively little effort that others will be able to use their work in subsequent research projects. While the TEI is too complex and open to different scholarly emphases to allow for unnegotiated exchange in all but the most simple cases – scholars with different interests might easily encode a common stretch of text using completely different TEI elements, for example, precluding the use of common stylesheets or other tools – the careful and detailed documentation the TEI provides ensures that users will always be able to understand TEI-compliant encoding. For this reason, the TEI standard is commonly recommended or required for archival purposes by scholarly projects funded by major national granting agencies including the National Endowment for the Humanities (NEH) in the United States, the Arts and Humanities Research Council (AHRC) in the United Kingdom, and the Deutsche Forschungsgemeinschaft (DFG) in Germany.

Capturing details of the text

Choosing a mark-up language is the first step in creating a digital text of a medieval manuscript. The second is setting about capturing the textual information this manuscript contains.

The process may look more difficult than it actually is. Digital texts may contain an immense amount of information: diplomatic transcriptions, normalised readings, lexical and grammatical information, links to facsimiles or other manuscripts, perhaps also collation information. Digital editions are commonly expected to provide far more information about witnesses and texts than was previously common in print editions. Print editors, traditionally, tend to stress selectivity: providing a single critical text (or single set of parallel texts) with a selective critical apparatus. They seldom reproduced diplomatic transcriptions of individual witnesses. Digital editors, on the other hand, work in a medium that stresses comprehensiveness: digital projects commonly include facsimiles and transcriptions of all available witnesses; critical texts (if they are included) tend to present the underlying evidence in a variety of different ways (see, for example, O'Donnell, *Cædmon's Hymn*, or, for Middle English, Peter Robinson's edition of the *Wife of Bath's Prologue*);[25] and their collations and critical

---

[25] Peter Robinson, ed., *The Wife of Bath's Prologue on CD-ROM*, Cambridge, Cambridge University Press, 1996.

apparatuses often allow the user to oversee all readings from all relevant witnesses.

In practice, the process by which this information is acquired is quite similar to that used in the pre-digital age for transcriptions and collation (cf., for example, the processes as discussed by Boyle and Haugen).[26] Information about the witnesses is collected in several passes: first codicological and historical information, then diplomatic information, and finally collations and other editorial analysis. The main difference between digital and print practice is the fate of the preliminary work of transcription and collation. In print, this work was seen almost invariably as a private prelude to preparing the print edition. Even when it was intended for publication, it often appeared as a separate volume distinct from the critical text (compare the texts of Elliott Van Kirk Dobbie's *The Manuscripts of Cædmon's Hymn* and his edition of the poem in the Anglo-Saxon Poetic Records)[27]. In digital practice, however, transcriptions and collations are almost always intended for publication and may replace the critical text altogether (see, for example, Robinson's edition of the *Wife of Bath's Prologue* and Kiernan's edition of *Beowulf*).[28]

The TEI provides specific elements for the transcription of primary texts. These include elements for indicating changes in scribe, for describing damaged or missing sections of text, for recording abbreviations, marking line breaks in the text, and describing unusual characters, among many other things. While the precise semantics of these elements are occasionally open to interpretation (there are, for example, a number of different ways of understanding an abbreviation or contraction), their general sense should pose no difficulty to anybody used to recording diplomatic features in type using a symbolic diplomatic transcription system.

The TEI transcription module also has some advantages over previous symbolic systems. For one thing its mark-up is explicit: abbreviations are

---

[26] Leonard E. Boyle, 'Optimist and recensionist: "common errors" or "common variations"?' in John J. O'Meara and Bernd Naumann, *Latin Script and Letters, A.D. 400–900: Festschrift presented to Ludwig Bieler on the occasion of his 70th birthday*, Leiden, E.J. Brill, 1976, pp. 264–73; Odd Einar Haugen, 'Parallel views: multi-level encoding of medieval Nordic primary sources', *Literary and Linguistic Computing*, 19.1, 2004, pp. 73–91.

[27] Elliott Van Kirk Dobbie, *The Manuscripts of Cædmon's Hymn and Bede's Death Song with a Critical Text of the Epistola Cuthberti de obitu Bedæ*, Columbia University Studies in English and Comparative Literature, 128, New York, Columbia University Press, 1937; Elliott Van Kirk Dobbie, *The Anglo-Saxon Minor Poems*, The Anglo-Saxon Poetic Records 6, New York, Columbia University Press, 1942.

[28] Kevin S. Kiernan, ed., *The Electronic Beowulf* [electronic text], London, British Library, 1999.

described as <abbr>, line breaks are described as <lb/>, and damage is described as <damage> so encoders and users generally do not need to consult a symbolic table in order to understand or remember the appropriate code (while the mark-up is more verbose, this is a minor problem in modern editing environments, most of which feature context sensitive tag-completion utilities). Perhaps more importantly, the TEI module allows encoders to capture information about the text and their knowledge of it in ways rarely, if ever, attempted in print. For example, all transcription elements allow encoders to identify both the person responsible for each encoding decision and the level of certainty with which the decision was made. Multi-person projects, especially those using student assistants, can easily review the work of individual participants for training or proof-reading purposes; and the ability to indicate certainty allows encoders an opportunity to record tentative interpretations of hypotheses about their sources either for publication or subsequent review.

Finally, the TEI transcription module allows encoders to integrate tightly different kinds of knowledge about their sources in recoverable ways. Thus, for example, segments written in a particular hand or script can be linked to biographical or palaeographic information collected elsewhere in the project: a user, searching a collection of texts for a specific scribe, is thus easily directed to the relevant examples; likewise, a scholar starting with a fragment of text in the transcription can instantly call up additional information or examples in the same script or copied by the same hand. Other modules allow encoders to associate more detailed information about place, biography, history, or script with these tags.

Editorial texts and collations

Once the text has been transcribed, it can be published as is or submitted for further processing. The TEI provides special elements for collating witnesses, and indicating normalisation, emendation, and other editorial processes. With the help of these elements, encoders can reuse their diplomatic transcriptions to construct reading texts or critical texts with a textual apparatus.

The TEI apparatus can be used to reproduce the typical format of a print textual apparatus. Each apparatus entry (<app>) can contain a single lemma (<lem>) and one or more witness readings (<rdg>). When several readings share some essential feature, they can be grouped using a reading group element (<rdgGrp>). Using these and other elements and attributes, the TEI also allows encoders to incorporate additional information beyond that usually found in a print textual apparatus. Reading groups, for example, can be characterised according to their significance using a convenient typology (such as orthographic vs. substantive); individual variants can be assigned

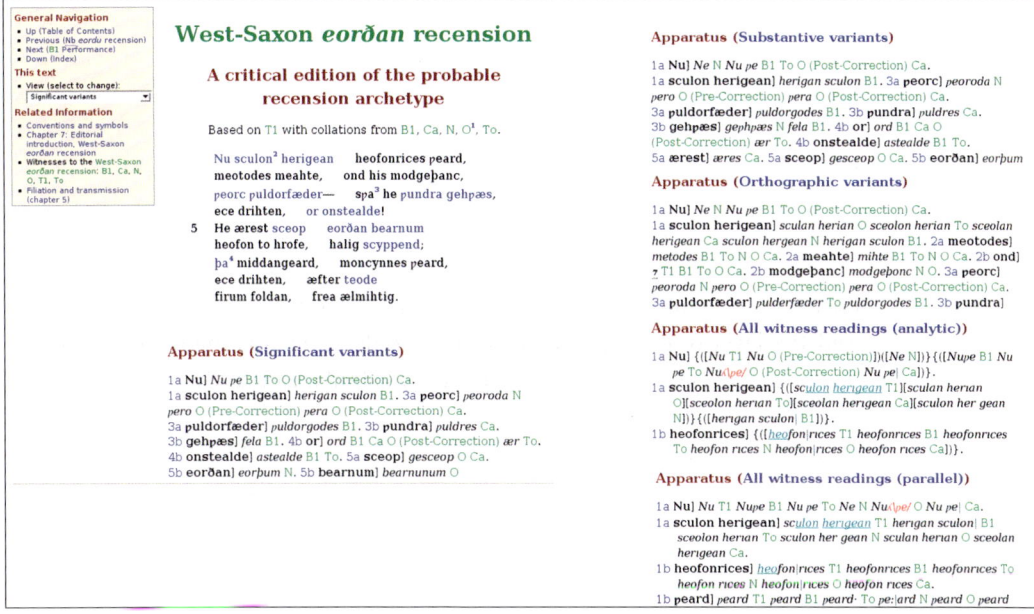

8.14 Screenshots showing different apparatus views from digital edition of *Cædmon's Hymn*. Users change the apparatus using the menu at left.

causes (such as overwriting or deletion), or distinguished by hand. In cases where variants are related to each other – for example a correction written over an earlier form – it is also possible to indicate the sequence in which the readings occurred.

The result of this is that the TEI apparatus model does far more than simply record print-style lists of variants. In O'Donnell's *Cædmon's Hymn*, the model is used to organise variants so that users can choose dynamically the level of detail they wish to see in the textual collations. Users can choose to see a diplomatic transcription of every reading in the poem, an ordered list of spelling variants, a list of variants that impact sense, syntax, or metre, or variants that have a potentially significant effect on the poem as a whole. In each case, the apparatus is produced from the same hierarchically organised file; differences between the various views are produced by applying different stylesheets to the same underlying data.[29]

It is even possible to dispense with the base text altogether. A 'Parallel Segmentation Method' allows the entire text to be encoded as a series of witness readings: instead of a single, critical text, the encoder produces a collation which can be manipulated in a variety of different ways: with appropriate stylesheets and information about individual manuscripts and groups of witnesses, readers using a text coded in this way are able to

---

[29] See O'Donnell, *Cædmon's Hymn*, paragraphs 7.2–7.9 for a discussion of these terms.

customise the text to match their research interests, producing a parallel text edition of the entire tradition, viewing different groups of manuscripts for comparison, creating diplomatic transcriptions of one or more individual manuscripts, or building editions based on any of a variety of different search criteria.[30]

Of course, depending on how well the initial capture has been done, this extremely flexible approach to the presentation of the text can be either extremely illuminating or terribly banal. Although the processes involved are relatively straightforward, successful implementation can require considerable disciplinary knowledge. Encoders who have devoted attention to the digitization of the text of their manuscripts can use this ability to attach rich information about scribal performance, manuscript provenance and dating, and linguistic information to guide their readers' interaction with the digital edition. Encoders who have devoted less attention to providing this type of information will provide their readers with plenty of choice but little advice on how to make the best of the options with which they are being presented: in such cases, the result will be little more effective than some of the efforts of scholars and librarians in the immediate aftermath of the Ashburnham House fire. Performed successfully, however, digitization can easily transcend the sources it mediates – providing users with experiences and research opportunities not even available to those within easy commuting distance of the great manuscript collections.

---

[30] There are as yet no editions that use this method with an Anglo-Saxon text. A method similar to this is used for Chaucer in Robinson's edition of the *Wife of Bath's Prologue*.

Further reading

The reading list below gives key reading material and electronic resources in each area of specialism covered in this book.

Introduction
For historical background on the period covered by this book:
Lapidge, Michael, Blair, John, Keynes, Simon and Scragg, Donald (eds), *The Blackwell Encyclopaedia of Anglo-Saxon England* (Oxford: Blackwell, 1999).

Chapter 1: Handling Anglo-Saxon manuscripts
For those who wish to pursue the topic of manuscript study across a broader period:
Clemens, Raymond and Graham, Timothy, *Introducing Manuscript Studies* (New York: Cornell University Press, 2007).

Chapter 2: The construction and writing of Anglo-Saxon manuscripts
Bishop, T.A.M., *English Caroline Minuscule* (Oxford: Clarendon Press, 1971).
Brown, Michelle P., *Manuscripts from the Anglo-Saxon Age* (London: The British Library, 2007).
Brown, T.J., 'Tradition, imitation and invention in Insular handwriting of the seventh and eighth centuries' in Janet M. Bately, Michelle P. Brown and Jane Roberts (eds), *A Palaeographer's View: selected writings of Julian Brown* (London: Harvey Miller, 1993), pp. 179–200.
Richards, Mary P. (ed.), *Anglo-Saxon Manuscripts: Basic Readings* (New York and London: Garland, 1994, repr. London: Routledge, 1994).
Roberts, Jane, *Guide to Scripts used in English Writings up to 1500* (London: The British Library, 2005), especially pp. 13–103.
Rumble, Alexander R. (ed.), *Writing and Texts in Anglo-Saxon England*, Publications of the Manchester Centre for Anglo-Saxon Studies 5 (Cambridge and Rochester, NY: D.S. Brewer, 2006).

Chapter 3: Manuscript sources of Old English prose
Ker, N.R., *Catalogue of Manuscripts containing Anglo-Saxon* (Oxford: Clarendon Press 1957, new edition 1991).

Pulsiano, Phillip and Treharne, Elaine (eds), *Anglo-Saxon Manuscripts and their Heritage* (Aldershot: Ashgate, 1998).
Pulsiano, Phillip and Treharne, Elaine (eds), *A Companion to Anglo-Saxon Literature* (Oxford: Blackwell, 2001, reprinted Wiley-Blackwell, 2008).
Richards, Mary P. (ed.), *Anglo-Saxon Manuscripts: Basic Readings* (New York and London: Garland, 1994, repr. London: Routledge, 1994).
Sisam, Kenneth, *Studies in the History of Old English Literature* (Oxford: Clarendon Press, 1953).
Szarmach, Paul E. (ed.), *Old English Prose: Basic Readings* (New York and London: Garland, 2000).

Chapter 4: Manuscript sources of Old English poetry
Caie, Graham, 'Codicological clues: reading Old English Christian poetry in its manuscript context' in Paul Cavill (ed.), *The Christian Tradition in Anglo-Saxon England* (Cambridge: D.S. Brewer, 2004), pp. 3–14.
Conner, Patrick, *Anglo-Saxon Exeter: A Tenth-Century Cultural History* (Woodbridge: Boydell and Brewer, 1993).
Kiernan, Kevin (ed.), *The Electronic Beowulf* (London: The British Library, 1999).
Muir, Bernard (ed.), with Nick Kennedy, *A Digital Facsimile of Oxford, Bodleian Library, MS. Junius 11*, Bodleian Digital Texts 1 (Oxford: Bodleian Library, 2004).
Muir, Bernard (ed.), with Nick Kennedy, *The Exeter DVD: The Exeter Anthology of Old English Poetry* (Exeter: University of Exeter Press, 2006).
O'Brien O'Keeffe, Katherine, *Visible Song: Transitional Literacy in Old English Verse* (Cambridge Studies in Anglo-Saxon England 4, Cambridge: Cambridge University Press, 1990).
O'Donnell, Daniel (ed.), *Caedmon's Hymn: A Multi-Media Study, Edition and Archive* (Cambridge: D. S. Brewer, 2005).
Scragg, D.G. (ed.), *The Vercelli Homilies and Related Texts*, Early English Text Society, original series 300 (Oxford: Oxford University Press, 1992).
Sisam, Celia (ed.), *The Vercelli Book: a late tenth-century manuscript containing prose and verse*, Vercelli Biblioteca Capitolaire CXVII, Early English Manuscripts in Facsimile 19 (Copenhagen: Rosenkilde & Bagger, 1976).
Wright, Charles D., 'More Old English poetry in Vercelli Homily XXI', in Treharne, Elaine and Rosser, Susan (eds), *Early Medieval Texts and Interpretations: Studies Presented to Donald G. Scragg* (Tempe, AZ: Arizona Center for Medieval and Renaissance Studies, 2003), pp. 245–62.

Chapter 5: A survey of Latin manuscripts
Bishop, T.A.M., *English Caroline Minuscule* (Oxford: Clarendon Press, 1971).
Dumville, David, *English Caroline Script and Monastic History: Studies in Benedictinism, A.D. 950–1030* (Woodbridge: Boydell and Brewer, 1993).
Gneuss, Helmut, *Handlist of Anglo-Saxon Manuscripts: A List of Manuscripts and Manuscript Fragments Written or Owned in England up to 1100,*

Medieval and Renaissance Texts and Studies 241 (Tempe, AZ: Arizona Center for Medieval and Renaissance Studies, 2001).
Gneuss, Helmut, *Books and Libraries in Early England* (Aldershot: Variorum, 1996).
Lapidge, Michael, *The Anglo-Saxon Library* (Oxford: Oxford University Press, 2006).

Chapter 6: Glosses and notes in Anglo-Saxon manuscripts
Derolez, R. (ed.), *Anglo-Saxon Glossography: Papers Read at the International Conference Held in the Koninklijke Academie voor Wetenschapen, Letteren en Schone Kunsten van België, Brussels, 8 and 9 September 1986* (Brussels: Paleis der Academiën, 1992).
Franzen, Christine, *The Tremulous Hand of Worcester: a study of Old English in the thirteenth century* (Oxford: Clarendon Press, 1991).
Graham, Timothy. 'Anglo-Saxon Studies: Sixteenth to Eighteenth Centuries' in Phillip Pulsiano and Elaine Treharne (eds), *A Companion to Anglo-Saxon Literature* (Oxford: Blackwell, 2001, repr. Wiley-Blackwell, 2008), pp. 415–33.
Gretsch, Mechthild, 'Winchester vocabulary and standard Old English: the vernacular in late Anglo-Saxon England', *Proceedings of the John Rylands University Library of Manchester*, 83 (2001), pp. 41–87.
Lapidge, Michael, 'The study of Latin texts in late Anglo-Saxon England [1], the evidence of Latin glosses' in Nicholas Brooks (ed.), *Latin and the Vernacular Languages in Early Medieval Britain* (Leicester: Leicester University Press, 1982), pp. 99–140.
Robinson, Fred C., 'Syntactical glosses in Latin manuscripts of Anglo-Saxon provenance', *Speculum*, 48 (1973), pp. 443–75.

Chapter 7: Manuscript art
Brown, Michelle P., *The Lindisfarne Gospels: society, spirituality and the scribe*, (London: The British Library, 2003).
Deshman, Robert, *The Benedictional of Æthelwold*, Studies in Manuscript Illumination 9 (Princeton: Princeton University Press, 1995).
Karkov, Catherine E., *Text and Picture in Anglo-Saxon England: narrative strategies in the Junius 11 manuscript*, Cambridge Studies in Anglo-Saxon England 31 (Cambridge: Cambridge University Press, 2001).
Netzer, Nancy, *Cultural Interplay in the Eighth Century: the Trier Gospels and the making of a scriptorium at Echternach*, Cambridge Studies in Palaeography and Codicology 3 (Cambridge: Cambridge University Press, 1994).
Noel, William, *The Harley Psalter*, Cambridge Studies in Palaeography and Codicology 4 (Cambridge: Cambridge University Press, 1995).
Withers, Benjamin C., *The Illustrated Old English Hexateuch, Cotton Claudius B.iv: the frontier of seeing and reading in Anglo-Saxon England* (London and Toronto: The British Library and University of Toronto Press, 2007).

Chapter 8: From manuscript to computer

Besser, Howard, Introduction to Imaging (2005: revised edition edited by Sally Hubbard with Deborah Lenart) http://www.getty.edu/research/conducting_research/standards/introimages/

Burnard, Lou, O'Brien O'Keeffe, Katherine and Unsworth, John (eds), *Electronic Textual Editing* (New York: MLA, 2006).

Galer, Mark and Horvat, Les, *Digital Imaging: essential skills* (Amsterdam and London: Elsevier/Focal Press, Third Edition, 2005).

Siemens, Ray and Schreibman Susan (eds), *A Companion to Digital Literary Studies* (Oxford: Blackwell, 2008).

TASI Website: http://www.tasi.ac.uk

TEI Consortium (ed.), 'A gentle introduction to XML', *TEI P5: Guidelines for Electronic Text Encoding and Interchange* (Oxford: Providence, Charlottesville, Nancy, TEI Consortium, 2007) http://www.tei-c.org/release/doc/tei-p5-doc/en/html/SG.html.

Glossary

acephalous 'headless'; the description of a text lacking its beginning
Adobe Flash software by Adobe
Adobe Shockwave software by Adobe
annal a chronicle entry covering one year
antiphon church music consisting of two parts responding to one another
antiphonary a text containing songs performed at **Mass** by the choir
Anglo-Latin Latin written in England or by an English author (at home or abroad); but see Chapter 5 note 1 for specific use of the term in that chapter
Anglo-Saxon minuscule a minuscule script used in England between 850 and 1100. There are three varieties: the earliest is pointed, the next square, the third round
Antique art a period of art covering classical Greek and Roman art and continuing up to about the fifth century AD
argumentum an explanatory introduction to a text
ascender the vertical stroke of a letter which extends above the top of a row of **minims**

Benedictine Reform a tenth-century movement patronised by King Edgar, involving a return to the monastic principles established by St Benedict of Nursia (*c*.480–543) which provoked an intellectual renaissance and resultant book production in England
benedictional a service book containing episcopal blessings, arranged according to the **liturgical year**
bifolium (plural *bifolia*) one sheet of **parchment** or **vellum**, folded to make two folia or **folios**

binding a complex process in the making of a *codex*, in which leaves of **parchment** or **vellum** are assembled into **quires**, stitched together, pressed and trimmed and attached to supporting cords or leather bands, which are in turn attached to wooden boards by means of channels and holes, secured by pegs; the boards are usually covered by leather outside and by **pastedowns** glued onto the inside.
bit-depth a term used in digital imaging to describe the amount of information an image can hold about an individual **pixel**, e.g. an '8-bit' image can have 256 different values (colours) for each pixel of an image
booklet a **quire** or a small, self-contained set of quires, stitched together, sometimes unbound, sometimes in a wrapper, which may have circulated independently before being bound into a *codex*
breviary a service book containing all the texts necessary for celebrating the **canonical hours**, mostly psalms and biblical readings
breviate psalter an abbreviated **psalter**
Byzantine culture and art, named from Byzantium, once the eastern capital of the Roman Empire. The influential, classically based art style was found throughout the eastern Mediterranean. It influenced late Anglo-Saxon art chiefly through **Carolingian** and **Ottonian** art

caesura the regular medial pause in lines of (classical) poetry. The term is used for the break between metrical units in the Old English poetic line and in printed texts is conventionally marked by a gap

calendar a text providing the feast days of the saints and fixed feast days of the Church in chronological order

canticles biblical songs of praise or thanksgiving, sung during the Daily **Office**

canon an ecclesiastical rule

canon tables, Eusebian canon tables a system of indicting the places of key passages in the four gospels in tabular form, sometimes elaborately decorated

Canonical Hours divisions of time established by the Christian Church at which specific portions of the **Divine Office** were received

Caroline script a style of script derived from Carolingian writing

Carolingian culture and art, named from Charlemagne, king of the Franks and Holy Roman Emperor (742–814). The art style is classically based, featuring naturalistic figures and acanthus plants. It flourished in the Frankish Empire (France, Germany, parts of Italy) in the eighth and ninth centuries

catchword the first word or words from the text on the first line of the following **folio** or **quire**, written at the foot of the preceding folio, or the last folio in a quire. The purpose was to preserve the correct sequence of folios in a quire, or of quires within a *codex*.

catechesis oral instruction of first principles of faith

Celtic culture and art, named from the Celtic peoples who inhabited Ireland and Wales. Irish Celtic art was influential in Northumbria through Christian missionary activity

chapter short lessons taken from scripture read during the Daily **Office**

charter a formal document recording a transaction such as a grant of land

circulus anni the liturgical cycle for the church year

codex a manuscript in the form of a book, composed of folded sheets of **parchment** or **vellum** stitched together at one edge

codicologist an expert on codicology

codicology the examination of the physical characteristics of a manuscript book or *codex*

collation (in **codicology**) the placing of leaves of a book in order prior to binding; (in editing) the assembly of different manuscripts for examination and comparison

collect a short prayer containing one main petition

collectar a service book containing the prayers (collects) for the hours and days of the **Office**

colophon a statement, usually at the end of a manuscript book, recording information such as where and by whom it was made

common-place book a book into which striking passages from texts are copied for personal use

computus calculations necessary to arrive at the correct date for Easter in a given year

construe mark symbol used in a method of syntactical **glossing** which identifed the structure of a Latin sentence

Copperplate see **Round**

copy-text the source text from which a new copy was made

cradle an angled support for a manuscript to prevent it from being damaged while it is examined or photographed

cursive a continuous script in which the pen is not lifted between letters; in the **Insular** system of scripts, the lowest grade of **minuscule**

decretal, papal a letter giving a pontifical decision on a matter of discipline, usually in answer to a question

descender the vertical stroke of a letter which descends below the row of **minims**

diacritic a mark placed above, or attached to, a letter in script to indicate pronunciation

diminuendo 'getting smaller'; a motif in **Insular** art whereby the opening of a text is ornamented with a large initial letter and script of larger-than-normal size, which reduces in blocks (such as line by line) until it reaches the normal size for the rest of the text

diplomatic transcription a method of transcribing a manuscript into modern type, indicating by symbols any additional material on each page

dittography erroneous repetition of a word, phrase or passage

digital file a computer file

digital image an image stored as a **digital** (computer) **file** that can be displayed and manipulated by software applications. Digital images have a variety of file formats such as **JPEG, GIF, TIFF**

digitization the conversion of analogue material to a **digital file**. Methods include using a flat-bed **scanner** to convert a photograph to a **digital image** (see also **scanning**) or by adding metainformation to a text file (see also **mark-up**)

Divine Office the cycle of services for each day (excluding **Mass**) for Benedictine monks, comprising the monastic hours of Matins, Lauds, Prime, Terce, Sext, None, Vespers and Compline

dry point, drypoint description of an insertion scratched into the surface of **parchment** or **vellum** with a pointed instrument, especially a **stylus**

endleaf *see* **endpapers**

endorsement a note written on the back of a manuscript

endpapers extra leaves at the beginning and end of a **codex**, inserted during **binding**, sometimes used as **pastedowns**

epistle a letter; in the context of church services, an extract from one of the letters of the apostles included in the New Testament

epitome an abridgement or summary of a text

escatalogical adjective used of theological matters such as death, judgement and post-death existence

evangelary a book containing the gospel readings for the **Mass**, arranged in order of the **liturgical year**

exegetical concerning exegesis, interpretation, especially of the Bible

exemplar a model (text or image) which is copied

explicit closing words of a text

expositio hymnorum a prose paraphrase of hymns

eyeskip scribe's omission of a word, phrase or passage

fibre-optic light a lighting technique which uses bundles of thin, flexible, coated glass fibres to give maximum light in places difficult to access

fitts numbered sections of certain Old English poems

florilegium a collection of selected texts; an anthology

flyleaf a blank leaf at the beginning or the end of a book

foliage decoration consisting of stylised leaves, buds and branches

foliate ornament consisting of foliage

foliation a method of numbering leaves within a *codex* by a sequence of **folio** numbers, in which each leaf is numbered once, with the addition of v for '**verso**' to refer to the back of the leaf, and sometimes of r for '**recto**' to refer to the front (cf. **pagination**)

folio one page of **parchment** or **vellum**, half of a *bifolium*; the front and back of a folio are usually assigned the same number and identified as **recto** and **verso** (e.g. folio 1r, 1v) rather than given sequential numbering (page 1, page 2).

formula letters samples for writing letters for specific occasions, such as expressing gratitude, demanding the return of something, or praising someone for good deeds

GIF (.gif) a **digital image** file format

GIMP Image Processing Software

gloss interpretation or translation of a text or part of a text, written between the lines or in the margin, in the form of a single word, a phrase or continuous text; usually written in ink, but sometimes scratched with a **stylus** ('**dry point**' **gloss**)

glossae collectae **glosses** collected into lists, which might remain grouped according to context, or organized according to theme or to simple alphabetical principles

glossator a person who has written translations or explanatory **glosses** into the margins or between the lines of an existing text

gospel book a book containing the four gospels (Matthew, Mark, Luke and John) and sometimes prefatory material and **canon tables**

Gothic Anglicana the English variety of **cursive** script used in documents *c.*1200–1600 and in less formal books *c.*1250–1500

Gothic Secretary a **cursive** script imported into England from France in the late fourteenth century, which became very popular for less formal writing by the mid-sixteenth century

Gothic Textura the formal book-script of the later medieval period *c.*1200–1550, used for bibles, etc.

hagiography legends of saints, especially miracles

half-sheet a single leaf of **parchment** bound in with the *bifolia* making up a **quire**

Half-Uncial a semi-majuscule script produced in churches associated with the Irish mission, with a distinctive form of *a* and **majuscule** frequently used for *N*, *R* and *S*

haplography the erroneous writing of something once which should have been written twice

hard point a pointed implement such as a **stylus**, used for constructing a **writing grid**, drawing, or glossing in a manuscript

Hiberno-Saxon art *see* **Insular art**

historiated initial a large letter opening a text in which the outline of the letter encloses a picture

homeoteleuton *see* **eyeskip**

homiletic adjective meaning pertaining to **homily**

homiliary a volume of **homilies** arranged according to the ecclesiastical year

homily an address delivered during **Mass**, interpreting the day's **epistle** or gospel reading (cf. **sermon**)

HTML HyperText Mark-up Language

Hybrid in the Insular system of scripts, a high-grade **miniscule** with some letter-forms borrowed from **Half-Unical**

hymnal a book or section of a book containing metrical (Latin) hymns sung during the **Divine Office**, arranged according to the **liturgical year**

incipit opening words of a text

incunabula early printed books, especially pre-1500

inhabited initial an opening letter decorated with living creatures

initial the first letter of a passage of text, sometimes enlarged, coloured and treated decoratively

Insular an adjective applied to the common features of the culture of the British Isles, especially England and Ireland

Insular art an art style of England, especially Northumbria, Iona and Ireland, transmitted via missionaries to the Continent; it combines Celtic motifs such as decorated script, spirals and red dotting, with Anglo-Saxon zoomorphic motifs and Roman (late Antique) naturalistic figures; roughly sixth to ninth century

Insular minuscule a form of **minuscule** script characteristic of the British Isles but not peculiar to any one region of Britain

interline the space between lines of text in which **glosses** are sometimes written

interlinear gloss **gloss** written between the lines of a text

interpretamentum (plural *interpretamenta*) an explanatory **gloss**, in English, Latin or both

introit anthem sung at the beginning of the **Mass**

IPR intellectual property rights

Italic script used by well-educated writers in Tudor England, originating in Italy

JPEG (.jpg) a **digital image** file format

lectionary a book of readings for use in the liturgy

lemma (plural *lemmata*) a word which is glossed

lexical gloss a **gloss** in the form of a synonym of the *lemma*

liber vitae a 'book of life' listing the members and benefactors of a monastic community who were to be remembered in prayers

ligature a link between adjoining letters in script

litany a series of prayers for help from a series of saints

littera notabilior an enlarged letter, sometimes coloured, employed at the opening of a clause

liturgical year the annual programme for public worship

liturgy the rites for public worship, including the Eucharist and the **Divine Office** or **Canonical Hours**

macron a straight line written over a vowel indicting pronunciation is 'long'

majuscule a script which uses large rounded capital letters, with few or no **ascenders** and **descenders** (cf. **miniscule**)

mandorla an almond-shaped halo round the whole body of a sacred figure in art

manumission freeing of a person or persons from slavery; the document recording this fact

mark-up the addition of metainformation about a text to a computer file using a recognised system such as **XML** or **SGML**.

Martyrology a manuscript listing the saints who died on each day of the year

Mass the religious ceremony (or service) central to Christianity, which is celebrated in church, and includes the Eucharist

membrum disiectum (plural *membra disiecta*) a fragment of an original manuscript which has been separated and is now in a different library

merograph a **gloss** written in abbreviated form

minim the smallest vertical stroke within a **minuscule** script, used to form letters such as *i, n, u* and *m*

minuscule a script (equivalent to lower case in printing) in which some letters are formed with **ascenders** and **descenders**

mise-en-page page lay-out

monastic hours *see* **Divine Office**

monumental square capitals an angular style of **majuscules** used for headings in **Insular** and early Anglo-Saxon manuscripts and related to script found on stone monuments and metalwork. The letter *A* with a broken bar is characteristic, as are angular forms of *C* and *G*

Night Office monastic prayers before dawn, which became part of Matins

offertory text spoken or sung in church while the congregation make their offerings

Office *see* **Divine Office**

offset text or image preserved, in reverse, on a surface to which it has been attached by glue or paste

origin the place where a manuscript was written (cf. **provenance**)

opening two facing pages of an open *codex*

orthography spelling

Ottonian culture and art, named from the German king and Holy Roman Emperor Otto I. The art style, a ninth- and tenth-century successor to **Carolingian** art, influenced by **Byzantine** art, also by Anglo-Saxon, featured elaborately decorated manuscripts with focus on portraits and figures

overline a mark of abbreviation consisting of a short, horizontal, suprascript line close to the point where a word has been abbreviated

pagination a method of numbering leaves within a *codex* by a sequence in which each side of the leaf is numbered separately, as in modern printed books (cf. **foliation**)

palaeographer an expert in **palaeography**

palaeography the classification and description of former styles of handwriting

palimpsest a manuscript in which an original text has been erased, sometimes by washing, and the manuscript re-used (the newer text being called 'the upper script'); remains of the original text (the 'lower script') may be revealed by ultra violet lighting

pandect a complete bible (Old and New Testaments) in one volume

parchment a general term for animal skin on which manuscripts are written; in specialist use the term is confined to sheep- or goatskin

passio an account of the life of a saint, particularly concerning suffering and martyrdom

pastedown parchment or paper pasted down on the inside of the wooden boards covering a bound **codex**, to conceal the grooves in the wood into which the ends of the leather binding bands were channelled. Pastedowns often consisted of re-used manuscript.

patristic pertaining to the teaching of the Church Fathers, early Christian writers (up to the eighth century)

paving letters letters of the alphabet used as **glosses** to a Latin text, to indicate word order for a translator

PDF format Portable Document Format; Adobe's proprietary **digital file** format for documents

penitential a rule book of penances for misdeeds

per cola et commata a system of setting out bibles and **gospel books** in which each verse and each of its subordinate clauses is begun on a new line

pericope an extract, especially a suitable passage for reading in church

pixel a picture element in computer imaging, hence a measure of the resolution of an image

pocket-book a very small manuscript, easily transported

pointing insertion of punctuation marks in the form of points, or dots

pontifical a liturgical book containing the order of service for sacraments exclusively carried out by popes and bishops

prayerbook a collection of prayers for private use, sometimes organized according to themes and accompanied by biblical texts

press-mark a library catalogue identification for a *codex* either written inside the book or written on a slip attached to the binding

pricking, prick mark a mark made in **parchment** or **vellum** with a sharp instrument as a guide to ruling, or as part of the construction of drawings

prognostic, prognostication a prediction of future events from natural phenomena such as the weather

Protogothic miniscule a development from **Caroline miniscule** used in the twelfth century

provenance the place where a manuscript was kept, often indicated as a monastery or monastic/cathedral city (cf. **origin**)

psalter a book of all the psalms, sometimes accompanied by other religious texts

punctus, punctus simplex a punctuation mark in the form of a dot, like a modern full stop or period

punctus elevatus a punctuation mark consisting of a dot and a tick-like line above it, often indicating an internal division of a sentence

punctus interrogativus a punctuation mark, consisting of a dot and sideways hook-shape above it, marking the end of a phrase containing a question

punctus versus a punctuation mark resembling a modern semi-colon, usually indicating a major pause, such as the end of a chapter

quadrivium the four advanced disciplines of the medieval school comprising arithmetic, music, geometry, and astronomy

quire a gathering of *bifolia* arranged one inside the other and stitched together to form a **booklet**

quire signatures or **numbers** numerals or letters written in sequence on the leaves of a manuscript to facilitate the internal ordering of a **quire** and the relationship of quires to one another

recto the front of a **folio**

regular clergy clergy living under a rule of chastity, poverty and obedience (i.e. monks)

responsory a short verse, usually taken from the Scriptures, sung in response to the lessons of **Mass** and **Office**

Round a cursive script developed from **Italic**, used in formal writing from the seventeenth century to the early twentieth; also known as **Copperplate**, because it could be learned from copy-books engraved on copper plates

rubric, rubrication a heading to a text, usually, but not always, written in red ink

runes letters of the Germanic alphabet designed for use in inscriptions but sometimes found in manuscript texts; the runic letters 'thorn' and 'wynn' were used in Old English texts for the sounds <th> and <w> respectively

running heading the title of the work, or the title and number of the chapter appearing on a page in a manuscript, added in the upper margin, often in coloured ink

rustic capitals a Roman **majuscule** script with a more curved and less rigid appearance than Square capitals

sacramentary a service book for **Mass**, containing both the fixed prayers and those which varied during the **liturgical year**

scanner equipment used to convert an analogue object into a **digital file**, chiefly the flat-bed scanner or the digital camera

scanning the process of converting an analogue object (usually, but not always, a page/folio or photograph) into a **digital file**

scholion or *scholium* (plural *scholia*) an extended explanation of a word or idea in a text, often placed in the margin

scribe the person who physically wrote a manuscript, mostly copyist rather than composer; sometimes also artist

scriptor a **scribe** known to have written more than one sequence of surviving text

scriptorium a location in an ecclesiastical establishment for the writing of manuscripts

semi-majuscule a script such as **Half-Uncial**, which includes letter-forms from both **majuscule** and **minuscule** scripts

sermon a moral address delivered during **Mass**, not directly arising from the **liturgy** of the day, though supported with biblical quotations (cf. **homily**)

Set a formal grade of handwriting in the **Insular** system, a good-quality **minuscule** with few **ligatures**

SGML Standard General Mark-up Language

signes de renvoi matching symbols appearing in the main text of a manuscript and in accompanying marginal material to aid cross-referencing

Southumbrian a term used of art from Mercia and Kent (south of the river Humber)

stemma a 'family tree' of manuscripts constructed to show their interrelationship including the possibility of members now missing

stylus an object of metal or bone like a long pin, with a point at one end for writing on wax tablets, **pricking** and **ruling** manuscripts and sometimes for annotating manuscripts ('**dry point**'); sometimes with a blunt triangular head for erasing – by smoothing wax or scraping skin

subpunct to mark a letter by putting a *punctus* ('point') underneath it, indicating that it should be omitted

suppletive gloss a gloss which completes the meaning of the main text by supplying additional words

syntactical gloss symbol placed over a Latin word of a sentence to indicate the word-order when translating into English, or a system of symbols placed above or below significant elements in a Latin sentence, to help comprehension of Latin constructions

TEI Text Encoding Initiative

textblock the leaves of a *codex* containing the text (as opposed to **pastedowns** and **flyleaves**)

TIFF (.tif) a digital image file format

tonsure monastic haircut imitative of Christ's crown of thorns. Different branches of the Church manifested this in different ways

trivium the three basic disciplines of the medieval school comprising grammar, dialectic (or logic), and rhetoric; this includes the study of poetic texts since these incorporate the disciplines of the *trivium*

troper a book of tropes, for chants in religious services, music or text

Uncial a script found in early Anglo-Saxon manuscripts with close links to Rome, consisting of rounded **majuscule** letters with characteristic shapes for A, D, E, G and M.

URL Universal Resource Locator. A protocol for indicating the location of a digital file. Web addresses of the type http://www.example.com/ are URLs.

vellum calfskin on which manuscripts are written; the term has more restricted use than **parchment**

vernacular native language, as opposed to Latin; in terms of Anglo-Saxon manuscripts, the Old English language

verso the back of a **folio**

vita ('life') an account of the life of a saint

watermark originally signifying patterns of letters, numbers or pictures inserted into individual handmade sheets of paper during manufacture, the term '(digital) watermark' is now used to identify data embedded in a digital image and not visible to the naked eye

web world wide web or **www**

www world wide web

writing grid a framework on a manuscript page ruled before writing commenced, consisting of horizontal lines for writing on and vertical lines marking the boundaries of the text

XML eXtensible Mark-up Language

Index of manuscripts

Numbers of illustrations appear in italics

AUSTRIA

St Paul (Carinthia) Stiftsbibliothek 21 (25.2.16)   144

BELGIUM

Antwerp, Plantin-Moretus Museum M.16.2   144, 145n.62

Brussels, Bibliothèque Royale 1650   168, *6.4*
  Bibliothèque Royale 1828–30   145n.62
  Bibliothèque Royale 8558–63   141
  Bibliothèque Royale 9850–52   131

DENMARK

Copenhagen, Kongelige Bibliotek G.K.S.1595   *12/*

FRANCE

Arras, Bibliothèque Municipale 1029   130

Avranches, Bibliothèque Municipale 29   125, 143
  Bibliothèque Municipale 236   155

Boulogne-sur-Mer, Bibliothèque Municipale 32   131, 133
  Bibliothèque Municipale 106   125–6, 130
  Bibliothèque Municipale 189   171

Épinal, Bibliothèque Municipale 72   145–6

Le Havre, Bibliothèque Municipale 330   123

Paris, Bibliothèque Nationale 7585   146n.63
  Bibliothèque Nationale, anglais 67   144n.58
  Bibliothèque Nationale, fonds latin 5237   258n.5
  Bibliothèque Nationale, fonds latin 8824 (*Paris Psalter*)   8, 11, 16, 58, *1.1*
  Bibliothèque Nationale, lat. 943   124
  Bibliothèque Nationale, lat. 987 (*Ramsey Benedictional*)   *2.9*
  Bibliothèque Nationale, lat. 2825   170–1
  Bibliothèque Nationale, lat. 4210   140
  Bibliothèque Nationale, lat. 4839   155n.79, 156
  Bibliothèque Nationale, lat. 5362   128, 142
  Bibliothèque Nationale, lat. 6401   155
  Bibliothèque Nationale, lat. 8085   148
  Bibliothèque Nationale, lat. 8092   151
  Bibliothèque Nationale, lat. 9389 (*Echternach Gospels*)   117
  Bibliothèque Nationale, lat. 9488   120n.19
  Bibliothèque Nationale, lat. 10575   124
  Bibliothèque Nationale, lat. 10837   138, 152n.75
  Bibliothèque Nationale, nouv. acq. lat 586   144, 154
  Bibliothèque Sainte-Geneviève 2410   133, 148

Rheims, Bibliothèque Municipale 9   217–8, *7.10*

Rouen, Bibliothèque Municipale 26   131, 133–4, 146n.65, 151
  Bibliothèque Municipale 274 (Y.6) (*Missal of Robert of Jumièges*)   121, 224
  Bibliothèque Municipale 1382   140
  Bibliothèque Municipale 1385   140
  Bibliothèque Municipale Y.7 (*Benedictional of Archbishop Robert*)   224

Saint-Omer, Bibliothèque Municipale 202   126

GERMANY

Berlin, Staatsbibliothek Preussischer Kulturbesitz, Grimm 132,1   130
Staatsbibliothek Preussischer Kulturbesitz, Grimm 132,2   145n.61
Staatsbibliothek Preussischer Kulturbesitz, Lat. fol.877   120

Darmstadt, Hessische Landes- und Hochschulbibliothek 4262   154n.76

Düsseldorf, Nordrhein-Westfälisches Hauptstaatsarchiv Z11/1   142
Universitätsbibliothek Fragm. K16:Z.3/1   131

Hanover, Kestner Museum, W.M. XXIa, 36 (*Eadwig Gospels*)   221–2, *2.11, 7.13–7.18*

Herrnstein near Siegburg, Bibliothek der Grafen Nesselrode 192   155

Karlsruhe, Badische Landesbibliothek, Aug. perg. 221   126
Badische Landesbibliothek, Fragm. Aug. 122   145n.59, 155n.79

Kassel, Gesamthochschulbibliothek, 2ºMs. theol.21   131
Gesamthochschulbibliothek, 2ºMs.theol.65   143

Köln, Historisches Archiv der Stadt, GB Kasten B   120n.19

Munich, Bayerische Staatsbibliothek Clm 6433   *1.7*
Bayerische Staatsbibliothek Clm 29336(1   148–9n.68
Bayerische Staatsbibliothek, Clm 29698(2   155–6

Münster in Westfalen, Staatsarchiv MSC. I.243   154n.76
Universitätsbibliothek, Fragmentenkapsel 1 no.3   142
Universitätsbibliothek, Fragmentensammlung IV.8   120

Würzburg, Cathedral Library M.p.th.q. 2   23, *1.6*
Universitätsbibliothek M.p.th.f.43   126, 131
Universitätsbibliothek M.p.th.f.68   118

HUNGARY

Miskolc, Levay Jozsef Library s.n.   150

IRELAND

Dublin, Royal Irish Academy s.n.   216
Trinity College 57 (*Book of Durrow*)   223
Trinity College 58 (formerly A I 16; *Book of Kells*)   205, 223, 265, 269
Trinity College 174   82

ITALY

Florence, Biblioteca Medicea Laurenziana, Amiatinus I (*Codex Amiatinus*)   2, 115, 208–10
Biblioteca Medicea Laurenziana, Plut.xvii.20   122

Vatican City, Biblioteca Apostolica Vaticana, lat. 3363   149
Biblioteca Apostolica Vaticana, Pal. lat. 259   126
Biblioteca Apostolica Vaticana, Reg. lat. 12 (*Bury Psalter*)   235
Biblioteca Apostolica Vaticana, Reg. lat. 338   125, 135
Biblioteca Apostolica Vaticana, Reg. lat. 489   143
Biblioteca Apostolica Vaticana, Reg. lat. 1671   147

Vercelli, Biblioteca capitolare CXVII (*Vercelli Book*)   23, 62–3, 80–1, 88, 94–5, 101–3, 105–6, 109, *4.3*

NETHERLANDS

Leiden, Bibliotheek der Rijksuniversiteit, Scaliger 69   155n.78
Bibliotheek der Rijksuniversiteit, Voss. Lat. Q.69 (*Leiden Glossary*)   178, 180

Utrecht, Universiteitsbibliotheek 32, Script. eccl. 484 (*Utrecht Psalter*)   6, 12, 23, 117, 162, 206, 213, 224, 231, 235, 241, *1.1, 1.3*

NORWAY

Oslo, Riksarkivet 207   123
Riksarkivet 208   123
Riksarkivet 210   123
Riksarkivet, Lat. fragm. 201   121n.24
Riksarkivet, Lat. fragm. 211   121n.24
Universitetsbiblioteket, Lat. fragm. 16   124n.32

RUSSIA

St Petersburg, Russian National Library, Lat. F.v.I.8 (*St Petersburg Gospels*)   21, 117

Russian National Library O.v.XIV.1   145n.59
Russian National Library Q.v.I.15   150
Russian National Library Q.v.I.18 (*St Petersburg Bede*)   142n.56, 216

SWEDEN

Stockholm, Kungliga Biblioteket (Royal Library)
  A.135 (*Codex Aureus*)   14, 117, 210–11, 7.2–7.4
  Riksarkivet Lösa Pergamentsomslag s. 9   124n.32

SWITZERLAND

Geneva, Bibliotheca Bodmeriana 175   144

St Gallen, Stiftsbibliothek 1394   120n.19

UK, ENGLAND

Cambridge, Corpus Christi College 12   183, 191, 2.8, 6.13
  Corpus Christi College 23   58, 148n.68, 156, 174–5, 5.6, 6.8
  Corpus Christi College 41   36, 71, 121, 200, 202–3, 3.5, 3.6
  Corpus Christi College 44   124
  Corpus Christi College 57   127, 140, 2.4, 6.10
  Corpus Christi College 69   126
  Corpus Christi College 140   71, 3.4
  Corpus Christi College 144 (*Corpus Glossary*)   146, 180–1, 2.6, 6.12
  Corpus Christi College 153   149
  Corpus Christi College 162   61, 63, 81, 86, 199n.26, 202, 6.19
  Corpus Christi College 173, Part I   32–3, 37, 75, 86n.31, 176, 192, 2.7, 3.7, 4.2
  Corpus Christi College 173, Part II (*Corpus Sedulius*)   171, 175–7, 6.9
  Corpus Christi College 178   82, 138–9n.49, 199n.26
  Corpus Christi College 183   179, 208, 214, 6.11
  Corpus Christi College 188   199n.26, 202
  Corpus Christi College 190   127, 140
  Corpus Christi College 191   191, 201, 6.20
  Corpus Christi College 198   81, 191, 199n.26
  Corpus Christi College 201   11, 61, 88, 108–111, 202, 4.6, 4.7
  Corpus Christi College 206   150
  Corpus Christi College 214   170–1, 6.6
  Corpus Christi College 221   145
  Corpus Christi College 223   148, 156
  Corpus Christi College 260   155
  Corpus Christi College 265   127
  Corpus Christi College 270   142
  Corpus Christi College 272   116–17
  Corpus Christi College 286   117
  Corpus Christi College 303   81, 182, 199n.26
  Corpus Christi College 307   130
  Corpus Christi College 326   143
  Corpus Christi College 352   170, 6.5
  Corpus Christi College 356, pt. iii   156
  Corpus Christi College 368   139n.49
  Corpus Christi College 383   6.14
  Corpus Christi College 389   263, 130
  Corpus Christi College 391 (*Portiforium of St Wulstan*)   16, 134
  Corpus Christi College 402   200
  Corpus Christi College 419   16, 199n.26, 202
  Corpus Christi College 421   16, 199n.26
  Corpus Christi College 422 (*Red Book of Darley*)   216–17, 7.9
  Corpus Christi College 449   144n.58
  Corpus Christi College 473   122
  Gonville and Caius College 144/194   151
  Gonville and Caius College 466/573   123
  Gonville and Caius College 734/782a   121
  Gonville and Caius College 820 (h)   115
  Jesus College 5 (Q.A.5)   123
  Magdalene College, Pepys 2981   114n.5, 115
  Pembroke College C8   122
  Pembroke College 46   122
  St John's College 82   135–6
  St John's College Ii.12.29   146n.64
  St John's College 101   141
  Trinity College B.1.30A   124n.32
  Trinity College B.4.27   133
  Trinity College B.15.33   146n.65
  Trinity College B.15.34   199n.26
  Trinity College B.16.3   151
  Trinity College O.2.30   125, 179
  Trinity College O.2.31   151
  Trinity College O.4.10   148
  Trinity College R.7.5   142n.56
  Trinity College R.15.32   150, 152, 154
  Trinity College R.17.1   160
  Trinity Hall 24   120
  University Library Dd.3.12   200n.28
  University Library Ee.2.4   140

University Library Ff.1.23   116, 160n.1, 161, *6.2*
University Library Ff.1.27   98
University Library Ff.4.43   140
University Library Ff.5.27   117
University Library Gg.3.28   80, 84, 199n.26, 201
University Library Gg.5.35   143, 148, 156, 178–9
University Library Hh.1.10   187, 200-202
University Library Ii.2.4   201
University Library Kk.3.18   200, 202, *6.21*
University Library Kk.5.16 (*Moore Bede*)   142n.56, *2.3–2.4*
University Library Ll.1.10 (*Book of Cerne*)   211–12, *7.5–7.7*

Canterbury, Cathedral Library and Archives, Add. 127/1   126
Cathedral Library and Archives, Add. 127/19   145
Cathedral Library and Archives, Add. 128/52   123
Cathedral Library and Archives Add. 172   136

Durham, Cathedral Library A.II.10   118, 216, 223
Cathedral Library A.II.16   *2.2*
Cathedral Library A.IV.19 (*Durham Ritual or Collectar*)   121, 136, 138, 165, *5.3*
Cathedral Library B.II.35   142n.56
Cathedral Library B.III.32   135, 144n.58, 165
Cathedral Library B.IV.6   115
Cathedral Library B.IV.9   148
Cathedral Library C.III.13   223
Cathedral Library C.III.20   223

Exeter, Cathedral, Dean and Chapter Library 3501 (*Exeter Book*)   5, 10, 88, 90–5, 99–103, 105, 189, 190, 257n.4, *4.1, 6.15*
Cathedral, Dean and Chapter Library 3507   153
Cathedral, Dean and Chapter Library FMS/1,2,2a   142

Hereford, Cathedral Library O.VI.11   *1.8*

Lincoln, Cathedral Library 182   127

London, British Library, Additional 11034   151, 155
British Library, Additional 24199   148n.68
British Library, Additional 28188   124
British Library, Additional 33241   143
British Library, Additional 34600   200n.28
British Library, Additional 34601   200n.28
British Library, Additional 37517 (*Bosworth Psalter*)   49, 116, 134–5, 138, 160n.1, *2.10, 5.4*
British Library, Additional 37777   115

British Library, Additional 40618   118
British Library, Additional 49598 (*Benedictional of Æthelwold*)   13–14, 224–5, 227, *7.19-7.21*
British Library, Additional 56488   134
British Library, Arundel 60   160n.1
British Library, Arundel 155   134, 152
British Library, Burney 277   135
British Library, Cotton Caligula A. xv   130, 152–3
British Library, Cotton Claudius A. iii   124
British Library, Cotton Claudius B. iv (*Old English Hexateuch*)   13, 51, 58, 187, 194, 197–8, 246, *1.4, 7.32*
British Library, Cotton Claudius B. v   121
British Library, Cotton Cleopatra A. iii   146
British Library, Cotton Cleopatra A. vi   144
British Library, Cotton Cleopatra C. viii   148n.68
British Library, Cotton Domitian A. i   178
British Library, Cotton Domitian i   145, 151
British Library, Cotton Domitian ix   145n.61
British Library, Cotton Faustina A. x   65n.4
British Library, Cotton Faustina B. iii   140
British Library, Cotton Galba A. xviii (*Galba Psalter*)   117, 152, 206, *7.23*
British Library, Cotton Julius A. ii   144n.58
British Library, Cotton Julius A. vi   135, 165, 239–41, *7.28-7.29*
British Library, Cotton Nero A. i   70, 187
British Library, Cotton Nero D. iv (*Lindisfarne Gospels*)   117, 163–5, 206, 208–9, 218, 221–3, 265, *6.3, 7.1, 7.11-7.12, 8.7*
British Library, Cotton Otho A. vi   261, *8.3*
British Library, Cotton Otho A. x   142
British Library, Cotton Otho A. xii   97
British Library, Cotton Otho B. xi   194, 200
British Library, Cotton Otho E. i   146
British Library, Cotton Tiberius A. iii   78, 138, 140, 166, 169n.10, *3.8*
British Library, Cotton Tiberius A. xiv   142n.56
British Library, Cotton Tiberius B.i   *2.12*
British Library, Cotton Tiberius B.iv   191-2, *6.16*
British Library, Cotton Tiberius B.v   57, 152, 154–5, 242–4, *5.7, 7.31*
British Library, Cotton Tiberius C.ii   142n.56, 179
British Library, Cotton Tiberius C.vi (*Tiberius Psalter*)   116, 160n.1, 233–5, *7.24-7.25*
British Library, Cotton Titus A.iv   138, 140n.50
British Library, Cotton Titus D.xxvi   138, 229
British Library, Cotton Titus D.xxvii   138, 229,

7.22
British Library, Cotton Vespasian A.i (*Vespasian Psalter*)   135, 160n.1, 216, *6.1, 7.8*
British Library, Cotton Vespasian A.viii (*New Minster Charter*)   14, 214, 227, 237–8, *7.27*
British Library, Cotton Vespasian B.vi   154n.76
British Library, Cotton Vespasian B.x   155n.78
British Library, Cotton Vespasian D.ii   127
British Library, Cotton Vespasian D.vi   116, 163n.4
British Library, Cotton Vespasian D.xii   135, 162n.3, 165
British Library, Cotton Vespasian D.xiv   11, 149, *1.2*
British Library, Cotton Vespasian D.xv   115
British Library, Cotton Vitellius A.vi   143
British Library, Cotton Vitellius A.vii   124
British Library, Cotton Vitellius A.xv (*Beowulf Manuscript*)   10, 16–17, 44, 88, 93, 95, 97, 101, 104–6, 109, 189, 242–3, 270, *4.4–4.5, 7.30, 8.10*
British Library, Cotton Vitellius A.xix   173, *6.7*
British Library, Cotton Vitellius C.iii   57
British Library, Cotton Vitellius D.xx   98
British Library, Cotton Vitellius E.xii   124
British Library, Cotton Vitellius E.xviii   116, 160n.1, *5.1*
British Library, Egerton 267   149
British Library, Egerton 1046   116
British Library, Harley 107   144n.58
British Library, Harley 213   125
British Library, Harley 603 (*Harley Psalter*)   12, 116, 205, *1.3*
British Library, Harley 647   154
British Library, Harley 2506   150, 154
British Library, Harley 2904 (*Ramsey Psalter*)   231
British Library, Harley 3020   125
British Library, Harley 3097   130
British Library, Harley 3271   63, 143, 144n.58, 145n.62
British Library, Harley 3376   146
British Library, Harley 3826   143, 145, 150,
British Library, Harley 5431   140, 152
British Library, Harley 5915   143, 144n.58
British Library, Henry Davis Collection, no. 59   189
British Library, Royal 1 E.vi   224
British Library, Royal 1 E.vii   115
British Library, Royal 1 E.viii   115

British Library, Royal 2 A.xx (*Royal Prayerbook*)   *2.5*
British Library, Royal 2 B.v   160n.1
British Library, Royal 4 A.xiv   123, 130
British Library, Royal 6 B.vii   150n.70
British Library, Royal 6 C.i   146n.63
British Library, Royal 7 C.iv   166
British Library, Royal 7 C.xii   61, *3.1*
British Library, Royal 8 F.xiv   148n.67
British Library, Royal 12 C.xxiii   150
British Library, Royal 12 D.xvii   156n.80
British Library, Royal 12 G.xii   144n.58
British Library, Royal 13 A.x   130
British Library, Royal 13 A.xv   130
British Library, Royal 13 C.v   142n.56
British Library, Royal 15 A.xxxiii   151
British Library, Royal 17 C.xvii   134
British Library, Sloane 1086   114n.5
British Library, Stowe 2   160n.1
British Library, Stowe 944 (*New Minster Liber Vitae*)   14, 236–8, *7.26*
College of Arms, Arundel 22   122
College of Arms, Arundel 30   148
Lambeth Palace Library 149   131, 133, 156, *5.2*
Lambeth Palace Library 414   141
Lambeth Palace Library 427   160n.1
Lambeth Palace Library 692   191
Westminster Abbey Library 36   123

Longleat House, Wiltshire, Library of the Marquess of Bath NMR 10589   146n.64

Manchester, John Rylands University Library, Lat. Fragm. 11   124n.32
John Rylands University Library, Rylands Latin 1550   *2.15*

Oxford, All Souls College SR 79.g.8   122
Bodleian Library, Auctarium D. infra 2.9   141
Bodleian Library, Auctarium D.2.14   117–18
Bodleian Library, Auctarium D.2.19 (*Macregol or Rushworth Gospels*)   117, 163
Bodleian Library, Auctarium F.2.14   145
Bodleian Library, Auctarium F.3.6   148
Bodleian Library, Auctarium F.4.32 (*Dunstan's 'classbook'*)   148, *2.10*
Bodleian Library, Barlow 35   131
Bodleian Library, Bodley 163   142
Bodleian Library, Bodley 340   68–9, *3.2*

Bodleian Library, Bodley 342   68–9, *3.3*
Bodleian Library, Bodley 343   182
Bodleian Library, Bodley 386   123
Bodleian Library, Bodley 441   187
Bodleian Library, Bodley 516   133
Bodleian Library, Bodley 579 (*Leofric Missal*)   121, 122n.30, 123–4, 138
Bodleian Library, Bodley 775   122
Bodleian Library, Digby 39   142
Bodleian Library, Digby 63   152
Bodleian Library, Digby 86   10
Bodleian Library, Digby 146   168
Bodleian Library, Douce 125   155
Bodleian Library, Douce 296   116
Bodleian Library, e Mus 66   18, 149, *1.5*
Bodleian Library, Hatton 20   78, 81, 191
Bodleian Library, Hatton 43   142n.56
Bodleian Library, Hatton 48   138, 139n.49, *2.1*
Bodleian Library, Hatton 76   66n.6
Bodleian Library, Hatton 114   75
Bodleian Library, Hatton 115   76
Bodleian Library, Junius 11 (*Junius Manuscript*)   94, 104, 107, 206, 246, 271, *7.33*–*7.34*, *8.11*
Bodleian Library, Junius 27   160
Bodleian Library, Junius 85/86   68–9
Bodleian Library, Junius 121   67, 81, 191
Bodleian Library, Lat. bib. c.8 (P)   116
Bodleian Library, Lat. class. c.2   148
Bodleian Library, Laud Misc. 381   199
Bodleian Library, Laud Misc. 482   70
Bodleian Library, Laud Misc. 509   194–5, 197–8, *6.18*
Bodleian Library, Laud Misc. 636   192, *6.17*
Bodleian Library, Rawlinson B.203   98
Bodleian Library, Rawlinson B.484   233
Bodleian Library, Rawlinson C.697   150
Bodleian Library, Selden supra 36*   135
Bodleian Library, Tanner 10   58

Corpus Christi College 197   138, 139n.49, 156, *5.5*
Queen's College 320   146n.63
St John's College 154   144

Ripon, Cathedral Library, frag. 2   135

Salisbury, Cathedral Library 134   151
Cathedral Library 150 (*Salisbury Psalter*)   65n.4, 152, 160n.1, 161n.2
Cathedral Library 180   117

Wells, Cathedral Library 7   138–9

Winchester, Cathedral Library 1   142

Worcester, Cathedral Library F.48   143
Cathedral Library F.173   123
Cathedral Library F.174   185
Cathedral Library Q.5   145n.59

UK, SCOTLAND

Edinburgh, National Library of Scotland, Advocates 18.7.8   114, 126

UK, WALES

Aberystwyth, National Library of Wales 735C   150

USA

Bloomington, Indiana University, Lilly Library, Poole 41   123

Columbia, University of Missouri, Ellis Library, Fragmenta manuscripta F.M.2   145

New Haven, Yale University, Beinecke Library 401   150
Beinecke Library M 826   142

New York, Pierpont Morgan Library 709 (*Judith Gospels*)   249–50, *7.35*

Princeton, Scheide collection 71   66

General index

Numbers of illustrations appear in italics

Aachen (Aix-la-Chapelle), Germany, synod held at 140
Abbadia San Salvatore, Italy 115
Abbo of Fleury, tenth-/eleventh-century abbot of Saint-Benoît-sur-Loire, *De differentia circuli et sphaerae* 152, extract from Hyginus 154, *Vita S. Eadmundi* 128
Abbo of Saint-Germain-des-Prés, ninth-/tenth-century monk 127, *Bella Parisiacae urbis* 143, 151, 178, *sermons* 127
abbreviation 15, 18, 28, 30, 42, 45, 55–7, 100, 168–9, 216, 273, 278, 281–2, 295, *2.4*
Abel, son of Adam and Eve 249, *7.34*
Abingdon Abbey 44, 178, *2.12, 2.14, 6.10*
Abraham, Old Testament patriarch *7.32*
acanthus 213–4, 292, *7.13–7.19, 7.21, 7.23, 7.27*
Adalbert of Metz, tenth-century deacon, *Speculum Gregorii* 132–3
Adam, biblical first man 241, 249
addition, of drawings 37; leaves 36; text 58, 107, 197, *3.6, 3.7*; metainformation 295; *see also* annotation; doodle; foliation; gloss; marginalia; pagination
Adelard of Ghent, eleventh-century monk of St Peter's, Ghent, *Vita S. Dunstani* 128
Adobe software 260, 291, 295
Adrevald of Fleury, ninth-century monk, *Historia translationis et miracula S. Benedicti* 128
Advent 119–20, 152
Advent Lyric I, Old English poem *4.1*
Æðilwald, bishop of Lindisfarne *see* Ethilwald
Ælfgifu/Emma, queen to (1) Æthelræd I (2) Cnut 13, 143, 236–7, 252, *7.26*
Ælfric, tenth-/eleventh-century abbot of Eynsham 65, 70–1, 80, 82, 84, 95, *3.1*; *Catholic Homilies* 61, 70–1, 80, 82–3, 124, 187, 201; *Colloquy* 60, 166; *De temporibus anni* 152; *Glossary* 60, 144, 145n.60, 185, 187, 200, 202; *Grammar* 60, 63, 64, 143–5, 185, 187, 200, 202; letter to Sigeweard 195; *Preface* to Genesis 198; *Vita S. Aethelwoldi* 128
Ælfsige, eleventh-century abbot of Bath 71
Ælfwine, eleventh-century dean and abbot of the New Minster, Winchester; patron, possible scribe and artist 229–30; *Ælfwine's Prayerbook* 229–30, *7.22*
Æthelbald, king of Mercia 194
Æthelthryth, St (Etheldreda), seventh-century queen and abbess of Ely 128, 130, 142
Æthelweard tenth-century scholar 113n.1; *Chronicon* 142
Æthelwold, tenth-century bishop of Winchester 44, 128, 138, 166, 204, 225, 227, 229, *Benedictional of see* Index of Manuscripts UK, England, London, British Library, Additional 49598; *Regularis Concordia* 108, 140–1, 166, 169, 227, 229, *3.8*; translation of the *Benedictine Rule* 65n.4, 166
Æthelwulf, ninth-century king of the West Saxons 224
Æthelwulf, ninth-century poet, *De abbatibus* 142
Aethicus Ister, fifth-century traveller, *Cosmographia* 155
Agroecius, fifth-century ?bishop of Sens, *De orthographia* 145
Aidan, St, seventh-century missionary from Iona to Northumbria 128
Alcuin of York, eighth-/ninth-century abbot of St Martin's, Tours 113n.1, 131, 148, 167, 224, 231; *De fide sanctae et individuae Trinitatis* 132; *De orthographia* 145, 150; *De trinitate ad Fredegisum*

132; *In Canticum canticorum* 125, 131–3, 138; *In Ecclesiasten* 125; *Interrogationes Sigewulfi in Genesin* 131–3; (?) *Vita S. Judoci* 128

Aldhelm, St, seventh-/eighth-century abbot of Malmesbury, bishop of Sherborne 113, 148, 154, 167; *Aenigmata* (riddles) 150; *De virginitate* 127, 150, 167–9, 180, 6.4

Aldred, tenth-century glossator of the *Lindisfarne Gospels* and the *Durham Ritual* 163–5, 220, 6.3

Alexander, Jonathan J.G. 20

Alfred, ealdorman, rescuer of manuscript 211

Alfred, reeve of Bath 197

Alfred, 'the Great', king of Wessex 6, 60, 114n.3, 119, 197, 241; Alfredian translations 60, 64, 78, 142, 149, 182–3, 201, 208, 221; Alfred's preface to translation of Gregory *Cura Pastoralis* 78, 118–19, 160, 183, 191, 6.13; Asser's *Life of King Alfred* 97; law-code 33, 37, 189; treaty with Guthrum 188, 6.14; will of 237

alliteration, in poetry 89–90; alliterative prose 88, 95

alphabets 125; Latin 38–9, 60, 125, 172–3, 295, 6.6; runic 38–9, 90, 101–2, 165, 296

alphabetical ordering 33, 53–4, 104, 158, 170–3, 180–1, 293

alterations 16, 53–4, 70, 85–6, 200, 3.2, 6.18

Altercatio duorum geometricorum 155

Ambrose, St, fourth-century bishop of Milan, *De apologia prophetae David* 131–2; *De excessu fratris* 131–2; *De Joseph patriarcha* 131–2; *De paenitentia* 131–2; *De patriarchis* 131–2; *Exhortatio virginitatis* 130; *Expositio de psalmo CXVIII* 132; *Hexameron* 132; *In Evangelium Lucae* 125; letters 131

Ambrosius Autpertus, eighth-century Italian writer 127

ampersand 50

analogue process 260

Ancrene Wisse, Middle English prose text 197, 200

Andreas, Old English poem 92, 101, 103–4, 106

angels 97, 216, 233, 235, 7.9; the Fall of the Angels 107, 249, 7.33

Anglicana script 57, 293

Anglo-Latin writers 112–13, 144, 150, 291

Anglo-Norman language 162

Anglo-Saxon Chronicle, The 60, 83–4, 95, 142–3, 188–9, 192, 195, 200; MS A 37, 75, 176, 192, 194–5, 197, 2.7, 3.7, 4.2; MS C 2.12; MS D 191–4, 6.16; MS E 192, 194–5, 197, 6.17; MS G 194–5, 197; Æthelweard's Latin translation of 142; poems in 98, 2.12, 4.2

Anglo-Saxon Manuscripts in Microfiche Facsimile 30, 86n.31

Anglo-Saxon Poetic Records 88, 281; *see also* Dobbie; Elliott Van Kirk

annotation 4–5, 10, 58–9, 64, 76, 80, 82, 84, 93, 157–8, 167, 185–8, 192, 194–5, 197, 200–1, 273, 3.1, 6.8, 6.14, 6.16–6.17, 6.21 *see also* gloss

Anonymous texts *De nominibus stellarum* 154; *Excerptiones de Prisciano* 144; grammatical treatises 145; homilies 82n.18, 124–5; *In psalmos* 132; *In evangelia* 132; *In Matthaeum* 132–3; *In epistolam ad Colossenses* 132; saints' lives 128; *Vita Ceolfridi* 125

ANSAX electronic discussion forum 263

antiphonary 291

Antique period, art 14, 204, 211, 239, 291, 294; authors 148–9, 167

Antonius Musa, first-century BC physician and botanist, *De herba vettonica* 155

Apollonius of Tyre, Old English prose text 61, 108

apostles 235, 293; Acts of 167; Gregory the Great as apostle 126; *see also Fates of the Apostles*

Apponius, fifth- to mid-seventh-century scholar, possibly Roman, *In Canticum canticorum* 132

Apuleius; Pseudo-Apuleius, fifth-century author, *Herbarius*, *De taxone liber* 155

Arabic 187

Arator, sixth-century Latin poet 148; *De actibus apostolorum* 167; *Historia apostolica* 18, 149, 151, 155, 157, 1.5

Aratus of Soli, third-century BC philosopher, *Phainomena* 154

Archimedes, third-century BC Greek mathematician 261; Archimedes Palimpsest project 261

argumentum 6, 291

arithmetic 151, 154, 296; *see also* Boethius; *computus*; mathematics

Arius, fourth-century heretic 222, 7.18

Arts and Humanities Research Council (AHRC), UK 280

ash, letter 39, 90

Ashburnham House, fire at 17, 94, 97, 253, 255, 284, 4.4

Asser, ninth-/tenth-century Welsh monk, bishop of Sherborne, *Life* of King Alfred 97

astronomy 112, 150–1, 154–5, 296

Athelstan, king of the English 14, 98, 165, 214

audio digitization 255, 268

Augustine of Canterbury, St, sixth-/seventh-century archbishop of Canterbury, missionary to the Anglo-Saxons 128, 210

Augustine of Hippo, St, fourth-/fifth-century bishop of Hippo, theologian 125, 167; *De adulterinis coniugiis* 132–3; *De civitate Dei* 132; *De consensu Evangelistarum* 132; *De mendacio* 131; *De orando Deo* 132; *De Trinitate* 132; *De videndo Deo* 132–3; *In epistolam Johannis ad Parthos* 132–3; *In Psalmos* 131; *Quaestiones Evangeliorum* 132; sermons 126; Pseudo-Augustine 125; *De Symbolo* 132
Austria 113, 144

B, unknown tenth-/eleventh-century author, *Vita S. Dunstani* 128
badge 31
Bald's *Leechbook*, Old English medical compilation 156n.80
Basil, St, 'the Great', fourth-century archbishop of Caesaria 127
Bath Abbey 71, *3.4*
Battle of Brunanburh, The, Old English poem 98, *2.12*
Battle of Maldon, The, Old English poem 75, 97–8
Bayeux Tapestry 235, 246, 258n.5
Bede (Beda), St., 'The Venerable', seventh-/eighth-century monk of Jarrow 113–14, 131, 148, 150n.69, 167, 192, 204, 218; *De die iudicii* 108, 151, 155; *De orthographia* 143, 145, 150; *De temporibus* 152; *De temporum ratione* 154; *Historia abbatum* 125; *Historia ecclesiastica* 5, 36, 58, 60, 71–2, 75, 95, 118, 121, 126, 128–9, 141–2, 152, 155, 179, 182–3, 187, 192n.23, 194, 200, 202–3, 216, 221, 254, *2.3–2.4*, *3.5–3.6*, *6.21*; *Homiliae in Evangelia* 125, 127; Homily on Benedict Biscop (*Homiliae in Evangelia* I.13) 125, 127; *In Apocalypsin* 131, 133, 156, *5.2*; *In canticum Habacuc* 135n.45; *In epistolas catholicas* 132; *In Evangelium Lucae* 132; *In proverbia Salomonis* 132; *Vita S. Cuthberti* prose 128, 173, *6.7*; *Vita S. Cuthberti* verse 128–30, 170–1, 179, *6.11*; Pseudo-Beda, *Quaestionum super Genesin dialogus* 132
Bede's Death Song, Old English poem 254
Bedford 188
Belgium 113
Benedict Biscop, seventh-century founder of monasteries of Jarrow and Wearmouth 125, 127, 131
Benedict, St, of Nursia, fifth-/sixth-century monastic leader 128, 131, 138, 141, 195; feast of 138; *see also* Benedictine Reform; *Benedictine Rule*
Benedictine order 160, 162, 178
Benedictine Reform 44, 80, 99, 108, 117–18, 138, 140–1, 166, 204, 214, 224–5
Benedictine Rule/*Rule* of St Benedict/*Regula Sancti Benedicti* 50, 65n.4, 99, 125, 127, 138–41, 152, 156, 166, 179–80, 182–3, 231, *2.1*, *2.14*, *5.5*
benedictional 121, 124–5, 224, *2.9*, *7.19–7.21 see also* Æthelwold; Robert of Jumièges
Beowulf, fictional king of the Geats 17n.15
Beowulf, Old English poem 16–17, 92, 95, 106, 189–90, 270, *4.4–4.5*, *8.10*; *see also* Electronic *Beowulf*; Index of Manuscripts UK, England, London, British Library, Cotton Vitellius A.xv
Bethurum, Dorothy, editor 84
Bible 39, 51, 64, 107, 112, 115, 117, 119, 124, 161, 165, 195, 197, 199–200, 224, 293–5; New Testament 107, 115, 132, 163, 180, 195, 233–5, 293, 295; Acts 167; John 165, 212, 222, 293, *7.6*; John 5:10 165; John 19:34 164, *6.3*; Luke 125, 293, *2.2*; Mark 165, 293, *7.12*; Matthew 133, 165, 293; Matthew 1:18 216; Old Testament 81, 107, 115–17, 119, 132–3, 163, 167, 180, 195, 198, 233–6, 295; Daniel 115; Daniel 3:57ff. 135; Ecclesiastes 116; Ecclesiasticus 115–16; Exodus 15:1ff 135; Exodus 22:15 198; Genesis 198, *7.33*, *7.34*; Genesis 33:18–34:31 198; Genesis 39:4 *1.4*; Hexateuch 64, 194, 197 (*see also* Index of Manuscripts UK, London, British Library Cotton Claudius B. iv); Kings 115; Machabees 115; Minor Prophets 115; Proverbs 116, 163n.4; Song of Songs 116; Wisdom 116; *see also* psalms; gospels
bifolium 34–5, 195, 291, 293
Bili of Alet, ninth-century deacon, *Vita S. Machuti* 128, 130
bilingualism 4
bilingual text 6, 34, 49–50, 57–8
Billfrith, anchorite of Lindisfarne, maker of the metal casing of the *Lindisfarne Gospels* 163, 220
binding 5, 19, 26, 31–2, 36–7, 102, 126, 135, 163, 252, 256–7, 291–3, 295–6
Birinus, St, seventh-century bishop of Wessex 128, 130, 142
bit-depth 258, 291
Blicking Homilies 66–7, 83
blot, blotting 54, *4.4*
Boethius, Anicius Manlius Severinus, fifth-/sixth-century Roman philosopher 148, 167; *The Consolation of Philosophy* 149, 167, 151, 155, 170–1, *6.6*; *De institutione arithmetica* 170, *6.5*, *De institutione musica* 155, metres 149; Pseudo-Boethius, *Geometria* 155 *see also* eBoethius Project
Boniface, St, seventh-/eighth-century missionary, bishop of Old Saxony, archbishop of Mainz 21; *Ars grammatica* 145; riddles 150

book supports 26, 257, 292, *8.1*
booklet 4–5, 34, 37, 71, 76–7, 99–100, 135, 140, 291, 296
bookworm 15
Boyle, Leonard E. 281
breviary (portiforium) 134–6, 291
British Isles 33, 41, 206, 294
Brown, Michelle 117n.12, 211–12, 216
Buckingham, Patricia 27
Burkhard, eighth-century bishop of Würzburg 21
Bury St Edmunds Abbey 235
Byrhtferth of Ramsey, tenth-/eleventh-century priest and monk, *Vita S. Ecgwini* 128; *Vita S. Oswaldi* 128
Byrhtnoth, tenth-century ealdorman of Essex 98
Byzantium, Byzantine art 214, 224, 231, 233, 291

Cædmon, seventh-century poet 2, 97; *Cædmon's Hymn*, Old English poem 5, 95, 97, 254, 258n.5, 267–8, 277n.22, 280–1, 283, *8.8–8.9, 8.14*
Caesarius, fifth-/sixth-century bishop of Arles 125; *In Apocalypsin* 132; sermons 127, 131; *sermo* 100 125
caesura 89, 90, 291
calendar 61, 116, 121, 125, 134, 138, 151–2, 232, 238–41, 243, 292, *5.4, 7.28–7.29*; metrical calendar 125, 135
Cambridge Songs (excerpts from Boethius's metres) 149
Cambridge 194–5, 200, 202n.29, 253; University 87, 200–1; Corpus Christi College 22, 159, 190, 200, 203; King's College 194; 22, 200; Parker Library 24; Trinity College 22, 200; University Library 22, 190, 200, 203; Wren Library 24; *see also* Index of Manuscripts UK, England, Cambridge
Camden, William, *Britannia* 186
camera 255–7, 262, 271, 296, *8.1–8.2*
canon (non-monastic clergyman) 3, 141; *Rule for Canons* 141, 191, 201, *6.20*
canon (ecclesiastical rule) 180, 185, 216, 292; Canon Law 140–1
Canon Table 117, 119, 221–2, 224, 292–3, *7.13–7.14*
canonical hours 134, 231, 291, 294
Canterbury 78, 81, 82n.18, 128, 141, 161–2, 166, 174, 178, 182, 210–11, 213, *2.13–2.14, 3.8*; archbishopric 178, 190, *2.10*; Christ Church Cathedral 12, 44, 49, 78, 80, 108, 162, 166, 171, 194, 211, 221, 224, 235, *2.11*; St Augustine's Abbey 6, 80, 101, 160, 170, 173, 178–9
canticle 16, 116, 134–136n.46, 160n.1, 162n.3, 231, 292
Caper, Falvius, second-century Latin grammarian, *De orthographia* 145

capital letters 51, 58, 91, 101, 103, 106, 108, 110, 138, 216, *8.12*; coloured 11, 51, 58, 81, 111; decorated 58, 81, 100; rustic 6, 224, 296, *2.11*; square 100–101, 103, 139, 295–6, *2.9*; *see also* initials
Capitulare monasticum 127, 140
carbon 37
Caroline script 6, 44–6, 49–50, 55, 156, 224, 292, 296, *2.9–2.11, 2.14, 5.1, 5.5*
Carolingian art and culture 6, 12, 14, 23, 162, 178, 204, 206, 208, 214, 224, 231, 235, 237, 241, 291–2, 295; Carolingian authors 144, 151
carpet page 206, 223, 267
Casley, David 98
Cassian, John, fourth-/fifth-century monk and ascetic, *De institutis monachorum* 141; *Collationes* 141
Cassiodorus, Flavius Magnus Aurelius Senator, fifth-/sixth-century statesman, monk, writer, founder of monastery of Vivarium at Squillace, Italy, *De anima* 132–3; *De computo paschali* 153; *De orthographia* 145; *In psalmos* 131–2, 220; *Institutiones* 220
catalogue, digital 264, 269, *8.4*; exhibition 21n.17; iconographic 10, 20; of Anglo-Saxon manuscripts 9, 30, 186, 182; of *Incipits* 9; of library 9, 20, 30, 32, 296
catchword 36–7, 121–122n.30, 292
Cato; Pseudo-Cato, *Disticha Catonis* 148–9, 151
CCD *see* Charge Coupled Device
Cecil, Sir William, Secretary of State 188
cellphone *see* mobile phone
Celtic art and culture *see* Irish art and culture
Celtic countries 118, 292
Cerne Abbas, Dorset 70, 80
chants 121–2, 134, 297
Charge Coupled Device (CCD) 256–7
Charlemagne, Emperor of the Franks, Holy Roman Emperor 44, 122, 224, 292
charm 5, 71–3, 75, 97, 121, *3.6*
charter 8, 60, 237, 292 *see also* Index of Manuscripts UK, London, British Library Cotton Vespasian A viii (*New Minster Charter*)
chemicals 17, 153
Chester-le-Street, Co. Durham 163, 165
Chi-rho, monogram of Christ's name 206, 209, 211, 216, 219, 237, *7.1, 7.4*
choir 120–2, 135, 291
Christ and Satan, Old English poem 107–8
Christ I, II, III, Old English poems 100, 102, 109, 189

Christ, Jesus 185, 234, 236–7, *7.24*, *7.27*; Ascension of 233, 235; Crucifixion of 229–30, 233, 235; Harrowing of Hell by 235; in Majesty 216, 232–3, *7.9*, *7.25*; *Logos* 221–2, *7.14*; Nativity of 233; Temptation of 107; wounds of 233
Christmas 10, 119–20, 122
Chrodegang of Metz, eighth-century bishop of Metz, *Regula canonicorum* 141, 191, 201, *6.20*
chronicle 291 *see also* Anglo-Saxon Chronicle
church, building for worship 3, 112, 138, 195, 204, 227, 237, 291, 293, 295, *7.20*
Church, the Christian institution 3, 39, 59, 63, 124, 163, 165, 178, 186, 190, 200, 204, 214, 223, 228, 234, 237, 292, 295, 297; *see also* Rome
Church Fathers 165, 295
Church of England 59, 186
church year *see* liturgical year
Cicero, Marcus Tullius, second-century Roman orator and philosopher 167; *Aratea* 146, 154; *Invectivae* 154n.77; *Philippicae* 146; *Somnium Scipionis* 146, 154n.77; *Topica* 146
Cilicia 178
Ciula, Arianna 260
classbook 176; *see also* classroom; Index of Manuscripts, UK, Oxford, Bodleian Library Auctarium F.4.32 (*Dunstan's 'classbook'*)
classical authors (Latin) 64, 112, 144, 146–7, 167, 291
classical art (Greek and Roman) 57, 211, 241, 291–2
classroom 4, 112, 134, 144–55, 157; *see also* classbook
Clemoes, Peter, editor 84, 86–7
clergy 56, 115–16, 125–7, 131, 231, 296
Cnut, king of England, Denmark and Norway 13, 143, 236–7, *7.26*
Cnut's Song, Old English poem 98
coat of arms 31
codex 1, 4–5, 18–19, 26, 29, 31–2, 35, 37, 92, 94, 102, 107, 174, 201, 252, 262, 264, 267, 291–3, 295–7; *see also* *Codex Amiatinus*; *Codex Aureus*; *Nowell Codex*; *Southwick Codex*
Codex Amiatinus see Index of Manuscripts Italy, Florence, Biblioteca Medicea Laurenziana, Amiatinus I
Codex Aureus see Index of Manuscripts Sweden, Stockholm, Kungliga Biblioteket (Royal Library) A.135
codicology 2, 28–9, 67, 99, 252, 261, 272, 292
Coleman of Worcester, scribe 82
collation 35–6, 54, 85, 195, 197, 252, 255, 267, 280–4, 292, *8.8–8.9*, *8.14*

collect 116, 134–5, 165, 292
collectar 134, 136, 138, 224, 292; *Durham Ritual* or *Collectar see* Index of Manuscripts UK, England, Durham, Cathedral Library A.IV.19
collector of manuscripts *see* Athelstan, Cotton, L'Isle, Parker
Cologne, Germany 124, 202
colophon 6, 54, 163n.5, 165, 220, 222, 292, *2.11*, *4.6*
colour 4, 6, 9–14, 16, 21, 27, 33–4, 37, 39, 51–2, 57–8, 81, 93, 110–11, 174, 204, 206, 213–15, 227, 229, 235, 237, 246, 258–60, 270, 273, 291, 294, 296
colour-depth *see* bit-depth
column, architectural 211, 227; text layout 6, 8, 34, 51, 53, 58, 83, 162, 164, 176, 181, 273–6, *1.1*, *2.6*, *6.3*, *6.9*, *6.12*
Commemoratio brevis de tonis 120
commentary 34, 53, 60, 131, 133, 144, 146, 151, 154, 220
Commune Sanctorum 120
communion 121–2
computer 243–85
computus 20, 121, 135, 151–2, 157, 292; *see also* Cassiodorus; Helperic of Auxerre; Hrabanus Maurus
confessional texts 64, 108
confessor, priest 70; saint 120, 233, *7.23*
Conner, Patrick, *Anglo-Saxon Exeter* 99–100
Conquest (Norman) *see* Normans
conservation weights 26
contact scanning 256, 258
contents, of a manuscript or art programme 9, 20, 30, 37, 61, 93–4, 101, 108, 113, 133, 233; tables and lists of 28, 32–3, 35, 42, 75, 201, 267, *2.8*
Continent *see* Europe
Copperplate script 296
copy, handwritten, of an earlier manuscript 8, 29, 33, 36, 44, 51, 56, 61–3, 65n.4, 66n.6, 70–1, 77–8, 80, 84–5, 87, 138, 141, 163, 170–5, 178–80, 183, 185, 187–8, 191–2, 194–5, 198, 201, 205, 216n.9, 254, 267, 292
copy, modern, of a manuscript 8, 10, 19–20, 22, 259–60, 263
copying 11–12, 54–5, 57, 66, 67, 69, 71–2, 76–8, 80–1, 95, 106, 108, 111, 167, 174, 198, 210, 220, 270
copyist *see* scribe
copyright 19, 27, 271
copy-text 66n.7–67, 77–8, 80–2, 292
Corbie, France 150
Coronation of Edgar, The, Old English poem 98, *4.2*
correction 53–4, 108, 254, 272–3, 276–7, 283
Cotton, Sir Robert 76, 97, 192, 194–5, 203, 242; Cotton

collection of manuscripts 9, 76, 94, 97, 194, 253 *see also* Index of Manuscripts, UK, London, British Library
Cotton, Sir Thomas 203
cover, of book 17–18, 31–2, 61, 149, 223, 243, *1.5*
cradle *see* book supports
Craig-McFeely, J. 260
crayon 59
Crediton 99
cross, in art 6, 13–14, *1.1*, *7.3*, *7.26*; prayers to 229
crucifixion 16, 107, 223, 229–30, 233, 235, 249, *7.22*, *7.35*
curse 32
cursive script 41, 44, 51, 292–4, 296
Cuthbert, St, seventh-century bishop of Lindisfarne 14, 165, 214; *Life of* 128, 130, 142, 170, 173, 179, *6.7*, *6.11*
Cuthswitha, seventh-/eighth-century abbess, probably of Inkberrow *1.6*
cycle of illustrations 205, 222, 233–5, 241–2, 244, *7.24*
Cynewulf, unidentified ninth-/tenth-century Anglo-Saxon poet 102
Cyprian, third-century bishop of Carthage, *Ad Quirinum testimonia* 132, 153
Cyprianus Gallus, fifth-century poet, *Pentateuchos* 132

damage to manuscripts 15–19, 25, 29, 31, 37, 53, 93–4, 97, 99–104, 107, 171, 175, 252, 257, 260–1, 272, 277, 281–2, 292, *4.4*, *4.4*, *8.3*
Danes *see* Vikings
Daniel, Old English poem 107
dashes, as glosses 173
date, of manuscripts, texts, binding, purchase 30–3, 36, 38, 54, 57, 89, 95, 97–8, 102, 104, 106–7, 114n.4, 117, 120, 123, 126, 130, 134, 141–2, 146n.64, 161, 176, 204, 206, 209, 211, 224, 278–9; of Easter 151–2, 194, 292; of image creation 263, 271; of Pentecost 152n.72
dating conventions 30
David, king of Israel, psalmist 6, 131–2, 216, 231, *7.8*
De nominibus stellarum 154
De septiformi spiritu see Wulfstan
Death of Edgar, The, Old English poem 98, *4.2*
decretal 180, 292
dedication, of church 227, 229, *7.20*
dedication page 208
Defensor, seventh-century monk of Ligugé, *Liber scintillarum* 165–6
deletion 18, 254, 273, 278, 283
Denewulf, bishop of Winchester 197

Deor, Old English poem 100
Descent into Hell, The, Old English poem 100
desktop publishing 255
Deutsche Forschungsgemeinschaft (DFG), Germany 280
dialect 52, 102, 113; Kentish 80; Mercian 160; Northumbrian 97; West Saxon 6, 97
dialectic 144, 150, 297
dictionaries 15, 158, 181, 188–189n.21, 190–1
digital edition 11, 101, 284, *8.14*
digital file 255–60, 262, 293
digital image 29–30, 93, 246n.39, 258–61, 263, 293, *8.6*
Digital Image Archive of Medieval Music manuscripts (DIAMM) 260
Digital Medievalist Community of Practice 279
digitization 5, 28, 252, 255–64, 273, 279, 284, 293, *8.1*–*8.2*, *8.4*, *8.6*, *8.11*
dimensions 9, 33, 195
diminuendo 58, 223, 292, *1.7*
Dinah, daughter of Jacob, Old Testament figure 198
Dionysius Exiguus, sixth-century monk, *Epistola de ratione paschali* 152
display manuscript 93, 210, 223–4, 229, 237–8
Dissolution of monasteries 60, 186, 190
Divine Office 160, 165, 292–5
Dobbie, Elliott Van Kirk, editor, *The Manuscripts of Cædmon's Hymn* 281; the Anglo-Saxon Poetic Records 88, 281
Donatus, Aelius, fourth-century Latin grammarian, *Ars maior* 144–5; *Ars minor* 151; commentaries on 144
donor, of manuscript 32, 107; portrait of 14, *7.35*
doodle 81
dots, as art 58, 233–5, *2.2*; as corrections 164n.6; as glosses 172–4; as punctuation 100–1, 296 (*see also punctus*); pixels 258
drawing (illustration) 6–8, 10–12, 14, 16, 23, 34, 57–8, 108, 148n.68, 154, 162, 212, 227, 229–30, 233–7, 240–3, 246, 249, 294, 296
Dream of the Rood, The, Old English poem 101–4, *4.3*
drypoint, dry point 93, 173n.13, 174, 177, 293, 297, *6.10*; *see also* hard point; stylus
Dunstan, St, tenth-century archbishop of Canterbury 44, 138, 204; Dunstan's 'classbook' *see* Index of Manuscripts UK, England, Oxford, Bodleian Library, Auctarium F.4.32; *Vita S. Dunstani* 128
Durham (*De Situ Dunhelmi*), Old English poem 98
Durham 80; *see also* Index of Manuscripts UK, England, Durham, Cathedral Library

Eadfrith, seventh-century bishop of Lindisfarne, scribe and probable artist of the *Lindisfarne Gospels* 163, 220
Eadwig Basan, scribe 44, 221-2, 224, *2.11, 7.13-7.18*; *Eadwig Gospels see* Index of Manuscripts Germany, Hanover, Kestner Museum, W.M. XXIa, 36
eagle 211-12
Ealhswith, queen to Alfred 241
Eanflæd, queen to Oswy of Northumbria 152
Early English Manuscripts in Facsimile 30, 86n.31
Early English Text Society 86n.31, 93
Easter 82, 120, 151-2, 154, 192n.23, 194, 292; Easter Tables 151
eBoethius project 261, *8.3*
ecclesiastical year *see* liturgical year
Echternach, Luxembourg 152n.75; *Echternach Gospels see* Index of Manuscripts France, Paris, Bibliothèque Nationale, lat. 9389
Edgar, king of England 44, 204, 229, 237, 291, *7.27*; 'Edgar's Establishment of Monasteries' 227; *see also Coronation of Edgar*; *Death of Edgar*
editing practice 82-8, 261n.10, 292
edition 1-3, 5, 9-11, 18, 20, 27-9, 34, 52, 83-9, 91-2, 95, 101, 107, 110-11, 122, 188-189n.21, 190, 195, 197, 200, 202-3, 252, 254, 258n.5, 263, 267-9, 277-8, 280-1, 284
Edition Production Technology software 261
Edward, 'the Confessor', king of England 78, 114n.3
Egbert, missionary 192n.23, 194
Electronic Beowulf 104, 264, 270, 281, *8.5, 8.10*
Elene, Old English poem 101-2
Elizabeth I, queen of England 188
Elphinston, John 98
Ely 182
emendation 8, 87, 282
endorsement 8, 293
endpaper 18, 293
epic literature 92, 113
Epiphany 138
episcopal letter 152
epistle 121, 125, 293-4
erasure 6-7, 53, 93, 202n.29, 278, *1.1, 4.4*
Essex 98
eth, letter 39, 90, 171
Ethilwald, eighth-century bishop of Lindisfarne, binder of the *Lindisfarne Gospels* 163, 220
etymology 144
Euclid, fourth-century BC Greek mathematician, *Euclides latinus* 155

Europe 3, 72, 162, 167, 214, 218, 231
Eutyches, sixth-century Greek grammarian, *Ars de uerbo* 145
evangelary 224, 293
Evangelists 117, 119, 217, 220, 222; evangelist portrait 210-11, 218-21 (*see also* John; Luke; Mark; Matthew); evangelist symbol 211-12, 219-20 (*see also* eagle)
Eve, biblical first woman 242, 249
exegesis 113, 125, 130-135n.45, 141, 150, 157, 205, 293
exemplar 54, 57-8, 60, 71, 102, 142, 167, 174-5, 180, 206n.2, 241, 253, 293
Exeter 90; Cathedral 99; Dean and Chapter Library 93; *see also* Index of Manuscripts UK, England, Exeter, Cathedral, Dean and Chapter Library 3501 (*Exeter Book*), 3507, FMS/1,2,2a
Exeter Book on DVD 268
Exhortation to Christian Living, An, Old English poem 108, 111, *4.6*
Exodus, Old English poem 107
explicit 66n.7, 107, 293
expositio hymnorum 135, 146, 157, 293
eXtensible Markup Language *see* XML

facsimile 1, 7-11, 20-2, 29-30, 86, 92-3, 101-2, 111, 187n.20, 195, 233n.27, 242, 246n.39, 254, 258-9, 263, 267-8, 270, 272-4, 280, *2.4*
Farmon, glossator, priest of Harewood 165
Fates of the Apostles, The, Old English poem 101-3
feast days 138, 292; *see also* Benedict; Christmas; Easter; Epiphany; Machutus; Mary; Pentecost
Felix of Crowland, eighth-century author, *Vita S. Guthlaci* 128
fibre optic lighting *see* light
Flanders 143, 214 *see also* Judith of Flanders
Flash software 265, 267, 291
flesh side (of parchment) 33, 35
flyleaf 32, 82, 293, *3.4*
Folcard, monk of Saint Bertin, abbot of Thorney, *Vita S. Botulphi* 128
foliation 35, 37, 293, 295
Ford, Alun 26n.20
Fourth Lateran Council 185
fragments of manuscripts 18, 29, 31-2, 66n.7, 70, 89, 111-12, 114-16, 120-4, 126, 130, 134-6, 138-139n.49, 142-144n.58, 146, 148-50, 154n.76-155, 223, 253-5
frame 16, 34, 97, 174-5, 213, 235, 237, 243-4, 297, *6.8, 7.19-7.21, 7.25, 7.27, 7.31*

France 17, 113, 117, 123, 126, 133, 135, 150, 152n.75, 154, 162, 170, 214, 292, 294
Frankish Empire 44, 292
Freising, Germany 23
Frisia 23
Frithegod of Canterbury, tenth-century Frankish scholar *Breviloquium Vitae Wilfridi* 128
Frithestan, tenth-century deacon, scribe, later bishop of Winchester 176
Fulbert, bishop of Chartres, tenth-/eleventh-century scholar 125

Gameson, Richard 11
Geats, fictional Scandinavian people 17n.15
genealogical texts 64, 194
Genesis, Old English poem 107, 242
geography 112, 155–6, 241
geometry 151, 155, 296; geometric art 204, 206
Germanicus, Claudius Caesar, first-century BC/first-century AD soldier and translator, *Aratea* 154
Germanus, St 179
Germany 21, 113, 118, 124, 135, 143, 280, 292
GIF (.gif) 259, 293
Gifts of Men, The, Old English poem 100
Gildas, fifth-/sixth-century Welsh priest, *De excidio Britanniae* 143
GIMP *see* Image Processing Software
Glastonbury Abbey 44, 81, 90, 182n.16, *2.10*
Gloria, liturgical prayer 119, 122
Gloria, Old English poem 109
gloss 5–6, 8, 10, 16n.14, 38, 42, 45, 60, 112, 116, 134–5, 146, 148–50, 157–203, *3.2*, *5.6*, *6.2*, *6.4*; accentual 53; construe mark 173–4, 292; continuous 49, 65n.4, 117, 160–6, *2.13*, *3.8*, *5.1*, *6.2–3*; drypoint or scratched 7, 9, 93, 177–8, *6.10*; grammatical 53; interlinear 2, 6, 34, 53, 58, 116, 138, 147, 160–6, *2.8*, *4.4*, *5.3*, *6.1–6.3*, *6.15*; interrogative 53; marginal 2, 53, 58; lexical 168; suppletive 169; syntactical 53, 17–4, *6.6–7*
glossary 34, 50, 53, 63, 143–6, 150, 158, 178–81; *see also* Ælfric
glossator 9, 116, 159; *see also* Aldred; Farmon; Owun; Tremulous Hand of Worcester
glue 15, 18, 149, 291, 295, *1.5*
Gneuss, Helmut, *Handlist of Anglo-Saxon Manuscripts* 9, 30, 112, 114nn.3–5, 115–17, 120, 122–8, 135
gold 14, 204, 213, 229, 236, *7.36*; gold ink 57, 211, 237; gold leaf 57

goose feather 37
Goscelin of Canterbury, eleventh-century Flemish monk, *Lives* of St Æthelburga, Augustine of Canterbury, Archbishop Deusdedit, Abbot Hadrian, Kenelm, Archbishop Laurentius, Letardus, Archbishop Mellitus, Mildred, Archbishop Theodore, and Wulfhilda 128
gospel book 39, 51, 71, 117–19, 216–18, 221, 223–4, 237, 251, 293, 295
gospels 71, 114n.5, 117–19, 121, 131, 163–5, 167, 197, 205, 217, 292–3; *see also* Bible; *Codex Aureus*; Eadwig Basan; Echternach; Judith of Flanders; Lindisfarne; *MacRegol* (or *Rushworth*) *Gospels*; Rheims; *West Saxon Gospels* and Index of Manuscripts
gradual 120n.17–122, 134
grammar 112, 158, 183, 185, 278, 297; grammatical texts 143–5; *see also* Ælfric; Boniface; Donatus; Eutyches; Priscian
Greek (language) 154, 219
Gregory I, 'the Great', St, sixth-century pope 216; *Cura Pastoralis* 78, 119n.14, 160, 182–3, 201, *2.8*; *Dialogues* 66n.6, 182–3; *Homiliae in evangelia* 125–6, 130; *Homiliae in Ezechielem* 125–6, 131; *Moralia in Job* 132
Gregory of Tours, sixth-century bishop of Tours, *De virtutibus S. Martini* 125, 128; *Historia Francorum* 125, 142–3
greyscale 258
gum 37
Guthlac A and *B*, Old English poems 100
Guthrum, Viking chief 188, *6.14*

Hadrian, sixth-/seventh-century abbot of St Augustine's, Canterbury 128, 178
hagiography 142, 294
Haimo of Auxerre, ninth-century monk 125, 127
hair side (of parchment) 33, 35
half-sheet 36, 294
Half-uncials 39, 41, 294, 297, *2.2*
hard point 6, 34, 294; *see also* drypoint; stylus
Harewood 165
Harley collection, British Library 9; *see also* Index of Manuscripts, UK, London
Haugen, Odd Einar 281
Hell 235, 237, 249; *see also* Christ: Harrowing of Hell; Descent into Hell
Helperic of Auxerre, ninth-century scholar, *De computo* 152
Helsinki, Finland 21

Hemming of Worcester, scribe 65, 67
Henry VIII, king of England 186
Hermannus Archidiaconus, ?eleventh-century Anglo-Saxon author, *Miracula S. Eadmundi* 128
Hiberno-Saxon art *see* Insular art
history 2, 4, 37, 67, 86–7, 93, 102, 107, 112, 141–3, 188, 192, 201, 203, 223, 225, 252, 272, 282
hole 15–16
Homiletic Fragment I, Old English poem 101, *4.3*
homiliary 16, 68, 75, 124–6, 182, 191, 294, *6.19*
homily 5, 23, 61, 64, 67, 69–70, 72, 75–6, 86, 108–9, 124–7, 130–1, 157, 182, 187, 197, 199, 294, 297, *3.2–3.3, 3.5–3.6*; *see also* Abbo of Saint-Germain-des-Prés; Ælfric; Ambrosius Autpertus; Augustine of Hippo; Basil; Bede; Blickling Homilies; Caesarius; Fulbert; Gregory I; Haimo of Auxerre; Origenes; Paul the Deacon; Vercelli Homilies; Wulfstan
Horace, Quintus Horatius Flaccus, first-century BC Latin poet and philosopher, *Carmina* 146
horologium 125
Hrabanus Maurus, eighth-/ninth-century abbot of Fulda, archbishop of Mainz, *De computo* 153; *De laudibus sanctae crucis* 151; *In epistolas Pauli* 125, 132; *In Hester* 132; *In Judith* 132; *In Matthaeum* 132
HTML *see* HyperText Markup Language
Hucbald of Saint-Amand, ninth-/tenth-century monk, *De harmonica instituone* 155
human decoration 58, 227
Husband's Message, The, Old English poem 92, 100–1
Hwætberht (Eusebius), Anglo-Latin author, possibly seventh-/eighth-century, riddles 150
Hyginus, Gaius Julius, first-century BC/first-century AD Latin author, *Astronomica* 152, 154
hymns 130, 134–5, 144, 146, 162n.3, 165, 189, 211, 293–4; *see also* Cædmon; *expositio hymnorum*; Sedulius
hymnal 134–5, 157, 224, 294
HyperText Markup Language (HTML) 272, 294

image processing 270–1, 293
incipit 9, 121, 212, 219, 294, *7.6, 7.12*
index 32–3, 35, 64n.3, 125, 158, 201–2, 275, 277, 280, *8.13*
initial 38, 88, 103; coloured 6, 11–12, 34, 58, 81, 110–11, 294, *1.2, 2.1, 4.6*; decorated 2, 20, 58, 138, 204, 216–16, 223–4, 233, *5.3*; enlarged 28, 51, 101, 103–4, 223, 292, *4.7, 8.10*; historiated 160, 215–16, 294, *7.8*; inhabited 58, 103, 215, 294, *1.7, 7.7*; marginal 6
initials, of owner 31
ink 16–17, 35, 37, 53, 58, 164, 173n.13, 174, 178, 202, 255, 261, 277, 293; black 37; coloured 6, 9–10, 12, 37, 52, 57–8, 161–2, 165, 211, 214, 296, *3.6*; ink drawing 14, 195, 204, 214, 229; ink ruling 34; recipes for 37
Inkberrow, Worcester 21
Innocent III, pope 185
Insular manuscripts 34–5, 51–2, 204, 205n.1, 216, 221, 223, 231, 233; Insular art 21, 206, 209, 211–12, 223, 231–3, 235, 292, 294, *1.7*; Insular script 6, 37, 41–2, 110, 113, 156, 292, 294–5, 297, *2.1–2.3, 2.5–2.6, 2.10, 5.1–5.3, 5.5*
interlace 39, 58, 103
International Society of Anglo-Saxonists (ISAS) 21
introit 121–2, 294
Iona 118, 192n.23, 194, 294
Ireland 38, 118, 165, 206, 292, 294
Irish (Celtic) art and culture 57, 118, 206, 209, 292, 294
Irish Sea 3
Irish script 42, 223
iron sulphate 37
Isidore of Seville, sixth-/seventh-century bishop of Seville, *De natura rerum* 153; *Etymologiae* 130, 133, 145–6, 153; *Quaestiones in Vetus Testamentum* 132–3
Israel the Grammarian, tenth-century scholar, *De arte metrica* 133
Italic script 51, 190, 294, 296
Italy 17, 21, 80, 94, 113, 115, 123, 131, 143, 170, 208, 292, 294
ivories 31

James, M.R., palaeographer and ghost-story writer 59
Jarrow, Northumbrian monastery 2, 97, 115, 125, 209–10, *2.3*
Jerome, St, fourth-century scholar and translator 142, 263; *Altercatio Luciferani et Orthodoxi* 132; *De viris illustribus* 153; *In Danielem* 132; *In Ecclesiasten* 21, 132; *In Evangelium Matthaei* 132; *In epistolas Pauli* 132; *Tractatus in Psalmos* 132; Gallican Psalter 6; *Vita S. Malchi* 128; *Vita S. Pauli Eremitae* 128, 130; Pseudo-Jerome, *Breviarium in Psalmos* 125, 132
jewels 31
Johannes Chrysostomus, St, fourth-/fifth-century archbishop of Constantinople, *De muliere Cananaea, De reparatione lapsi, De compunctione cordis* 132–3
Johannes Constantinopolitanus 132–3
Johannes Diaconus of Rome, ninth-century scholar, *Vita S. Gregorii* 128
John, St, 'the Evangelist' 211–12, 219, 222, 230, 233, *2.11, 7.2, 7.5, 7.17- 7.18, 7.22, 7.35 see also* Bible

Joscelyn, John, chaplain and secretary to Archbishop Matthew Parker, lexicographer 190–2, 194, 202, 6.16
Josephus, Flavius, first-century Jewish historian, *De bello Judaico* 143
JPEG (.jpg) 14n.11, 259, 293–4
Judas Iscariot, biblical figure 172
Judith, daughter of Charles the Bald, wife of Æthelwulf 224
Judith of Flanders, wife of Earl Tostig of Northumbria 224–51; *Judith Gospels see* Index of Manuscripts USA, New York, Pierpont Morgan Library 709
Judith, Old English poem 92, 104, 106
Juliana (*The Passion of St Juliana*), Old English poem 100, 102
Junius, Francis, seventeenth-century scholar 107
Justinus, Marcus Junianus, Latin historian, date uncertain, epitome of Pompeius Trogus's *Historiae Philippicae* 143
Juvenal, Decimus Junius, first-/second-century Roman poet, *Satirae* 146, 148; Glosses on the *Satirae* 146
Juvencus, Caius Vettius Aquilinus, fourth-century Spanish priest and poet 148; *Evangelium libri quattuor* (*Libri Evangeliorum*) 133, 149, 167

Kent 161, 210, 297
Ker, Neil Ripley, *A Catalogue of Manuscripts containing Anglo-Saxon* 9, 16n.13, 30, 86, 182
Kiernan, Kevin, editor 17, 93, 104, 261, 281
Kim, Susan 242

L'Isle, William, Fellow of King's College, Cambridge 194–5, 197–9, 202, 6.17–6.19; *A Saxon Treatise Concerning the Old and New Testament* 195
La Coruna, Spain, SELIM conference at 85
labours of the months 239–41, 7.28–7.29
Lachmann, Karl, Lachmannian stemma 85
Lactantius, Lucius Caecilius Firmianus, fourth-century Christian apologist and poet 148; *De ave phoenice* 149
Laidcenn Mac Baith of Cluain-ferta-Molua, seventh-century Irish scholar, *Egloga de Moralibus in Job* 132
Lambarde, William 188–9
Lambeth Palace, London residence of the archbishop of Canterbury 190 *see also* Index of Manuscripts UK, London, Lambeth Palace Library

Lantfred of Winchester, tenth-century Frankish author, *Translatio et miracula S. Swithuni* 128
laptop 15, 24
Laud, William, archbishop of Canterbury 194
law 19, 60, 64, 108 *see also* Alfred; Wulfstan
Lea, River 188
lead 26, 34, 201
leather 26, 31, 34, 291, 295
lectionary 122, 294
lector 120–2, 178
Leeds 165
legendary 127
Leland, John, antiquary 186
lemma 53, 116, 146, 166n.9, 168–9, 178–9, 181, 186, 282, 294
Lent 120, 152
Leo I, pope 167
Leofric, bishop of Exeter 99; *Leofric Missal see* Index of Manuscripts UK, England, Oxford, Bodleian Library, Bodley 579
lessons 120, 134, 292, 296
letter (character) 1–2, 6, 19, 22, 36, 39, 41, 44–6, 50–5, 58, 70, 77–8, 81, 87, 90–1, 95, 102–4, 138, 156, 164n.6, 170–3, 180–1, 184–5, 189, 192, 212, 215, 223, 276, 291–2, 294–7, 2.2, 2.4, 2.9, 2.14, 4.4, 6.6, 8.12; *see also* initial; script
letter (epistle) 131, 140, 152, 194, 200n.28, 292–3; *see also* Ælfric; Radulf
liber vitae 236, 294, *New Minster Liber Vitae see* Index of Manuscripts UK, England, London, British Library, Stowe 944
Lichfield 211
Life of saint *see Vita*
ligature 41, 44, 55, 294, 297, 2.4
lighting 1, 8, 16, 19, 281, 252, 257; charge coupled device 256; fibre optic cold light 24, 29, 177–8, 293, 6.10; multispectral imaging 261; video spectral comparator 24; ultra violet 24, 261, 295; X-ray fluorescence 261
Lindisfarne 163, 165; *Lindisfarne Gospels see* Index of Manuscripts UK, England, London, British Library, Cotton Nero D.iv
line break 95, 278, 281–2, 4.12
list 277, 283; ANSAX 263; bulleted 272–3; chapter 179, 2.11; donations 99; episcopal 37; glossary 63, 146, 178–80, 293; lexicographical 191; liber vitae 236–7, 294; martyrology 178, 295; of classical authors 146; of contents 28, 32–3; of exigetical and theological texts 131–2; of Roman emperors 140; of saints' lives

128; of scriptors and their work 65n.5; of years *3.7*; papal 37; regnal 37, 237; relics 71; TEI 279n.24; *see also* Gneuss; Ker
litany 116, 134, 211, 294
liturgy, liturgical text 64, 112–13, 116–17, 119–27, 138, 151–2, 157, 160, 166n.9, 223–4, 231, 294, 296, 297, *5.1–5.3*
liturgical year 61, 151–2, 165, 291, 292–4, 296
Lock, A. 260
Loire, France 149
London 81; British Library 22; *see also* Index of Manuscripts UK, London
Lord's Prayer II, Old English poem 11, 111
Lot's wife, biblical figure 169
Lucretius, Titus Lucretius Carus, first-century BC Roman poet/philosopher 85
Luke, St, Evangelist, 222, *7.17*; *see also* Bible
lunar month 152
Luxembourg 113
lyric 113

machine-readable text 255–6
Machutus, St, sixth-century Welsh bishop of Aleth 130; feast of 130
Macregol Gospels see Index of Manuscripts UK, England, Oxford, Bodleian Library, Auctarium D.2.19
Macromedia Flash 265
magnifying glass 15, 29
majuscule 39, 51, 58, 294–7
Maldon, Essex, battle of 75, 97; *see also Battle of Maldon, The*
Malmesbury 108
Manchester database of script and spellings 28, 65n.5, 70n.12
manumission 71, 295
manuscripts see Index of Manuscripts pp. 296–301
margin, construction and original use of 6, 28, 34, 77, 103–4, 110, 235, *3.7, 4.4*
marginalia, additions placed in manuscript margins 2, 5, 18, 32, 52–3, 58–60, 64, 70–2, 75, 80–2, 85, 97, 102, 121, 151, 159, 167–171, 174, 184–5, 187–9, 192, 194, 197–202, 211, 254, 272–3, 276, 293, 296–7. *2.12, 3.5, 3.7, 6.5, 6.18–6.19, 6.21*
Mark, St, Evangelist 222, *7.16 see also* Bible
mark-up systems 252, 256, 268–9, 272–82, 293–5, 297
Martial, Marcus Valerius Martialis, first-century Spanish Latin poet, *Epigrammata* 146, 148
Martianus Capella, fifth-century African Roman writer 151, *De nuptiis Philologiae et Mercurii* 143, 149, 151–2, 154
Martin, St, 125; *see also* Gregory of Tours; Sulpicius Severus
martyrologies 127, 178, 295, *6.10*
Martyrology, Old English 121
Marvels of the East, see *Wonders of the East*
Mary, St, Virgin 8, 228–9, 233, 235–7, *7.22, 7.26, 7.35*; cult of 228–9; Dormition of 228, *7.21*; feast of the Purification of 138; hymn to 189
Mass 113, 119–22, 126–7, 133–4, 138, 157, 160, 216, 291, 293–7
mathematics 112, 170 see also arithmetic; *computus*
Mathilda, tenth-century abbess of Essen 143
Matthew, St, Evangelist 219, 221, *7.10–7.11, 7.15 see also* Bible
Maxims I, Old English poem 100
medicine 60, 64, 72, 112–13, 121, 155–6; *see also* Quintus Serenus
Mediterranean culture 210, 291
Melbourne, University of, Ductus Project, Evellum software 20
membrum disiectum, membra disiecta 114–16, 118, 120, 121n.24, 123, 124n.32, 127, 130, 135, 140, 142–6, 148n.67, 150, 295
Memoriale qualiter 140
memory, memorisation 3–4, 11, 116, 118, 134, 205; memory card 255
Mercia 161, 210–12, 297, *2.1; see also* Æthelbald; dialect
Merovingian cursive script 44
metal 31, 34, 38, 93, 163, 174, 177, 297; ornamental metalwork 204, 206, 209, 295
metrics 144
microfiche 1, 30, 86n.31, 233n.27
microfilm 1, 8–9, 19, 25, 223n.27, 257–60
Microsoft Word 255, 273
Middle English language 181–5, 197, 200, 280; Middle English period 51, 123, 183
miniature 34, 205, 211, 216–17, 224, 227, 229, 231, 233, 235–7, 244, 246, 249, 251; *see also* drawing
minims 45, 49, 54, 291–2, 295
Minster-in-Thanet, monastery 211
minuscule 39, 41–4, 58, 212, 295, 297; Anglo- (English) Caroline 6, 44–5, 292, *2.9, 2.11*; Anglo-Saxon 22, 42, 44–5, 49–50, 100–101, 106, 110, 291, *1.7, 2.7–2.8, 2.12–2.14*; Caroline 44–5, 49–50, 224, *2.10*; Insular 6, 31, 41, 292, 294, *2.3, 2.5–2.6*; Protogothic 51; vernacular 6
mirror 15, 18; mirror-image 16, *1.5*

mise-en-page (page design) 100, 110–11, 255, 272, 295
missal 120–4; *see also* Index of Manuscripts France, Rouen, Bibliothèque Municipale 274 (Y.6) (*Missal of Robert of Jumièges*); UK, England, Oxford, Bodleian Library, Bodley 579 (*Leofric Missal*)
missionaries 3, 60, 117, 204; Anglo-Saxon missions to the Continent 23, 42, 113, 118, 120, 131, 143, 156, 291, *1.6*; Italian to England 38, 115, 118, 131, 210; Iro-Scottish to Northumbria 38–9, 115, 156, 292, 294; *see also* Boniface; Egbert; Germanus
Modoin, ninth-century bishop of Autun, *Ecloga* 155
monasticism 2, 4, 60, 64–5, 77, 80, 98–100, 102, 108, 112, 119, 134–5, 138, 146, 160–1, 163, 166, 182, 186, 194, 209, 223, 291, 293–5; *see also* Æthelwold; Benedictine Reform; Benedictine Rule; *Capitulare monasticum*; *Memoriale qualiter*; Smaragdus
monk 1, 3, 56, 65n.4, 81, 94, 112, 115, 118–19, 127, 131, 134–5, 139, 141, 157, 160, 166, 178, 192n.23, 293, 296, *1.2*; *see also* Defensor; Eadwig Basan; Hadrian; Theodore
Monkwearmouth *see* Wearmouth
Mont-Saint-Michel, France 143
Morris, Richard, editor 83
Muir, Bernard, editor, *The Exeter Anthology of Old English Poetry* 93, 99–100; *MS Junius 11* 11, 94, 108
music 34, 112, 151, 155, 291, 296–7; *Musica Enchiriadis* (anonymous) 155; *see also* Boethius; Digital Image Archive of Medieval Music
MyPictureMarc by Digimarc 272n.20

Napier, Arthur, editor 83, 85
National Endowment for the Humanities (NEH), USA 280
Nemesianus, Marcus Aurelius Olympus, third-century Latin poet, *Cynegetica* 156
Netherlands, The 113
nib 37, 54
Night Office (Nocturns) *see* Office
non-contact scanning 256–7, *8.1–8.2*
Normans, pre-Conquest 78; Norman Conquest 23, 64, 112, 126, 127n.36, 143–4, 160n.1, 162, 181, 224; Norman culture and period 23, 71, 82, 114n.4, 130, 206, 145, 150n.70, 235; Norman script 45
Northumbria 115, 118, 131, 163, 204, 208–9, 211, 223, 251, 292, 294, *2.2–2.3*
Nowell, Laurence, antiquarian 188–90, *4.4, 6.15*
Nowell Codex see Index of Manuscripts UK, England, London, British Library, Cotton Vitellius A.xv (*Beowulf Manuscript*)

O'Donnell, Daniel Paul 95
oak galls 37
offertory 121–2, 295
Office 113, 116, 119n.16, 127, 133, 157, 160, 165, 292–6; Daily Office 134–8; Friday Office 135n.45; Night Office 126, 295; Sunday Office 135; Thursday Office 135
offset 15–16, 18, 295, *1.5*
Ohlgren, Thomas, *Iconographic catalogue* 10, 20
Ohthere, voyager 155
Old Saxony 23
Optantius (Optatianus) Porphyrius Publilius, fourth-century Latin poet, *Carmina* 146
Orchard, Andy, *Pride and Prodigies* 243
Origenes, second-/third-century Egyptian theologian, *Homiliae in Genesin*, *Homiliae in Exodum*, *Homiliae in Leviticum* 130
Orosius, Paulus, fourth-/fifth-century Spanish (now Portugal) Christian historian, 'de situ Babylonis' 142; *Historiae aduersus paganos* 142, 155, 180–1, 187
orthography 52, 144, 200, 295
Osbern of Canterbury, eleventh-century monk of Canterbury and Bec, *Vita et translatio S. Alphegi*, *Vita S. Dunstani* 128
Oswald, St, tenth-century bishop of Worcester, archbishop of York 44, 138, 161
Oswald, St, king of Northumbria 118, 130, 142
Oswy, king of Northumbria 152
Ottonian art 204, 214, 291, 295
Ouse, River 188
overline 55, 295
Ovid, Publius Ovidius Naso, first-century BC/first-century AD Latin poet, *Amores* 146; *Ars amatoria* 146, 148, *2.10*; *Metamorphoses* 146–7
owners of manuscripts 7, 16, 23, 31–2, 71, 77, 82, 97, 112–13, 158, 163, 186, 189, 192, 251, 272, *1.6*
Owun, glossator 165
Oxford 253; Bodleian Library 22, 27, 94, 107; Bodleian Library digitization project 264; Duke Humphrey Library 94; Oxford University Press 93; *see also* Index of Manuscripts, UK, Oxford

pagination 35, 37, 293, 295
palimpsest 24, 112, 114, 120, 126, 148, 261, 295
pandect 115, 295
paper 1, 16, 19, 27, 31–3, 35, 195, 197, 263, 295, 297; *see also* endpaper
Parallel Segmentation Method 283

parchment 1, 9, 15–16, 18–19, 29, 31–5, 54, 60, 67, 70, 75, 93, 99–100, 158, 174, 177–8, 195, 211, 262, 291–7
Paris, siege of 143, 178; *see also* Index of Manuscripts France, Paris
Parker, John, lexicographer 59, 191
Parker, Matthew, archbishop of Canterbury, Master of Corpus Christi College, Cambridge 7, 59, 190, 192, 203
Paschasius Radbertus, eighth-/ninth-century abbot of Corbie, *De corpore et sanguine Domini* 132
passio 124, 295
pastedown 18, 31–2, 112, 114, 149, 291, 293, 295, 297, *1.5*
Pastoral Care 83, 160, 182–3, 201; *see also* Alfred; Gregory I
Pater Noster, Old English poem 110, *4.7*
Paterius, sixth-/seventh-century bishop of Brescia, *De expositione Veteris et Novi Testamenti* 132
patrons, patronage 38, 108, 204–5, 224–5, 227, 231, 241, 246, 249, 251, 291
patron saints 227, 237
Paul the Deacon, (Paulus Diaconus), eighth-century monk and historian 125; Homiliary 125–6
Paul, St, apostle 125
Paul, St, 'the hermit' *see* Jerome
Pavia, Italy 167
paving letters 170, 172, 295
PDF *see* Portable Document Format
pedagogy 157, 160, 167
Pelagius, fourth-/fifth-century monk and heretic, *In epistolam Pauli ad Philippenses* 132; Pelagian heresy 179
penance 64, 102, 111, 231, 295
pencil 15, 35
penitential 70, 108–9, 140, 182, 295
Pentecost 120, 152n.72
pen-trial 81
per cola et commata 51, 295
Perigrinus, scribe 23, *1.7*
Persius, Aulus Persius Flaccus, first-century Latin poet, *Satirae* 146, 148; Commentary on the *Satirae* 146
Peter, St, apostle 236–7
Peterborough 192; *Peterborough Chronicle* 192 *see also* Anglo-Saxon Chronicle, The: MS E
Petrocellus, medical writer, thought to be eleventh-century but possibly earlier (ninth-century?) 156
Philippus Presbyter, fifth-century scholar, disciple of St Jerome, *Commentarii in librum Job* 132
philosophy 113; *see also* Boethius
Phoenix, The, Old English poem 100

photograph 7–8, 10–11, 15–16, 19, 22, 25, 27, 29, 159, 254; digital photography 19, 29, 255–8, 270, 274, 293, 296; ultra violet 16, 261; under fibre-optic light 178, *6.10*; X-ray fluorescence 261
pigment 201, 204, 261
pixels 258–9, 291, 296
place names 91, 186, 188
plain text 255
Pliny the Elder, Gaius Plinius Secundus, Roman soldier, administrator and scholar, *Naturalis historia* 146, 152
plummet *see* lead
pocket-book 68, 70, 296
Pompeius Trogus, Gnaeus, fourth-century BC Latin historian, *Historiae Philippicae* 143
pontifical 112, 121, 123–4, 224, 296
Portable Document Format (PDF) 277, 295
prayer 64, 116, 119–20, 133–4, 165, 211, 229–31, 233, 237, 292, 294–6, *2.5, 7.7*; *see also* Lord's Prayer II; Pater Noster; *Summons to Prayer, A*; Office
prayerbook 224, 296; *see also* Ælfwine; Index of Manuscripts UK, England, London, British Library, Royal 2 A.xx (*Royal Prayerbook*)
prayer mats 223
preparation of skin 33
Prescott, Andrew 253
press-mark 31–2, 296
pricking 9, 33–4, 296–7
Primasius, sixth-century bishop of Hadrumetum and primate of Byzacena, Africa, *In Apocalypsin* 132
Priscian, fifth-/sixth-century Latin grammarian 144, 154; *Institutio de nomine, pronomine et uerbo* 144–5, 151; *Institutiones grammaticae* 144–5; *Periegesis* 155–6; anonymous *Excerptiones de Prisciano* 144; Pseudo-Priscian, *Carmen de sideribus* 154–5
Proba, possibly Faltonia Betitia, fourth-century, female Latin writer, *Cento Vergilianus* 149
prognostic 10–11, 20, 60, 76, 296, *1.2*
Prosper of Aquitaine, Tiro Prosper, fourth-/fifth-century, lay Christian writer 148, 167; *Epigrammata* 149, 167
provenance 31–2, 37, 59, 80–1, 98, 120, 138, 151, 215, 263, 270–2, 284, 295–6
Prudentius, Aurelius Prudentius Clemens, fourth-/fifth-century Spanish Christian poet; *Apotheosis* 149; *Cathemerinon* 149, 171; *Contra Symmachum* 148; *Dittochaeon* 148–9; *Hamartigenia* 148–9; *Peristephanon* 149; *Psychomachia* 58, 148–9, 156, 167, 174–5, *5.6, 6.8*

psalm 6, 64, 116–7, 119, 134, 144, 146, 160, 162–3, 197, 205, 231, 233, 235, 254, 291, 296, *1.1*, *1.3*, *6.1–6.2*; see also Ambrose; Augustine of Hippo; Bible; Cassiodorus; Jerome; psalter

psalter 16, 34, 65n.4, 116, 134–6, 152, 157, 160–3, 211, 224, 231–5, 291, 296; Romanum 6, 116n.8; Gallicanum 6, 116n.8; Hebraicum 116n.8; see also Index of Manuscripts France, Paris, Bibliothèque Nationale, fonds latin 8824 (*Paris Psalter*); Italy, Vatican City, Biblioteca Apostolica Vaticana, Reg. lat. 12 (*Bury Psalter*); Netherlands, Utrecht, Universiteitsbibliotheek 32, Script. eccl. 484 (*Utrecht Psalter*); UK, England, Cambridge, Trinity College MS R.17.1 (*Eadwine Psalter*); London, British Library, Additional 37517 (*Bosworth Psalter*); Cotton Galba A.xviii (*Galba Psalter*); Cotton Tiberius C.vi (*Tiberius Psalter*); Cotton Vespasian A.i (*Vespasian Psalter*); Cotton Vitellius E.xviii; Harley 603 (*Harley Psalter*); Harley 2904 (*Ramsey Psalter*)

Pseudo-Apuleius see Apuleius
Pseudo-Augustine *see* Augustine
Pseudo-Boethius *see* Boethius
Pseudo-Cato *see* Cato
Pseudo-Jerome *see* Jerome
Pseudo-Linus, second-century apocryphal writer, *Martyrium S. Petri et Pauli*
Pseudo-Priscian *see* Priscian
publication of manuscripts 27, 190, 195, 265, 272–3, 277, 281–2 see also editing practice; edition
punctuation 1, 6, 10, 18–19, 51–2, 70–1, 88–9, 91–2, 95, 97, 100–104, 108, 110–11,185, 296, *4.6–4.7*
punctus, *punctus elevatus* 6, 52, 296; *punctus interrogativus* 52, 71, 296; *punctus simplex* 51, 91, 104, 110, 296; *punctus versus* 52, 110, 296; subpunct 53, 297
purple 14, 81, 211, 237, *7.3*

quadrivium 112, 151–5, 296
quill 37, 161, 174
quire 16, 28, 31, 34–7, 54, 62–3, 66, 75–6, 93, 99, 102, 104, 291–2, 294, 296; quire number/signature 36, 102, 104, 296, *2.1*, *2.3*, *4.3*; quiring 9

Rabanus Maurus *see* Hrabanus Maurus
Radulf of Liège and Ragimbold of Cologne, correspondents in 1025, 'Letters on geometry' 155
reagent *see* chemicals
recycling of manuscripts 18

red 11, 13, 52, 58, 81, 110, 138, 161, 162n.3, 165, 235, 276, 294, 296, *1,7*, *2.1*; red crayon 59; red lead 201
Red Sea 242
refectory 112, 138, 157
Reformation 18, 59, 120, 123
Regula Benedicti see Benedictine Rule
Regularis Concordia see Æthelwold
Remigius of Auxerre, ninth-/tenth-century monk, commentaries 151, 154
repair of books and manuscripts 16
Resignation A and *B*, Old English poems 100
responsory 116, 134, 296
restoration, digital 260–1
Rheims, France 23, 116, 214; see also Index of Manuscripts France, Rheims, Bibliothèque Municipale 9 (*Rheims Gospels*)
riddles 15, 99–100, 150; *Riddle 47* 15; *Riddle 60* 101; see also Aldhelm; Boniface; Eusebius; Symphosius; Tatwine
Robert of Jumièges, archbishop of Canterbury, Benedictional of 224; Sacramentary of 112, 224
Robinson, Fred C., editor 254
Robinson, Peter, editor 280–1
Rochester 80, 86, 182, *1.2*
rodents 171
Roman culture 38–9,140, 188, 209, 214, 291, 294
Rome, Italy 38–9, 94, 155, 167, 178, 211, 297; Church of Rome 186, 190
rubric, rubrication 8, 11, 34, 38, 52, 111, 201, 237, 273, 277, 296, *2.1*, *2.9*
Rufinus of Aquileia, Tyrranius, fourth-/fifth-century monk, historian and translator, *Historia monachorum* 143
ruling 33–4, 174, 177, 296–7
runes see alphabet: runic
running heading 28, 52, 296
Rushworth, John, deputy clerk to the House of Commons 163; see also Index of Manuscripts UK, England, Oxford, Bodleian Library, Auctarium D.2.19 (*Macregol* or *Rushworth Gospels*)
Ruthwell Cross, Dumfries and Galloway, Scotland 101, 208, 235

sacramentary 112, 119–24, 134, 138, 157, 224, 296
Saint-Amand, Belgium 141; see also Hucbald
Saints' Lives see *Vitae* and individual authors
Saint-Vaast, Arras 121, 123

Salisbury 82; *see also* UK, England, Salisbury, Cathedral Library
salvation 100, 102, 107, 111, 141
Sanctorale 120
Satan 235; *see also* Christ and Satan
Sawley, Yorkshire, monastery 98
scanner 256–8, 293, 296, *8.1–8.2*
scholium, scholia 150, 169–70, 296, *6.5*
scientific texts 64, 113, 133, 153
Scolica Enchiriadis (anonymous) 155
Scots (people) 165
scribe 2, 4, 6–11, 15, 18, 23, 30, 34, 36–7, 44–6, 50–8, 60–1, 63–7, 70, 71n.14, 75–8, 80–2, 84, 86, 90–2, 95, 99–108, 110–11, 113–14, 117, 138, 156, 159, 161, 162n.3, 165, 167, 170, 174–5, 179, 197, 218, 222–4, 229, 261, 272, 278, 281–2, 293, 296–7, *1.5*, *1.7*, *2.10–2.11*, *3.6–3.7*, *4.4–4.7*; evangelist 218, *7.11*, *7.15–7.18*; female 65; secular 56; *see also* Ælfric; Ælfwine; Aldred; Coleman; Eadfrith; Eadwig Basan; Farmon; Frithestan; Hemming; *Peregrinus*; Tremulous Hand of Worcester; Wulfstan; Wulfwine
script 1, 4, 7, 18, 28, 30, 32, 38, 41, 45, 53–4, 56–7, 64–5, 70, 77, 80, 90–1, 95, 100, 104, 107–8, 110, 114, 126, 148, 156, 159, 182–4, 187, 189, 272–3, 282, 292, 294; script size 6, 58, 161, 174, *1.7*; *see also* Anglicana; Copperplate; cursive; Half-Uncials; Italic; Irish; majuscule; minuscule; Secretary; Textura; Uncial; Welsh
Secretary script 51, 197, 294
Sedulius, fifth-century Latin Christian poet 148; hymns 151; *Paschale Carmen (Carmen Paschale)* 149, 167; *Paschale opus* 167; *see also* Index of Manuscripts UK, England, Cambridge, Corpus Christi College 173, Part II (*Corpus Sedulius*)
Serenus, Quintus Serenus, second-/third-century Roman poet, *Liber medicinalis* 156
Sermo Lupi see Wulfstan
Servius, Maurus Servius Honoratus, fourth-century grammarian and commentator, *In Aeneida* 146–7
Sextus Placitus, obscure Latin writer, *Liber medicinae ex animalibus* 155
SGML *see* Standard General Markup Language
Shaftesbury 65n.4
Shakespeare, William, *Pericles* 61
Shechem, Old Testament figure, Shechemites 198, 200
Shockwave software 267, 291
Sigeric, tenth-century archbishop of Canterbury 155
Sigeweard, ealdorman, letter to 195

signature, of owner, donor 32; *see also* quire: quire signature
signes-de-renvoi 53, 170, 194, 297, *6.5*
silver 211
Skeat, W.W., editor 95
slide 257
Smaragdus, Ardo, eighth-/ninth-century abbot of Aniane, *Diadema monachorum* 127, 140–1; *Expositio in Regulam S. Benedicti* 140
snake ('book snake') 26, *1.8*
Solomon and Saturn, Old English text surviving in prose and poetic versions 121, 216n.10
Soul and Body I, Old English poem 101
Soul and Body II, Old English poem 100
Southumbrian art 210–11, 297, *2.5*
Southwick Codex *see* Index of Manuscripts UK, England, London, British Library, Cotton Vitellius A.xv (*Beowulf Manuscript*)
Spain 170
spelling variants 18, 52, 55, 95, 97, 102, 192, 198, 283; *see also* orthography
Spelman, Sir Henry, historian 200; *Concilia, decreta, leges, constitutiones, in re ecclesiarum orbis Britannici* 200
SPI *see* System for Palaeographical Inspections
St Gallen Abbey, Switzerland 178; *see also* Index of Manuscripts Switzerland, St Gallen, Stiftsbibliothek 1394
St Petersburg, Russia 21n.17; *see also* Index of Manuscripts Russia, St Petersburg, Russian National Library, Lat. F.v.I.8 (*St Petersburg Gospels*); O.v.XIV.1; Q.v.I.15; Q.v.I.18 (*St Petersburg Bede*)
stamp (library) 32
Standard General Markup Language (SGML) 276n.21, 297
standards of practice in manuscript storage and conservation 25
Statius, Publius Papinius, first-century Latin poet, *Thebais* 146
Stephen of Ripon, eighth-century English writer, *Vita S. Wilfridi* 128
stiffening material 32
stone, foundation stones 123; gemstones 163; inscriptions on stone 38, 295
stub, of manuscript leaf 9
stylus 9, 174, 177, 293–4, 297; *see also* drypoint; hard point
subpuncting *see punctus:* subpunct

Sulpicius Severus, fourth-/fifth-century lawyer and monk, *Vita S. Martini* 125, 128, 130
Summons to Prayer, A, Old English poem 108, 110–11, *4.6–4.7*
Sunday 24, 82, 119–20, 135, 138, 152, *1.2*
surrogates 257–9
Survey of Manuscripts Illuminated in the British Isles 10, 20
Sweet, Henry, editor 83
Swithun, St, ninth-century bishop of Winchester 214, 227, *7.19*; *see also* Lantfred; Wulfstan
Symphosius, fourth- or fifth-century Latin author, *Aenigmata, Riddle 16* 15n.12
synod *see* Aachen, Whitby, Winchester
System for Palaeographical Inspections (SPI) 260

Talbot, Robert, prebendary of Norwich Cathedral 187–8, *2.12, 6.14*
Tatwine, eighth-century archbishop of Canterbury, riddles 150
tearing of manuscripts 1, 15, 26, 33
TEI *see* Text Encoding Initiative
Temple, Elżbieta 20
Temporale 119–20
Terence, Publius Terentius Afer, second-century Roman dramatist, *Comediae* 146
Text Encoding Initiative (TEI); *Guidelines* 252, 256, 258, 279–80, 297
textblock 31, 33–7, 297
Textura script 51, 294, *2.15*
Thames, River 188, 190
The Grave, Old English poem 98
Theodore of Mopsuestia, fourth-/fifth-century bishop of Mopsuestia (now Turkey), *Commentarii in epistolas Pauli* 132
Theodore, seventh-century archbishop of Canterbury 178; *see also* Goscelin
theology 130–3, 185, 204, 233, 293, *1.7*
Thompson, Susan D. 8
thorn branches 37
thorn, letter 39, 78, 90, 171, 276, 296
Thorney Abbey, Cambridgeshire 182
Thorpe, Benjamin, editor 83–4
TIFF (.tif) 14n.11, 259, 293, 297
titles, of medieval books, texts or chapters 31, 52, 61, 92, 101, 121nn.20,22,154, 179, 189n.21, 201, 296, *6.20*; of modern works 27, 61, 278
Tolkein, J.R.R. 7
tonsure 123, 192n.23, 194, 297

translation 6, 53, 58, 64, 65n.4, 66n.6, 71–2, 81, 119n.14, 121, 138, 141–2, 149, 154, 157–8, 160–7, 169, 182–3, 186, 189–91, 194–5, 197–8, 201, 219–20, 231, 254, 268, 293, *2.8*
treaty between Alfred and Guthrum 188, *6.14*
Treharne, Elaine 11
Tremulous Hand of Worcester 59, 80, 183–6, 191, *2.8, 6.13*
Trinity 185
trivium 112, 144–51, 155, 297, *5.6*
trope, literary theme 278; song added to liturgy 122, 178
troper 122, 224, 297; *Winchester Troper see* Index of Manuscripts UK, England, Cambridge, Corpus Christi College 473; Oxford, Bodleian Library, Bodley 775
Tuckley, Chris 26
Turning the Pages system of digitization 265, *8.7*
tironian *nota* 50

Uncial script 6, 39, 160, 297, *2.1, 2.9*
underlining 53, 59, 190–2, 199, 272–3, *2.12, 6.19*
unfinished manuscripts 206, 246, 249
Universal Resource Locator (URL) 263, 297
URL *see* Universal Resource Locator

vellum 1, 7, 9–10, 33, 204, 291–3, 296–7
Venantius Fortunatus, Venantius Honorius Clementianus Fortunatus, sixth-century Latin poet, *Carmina* 149
Vercelli Homilies 23, 63, 101–2; *Homily IX* 101; *see* Index of Manuscripts Italy, Vercelli, Biblioteca capitolare CXVII (*Vercelli Book*)
Vercelli, Italy 94; *see also* Index of Manuscripts Italy, Vercelli, Biblioteca capitolare CXVII (*Vercelli Book*)
video digitization 255, 268
video spectral comparator 24
Vigilius, pope 167
Vikings 97–8, 117, 143, 160, 163, 178, 188, 211, 224, 242
vine-scroll 208, 235
vinegar 37
Virgil, Publius Vergilius Maro, first-century BC Latin poet 167; *Aeneid* 146–8; *Bucolica* 146–7; *Georgica* 146–7; *see also* Proba; Servius
Vitae, Lives of saints 297; Æthelburga 128; Æthelthryth 128; Æthelwold 128; Aichard 125; Aidan 128; Alphege 128; Augustine of Canterbury 128; Bavo 125; Benedict 128; Birinus 128; Botulph

128; Ceolfrith 125; Cuthbert prose 128; Cuthbert verse 128, 130; Deusdedit 128; Dunstan 128; Eadmund 128; Ecgwin 128; Gregory I 128; Guthlac 125, 128, 130; Hadrian 128; Judoc 128; Kenelm 128; Laurentius 128; Letardus 128; Machutus 128, 130; Malchus 128; Martin 125, 128, 130; Mellitus 128; Mildred 128; Oswald, king of Northumbria 128; Paul 'the hermit' 128, 130; Peter and Paul 128; Philibert 125; Swithun 128; Theodore 128; Walaric 125; Wilfrid 128; Wulfhilda 128

virgin saints 120, 223, *7.23* see also Mary

vocabulary 53, 55, 97, 145, 158, 164, 167, 178, 182–3, 185–6, 200

Vulgate, St Jerome's Latin translation of the bible 198, *2.2, 2.11*

Wærferth, ninth-/tenth-century bishop of Worcester, translator 66n.6

Wales, Welsh culture 150, 292

Wanderer, The, Old English poem 89–92, 100, 110

Wanley, Humfrey, *Librorum vett. septentrionalium ... catalogus historico-criticus* 202n.29

water, as ingredient for ink 37; water damage to manuscripts 94, 104, *4.1*

watermark 33, 269, 272, 297

Watling Street 188

wax tablet 70, 177, 297

Wearmouth (Monkwearmouth), Northumbrian monastery 2, 115, 125, 209–10, *2.3*

websites 3, 24, 65n.5, 70n.12, 87, 246n. 39, 266, 277

Weingarten Abbey, Germany 251

Welsh script 42

Werburgh, rescuer of manuscript 211

Werden, Germany 120

West Midlands 182

West Saxon Gospels 164, 187; *see also* Index of Manuscripts UK, Oxford, Bodleian Library, MS Bodley 441

Westminster 94; Little Dean's Yard 253; School 253; *see also* Ashburnham House; Index of Manuscripts UK, England, London, Westminster Abbey Library 36

Whale, The, Old English poem 100

Wheelock, Abraham, librarian and lecturer 187, 200–3, *6.20–6.21*

Whitby, Synod of 152

Wieland, Gernot *1.5*

Wife of Bath's Prologue, The (Geoffrey Chaucer, *The Canterbury Tales*) 280–1, 284n.30

Wife's Lament, The, Old English poem 92

William I, 'the Conqueror', king of England 114n.3

Winchcombe 161

Winchester 80–1, 108, 161, 166n.9, 175, 182, 204, 206, 214, 227–9, 237, *2.7*; New Minster 13, 44; Old Minster 44, 227, *2.9*; Synod of Winchester 138; Winchester Style 204, 213–14, 224, 233; *see also* Æthelwold; Denewulf; Frithestan; Lantfred; troper: *Winchester Troper*; Index of Manuscripts UK, England, Winchester, Cathedral Library 1

wine 37

Wonders of the East (*Marvels of the East*), Old English and Latin prose text 57, 81, 155, 242–4, *7.30–7.31*

wood, use of 26, 34, 295; illustration of cutting wood 241, *7.29*

Worcester 44, 65, 67, 75–6, 78, 80, 82, 108, 123, 182, 185, 191–2, 211, *1.6, 2.8, 6.13*; Cathedral 59, 182; *see also* Tremulous Hand of Worcester; Wærferth; Index of Manuscripts UK, England, Worcester, Cathedral Library

word division, word separation 91, 95, 184–5

World Wide Web (WWW) 11, 30, 259, 263–4, 272–4, 276–7, 297, *8.4, 8.12–13*

Wright, Charles D. 95

writing grid 9, 34, 90, 110, 114, 294, 297

Wulf and Eadwacer, Old English poem 100

Wulfstan, tenth-/eleventh-century archbishop of York, bishop of Worcester 65, 70, 83–4, 202; Canon Law Collection 140; common-place book (*see also* Index of Manuscripts UK, London, British Library Cotton Nero A. i) 70, 187; *De septiformi spiritu* 85; homilies 127; Homily Ia 127; Homily VIIIa 127; *Narratio metrica de S. Swithuno* 128; *Sermo Lupi* 84; *Vita S. Aethelwoldi* 128

Wulfstan, voyager 155

Wulfwine, scribe 6

Würzburg, Germany 23, 118, *1.6*; *see also* Index of Manuscripts Germany, Würzburg, Cathedral Library, Universitätsbibliothek

WWW *see* World Wide Web

wynn, letter 39, 78, 90, 171, 296

XML (eXtensible Markup Language) 252, 272, 277–8, 295, 297

X-ray 261

zoomorphic decoration 39, 103, 294, *1.7, 2.5*

Contributors

Maria Cesario is Lecturer in Medieval English at Brasenose College, University of Oxford, UK, having previously worked as a part-time lecturer at the University of Birmingham and part-time tutor at the University of Manchester. She completed her PhD on prognostic texts at the University of Manchester in 2007. She is now carrying out a detailed survey of all *Revelatio Esdrae* material produced in England c. 900–c. 1500, in Latin, French, Old English and Middle English, and a study of its use in determining the dates of the Church year.

Timothy Graham is Professor of History and Director of the Institute for Medieval Studies at the University of New Mexico, USA. A specialist in Anglo-Saxon manuscripts and their early modern use, he has frequently taught courses on palaeography and codicology and has co-directed National Endowment for the Humanities summer seminars on 'Old English Literature in its Manuscript Context' (at Corpus Christi College, Cambridge) and 'Anglo-Saxon Manuscripts and Texts' (at the British Library, London). He is editor of *The Recovery of Old English: Anglo-Saxon studies in the sixteenth and seventeenth centuries* (2000) and co-author of *Introduction to Manuscript Studies* (2007).

Catherine E. Karkov is Professor of Art History at the University of Leeds, UK. She is particularly interested in issues of gender and postcolonialism in Anglo-Saxon art, and is co-director of the Visionary Cross project. Her recent books include *The Ruler Portraits of Anglo-Saxon England* and *Text and Picture in Anglo-Saxon England: narrative strategies in the Junius 11 Manuscript*.

Stuart D. Lee is Director of Oxford University's Computing Services; Reader in E-learning and Digital Libraries; and a teaching member of the English Faculty, University of Oxford, UK, where he teaches Old English. He publishes on Old English and the fiction of J.R.R. Tolkien. He has also worked extensively in the fields of e-learning and digital libraries, supervising major digitization projects on the British First World War poets, and has written two books in this area on Digital Imaging and Electronic Collection Development.

Daniel Paul O'Donnell is Associate Professor of English at the University of Lethbridge, Canada. He is Chair of the Text Encoding Initiative (http://www.tei-c.org/), Founding Director of *Digital Medievalist* (http://www.digitalmedievalist.org/)

and Chair of the Medieval Academy of America's Electronic Editions Advisory Board. His print-and-digital edition of *Cædmon's Hymn* was published by the Medieval Academy and Boydell and Brewer in 2005. It received honourable mention in the MLA's competition for the Best Critical Edition published in 2005 or 2006.

Alexander R. Rumble is Reader in Palaeography at the University of Manchester, UK and Director of the Manchester Centre for Anglo-Saxon Studies. His teaching includes Palaeography, Anglo-Saxon History and Old English. His major publications relate to Anglo-Saxon Winchester (*Property and Piety in Early Medieval Winchester*), the Domesday manuscripts and English place-names. He is currently editing the Anglo-Saxon charters of the Old Minster, Winchester.

Donald Scragg is Professor Emeritus of the University of Manchester, UK. He was founder and first Director of the Manchester Centre for Anglo-Saxon Studies; was founder and is currently President of Teachers of Old English in Britain and Ireland; is Vice-President of the English Place-Name Society; and former President of the Simplified Spelling Society. His extensive publications include a wide range of subjects in Old English language and literature, and manuscripts containing Anglo-Saxon.

Elaine Treharne is Professor of Early English at Florida State University, USA and Co-Director of the AHRC-funded project, 'The Production and Use of English Manuscripts, 1060 to 1220' (Universities of Leicester and Leeds). She has published extensively on Old and Middle English texts and their contexts, and is currently writing a book for OUP on the ideology of Early English. Her new research project will investigate the emergence of modern manuscript studies. She is an editor for *Review of English Studies*, *Speculum*, and *Literature Compass*, General Editor (with Greg Walker) for the new Oxford Textual Perspectives series, and is Former Chair and President of the English Association.

Gernot R. Wieland is Professor in the Department of English, University of British Columbia, Canada. He is author of *The Latin Glosses on Arator and Prudentius in Cambridge, University Library Ms. Gg.5.35* (1983), editor of *The Canterbury Hymnal: Edited from British Library Manuscript Add. 37517* (1982) and of *Waltharius* (1986), as well as co-editor of several Festschriften (1999, 2001, and 2006). His research concentrates on the Anglo-Saxon manuscripts of Prudentius's *Psychomachia*, of which he has examined the textual transmission, the Latin and Old English glosses, the illustrations, and the captions to the illustrations. At present he works on the Anglo-Saxon manuscripts containing Arator's *Historia apostolica*.